THE DOME OF URYNE

EARLY ENGLISH TEXT SOCIETY
O.S. 354
2019

In the bygynnyng thou schalt take heede to þ that longeth
to the doome of vryne to the substaunce to the colour as
the regions. And to the contentz / ffirst loke to the substaunce
Whether hit is thikke or thynne other by rekene bothe // yf
the vryne be þ thanne schalt thou see thorugh the
vryne the poynt of thi fynger And that thynnesse by
tokeneth a bad splen and a badde stomake & hat in the
bowelles // And yf hit be thikke that thou may nought see
thorugh hit by tokeneth wynd in the stomake & in the
hed and in the bowelles // And yf hit be by twyxt thikke
and thynne hit tokeneth swellyng of the galle // the
secunde that . thou schalt take heed to ye cold of the
vryne as seyn these maistres they ben xx colours in the vryne / the firste colour ye whyt as cley was of the welle
this colour by tokeneth indigeston as a badde stomake & a
badde lyuer // And yf thou see in this vryne manye thyn-
nyng benmys hit by tokeneth a postem in the mylte / the
secunde colour ye white as whey yf this vryne be doubl
thyk and litel in quite which white contentz hit
tokeneth the flux // the thridde colour ye white zolow a
bryth horn of a lantne this vryne litel in quite & ofte
made tokeneth that the sek may nought kepen his vryne
and this colour ys neue knyt with thikke substaunce / the
ferthe colour ye a whit pisser this vryne yif hit be
thyke in substaunce with oute ganel in the bottom hit
tokeneth colica passio / the fifte colour ys as broth of flessh
that ys half withyn. this vryne yf hit be litel in quite

The Dome of Uryne: London: British Library, MS Sloane 374, f. 5ᵛ
© The British Library Board

THE DOME OF URYNE

A READING EDITION OF
NINE MIDDLE ENGLISH UROSCOPIES

EDITED BY

M. TERESA TAVORMINA

Published for
THE EARLY ENGLISH TEXT SOCIETY
by the
OXFORD UNIVERSITY PRESS
2019

OXFORD
UNIVERSITY PRESS

Great Clarendon Street, Oxford, OX2 6DP,
United Kingdom

Oxford University Press is a department of the University of Oxford.
It furthers the University's objective of excellence in research, scholarship,
and education by publishing worldwide. Oxford is a registered trade mark of
Oxford University Press in the UK and in certain other countries

First edition published in 2019

Impression: 1

British Library Cataloguing in Publication Data

Data available

ISBN 978-0-19-884532-4

Typeset by John Waś, Oxford
Printed in Great Britain
on acid-free paper by
TJ International Ltd, Padstow, Cornwall

In memory of Lister Matheson,
who gave me my first manuscript catalogue

PREFACE

Of the various subgenres of Middle English medical writing, one of the most extensive—after the ubiquities of recipe collections and herbal texts—is that devoted to uroscopy, the examination of urine for diagnostic and prognostic purposes. The pervasive incidence of uroscopy in medieval medical manuscripts is unsurprising, given the centrality of the procedure in contemporary medical practice, captured vividly by the urine flask's familiar iconographic role as the mark of the physician. It is similarly unsurprising that non-academic medical practitioners, as well as their patients, would have provided a ready audience for synopses of the complex, often lengthy, sometimes cryptic material in Latin uroscopic treatises, in the hope of a better understanding of physical afflictions and more informed remedies for such ailments. Indeed, the process of vernacularization is of particular interest in the case of uroscopy, as it appears that the post-medieval decline in uroscopy's reputation among learned practitioners may be related to its increasing dissemination in practical summaries and overviews such as the texts edited below.

What is somewhat unexpected, however, is the prolonged editorial neglect suffered by this important branch of English vernacular medical writing. Whether rooted in distaste for the subject matter or dismay at the seemingly endless variations among the many uroscopic texts—well over 125 distinct texts with hundreds of witnesses—in Middle English medical and occasional non-medical manuscripts, only a handful of these uroscopies has been edited to date. The goal of this volume is to make available several of the most common shorter uroscopies, texts chosen both for their popularity among compilers of medical manuscripts and for their combined value as a précis of those aspects of uroscopy seen by translators, writers, and readers as most important to know.

Much of the specialized medical content and terminology in the texts edited here will be unfamiliar to many readers of Middle English texts, and even to historians of medicine whose research has not focused on uroscopy and other medieval diagnostic procedures. In the light of this unfamiliarity, the explanatory and glossarial materials in this volume are somewhat more extensive than the norm in most EETS editions. Two sets of explanatory comment are provided, the first primarily focused on textual matters, the second on medical content and sources, and the Glossary includes both the technical terminology and (for readers who may not be Middle English specialists) a number of 'ordinary' Middle English words and grammatical forms.

This edition is the result of more than twenty years of work on several different projects, over the course of which I have been helped and supported by many colleagues and institutions. The deepest debts that I owe are to Linda Ehrsam Voigts and the late Lister M. Matheson, without whom I could never have begun the long process of collecting Middle English uroscopy texts nor made sense of many of the more difficult aspects of those texts. Ruth Harvey has been a most generous and supportive fellow-worker in the vineyard for nearly twenty years, sharing her wide knowledge of Henry Daniel and his commentators without stint, as well as her warm hospitality during many visits to Toronto. Over the last five years, I have also learned a great deal from the other collaborators in the Toronto Henry Daniel Project, including Sarah Star, Jessica Henderson, C. E. M. Henderson, Faith Wallis, Jake Walsh Morrissey, Peter Murray Jones, and Nicholas Everett.

For more general advice and support on Middle English manuscripts and medieval medical texts, I am very pleased to thank the late E. G. Stanley, Ralph Hanna, George Keiser, Tony Hunt, Laurence Moulinier-Brogi, Peter Murray Jones, Monica H. Green, Daniel Wakelin, Laurence Eldredge, Lea T. Olsan, Kari Anne Rand, Margaret Connolly, Laura Nuvoloni, and Javier Calle-Martín. This edition has also been much improved by the wise and patient counsel of Helen Spencer and Ralph Hanna and the vigilant copy-editing of Bonnie Blackburn.

Very few editions can come to fruition without the aid of libraries and librarians, and this volume is no exception. For access to the texts edited here, I am most grateful to the British Library, the Bodleian Library, the Wellcome Library for the History and Understanding of Medicine, and the libraries of Gonville and Caius College and Corpus Christi College, Cambridge. Permission to publish the images reproduced in this book has been kindly granted by the British Library; the Bodleian Library; the Wellcome Collection; the Parker Library, Corpus Christi College, Cambridge; and the Master and Fellows of Gonville and Caius College, Cambridge. The staff at all the above-named libraries have been unfailingly helpful, but I am glad to extend special thanks to Mark Statham at Gonville and Caius; Elma Brenner, Amanda Engineer, and Anna Hoffman at the Wellcome; and Susan L'Engle at the Vatican Film Library at St. Louis University. Finally, it gives me great pleasure to thank both the Interlibrary Loan staff and my career-long colleague and friend in the reference and collections departments of the Michigan State University Library, Agnes Haigh Widder, who have located, borrowed, or ordered hundreds of hard-to-find articles and books for me for more than four decades.

January 2019   M.T.T.

CONTENTS

LIST OF ILLUSTRATIONS

PLATES

FIGURES

LIST OF TABLES

SIGLA

Witnesses to the uroscopy treatises edited in this volume are found in 121 manuscripts and three early printed editions. Because of the large number of witnesses, a summary list of sigla and shelfmarks for all manuscripts of the texts is provided here. Detailed descriptions of the eight manuscripts used as base texts for the editions (Ad2, Cc, Gc4, Ld, S10, S15, S42, W12) are given in §II of the Introduction.

The system of alphanumeric sigla used here corresponds to that presented in Tavormina 2014: Appendix B. Each collection represented is assigned a one- or two-letter siglum, depending on how many manuscripts including English uroscopic material the collection contains, except for the Bodleian Additional manuscripts, which are indicated by the letters 'Add', in distinction from the British Library Additional manuscripts, signified by 'Ad'. For the manuscripts within a given collection, the alphabetic part of the siglum is followed by Arabic numerals that increase with the alphanumeric order of the shelfmarks, unless there is only one manuscript with Middle English uroscopic material in the collection, in which case no numeral is attached. When there is more than one copy or form of a text in a given manuscript, the versions are distinguished (if necessary) by a terminal 'a', 'b', etc. 'Missing' sigla in the list below (e.g. A1, A2, Ad3, etc.) reflect manuscripts that do not contain the texts edited in this volume. The three print witnesses, though cited rarely in the volume, are signified by single capital letters in italic.

MANUSCRIPTS

Siglum	Shelfmark	Texts included
A3	Oxford, Bodleian Library, MS Ashmole 1393	B, C, E
A6	Oxford, Bodleian Library, MS Ashmole 1405	I
A7	Oxford, Bodleian Library, MS Ashmole 1413	A, F, G
A8	Oxford, Bodleian Library, MS Ashmole 1438, Part I	C, D, E, G
A9	Oxford, Bodleian Library, MS Ashmole 1438, Part II	D, E, I

A10	Oxford, Bodleian Library, MS Ashmole 1444	C, G
A11	Oxford, Bodleian Library, MS Ashmole 1447	I
A13	Oxford, Bodleian Library, MS Ashmole 1477, Part III	E
A14	Oxford, Bodleian Library, MS Ashmole 1477, Part X	F, I
Ad1	London, British Library, MS Additional 4698	B, C, D
Ad2	London, British Library, MS Additional 4898	E
Ad4	London, British Library, MS Additional 10440	I
Ad6	London, British Library, MS Additional 19674	G
Ad7	London, British Library, MS Additional 30338	I
Add2	Oxford, Bodleian Library, MS Additional B.60	I
Add3	Oxford, Bodleian Library, MS Additional C.246	C, D
Ar	London, British Library, MS Arundel 42	E
Cc	Cambridge, Corpus Christi College, MS 388	E
Co1	Durham, University Library, MS Cosin V.III.10	I
Co3	Durham, University Library, MS Cosin V.V.13	H, I
Cp	New York, Columbia University Library, MS Plimpton 254	E
Cu1	Cambridge, University Library, MS Dd.5.76	I
Cu3	Cambridge, University Library, MS Dd.10.44	D, H, I
Cu4	Cambridge, University Library, MS Ee.1.13	H
Cu5	Cambridge, University Library, MS Ee.1.15	A, B, C

Cu6	Cambridge, University Library, MS Ff.2.6	E
Di1	Oxford, Bodleian Library, MS Digby 29	A, B, C, G, I
Di2	Oxford, Bodleian Library, MS Digby 75	A, B, C (2×)
Di3	Oxford, Bodleian Library, MS Digby 95	I
Eg3	London, British Library, MS Egerton 2433	A, F
Gc1	Cambridge, Gonville and Caius College, MS 84/166	B (2×), C (2×), F (2×)
Gc4	Cambridge, Gonville and Caius College, MS 336/725	A, B, C (2×), G
Gc6	Cambridge, Gonville and Caius College, MS 451/392	H
Gc7	Cambridge, Gonville and Caius College, MS 457/395	A, B, C
Gw3	Glasgow, University Library, MS Hunter 328	I
H1	London, British Library, MS Harley 218	H, I
H2	London, British Library, MS Harley 1010	A
H4	London, British Library, MS Harley 1612	H
H5	London, British Library, MS Harley 1735	H, I
H6	London, British Library, MS Harley 2274	I
H7	London, British Library, MS Harley 2375	B, C, H
H8	London, British Library, MS Harley 2390	A
H9	London, British Library, MS Harley 2558	I
H10	London, British Library, MS Harley 3383	A, B, C
H11	London, British Library, MS Harley 3407	I

H12	London, British Library, MS Harley 3810	I
H13	London, British Library, MS Harley 5401	I
Hg1	San Marino, Huntington Library, MS HM 64	B, I
Ht	Oxford, Bodleian Library, MS Hatton 29	D, E, I
Je	Cambridge, Jesus College, MS 43 (Q.D.1)	C, G
Ld	Oxford, Bodleian Library, MS Laud misc. 553	A, B, C
Lm2	London, Lambeth Palace Library, MS 444	I
Nm1	Bethesda, National Library of Medicine, MS E 4	C, G
Nm2	Bethesda, National Library of Medicine, MS E 30	B, C, E, G
Nm3	Bethesda, National Library of Medicine, MS E 49	H, I
Nw1	Aberystwyth, National Library of Wales, MS Peniarth 388C	D
Nw2	Aberystwyth, National Library of Wales, MS Sotheby C.2	F, I
Oa	Oxford, All Souls College, MS 81	I
Om	Oxford, Magdalen College, MS 221	C, G, I
Pe1	Cambridge, Magdalene College, MS Pepys 878	B, C
Pe2	Cambridge, Magdalene College, MS Pepys 1307	I
Pe3	Cambridge, Magdalene College, MS Pepys 1661	A, B, C
Pm	New York, Morgan Library, MS Bühler 21	E, I
Ra2	Oxford, Bodleian Library, MS Rawlinson C.81	G, I
Ra3	Oxford, Bodleian Library, MS Rawlinson C.299	D
Ra4	Oxford, Bodleian Library, MS Rawlinson C.506	I

Ra5	Oxford, Bodleian Library, MS Rawlinson D.248	I
Ra6	Oxford, Bodleian Library, MS Rawlinson D.1210	A, H
Ra7	Oxford, Bodleian Library, MS Rawlinson D.1221	I
Ro1	London, British Library, MS Royal 12 G.iv	E (3x)
Ro2	London, British Library, MS Royal 17 A.iii	E
Ro3	London, British Library, MS Royal 17 C.xv	D, G, I
Ro4	London, British Library, MS Royal 17 C.xxiv	I
Ro6	London, British Library, MS Royal 18 A.vi	A, C, G, I
Ry1	Manchester, John Rylands Library, MS Eng. 404	C
Ry2	Manchester, John Rylands Library, MS Eng. 1310	I
S1	London, British Library, MS Sloane 5	B (2×), C, E, H
S2	London, British Library, MS Sloane 7	F
S5	London, British Library, MS Sloane 120	B
S6	London, British Library, MS Sloane 121	A, B, C, D
S9	London, British Library, MS Sloane 135	A
S10	London, British Library, MS Sloane 213	H
S12	London, British Library, MS Sloane 297	I
S13	London, British Library, MS Sloane 340	A
S14	London, British Library, MS Sloane 357	E
S15	London, British Library, MS Sloane 374	I
S16	London, British Library, MS Sloane 382	I

S20	London, British Library, MS Sloane 635	C, F, H
S21	London, British Library, MS Sloane 706	A, B
S23	London, British Library, MS Sloane 783B	B
S24	London, British Library, MS Sloane 963	E (2×)
S28	London, British Library, MS Sloane 1317	E
S29	London, British Library, MS Sloane 1388	A, C, D, E (2×), G, I
S32	London, British Library, MS Sloane 2270	H
S35	London, British Library, MS Sloane 2584	A, B, C, E
S36	London, British Library, MS Sloane 3160	A
S40	London, British Library, MS Sloane 3466	D
S42	London, British Library, MS Sloane 3542	B, D
Se	Oxford, Bodleian Library, MS Selden Supra 73	I
Sh	Sheffield, Central Library, Jackson Collection MS 1302	I
Sj3	Cambridge, St John's College, MS K.49	I
St	Stockholm, Royal Library, MS X.90	I
Su	Woking, Surrey Historical Society, MS LM 1327/2	E
T2	Cambridge, Trinity College, MS O.1.65	C
T7	Cambridge, Trinity College, MS O.7.20, II	A, B, C, I
T8	Cambridge, Trinity College, MS O.8.35	I
T11	Cambridge, Trinity College, MS R.14.32	A, B, C
T12	Cambridge, Trinity College, MS R.14.39, II	D
T13	Cambridge, Trinity College, MS R.14.39, III	A, B, C, E, I

T14	Cambridge, Trinity College, MS R.14.51	E
T15	Cambridge, Trinity College, MS R.14.52	C, G
W1	London, Wellcome Library, MS 7	C, G, I
W4	London, Wellcome Library, MS 404	A (2×)
W6	London, Wellcome Library, MS 408	A, B, C
W7	London, Wellcome Library, MS 409	I
W8	London, Wellcome Library, MS 537	A, B, C, I
W9	London, Wellcome Library, MS 564	I
W10	London, Wellcome Library, MS 784	C, G
W11	London, Wellcome Library, MS 7117	G
W12	London, Wellcome Library, MS 8004	B, C, F
Yo	York, York Minster Library, MS XVI.E.32	A, B, C, E

PRINT WITNESSES

Siglum	Title	Texts included
S	*The Seynge of Uryns* (London: J. Rastell for Richard Banckes, 1525). STC2 22153; multiple later editions	I
J	*The Judgement of All Urynes* (London: Robert Wyer, ?1555). STC2 14834	I
K	*The Boke of Knowledge of Thynges Vnknowen Aparteynynge to Astronomye* (London: Robert Wyer, ?1554). STC 11930.7	H

ABBREVIATIONS

AN	Anglo-Norman
AND	*The Anglo-Norman Dictionary Online Edition*, ed. W. Rothwell, D. A. Trotter, G. De Wilde, H. Pagan, et al. (Aberystwyth, 2001–), http://www.anglo-norman.net/gate/
BL	London, British Library
Bodl.	Oxford, Bodleian Library
Briquet	C.-M. Briquet, *Les Filigranes: Dictionnaire historique des marques du papier dès leur apparition vers 1282 jusqu'en 1600*, 4 vols. (Leipzig, 1923)
BRUO	A. B. Emden, *A Biographical Register of the University of Oxford to A.D. 1500*, 3 vols. (Oxford, 1957–9)
CUL	Cambridge, University Library
De Renzi	*Collectio salernitana, ossia Documenti inediti, e trattati di medicina appartenenti alla Scuola medica salernitana*, ed. S. De Renzi, 5 vols. (Naples, 1852–9)
DMLBS	*Dictionary of Medieval Latin from British Sources*, ed. R. E. Latham, D. R. Howlett, and R. K. Ashdowne (Oxford, 1975–2013), http://logeion.uchicago.edu/
eLALME	See *LALME*
eTK	L. Thorndike and P. Kibre, *A Catalogue of Incipits of Mediaeval Scientific Writings in Latin*, online rev. edn., https://cctr1.umkc.edu/cgi-bin/medievalacademy
eVK2	L. E. Voigts and P. D. Kurtz, *Scientific and Medical Writings in Old and Middle English: An Electronic Reference*, rev. edn. (2014), https://cctr1.umkc.edu/cgi-bin/medievalacademy
'Guide'	M. T. Tavormina, 'Uroscopy in Middle English: A Guide to the Texts and Manuscripts', *Studies in Medieval and Renaissance History*, ser. 3, 11 (2014), 1–154. Also cited as Tavormina 2014
Heawood	E. Heawood, 'Sources of Early English Paper-Supply', *The Library*, ser. 4, 10 (1929–30), 282–307, 421–54
IMEP	A. S. G. Edwards et al., *The Index of Middle English Prose* (Cambridge, 1984–)
LALME	A. McIntosh, M. L. Samuels, M. Benskin, et al. *A Linguistic Atlas of Late Mediaeval English*, 4 vols. (Aberdeen,

	1986), http://www.lel.ed.ac.uk/ihd/elalme/elalme.html (=*eLALME*)
Manual 6	A. Renoir and C. D. Benson, *John Lydgate*, A Manual of the Writings in Middle English, 6 (fasc. XVI), ed. A. E. Hartung (New Haven, Conn., 1980)
Manual 10	G. R. Keiser, *Works of Science and Information*, A Manual of the Writings in Middle English, 10 (fasc. XXV), ed. A. E. Hartung (New Haven, Conn., 1998).
ME	Middle English
MED	*Middle English Dictionary*, ed. H. Kurath, S. M. Kuhn, and R. E. Lewis (Ann Arbor, Mich., 1952–2001), http://quod.lib.umich.edu/m/middle-english-dictionary/dictionary
ModE	Modern English
NIMEV	J. Boffey and A. S. G. Edwards, *A New Index of Middle English Verse* (London, 2005)
ODNB	*Oxford Dictionary of National Biography* (Oxford, 2004–), http://www.oxforddnb.com
OE	Old English
OED	*Oxford English Dictionary Online*, ed. J. Simpson, http://www.oed.com
OF	Old French
Piccard	G. Piccard, *Die Wasserzeichensammlung Piccard* (= Piccard Online), ed. Peter Rückert, Gerald Maier, et al. (Stuttgart, 1951–), https://www.piccard-online.de
Sloane Cat.	British Library, *Catalogus Librorum Manuscriptorum Bibliothecæ Sloanianæ*, 19 vols., in manuscript except for vol. i, n.d.
TCC	Cambridge, Trinity College
Walther	H. Walther, *Proverbia sententiaeque latinitatis Medii Aevi*, 6 vols. (Göttingen, 1963–9)

UROSCOPIC TEXTS: ABBREVIATIONS
AND SHORT TITLES

1&2U	*The First and Second Urines* (in **DU**)
15D	*Fifteen Discretions of Urine*
20C	*The Twenty Colours* (in **DU**)
20Col	*Twenty Colours by Digestion Groups*
20J	*Twenty Jordans*; also as Twenty-Jordan Series

3Reg	*The Third Knowledge of Urine: The Regions* (in **DU**)
4Con	*On the Four Contents of Urine* (in **DU**)
4Th	*Four Things that Belong to the Doom of Urine* (in **DU**)
Cleansing	*Cleansing of Blood*
CogPr	*Ad Cognoscendum Pregnantes* (in **DU**)
CplG	*Where the Complexions Are Generated* (in **DU**)
CplU	*The Complexions of Urine* (in **DU**)
DU	*The Dome of Uryne*
gra	*De gradibus* (in **DU**)
GrCon	*Urine that Has Great Contents* (in **DU**)
JP	*Judicium Perfectum Omnium Urinarum* (in **DU**)
LdH	*Lettre d'Hippocrate*
lun	*De etate lune* (in **DU**)
MWB	*Urines of Man, Woman, and Beast* (in **DU**)
pul	*To Know the Pulse* (in **DU**)
sig	*De signis* (in **DU**)
ST	*Six-Token List*
Ten Cold	*Ten Cold Ten Hot*
UMort	*Urina Mortis tam Hominum quam Mulierum* (in **DU**)
UMul	*Urina Mulieris* (in **DU**)
URufa	*Urina Rufa*
WBp	*Urine White and Brown* (Phlegm variant)
WBw	*Urine White and Brown* (Woman variant)
WR	*Urine White and Red*

INTRODUCTION

I. SCOPE OF EDITION

The texts selected for this volume are among the most broadly disseminated but still unedited urine treatises in Middle English. They range in date from the 1330s to the fifteenth century, probably no later than mid-century. Most of them are preserved in compendia containing various other practical medical texts, including phlebotomies, recipe collections, lunaries, plague treatises, and others; they offer concrete evidence of George Keiser's observation that 'the great majority of [Middle English] medical miscellanies contain at least one treatise on uroscopy' (Manual 10: 3661). Although the nine texts included here are anonymous, they serendipitously reflect the three major languages of medicine in medieval England, six of them with source texts in Latin and French, together with three that appear to be native compositions.

The treatises edited below are the following (for more detail on their content, see §III below):[1]

- A. *Twenty Colours by Digestion Groups* (a list of the standard late medieval urinary colours)
- B. *Urina Rufa* (a series of uroscopic signs and their diagnostic or prognostic significance)
- C. *Cleansing of Blood* (a summary of the main humoral and other correspondences on which uroscopic analysis is founded)

Texts A–C are derived from Latin originals found in both English and Continental contexts.

- D. *Urine White and Red*
- E. *Urine White and Brown* (Woman variant)
- F. *Urine White and Brown* (Phlegm variant)

Texts D–F are three related series of uroscopic signs, derived from Anglo-Norman or Old French originals and including the earliest attested Middle English uroscopy.

---

[1] Titles for the first eight texts are editorial, though those for texts B–G are based on words and phrases related to urine near the beginning of the texts or (for G) the beginning of the uroscopic material in the text. The title of text I, *The Dome of Uryne*, appears both in the opening sentence of the text and in an internal explicit (see lines I/1–2 and I/145 below). The nine texts correspond to the following items in Tavormina 2014: A=item 3.1, B=3.2, C=3.3, D=4.2, E=5.2.1, F=5.2.2, G=6.2, H=6.3, I=2.2.

    G. *Rufus Subrufus* (a listing of colours and their diagnostic implications, combined with a series of medical recipes for the ailments mentioned)

    H. *Ten Cold Ten Hot* (a brief compendium of summary paragraphs about humoral and astromedical correspondences, urinary colours, contents, etc.; like *Cleansing of Blood*, it provides a conceptual framework within which to understand the more practical, applied uroscopy of texts B and D–G)

    I. *The Dome of Uryne* (a larger compendium of uroscopic and related texts that contains both practical and theoretical components; in its fullest form, it includes segments on the colours and contents of urine, the humours, age of the moon, degrees of hot and cold, pulse, urines of death, women's urines, differences between men's and women's urines, and so on)

Although they are clearly rooted in the Latin and, to a lesser extent, the French uroscopic traditions, texts G–I appear to have been composed in English.

As a group, these texts provide an overview of the best-known elements of English vernacular uroscopy. They generally eschew detailed theoretical explanations, but are grounded firmly in Galenic humoralism and derived directly and indirectly from canonical Latin uroscopies, most notably Giles of Corbeil's *Carmen de urinis*, but also the works of Isaac Israeli, Theophilus Protospatharius, Gilbertus Anglicus, and others. Together they occur in over a hundred manuscripts, often with each other and with other practical medical texts: recipe collections, herbals, phlebotomies, and regimens of health. They contain a high concentration of medical vocabulary, some of it uncommon even in other medical texts (e.g. the technical terms for the colours, regions, and contents of urines), and some of it (such as names of sicknesses and the *materia medica* included in remedies) known from other sources but reinforced in the diagnostic and prognostic setting by these texts. Their frequent use of natural metaphors to help define particular colours and contents is also of interest from a lexical/semantic standpoint. They offer a window on the day-to-day application of uroscopic diagnosis by ordinary practitioners in the Middle Ages, and thus on one of the central arenas of healer–patient interaction in the period.

II. DESCRIPTIONS OF BASE MANUSCRIPTS

The nine texts in this edition occur in the following manuscripts; folio references for all individual witnesses to the texts will be found in Tavormina 2014.[2] For texts A, B, and C, which frequently appear together, sigla in bold indicate the sixteen manuscripts containing all three texts; double underlining indicates the one manuscript (S21) with only texts A and B, single underlining indicates the eight manuscripts with only texts B and C, and italics indicate the two manuscripts (*Ro6*, *S29*) with only texts A and C.[3] Twenty-three manuscripts present only one of the three texts. For the manuscript sigla, see pp. xv–xxi above.

Text A (*Twenty Colours*; 29 witnesses, 28 MSS): A7, **Cu5**, **Di1**, **Di2**, Eg3, **Gc4**, **Gc7**, H2, H8, **H10**, Ld, **Pe3**, Ra6, *Ro6*, **S6**, S9, S13, S21, *S29*, S35, S36, T7, **T11**, **T13**, W4 (2 forms of the text: prose and diagram with captions), **W6**, **W8**, **Yo**

Text B (*Urina Rufa*; 31 witnesses, 29 MSS): A3, Ad1, **Cu5**, **Di1**, **Di2**, Gc1 (2 copies: Gc1a, Gc1b), **Gc4**, **Gc7**, H7, **H10**, Hg1, Ld, Nm2, Pe1, **Pe3**, S1 (2 forms of the text: S1a, S1b), S5, **S6**, S21, S23, S35, S42, T7, **T11**, **T13**, **W6**, **W8**, W12, **Yo**

Text C (*Cleansing*; 41 witnesses, 38 MSS): A3, A8, A10, Ad1, Add3, **Cu5**, **Di1**, **Di2** (2 forms: Di2a, Di2b), Gc1 (2 copies: Gc1a, Gc1b), **Gc4** (2 forms: Gc4a, Gc4b), **Gc7**, H7, **H10**, Je, Ld, Nm1, Nm2, Om, Pe1, **Pe3**, *Ro6*, Ry1, S1, **S6**, S20, *S29*, S35, T2, T7, **T11**, **T13**, T15, W1, **W6**, **W8**, W10, W12, **Yo**

Text D (*Urine White and Red*; 14 witnesses, 14 MSS): A8, A9, Ad1, Add3, Cu3, Ht, Nw1, Ra3, Ro3, S6, S29, S40, S42, T12

Text E (*Urine White and Brown: Woman*; 26 distinct witnesses, 24 MSS): A3, A8, A9, A13, Ad2, Ar, Cc, Cp, Cu6, Ht, Nm2, Pm, Ro1 (3 copies of same text), Ro2, S1, S14, S24 (2 copies of same text), S28, S29 (2 forms: S29a, S29b), S35, Su, T13 (2 forms: T13a, T13b), T14, Yo

Text F (*Urine White and Brown: Phlegm*; 9 witnesses, 8 MSS): A7, A14, Eg3, Gc1 (2 forms: Gc1a, Gc1b), Nw2, S2, S20, W12

---

[2] Note the following additions and corrections to the information in Tavormina 2014: in item 2.0, *The Dome of Uryne*, correct the title *Judgement of Urynes* (pp. 24, 28) to *Judgement of All Urynes*; in item 5.2.1, *Urine White and Brown* (Woman), correct the folio run in BL Add. 4898 to 116ᵛ–117ʳ and add note to TCC R.14.39 indicating that it contains two separate forms of the text, bringing the total number of witnesses to twenty-nine, with twenty-six of them distinct; in item 6.3, *Ten Cold Ten Hot*, add the print witness, *The Boke of Knowledge of Thynges Vnknowen* (London: Robert Wyer, ?1554, ?1556).

[3] S29 (Sloane 1388) does contain a copy of the Latin version of *Urina Rufa*.

Text G (*Rufus Subrufus*; 18 witnesses, 18 MSS): A7, A8, A10, Ad6, Di1, Gc4, Je, Nm1, Nm2, Om, Ra2, R03, R06, S29, T15, W1, W10, W11

Text H (*Ten Cold Ten Hot*; 14 witnesses, 14 MSS): Co3, Cu3, Cu4, Gc6, H1, H4, H5, H7, Nm3, Ra6, S1, S10, S20, S32. Also occurs in a printed version, *The Boke of Knowledge of Thynges Vnknowen* (*K*; two printings, ?1554, ?1556), from which Nm3 was copied.

Text I (*The Dome of Uryne*; 55 witnesses, 54 MSS): A6, A9, A11, A14, Ad4, Ad7, Add2, Co1, Co3, Cu1, Cu3, Di1, Di3, Gw3, H1, H5, H6, H9, H11, H12, H13, Hg1, Ht, Lm2, Nw2, Nm3, Oa, Oc, Om, Pe2, Pm, Ra2, Ra4, Ra5, Ra7, R03, R04, R06, Ry2, S12, S15, S16, S29 (2 forms: S29a, S29b), Se, Sh, Sj3, St, T7, T8, T13, W1, W7, W8, W9. Also occurs in two printed versions, *The Seynge of Uryns* (*S*; with several reprints, 1525–75) and *The Judgement of All Urynes* (*J*; 1555); Nm3 is copied from the 1540 printing of *S*.

Because of the large number of witnesses to the texts, descriptions are limited here to the eight base manuscripts for those texts (Ad2, Cc, Gc4, Ld, S10, S15, S42, W12).

Overall page dimensions in the following descriptions are given in millimetres (height × width). It should, however, be noted that page size in these manuscripts can be variable, due in part to the degree of wear that many of them have seen and in part to the fact that they were often written by several scribes, sometimes over an extended period of time, or compiled from separate booklets of different sizes. When manuscripts are made up of both vellum and paper, the material with the larger number of leaves is given first. Parts of composite manuscripts are labelled with capital Roman numerals; capital letters are used to distinguish scribal hands where necessary. The language (i.e. English dialect identifications) of the manuscripts is briefly reported in the descriptions and then more fully discussed in §VI below. Watermarks have been compared to the reference collections compiled by Piccard ('Piccard Online'), Briquet, and Heawood. Though smaller in total extent than Piccard, Heawood's and Briquet's collections often record marks that are closer to those described below than their analogues in the Piccard database, thanks to the geographical origins of Heawood's and Briquet's source materials. As will be seen, the manuscripts illustrate the linguistic and topical heterogeneity of late medieval medical miscellanies, bringing together English, Latin, French, and mixed-language texts and combining uroscopy with recipe collections, herbal treatises, regiminal advice, bloodletting, astrological medicine, plague treatises, surgical texts, and the occasional religious or historical piece, in hands that range from highly formal and professional to careful but less elaborate to informal, possibly amateur writing.

Ad2: London, British Library, MS Additional 4898

s. xv. Vellum (with paper flyleaves). Ff. xv (iii modern, xii early modern)+ 140+xv (xii early modern, iii modern). Minor flaws (narrow holes) in original parchment on ff. 78, 139. The old front cover of the manuscript, with the initials 'E. H.', has been attached to the inside front cover.

DIMENSIONS: *c.* 192 × 130 mm; writing area: *c.* 140–5 × 85–8 mm. LINES/PAGE: *c.* 30–5.

HAND: One main scribe to f. 139^r, in a carefully written anglicana hand with secretary *a*. The scribe usually uses *y* for both *y* and *þ* (with the occasional appearance of *þ*), and *ʒ* for both *ʒ* and *z*. Miscellaneous English recipes and Latin notes added in later, less careful hands on ff. 81^v, 85^v, 86^r, 130^{rv}

WATERMARKS: Front flyleaves i–xii, rear flyleaves i–viii: pot or vase, with cover or crown, single handle, and crescent (or four-petalled flower, rarely) on top; indistinct letters or designs on bowl. Similar but not identical to Heawood, fig. 170 (mid- to late s. xvi); cf. Piccard 31439–68 (1534–62); Briquet 12803 (1586), 12806 (1600), 12519 (1536), 15266 (1567). Dates are consistent with the old binding for Edward Hoby.

CONTENTS

1. f. 1^{rv}: Three fragmentary English recipes on a heavy vellum leaf, probably originally a flyleaf; inc. 'For a fe⟨uer . . .⟩ smalleach ⟨. . .⟩ & rew'.

2. f. 2^r: Astromedical correspondences of signs, qualities, humours, etc.; *inc.* 'Aries Leo Sagittarius hot & drye attractivis'; eVK2 1068.25.

3. f. 2^r: Worm-charm; *inc.* 'Sent peter met with sent ?josmos & asked hem wer he had ben & he sayd yn the lond of wormys . . . & sle hem all to ix from nyne to viij . . .'.[4]

4. f. 2^v: Two French recipes for bragot and two Latin recipes for theriac and balsam; *inc.* 'Pernez vj galounes de bone ceruose . . . Mellis clara j quart' cassia fistula li. j'.

5. ff. 3^r–8^r: Latin recipes, mainly medical but with a few for colours and depilatories; *inc.* 'Sume radicem celidon' lj. semis anisij apij petroselini ana'.

---

[4] Charms involving holy personages (e.g. St Peter, St George, Job) and worms, as well as counting-down charms, occur sporadically throughout the English and Continental charm traditions, according to Lea Olsan (personal communication, Oct. 2015). Another charm involving 'Saint Job' and worms occurs in S42 item 5 (f. 36^v).

6. f. 8^{rv}: English medical recipes; *inc.* 'Ferst ley hym in a beed & hys heed lowe'; eVK2 1666.50.

7. ff. 9^{r}–25^{v}: Latin/English herbal and medical synonymy; *inc.* 'Amarusta anglice maythe amerok hondesfenl'.

8. ff. 25^{v}–26^{r}: Latin note on medical/herbal degrees; *inc.* 'Nota quod dicimus illam medicinam esse calidam in primo gradu'. Serves as a prologue to the medical recipes that follow. See Ad2 item 16.

9. ff. 26^{r}–32^{v}: Latin medical recipes; *inc.* 'Branka vicina semen lini fenugrecum omnia'.

10. ff. 33^{r}–38^{r}: John of Burgundy, *De epidemia*, with astrological prologue; *inc.* 'Isydorus eth. libro 4 c^{o} 9° sic ait Medicine curacio spernenda non est . . . Qvoniam omnia inferiora tam elementa'; eTK1290H-I, 1290K. See Gc4 item 43.

11. ff. 38^{r}–40^{v}: Master John Landryne, 'docto[r] in phisica & magist[er] in theologia', *Regimen sanitatis*; *inc.* 'Caueatis a tardis excessibus & potibus'. For Landryne (Landreyn), M.D., M.Th., D.Th. (*c.*1349–1409), see *BRUO* ii. 1090, Talbot and Hammond 1965: 160, Ussery 1971: 10–11, 48–9 (none of these sources records this treatise). To f. 38^{v}, the text is the same as a text in Sloane 3153, ff. 20^{v}–21^{r}, with the heading 'Quomodo homo debet se gubernare ut sit sanus in corpore, per Johannem Landre doctorem in fisica et magistrum in theologia' (see Getz 1990: 266).

12. ff. 41^{r}–42^{v}: 'Dilectissime frater' plague text; *inc.* 'Dilectissime frater vt intellexi multum times'; eTK 0431K, 0704L. See Gc4 item 45, S10 item 26.

13. ff. 42^{v}–68^{v}: *Tractatus de modo faciendi olea* (Latin recipes for oils, with additional medical recipes, virtues and uses of herbs, prognostics, etc.; at least one English heading, on a remedy for morphea, f. 45^{r}); *inc.* 'Quod omnia olea que sunt frigida de floribus'.

14. ff. 69^{r}–77^{v}: English medical recipes; *inc.* 'Tak and sethe verueyne & of betayne'; eVK2 5034.00. Recipes numbered in margins by original scribe, 1–80.

15. ff. 77^{v}–115^{r}: English medical and clothworking recipes; *inc.* 'Tak an handful of rue and anoþer of betayne'; eVK2 4953.25, 6356.75, 6243.75. Recipes numbered in margins by original scribe, 81–265; no visual break between items 14 and 15, which were presumably seen as a single text by the scribe. Eight Latin medical recipes embedded on f. 109^{rv}, six of them included in the marginal count.

16. f. 115^{rv}: English note on medical/herbal degrees; *inc.* 'We seyn þat

medycyne or þat herbe to ben in þe ferste degre hoot'; eVK2 7913.50. Content and phrasing similar to parts of Ad2 item 8.

17. ff. 115ᵛ–116ʳ: *Three Things of Inspecting Urines*; *inc.* 'He þat xal lokyn þe vrine hym byhoueth'; eVK2 2112.75; 'Guide' 11.3.

18. f. 116ʳᵛ: *The Doom of Urine Shalt Thou Cast in Four*; *inc.* 'Aftyr þese consideraciouns þe dom of þe vrine schal þou caste'; 'Guide' 7.4. Run in directly with item 17.

19. ff. 116ᵛ–117ʳ: *Urine White and Brown* (Woman variant); *inc.* 'Vrine at morwe whiȝt and aftyr mete broun'; 'Guide' 5.2.1. Run in directly with item 18. **Text E.2 below.**

20. f. 117ʳ: English recipe for 'euel in [þe] wombe'; *inc.* 'Qwo so haue euel in hys wombe nym þe ⟨jo⟩os of weybrede'. A two-line recipe run in directly with item 19.

21. ff. 117ᵛ–129ʳ· Latin medical recipes, *inc.* 'Recipe litargirij & tere & pulueriza'. Includes embedded text on signs of conception, *inc.* 'Sicut scribitur in tractatu de secretis mulierum' (f. 120ʳᵛ), which shares most of its content with ps.-Albertus Magnus, *De secretis mulierum*, ch. 7, ed. Barragán Nieto (2012: 422–41).

22. f. 129ʳᵛ: Latin medical verses on weights and measures, herbs, medicines, etc.; *inc.* 'Grana quater quinque scripuli pro pondere pone'; eTK 0589G.

23. ff. 129ᵛ–130ᵛ: Prognostics by New Year's Day; *inc.* 'ȝif þe firste day of geneuer be Sunday'; eVK2 2650.00; Manual 10: 3624, 3782–3. See also S10 item 18 (ch. [1]), W12 item 42.

24. f. 130ᵛ: On the nature of Saturn; *inc.* 'Wyte þou þat saturne is þe heyeste planete'; eVK2 8177.75; cf. eVK2 3136.50, 3696.00; Manual 10: 3617, 3768–9. See also Gc4 item 20, S10 item 18 (astromedical compendium, end of ch. 1), W12 item 41.

25. ff. 131ʳ–136ᵛ: Alphabetical Latin index to volume by original scribe, distinguishing numbered recto and verso pages with *a* and *b*, as in running heads *passim*; *inc.* 'Aqua pro oculis fo. 3.a / 19.a. Aqua preciosa pro oculis .53.b. / 112.a. / 112.b./' The uroscopies on ff. 115ᵛ–117ʳ are indexed as 'Vrinarum iudiciale 90 per totum' (f. 136ʳ), though '89.b., 90 per totum, 91.a.' would be more accurate. Explicit on f. 136ᵛ: 'Explicit tabula super medicinas in hoc libro contentas'.

26. ff. 136ᵛ–139ʳ: Latin and English medical and metallurgic recipes; *inc.* 'Tak a pound of oyle de olyue'; eVK2 4817.25.

27. ff. 139^r: Four English medical recipes and one Latin recipe; *inc.* 'Tak þe ȝelke of an hennes ey'; eVK2 6314.25. In a later hand.

28. f. 139^v: Miscellaneous Latin recipes, notes on measures, and a circular diagram for calculating the dominical letters, in later medieval hand(s). In post-medieval hands: a guide to the Arabic numeral forms used by the original scribe and two s. xvi/xvii English recipes for vomit and ague, in the hand also seen in the margin on f. 81^v, where it provides another anti-ague remedy.

29. f. 140^r: Pen trials with broad-nibbed pen; 'Helpe lord' in lighter ink, much finer pen.

f. 140^v Blank.

COLLATION: 1^8 2–12^{12}.

LANGUAGE: West Norfolk, though mixed with more standard forms.

TEXTUAL PRESENTATION: Texts in long lines. Two- to three-line initials and six- to seven-line initial *I/J*s to the left of text, in blue with red pen flourishing; small (one-line) initials and paraphs in alternating red and blue. Centred headings for many recipes. Marginal notes by original scribe in black underlined with red; red underlining of phrases in text and of headings to many of the English recipes. Running heads '.B.' (verso pages) and '.A.' (recto pages) in black ink touched with red, on ff. 2^v–8^v, 26^r–130^v, and 137^r–139^r. The same folios have also been numbered on the recto page, probably by the original scribe (his unusual 2-shaped form of Arabic '9' also appears in marginal numberings within the main text), in anticipation of the generally accurate index on ff. 131^r–136^v: ff. 26–130 are numbered 1–104 (with 31 doubled), ff. 137–9 are numbered 111–13, and ff. 3–8 are numbered 116, 115, 118, 117, 119–20, though the text itself is ordered correctly.

PROVENANCE, OWNERSHIP, OTHER NAMES AND DATES: Edward Hoby (1560–1617): motto and signature 'Fato quam voto | Edw' Hoby' on flyleaf vi^v, old front cover with Hoby's initials now attached to inside front cover; Sir Joseph Banks: donation note 'Presented by Joseph Banks, Esq., 11th. Feb. 1780' on flyleaf ix^r. Other names: 'Butt*es*' (f. 1^v); in a late medieval hand, 'Neale' (f. 2^r).

'Butt*es*' may be Sir William Butts of Norfolk, physician to Henry VIII, or a member of his family (Martin and Davies 2016, *ODNB*), though the surname and its variant 'But(t)' can be found in several different counties from the fourteenth to sixteenth centuries. For William Butts and his family, which might have included the John But who completes the A text of *Piers Plowman* in Bodleian Library, Rawlinson poet. 137, see Steer

1946; Hanna 1993: 28–31; *ODNB*, s.n. 'Butts, Sir William'; and R. Adams 2013a: 25–7, 2013b: 250–4. Hanna provides the fullest list of candidates for John But, revealing the geographical range of the name. The East Anglian language of the manuscript enhances the possibility that the manuscript passed through the hands of the Butts family at some point. The sixteenth-century Hoby family (Philip, Thomas, and Thomas's son Edward) could have crossed paths with the Butts family (William or his sons William, MP, Thomas, or Edmund) in court or possibly university or bibliophilic circles.

William Butts senior is considered a likely owner of the copy of *Piers Plowman* B in Bodleian Library, Rawlinson poet. 38 (R. Adams 2014: Introduction); his full name is carefully written at the end of the poem, just above the rubricated passus number on f. 101^r. It must be noted, however, that the letter forms of the initial *B* and the final *es* abbreviation in the Rawlinson manuscript and Ad2 are not entirely identical, which may weaken the identification of the somewhat less formal signature in Ad2.

DESCRIPTIONS: British Library, *Catalogue of Additions . . . Manuscripts 4101–5017* (1977): 272–3.

Cc: Cambridge, Corpus Christi College, MS 388

*c.*1320–30. Vellum. Ff. iii+54 (+narrow stub now numbered f. 35a)+iii. Folio 15 significantly imperfect at top outer corner; lower outer corner of f. 35 slightly imperfect; lower edges of ff. 37, 42 slightly imperfect; large hole in outer column of f. 38; small holes in left margin of f. 14 and lower margins of ff. 34, 35, 49.

DIMENSIONS: *c.*234×152 mm (ME uroscopy leaves *c.*228×152 mm); writing area: *c.*182×114 mm (ME uroscopy: *c.*189–96×124–30 mm). LINES/PAGE: *c.*38–41 (ME uroscopy 40–4).

HAND: One main hand, using an informal textura for most of the manuscript, with some anglicana letter forms in the ME recipe written in a lighter ink on f. 49ra, and a 'fully Anglicana' script for the uroscopy on ff. 53vb–54rb, but with all three scripts 'most probably by the same hand' (Benskin in Hunt 2001: 198–9). The scribe uses *y* for both *y* and *þ*, and *ʒ* for both *ʒ* and *z* (and occasionally *þ*). For more details on the scribe's orthography, see Benskin in Hunt 2001: 208–15.

CONTENTS

1. f. 1$^{ra–b}$: *Liber Ypocracii Galieni Sclepei* (verse prologue to *Lettre*

d'Hippocrate); *inc.* 'Ypocras se livere fyt / A le emperour Cesar myt'. Items 1–4, 6–7 are all edited in T. Hunt 2001.

2. ff. 1rb–2va: *De urinis secundum Magol*; *inc.* 'Urina viri sani est pura et aurei coloris'.

3. ff. 2va–3ra: Uroscopy section of *Lettre d'Hippocrate*; *inc.* 'Si le urine seyt blanche de tut le matyn'.

4. ff. 3ra–35va: Recipe section of *Lettre d'Hippocrate*, in French, English, and Latin; *inc.* 'Pernes ii unces de betoyne e iii unces de here te[re]stre'; eVK2 2131.00. Mixed French–English–Latin collection of 702 recipes.

5. f. 35$^{va–b}$: ps.-Galen, *Regimen by Months*; *inc.* 'In mense ianuarii ieiuno stomaco'. Atelous; Latin equivalent to 'Diet and Bloodletting: A Monthly Regimen' (Version A), ed. Mooney 1994. See Gc4 item 31, Ld item 13, S42 item 17.

6. f. 36$^{ra–va}$: Index to following recipes; *inc.* 'For werk of hefd / For werk of eris'.

7. ff. 36va–48vb: Medical recipe collection, mainly in English (*Medicine de tractatibus Ypocracii Gallieni et Sclepeii*); *inc.* 'Quo so haues werk and turning in his hed'; eVK2 3464.00, 2556.00; Manual 10: 3656, 3841. The earliest known version of the Middle English *Liber de Diversis Medicinis* (Keiser 2004: 238; 2005: 39–40). See S10 item 24.

8. f. 48vb: Medical recipes in Latin (one with English heading); *inc.* 'Accipe de radice altee & centauria'. Atelous.

9. f. 49$^{ra–b}$: Latin–English–French botanical/medical synonyms; *inc.* 'Millefolium a[nglice] milefolye stancrop a[nglice] crachecunte'.

10. f. 49ra: English medical recipe; *inc.* 'Tack muleyn and well it in sqwet mylck'; eVK2 5252.00.

11. f. 49$^{va–b}$: *Virtutes xij singnorum lunacionum*; *inc.* 'Nil capiti facies aries dum luna refulget'. Extract from *Flos medicine schole Salerni* (De Renzi i. 486–7, v. 53).

12. ff. 50$^{ra–vb}$: Latin medical recipes; *inc.* 'Recipe succum selodonii ?auoglosse ana cum modico sale'.

13. ff. 50vb–52ra: *Secreta medicine .H. Sampsonis de Clouburnel*; *inc.* 'Seus sunt lez erbes quy sunt appelle'. Anglo-Norman medical recipes, also found in part in Oxford, Bodleian Library, MS Bodley 761, ff. 11^{v}–21^{r} (at f. 12^{rv}), with the same attribution. Clouburnel identified by Jacquart (1979: 114) as Clos Bruneau, Paris (near the University of Paris).

14. ff. 52ra–53vb: *Nomina herbarum et earum virtutes* (Latin/Anglo-

Norman/English); *inc.* 'Garofila latine ro[manic]e garofle a[nglice] erbe ?manne'.

15. ff. 53vb–54rb: *Urine White and Brown* (Woman variant); *inc.* 'He[r] mayst þou knowen vrins be coloures vrine qwyt at morwen'; eVK2 7835.00. The earliest known version of any Middle English uroscopy. **Text E.1 below.**

COLLATION: 1–4^8 5^4 (including f. 35a) 6^8 ?7^8 (–6) 8^4. James (1912) analysed the last two quires as having eight and three leaves respectively, but Rand (2009) reports a missing leaf in quire 7 between ff. 48 and 49 (with a textual break between items 8 and 9 above), and notes further that ff. 44–6 'appear to be singletons' (*IMEP* 20: 115).

LANGUAGE: English texts from 'the borders of the East Midlands and East Anglia', and more specifically 'a small area in Ely and West Norfolk', with occasional, clustered traces of S. Lincolnshire language (Benskin, in Hunt 2001: 200–7, 228).

TEXTUAL PRESENTATION: Double columns; two- to five-line blue initials, two-line red initials; blue and some red paraphs; red pen flourishing on blue initials; red touching of ascenders in top line; lengthened descenders with decorative cross-strokes in bottom line; rubrication of titles and headings (rubrication and coloured paraphs end at f. 49^v); occasional marginal *nota* marks in red or brown ink.

PROVENANCE, OWNERSHIP, OTHER NAMES AND DATES: A name or phrase on f. 54^v, partly pasted over, appears under ultraviolet light to read 'ffa??s fflemyng'. Given by Archbishop Parker (see James 1912: i. xxxvi, Appendix to the Introduction).

DESCRIPTIONS: Nasmith 1777: 375; James 1912: ii. 238–9; Wilkins 1993: 103–5; T. Hunt 2001: 85–8; Rand 2009 (*IMEP* 20): 101–16, 144–5, 150.

Gc4: Cambridge, Gonville and Caius College, MS 336/725

s. xv$^{1/2}$–s. xv^{ex}. Vellum. Ff. ii+172+iii (new foliation 1–172 as of rebinding in 2008; many earlier editions and studies cite the older foliation, from 1–167 with additional leaves after old ff. 49, 52, 86, 92, 97, 124; old folio number 77 omitted).

Composite manuscript, in three parts. Part I: ff. 1–107, s. xv$^{1/2}$; Part II: ff. 108–62, s. xv^{ex}; Part III: ff. 163–72, s. xv^{ex}.

DIMENSIONS: *c.*242×176 mm; writing area variable: *c.*155–70×*c.*97–105 mm. LINES/PAGE: usually 33, occasionally fewer (30–2).

HANDS: Two main hands, with a third adding astronomical tables on ff. 163–72. Part I in bastard anglicana with frequent secretary *g* ('a careful, uniform, textura semiquadrata hand'; Voigts 1994: 128); part II mainly in secretary with some use of anglicana *a* and bastard secretary display script; Latin texts in part II have a greater admixture of anglicana forms of *a* and *g* than their English counterparts. Part III with mixed anglicana and secretary forms and bastard secretary display script.

CONTENTS

Certain folio runs in the first two parts of the manuscript are twins to selected portions of Takamiya MS 33, which was written by the same scribe as Gc4 part II. In part I, ff. 60ʳ–63ʳ = Takamiya 33, ff. 51ʳ–53ᵛ; ff. 96ʳ–97ᵛ = Takamiya 33, ff. 54ʳ–55ᵛ. In part II, ff. 108–57 are related to the 'Sloane Group' manuscripts identified by Voigts (1990) and are a twin to Takamiya 33, ff. 1–50. The texts on ff. 79ʳ–98ʳ in the Caius manuscript also occur in Sloane 340, ff. 39ᵛ–72ᵛ, though in a different order and interrupted by non-shared material on ff. 65ᵛ–70ʳ.

Part I

1. ff. 1ʳ–42ᵛ: Guy de Chauliac, *Chirurgia magna*, version 4 (*MED* and Manual 10; = version 3 in Wallner 1970 edition and Rand Schmidt 2001 (*IMEP* 17)): prologue, introductory *capitulum singulare*, rubrics, and book 1 (anatomy); *inc.* 'Afftir þat I haue first 30lden þankyngis'; eVK2 0756.00, 3638.00, 7644.00, 1881.00; Manual 10: 3646–8, 3831–2.

2. ff. 43ʳ–44ʳ: Richard of Wallingford, *Declaraciones Abbatis Sancti Albani super Kalendarium Regine*, sections 1–8; *inc.* 'Iff þer be maad a questioun of þe natiuite'; eVK2 2691.00. See also Gc4 item 32, W12 item 22.

3. ff. 44ʳ–45ʳ: Astronomical calculations of the position of the sun from 1381 onward; *inc.* 'And for as miche as of þe grees'; eVK2 1949.00, 8183.00.

4. ff. 45ʳ–54ᵛ: *The Four Elements*, chs. 1–4; *inc.* 'It is to vndirstonde þat eueri man'; eVK2 3209.00, 2488.00; 'Guide' 8.2.2c.

5. f. 55ʳᵛ: Table of contents for following treatise; *inc.* 'The j chapitre is of medicyns symple digestiuis'.

6. ff. 55ᵛ–65ʳ: Treatise on digestive and evacuative medicines; *inc.* 'Forsoþe sume goode freendis þe whiche trowide me'; eVK2 1965.00, 3571.00.

7. ff. 65ᵛ–68ᵛ: *The Golden Table of Pythagoras*; *inc.* 'Maister pictagorus þe noble philosophre'; eVK2 3536.00; Manual 10: 3625–6, 3786. Cf. S42 item 15, W12 item 5.

8. ff. 69ʳ–72ʳ: *Rufus Subrufus*; *inc.* 'Here bigynneþ a tretice of a mannys or of a wommans vrine'; eVK2 2193.00, 1797.00; 'Guide' 6.2a. **Text G below.**

9. f. 72^r: *Cleansing of Blood*; *inc.* 'Eueri vrine is a clensinge of blood'; Manual 10: 3662, 3852–3; 'Guide' 3.3.2a. Cf.Text C below; incomplete.

10. ff. 72^v–75^r: Treatise on inspection of urines; *inc.* 'Alle þo men þat wolen be trewe iugis'; eVK2 0839.00, 7798.00; 'Guide' 11.4.

11. ff. 75^v–76^r: *Cleansing of Blood*; *inc.* 'Eueri vryne is clensynge of blood'; eVK2 1579.00; Manual 10: 3662, 3852–3; 'Guide' 3.3.1b. Cf.Text C below.

12. f. 76^{rv}: *Urina Rufa*; *inc.* 'Uryne rufa signifieþ heele & good disposicioun'; eVK2 7818.50, 7810.50; Manual 10: 3662, 3852–3; 'Guide' 3.2.1c. Cf.Text B below.

13. f. 77^r: Erased, but originally contained a copy of the same material found on f. 72^r (the end of *Rufus Subrufus* and incomplete *Cleansing of Blood*); *inc.* 'a3ens Take oold schoon & stynkynge . . . Eueri vrine is a clensinge of blood'.

14. ff. 77^v–78^r: *Twenty Colours by Digestion Groups* (wheel diagram; no flasks); *inc.* 'Whi3t colour of vrine as þe watir of a welle'; eVK2 8106.50; Manual 10: 3662, 3852–3; 'Guide' 3.1.2a. Text A.2 below.

ff. 78^v–79^v: Blank.

15. ff. 80^r–98^v: Henry Daniel, *Liber Uricrisiarum* (Seventeen-Chapter Abridgement); *inc.* 'Uryne is as myche to seie as oon in þe reynes' (prec. by a table of contents, f. 80^{rv}); eVK2 7788.00; Manual 10: 3661, 3851–2; 'Guide' 15.3.

16. ff. 98^v–99^r: *Twenty Jordans* (Lactea incipit; abridged 10-colour version, also found in Sloane 340, ff. 73^v–74^r); *inc.* 'Lactea is as whey & bitokeneþe if he slepiþ not'; eVK2 3320.00; Manual 10: 3662, 3852; 'Guide' 1.4.

17. f. 99^r: *For to Know a Beast's Water from a Man's*; *inc.* 'The beestis watir wole be whi3t þicke'; eVK2 6607.00, 'Guide' 7.3.3.

18. ff. 99^r–100^v: Latin list of compound medicines; similar but not identical to text in Sloane 282, f. 188^{rv}(*inc.* 'Electuaria calefacientia diamargariton'; eTK 0412C, 0495D). Possibly derived from the *Antidotarium Nicolai*, though not arranged alphabetically (cf. eTK 0165A, 0165D, 0165G, 0490B, 0490C*).

19. ff. 101^r–102^r: *Tractatus de Physica et Chirurgia*; *inc.* 'This rule is vndirstonden as to my witt'; eVK2 7464.50; 'Guide' 14.2.3a.

20. f. 102^{rv}: On the nature of Saturn; *inc.* 'It is for to vndirstonde þat saturnus'; eVK2 3136.50; cf. eVK2 8177.75, 3696.00; Manual 10: 3617, 3768–9. See also Ad2 item 24, S10 item 18 (astromedical compendium, end of ch. [1]), W12 item 41.

21. ff. 102ᵛ–105ʳ: *Book of Ipocras of Life and Death*; *inc.* 'In þis book he techiþ for to knowe'; eVK2 3064.00, 8015.00; Manual 10: 3623, 3779.

22. f. 105ʳ: 'For to know all manner of sores' (on wounds and zodiacal signs); *inc.* 'If þou se a soor or apostyme'; eVK2 2704.00.

23. f. 105ᵛ: *Tabula ad sciendum quis planeta signat in omni hora*; *inc.* 'Dies Dominicus Dies lune Dies Martis'. Table of planetary hours.

24. f. 106ʳ: On planetary aspects (with diagram); *inc.* 'It is to knowe þat ech signe þat biholdiþ'; eVK2 3190.50.

25. f. 106ᵛ: Correspondences of signs, planets, elements, complexions, ages, seasons, qualities (Latin); *inc.* 'Signa Aries Leo Sagitarius Planete Mars Sol Elementum Ignis'.

26. f. 107ʳᵛ: *Eleven Manners of Urine for a Woman*; *inc.* 'Uryne of a woman þat is cleer schynynge'; eVK2 7806.00; 'Guide' 7.2.4. Signs drawn from both the *Lettre d'Hippocrate* (or one of its English derivatives) and *Urina Rufa*.

Part II

27. ff. 108ʳ–128ʳ: Excerpts from John Lydgate and Benedict Burgh, *Secrees of Old Philisoffres*; *inc.* 'It is to be titelled how preved withoute obstacle'; eVK2 3177.00; Manual 6: 1896–9, 2152–4; *NIMEV* 935.

28. f. 128ᵛ: Governance of the limbs by zodiacal signs; *inc.* 'The gret clerkis of astronomye sayn that euery lyme'; eVK2 6834.00.

29. ff. 128ᵛ–130ᵛ: Treatise on the zodiacal signs; *inc.* 'Aries is the signe of a ram which rayneth'; eVK2 1066.50.

30. f. 130ᵛ: Correspondences of signs, directions, qualities, complexions; *inc.* 'Aries Leo and Sagittarius thes thre'; eVK2 1072.50.

31. f. 131ʳᵛ: ps.-Galen, *Regimen by Months*; *inc.* 'In the monthe of Janyver ffastynge'; eVK2 2961.00; Manual 10: 3659, 3849–50. See also Cc item 5, Ld item 13, S42 item 17.

32. f. 132ʳ: Richard of Wallingford, *Declaraciones Abbatis Sancti Albani super Kalendarium Regine*, section 1 (= lines 1–22 of English translation on f. 43ʳ above); *inc.* 'Nota pro kalendario quod si fiat questio'; eTK 0931P (this MS), 1448E–F.

33. ff. 132ᵛ–136ʳ: On the planets and nativities; *inc.* 'Ther bee 7 planetis in the firmament'; eVK2 2202.00, 7141.00.

34. ff. 136ᵛ–137ʳ: On the spheres and planets; *inc.* 'Formalis mundi machina consistit in 12'.

35. ff. 137^v–141^r: On signs of excess and remedies therefor; *inc.* 'Omne enim corpus humanum cum sit ex quatuor'.

36. ff. 141^v–142^r: *Practica Urinarum; inc.* 'It is to vnderstonde who so will loke an vryne'; eVK2 3229.00; Manual 10: 3662, 3852; 'Guide' 11.2.

37. ff. 142^v–144^v: *Twenty Jordans* (Rubea incipit; illustrated); *inc.* 'Rubea a feuere thurgh chafyng of the leuer'; Manual 10: 3662, 3852; 'Guide' 1.2.

38. f. 144^v: *Expositiones colorum urine; inc.* 'Color rubeus est quasi flamma ignis'; eTK 0235B.

39. ff. 144^v–145^r: Latin recipes for *aqua mirabilis* (2) and *puluis diureticus* (called *puluis Walteri* in explicit); *inc.* 'Recipe galang' gariofi' quibub' zinziber mellilot".

40. ff. 145^r–148^v: ps.-Aristotle, *Regimen sanitatis; inc.* 'Aristo[te]les autem scribens Alexandro magno ait O alexander'; eTK 0135M.

41. ff. 148^v–149r: *Tractatus de mirabilibus aque ardentis rectificati; inc.* 'Ab origine mundi vniuersa naturaliter phisicancium multitudo'.

42. f. 149^{rv}: Brief Latin recipe for *pulvis contra cardiacam passionem & nimiam debilitatem; inc.* 'Recipe camphor' Muse ana [ounce] j Rasure eboris'.

43. ff. 149^v–153^r: John of Burgundy, *De epidemia*, without astrological prologue; *inc.* 'Ego Johannes de Burgundia diuino auxilio inuocato'; eTK 0488P, 1290H-I.

44. ff. 153^r–155^v: John of Burgundy, *Medicine against the Pestilence Evil* (Four-Chapter Plague Treatise); *inc.* 'This clerke seith in the first chapitre'; eVK2 2175.00, 7380.00; Manual 10: 3662–4, 3856–9.

45. ff. 155^v–157^v: 'Dilectissime frater' plague text (adaptation of John of Burgundy, *De epidemia*); *inc.* 'Dilectissime frater vt intellexi multum'; eTK 0431K, 0704L. See Ad2 item 12, S10 item 26.

f. 158^r blank.

46. f. 158^v: Astronomical volvelle with labels in mixed Latin and English.

47. f. 159^r: Vein man with labels in Latin.

48. f. 159^v: Zodiac man with bloodletting warnings for each sign, labels in Latin.

49. ff. 160–2: Originally blank, with later sketches of dog and ?hare on 160^v and crude later sketches of four heads on 161^r.

Part III

50. ff. 163^r–172^r: Latin astronomical tables and instructions in another hand; *inc.* 'Pro figura erigenda primo quere signum'.

COLLATION: Part I: $1-5^8$ 6^2 $7-9^8$ 10^{10} (–10) 11^4 (unsigned) $12-14^8$ 15^4; Part II: $1-6^8$ 7^8 (–6); Part III: 1^{10} (unsigned).

Most of the gatherings in the manuscript carry signatures in the hand of the part II scribe (part I: a–h, j–k, l–o; part II: a, c–h) and catchwords by the original scribes of each part. No apparent textual loss at transition between quires a and c in part II.[5]

LANGUAGE: Broadly East Midland, possibly with deliberate normalization of forms towards the 'Type I' variety of Middle English described by Samuels (1963: 84–7) and in *LALME* i. 40.

TEXTUAL PRESENTATION: Most texts in long lines, with a handful of list-based texts in double columns (ff. 55^r–65^r, 99^r–100^v, 106^v) or figures of division (73^{rv}); rime royal stanzas (ff. 108^r–128^r); short line captions under flasks in *Twenty Jordans* (ff. 142^v–144^r). Two- to six-line initials in gold leaf with blue and red decoration (blue, red, and green in part II). Border decoration in part I uses red pen-flourishing, usually either erased or drawn over with a later programme of decorative floral borders matching those in part II. One-line initials in red and blue, often alternating; a few decorated initials in the same black ink as the main text. Alternating red and blue paraphs and line fillers. Rubrication of titles and headings; rubrication of alternating words or columns in tables for legibility. Red underlining of some texts, both Latin and English, highlighting selected significant content; red brackets in figures of division.

ILLUSTRATIONS: Spheres of life and death, square of truth and falsehood in *The Golden Table of Pythagoras* (ff. 67^r, 68^{rv}); flasks in margins of *Rufus Subrufus* (f. 69^{rv}); illustrated format of *Twenty Colours by Digestion Groups* (ff. 77^v–78^r); astronomical tables and charts, items 23–5 above (ff. 105^v–106^v); flasks in *Twenty Jordans* (ff. 142^v–144^r); volvelle (f. 158^v), vein man (f. 159^r), zodiac man (f. 159^v), astronomical tables in item 50 above (ff. 163^v–172^r).

PROVENANCE, OWNERSHIP, OTHER NAMES AND DATES: 'John Bank*es*' written very lightly on f. 162^v, in s. ?xv^{ex}/xvi^{in} hand. Donated by William Moore (d. 1659).

DESCRIPTIONS: James 1907–14: i. 378–80; Rand Schmidt 2001 (*IMEP* 17): 60–72, 123; Voigts 1990: 50–3; Honkapohja 2017: 47–9.

---

[5] I follow the signature system as a guide to original collation, leading to one minor difference with James (1907–14: i. 378), who takes sigs. f and g (my part I quire 6 and 7) as a single ten-leaf gathering. Honkapohja follows James in this detail and also distributes leaves in sig. k and the unsigned quire after sig. k slightly differently from James's and my collations (2017: 47). Both James and Honkapohja treat part III as the last quire of part II.

Ld: Oxford, Bodleian Library, MS Laud misc. 553

s. xv. Vellum, except for paper ff. i–ii, 77–8. Ff. iii+81 (foliated to 78, with doubles of ff. 14, 15, and 23; ff. 76–8 blank; some irregularly shaped leaves).

DIMENSIONS: *c.*255×175 mm; writing area variable, *c.*190–230×*c.*120–65 mm. LINES/PAGE variable, 28–41 ll./p.

HANDS: Several distinct anglicana hands. The uroscopy, regimen, lunary, and recipe texts on ff. 30ᵛ–74ᵛ are written in two alternating hands using anglicana scripts.

WATERMARKS: Ff. i and 77 (flyleaves): similar to 'Post or Pillar' in Heawood 1950: 142, pl. 476 (#3487, dated 1636).

CONTENTS

1. ff. 1ʳ–4ᵛ: Papal bull from Innocent VI to Thomas de Shifford, concerning provision of a canonry of Hereford (dated [9] kal. Febr, 3 Inn VI = [?] Jan. 1355).

2. ff. 5ʳ–6ᵛ: English culinary recipes; *inc.* 'Nym resons & do out þe stones'; eVK2 3658.00; Manual 10: 3679, 3888. Atelous.

3. f. 7ʳᵛ: Latin prognostics by the twelve days and nights of Christmas; *inc.* 'Dicendum quod si dies Natalis domini' (prol.); 'Hec sunt signa duodecim noctium a natiuitate domini' (text). Atelous.

4. ff. 7ᵛ–19ʳ: *Agnus Castus*; *inc.* 'Agnus castus ys an herbe þat clupeth tout-sane'. Letters A, C–S; *des.* 'Explicit liber de uirtutibus herbarum'; eVK2 0769.00; Manual 10: 3642, 3822–3. Incomplete.

5. f. 19ᵛ: English medical recipes; *inc.* 'Tak twey part of led lytarge o part frankencens and iij part mastyk'; eVK2 6420.00.

6. ff. 20ʳ–23bᵛ: *Book of Medicines* ('þe Vertu of Herbes'); *inc.* 'Quintefoile & five leef þus al on . . . ⟨h⟩ote & d⟨rye⟩ in þe ij degre'; eVK2 4052.00, 0311.00; Manual 10: 3643, 3823.

7. ff. 24ʳ–29ᵛ: English medical recipes; *inc.* 'smale in a morter & seþe hem in fayre water'; eVK2 5366.00. Acephalous and atelous.

8. f. 30ʳ: Latin and English medical recipes; *inc.* 'Accipe vnam libram ordei puri & coque . . . Tak smalache percyle lythywert'. Heading for following text in a sprawling display script near bottom of page, between Latin and English recipes: 'Here begyneth ypocraces bok', with interlinear note in later hand, 'of this I haue hird'.

9. f. 30ᵛ: *Letter of Ipocras*: Verse Prologue, 'Man Beast and Bird' overview, 'Six-Token List'; *inc.* 'Ypocras this boke made 3are / and sende to þe emperur Sesar . . . Eueryche man beste & bryd þat body hath . . . þylke man

ys hole þat hys vreyne in morwe tyde ys wyȝte & after mete & tofore wyt or rede'; eVK2 8204.00, 1549.00, 7320.00; Manual 10: 3655, 3662, 3840, 3852–3; *NIMEV* 1605; 'Guide' 4.1.1; Keiser 2003: 310–14.

10. ff. 30ᵛ–31ʳ: *Twenty Colours by Digestion Groups*; *inc.* 'Vrina subrubea as crocus occidentalis'; Manual 10: 3662, 3852–3; 'Guide' 3.1.1a. **Text A.1 below.**

11. ff. 31ʳ–32ʳ: *Urina Rufa*; *inc.* 'Vrina rufa signefieth hel[þ] and gode disposicion'; eVK2 0533.00, 7811.00; Manual 10: 3662, 3852–3; 'Guide' 3.2.1a. **Text B below.**

12. f. 32ʳᵛ: *Cleansing of Blood*; *inc.* 'Eche vrine is þe clansyng of blod'; eVK2 1520.00, 7801.00; Manual 10: 3662, 3852–3; 'Guide' 3.3.1a. **Text C below.**

13. ff. 32ᵛ–33ʳ: ps.-Galen, *Regimen by Months*; *inc.* 'In þe monthe of Janyuer fastyng'; eVK2 2962.00; Manual 10: 3659, 3849–50. See Cc item 5, Gc4 item 31, S42 item 17.

14. ff. 33ʳ–34ᵛ: Latin lunary; *inc.* 'Luna prima dies [?vtib *canc.*] est vtilis omnibus agendis'. Similar to Weisser's text Ef₂L (1982: 209–14).

15. ff. 34ᵛ–74ᵛ: *Letter of Ipocras* medical recipes; *inc.* 'For eche of þe hed het hulle wort and eisel'; English and occasional Latin; eVK2 2128.00, 1825.00, 6122.00. Incomplete: syntactic breaks and apparent loss of leaves between ff. 45ᵛ and 46ʳ, 55ᵛ, and 56ʳ.

16. f. 74ᵛ: Incomplete list of books and chapters in *Ypocraces Bok*, 1.1–2.4 (ff. 30ᵛ–47ʳ); *inc.* 'De cognicione quatriplicis vrine & diffinicionibus humorum'. Latin and English.

17. f. 75ʳᵛ: Page from a s. xv missal, Sarum Use (Epistle, Alleluia, and Gospel for the First Sunday after the Octave of Easter; Communion for the Octave of Easter: 1 John 5: 5–10, John 20: 26, 1 Cor. 5: 7–8, John 20: 19–25); Dickinson 1861–83: 385–7.

ff. 76–8 blank.

COLLATION: The manuscript may be a combination of several booklets, written in several hands and with a number of missing leaves: the English culinary recipes (ff. 5ʳ–6ᵛ), Latin weather prognostications (f. 7ʳᵛ), and *Agnus Castus* (ff. 7ᵛ–19ʳ) may have comprised one unit; the *Book of Medicines* (f. 20ʳ–23bᵛ; f. 20ʳ appears more worn than the preceding page) and recipe text (ff. 24ʳ–29ᵛ) a second; and *Ypocraces Bok* (ff. 30ʳ–74ᵛ) a third.

To f. 29, the quiring is irregular, with quires of different sizes and missing leaves (possibly 1⁴ 2?⁸ (?–3, –5, –6) 3¹⁶ (–2, –6, –11, –15) 4⁴ (–3) 5⁴ (–3, –4) 6⁸ (–5, –6)). Ff. 30–66 are quired in eights, with only three lost leaves (7–8⁸ 9⁸ (–1) 10⁸ (–4, –5) 11⁸). The rest of the manuscript (ff. 67–74) is again irregularly quired (possibly 12^6 (–4 to –6) 13^2 $14^{?4}$; two singletons and a bifolium as rear flyleaves). No catchwords or signatures.

LANGUAGE: Herefordshire (Hand A, ff. 1^r–19^r); Gloucestershire (Hands C and D alternating, ff. 30^v–74^v). *LALME* i. 150, iii. 149, 164. LPs 7310 (A), 7211 (C/D).

TEXTUAL PRESENTATION: Variable from text to text, especially in the texts preceding *Ypocraces Bok*. Mainly blue initials, sometimes flourished with red, mainly one to three lines deep; alternating red and blue paraphs. Red and blue crosses in charms; some charms struck through by later hands. In *Ypocraces Bok* (ff. 30^v–74^v), the book number or an abbreviation ('P' = 'Primus'; 'S' = 'Secundus') and the letter 'L' are used as running verso/recto headers, usually in blue and red respectively; marginal notes, sometimes rubricated, indicate chapters within the books in the recipe collection. Occasional red underlining and red manicules.

PROVENANCE, OWNERSHIP, OTHER NAMES AND DATES: Ownership notes: 'Robert Okeham ys booke' (74^v; s. xvi); 'Liber Guil: Laud Archiepiscopi Cant. & Cancellar: vniversit' Oxon. 1637.' (2^r). Other names: 'Helias' (2^v), 'Alysander Bayis' (4^v; s. xv), 'Iames' (5^r), 'John Cokk*es* of ⟨. . .⟩' (6^r; s. xv), 'Clement' (47^r, twice; s. xv/s. xvi); recipe heading, 'A prowyd myddesson for the tovthe ache pprowyd by John wyllson of bakham þe keppere' (3^v; s. xv/s. xvi).

John Cokkes or Cokkys is the name of a well-known mid-fifteenth-century physician with Oxford associations (Talbot and Hammond 1965: 134–6; Getz 1990: 265; *BRUO* i. 457; Jones 1994: 106–7 and *ODNB*, s.n. 'Cokkys, John'). Wyllson may be John Wilson, barber of London and Warden of the Barbers' Company in 1476 and 1486 (Young 1890: 3). For 'Bakham', a place name as yet unidentified, perhaps read 'Peckham' (now a district in southeast London)?

DESCRIPTIONS: Madan, Hunt, et al. 1895–1953: no. 1118; Coxe 1852: ii. 398–9, p. 570 (Hunt's notes); Brodin 1950: 97–8, 103; Ogilvie-Thomson 2000: 56–71.

S10: London, British Library, MS Sloane 213

s. xv (early?). Vellum (with paper flyleaves). Ff. iv+164+iv. An older foliation with two leaves numbered 76 has been corrected; in the corrected numbering, a blank leaf after f. 160 has been left unnumbered (its old number 160 crossed out, but no new number given).

DIMENSIONS: $c.270 \times 185$–93 mm; writing area: 201×142–3 mm (columns $c.65$–8 mm wide). LINES/PAGE: 46.

HANDS: Two principal hands, both anglicana formata, both hands using *y* for both *y* and *þ*: Hand A on ff. 5^r–41^r, 47^r–124^r; Hand B (with different descender shapes for *q*, *þ/y*) on ff. 124^v–159^r. Hand A provides the heading to 'Quid pro quo' on f. 134^v, but the text is by Hand B. Two other hands, one a current anglicana and the other a current secretary, contribute the *Isagoge* text on ff. 41^v–46^v; the change of hand occurs on f. 42^r, line 17. Miscellaneous later hands on ff. 1^r–4^v, 109^v–110^r, 161^{rv}, 163^r (recipes, plague treatise, weights and measures, etc.).

CONTENTS[6]

f. 1^r: Blank except for shelfmarks (four different marks, two of them crossed out).

1. ff. 1^v–3^v: Middle English and Latin medical recipes; eVK2 5373.00.

2. f. 3^r: Miscellaneous Latin medical texts: ophthalmic recipes; prayers for physicians; Latin verses (excerpts from Giles of Corbeil, *Carmen de urinis*; moral on hope and fear from Aesopic fable 'The Hares and the Frogs'; miscellaneous medical verses, at least partially from *Flos medicine*).

ff. 3^v–4^r: Blank.

3. f. 4^v: Originally blank; now containing a paste-in 'Elenchus Tractatuum quæ hoc MSS. continentur'.

4. ff. 5ra–24va: Odo de Meung-sur-Loire (attrib.), *Macer Floridus de viribus herbarum*. Latin verse herbal; *inc.* 'Herbarum quasdam dicturus carmine vires'. English synonyms included in a number of chapter headings. Ends on f. 24va with short prose paragraph on the humours and their correspondences; *inc.* 'Quatuor sunt humorum genera humano corpore'; eTK 0609K, 0610A, 0610C–D.

5. ff. 24vb–32va: *Le lapidaire en vers* (Anglo-Norman); *inc.* (Prol.) 'Cil ke eiment pieris de pris / Deiuent sauoir quele ad le pris'; (text) 'Li ancien nus uoit disant / E enz es liures trouom lisant'; Dean 1999: 197 (no. 357).

6. ff. 32vb–36va: Marbode of Rennes, *De lapidibus*. Latin verse lapidary; *inc.* 'Evax rex arabum fertur scripsisse neroni'; eTK 0530B–C.

7. ff. 36va–37rb: Anonymous Latin verses on the properties of sixteen precious stones; *inc.* 'Capnites specie cristallinus optima gemma'.

8. f. 37$^{ra–b}$: Marbode of Rennes, Epilogue to *De lapidibus* (verses on ring

---

[6] Sloane 213 diverges from the other base manuscripts for this edition in the relative sophistication of the Latin texts it contains, including such works as the *Isagoge* of Ḥunayn ibn 'Isḥāq (Johannitius), Ibn Zuhr's regimen of health, Abū al-Ṣalt's treatise on simples, John of St-Amand's *Areolae*, and Honorius Augustodunensis's *Imago mundi* (items 12–15, 20 below).

and gem); *inc.* 'Arulus [*lege* Anulus] vt gemmam digitis aptandis hiberem [*sic*]'.

9. f. 37rb: *De virtutibus lapidum*; *inc.* 'In quocunque lapide inueneris arietem leonem sagittarium insculpi'; eTK 0715G–I. Miscellaneous notes on the virtues of engraved gems, jet, and ceraunius/pyrope.

10. ff. 37rb–38ra: Otto of Cremona (attrib.; sometimes attrib. to Giles of Corbeil), *De simplicibus aromaticis*, part 1 (verse; titled *De eleccione specierum*;); *inc.* 'Res aloes lignum preciosa sit hoc tibi signum'; eTK 0505G, 1351B.

11. ff. 38rb–41rb: *De variis morbis et medicamentis*; *inc.* 'Aiunt medici & hij qui de arborum & herbarum scribere naturis'; eTK 0072L.

12. ff. 41^v–46^v: Johannitius, *Isagoge*; *inc.* 'Medicina diuiditur in 2as partes s. in theoricam & practicam'; eTK 0738I, 0856E–F*. In long lines and different hands from preceding and following texts.

13. ff. 47ra–51vb: Ibn Zuhr (Avenzoar), *Regimen sanitatis (Kitab al-Taysir)*; *inc.* 'Capitis cutis conseruabitur si eam balneaueris prius cum melle'; eTK 0187J.

14. ff. 51vb–63vb: Abū al-Ṣalt ('Abulzale'), *Liber de medicinis simplicibus*, trans. Arnau de Vilanova; *inc.* 'Iuiube sunt temperate sed declinant aliquantulum'; eTK 0801K.

15. ff. 63vb–91ra: John of St-Amand, *Areolae*; *inc.* 'Sicut dicit Galienus primo simplicium medicinarum'; eTK 1484A–C.

16. ff. 91ra–109vb: *Treatise of Oils and of Waters Medicinable*; *inc.* 'Take a vessele of erthe þat be made in þe maner of a Juste'; eVK2 2314.00, 4902.00.

17. ff. 109vb–110ra: Latin medical recipes in a later hand.

f. 110^{rv} originally blank.

18. ff. 111ra–121ra: Astromedical compendium, divided into unnumbered chapters signalled by two- to three-line initials (1–5, 7–8) and/or headings referring to the 'suyng chapitere' (1–5) or announcing 'Here sues . . .' (6–8). Sections of the compendium, with some omissions and rearrangements, also appear in Harley 1735 (John Crophill's notebook), Sloane 2270 (John Eames's Book), and W12 (see below).

ch. [1] (f. 111^{ra–va}): Prognostics by New Year's Day ('Prophecies of Esdras'); *inc.* 'If þe first day of Januere be sononday'; eVK2 2648.00; Manual 10: 3617, 3624, 3768–9, 3782–3. Also in Ad2 item 23, W12 item 42. Ends with a paragraph on the nature of Saturn that also circulates on its own, as in Ad2 item 24, Gc4 item 20, W12 item 41.

ch. [2] (f. 111^{va-b}): Prognostics by thunder; *inc.* 'Thondere in Januere signyfies þat same 3ere grete wyndes'; eVK2 7561.00; Manual 10: 3624, 3783–4. Also in W12 item 43.

ch. [3] (ff. 111vb–113ra): Perilous days, seasonal regimen, days for bleeding, governance of limbs by zodiacal signs; *inc.* 'Wite þou þat in ilk monethe ere tuo disemoles'; eVK2 8177.00, 1818.00, 2794.00, 1183.00, 1177.00, 1237.00, 0748.00, 1349.00; Manual 10: 3642, 3780. Also in W12 item 40.

ch. [4] (ff. 113ra–115ra): Lunary; *inc.* 'Lune j es profitable for alle thynges to be done'; eVK2 3427.00. Discussed by Taavitsainen (1988: 73–4, 127–9).

ch. [5] (ff. 115rb–117ra): On the spheres, planets, planetary hours, zodiacal signs; *inc.* 'Aboue þe 4 elementes ere 9 speres'; eVK2 0717.00, 1543.00, 4492.00.

ch. [6] (ff. 117ra–118va): On various components of the macrocosm and microcosm; *inc.* 'And wite þou þat in ilk man and ilk womman regnes'; eVK2 8176.00; 'Guide' 6.3. **Text H below**, *Ten Cold Ten Hot*, is embedded at the end of this chapter.

ch. [7] (ff. 118va–120ra): Certain Rules of Physiognomy; *inc.* 'Alexander þe grete conquerour in alle his conquest & werres'; eVK2 0802.00.

ch. [8] (ff. 120ra–121ra): Onomastic prognostications; *inc.* 'Take tuo names of men whilk are gyuen þem'; eVK2 6412.00, 6199.00, 1464.00, 0878.00. Also in W12 item 44.

19. ff. 121ra–124^r: *Treatise of Geometry*; *inc.* 'Geometri es saide of þis greke worde geos'; eVK2 2019.00; Manual 10: 3639–40, 3811.

20. ff. 124va–130va: Honorius Augustodunensis, *Imago mundi*, bk. 1, chs. 1–109; *inc.* 'Mundus dicitur quasi vndique motus'; eTK 0047C, 0893G.

21. ff. 130va–134rb: Latin medical recipes, with index on ff. 133vb–134rb; *inc.* 'Diagridium ita conficitur mense augusti luna decrescente'.

22. ff. 134va–135vb: *Quid pro quo*; *inc.* '[C]irca ea que sunt utilia in curacionibus'; eTK 0206A.

23. ff. 135vb–138rb: English medical recipes; *inc.* 'Tak a pond of þe burgeons of þe popyltre'; eVK2 4822.00.

24. ff. 138rb–159ra: English medical recipes; *inc.* 'Here beginnes gode medicines for diuers euilles' (prol.), 'Tak betoyne or verueyne or filles or wormod' (text); eVK2 5140.00; Manual 10: 3656, 3841. Occasional Latin remedies. A copy of the *Liber de Diversis Medicinis*. See Cc item 7.

25. ff. 159ra–160rb: Latin/English synonymy, A–F; *inc.* 'Atanasia est quedam confeccio / Atriplex meldes'. Breaks off after a single entry for F.

ff. 160^{v}–160(bis)^{rv} blank. Old folio number 160 has been crossed out on 160(bis)^{r}, but no new number given on the blank page.

26. ff. 161^{rv}: 'Dilectissime frater' plague text (without the usual epistolary prologue); *inc.* 'In primis caueas omnem nimiam replecionem'; eTK 0431K, 0704L. See Ad2 item 12, Gc4 item 45.

27. f. 161^{v}: Two faint English recipes; *inc.* 'Take wormewode marcure dayses waybrede'.

f. 162 blank

28. f. 163^{r}: Latin treatise on medical weights and measures; *inc.* 'Oportet ad huc pondera medicaminum mensurasque eorundem cognoscere'.

COLLATION: 1^4 2–6^8 7^2 8–17^8 18^1 19^{10} 20–22^8 23^4 (–1).

Surviving signature letters and numbers suggest a system running from a–e, f–q in quires 2–6, 8–19. Although quire 19 (ff. 128–37) appears to be a complete gathering of ten leaves, with a catchword on f. 137^{v}, the singleton leaf comprising quire 18 and the first three leaves of quire 19 are signed continuously as q j through q iiij. Quire 7 contains only the end of the single-column *Isagoge* text that fills up the last 3½ folios of quire 6 (ff. 41^{v}–44^{v}); there is no catchword on either quire 6 or 7.

LANGUAGE: Hand A (ff. 91^{r}–109^{v}, 111^{r}–124^{r}) from Nottinghamshire (*LALME* iii. 403–4; LP 504); Hand B (ff. 135vb–195rb) shows a 'mixture of elements from N and S Lincs' (*LALME* i. 115).

TEXTUAL PRESENTATION: Double columns throughout, except ff. 1^{r}–4^{v}, 41^{v}–46^{v}, and 160^{v}–163^{v}. No running heads; very few original marginalia, aside from f. 111^{rv}, where days of the week and months are noted in prognosticatory texts. Extensive rubrication of main headings and internal section headings.

Initials vary in style and colour in different parts of the manuscript: dark blue initials with red pen flourishing in quires 2–6 and 14–23; in quires 8–13, bluish-green initials with red flourishing and red initials with green flourishing. Most initials are two lines deep, except for long *I/J* initials about ten lines long to the left of the text block. Alternating red and blue paraphs; some texts have non-decorated, one-line initials alternating red and blue.

PROVENANCE, OWNERSHIP, OTHER NAMES AND DATES: Dated ownership note on f. 6^{r}: 'Ex Bibl. Petr. de Cardonnel. MDCL'; the same information in the lower margin of f. 3^{r} in a later hand, similar to that of the 'Elenchus' pasted on f. 4ᵛ. Donated by Hans Sloane to the British Museum. Pierre de Cardonnel was a Norman printer and merchant (1614–67) who owned a number of books of English provenance and many books on medicine and science; for a detailed study, see Malcolm 2002.

DESCRIPTIONS: *Sloane Cat.*: i. 32–3; Pannier 1882: 298–9; Manzalaoui 1977: xxvi; Taavitsainen 1988: 73–4; McVaugh in Martínez Gázquez et al. 2004: 437–8; Dean 1999: 197 (for the OF lapidary only).

S15: London, British Library, MS Sloane 374

s. xv²ᐟ⁴. Paper (except ff. 96–8, a s. xvi index to the book on parchment). Ff. ii+98+ii. Leaves missing between ff. 23/24, 46/47, 85/86, and 91/92.

DIMENSIONS: *c*.204×127 mm; writing area: *c*.145–50×93–100 mm. LINES/PAGE: 24–9.

HAND: One neatly written main hand (ff. 1–94), anglicana with secretary *a* and occasional secretary *g*. Display script in bastard anglicana, mainly with secretary *g*.

WATERMARKS: Ff. 1–46, 75, 86: Dragon/Basilisk/Wyvern (Heawood 1929–30, fig. 88 (dated 1453); cf. Piccard 123927–4047 (dates 1370–1510); Briquet 2628–67, esp. 2660, 2666 (dated 1392, 1442)). Ff. 71–4, 76, 89: an unidentified mark with a triangular shape at one end.

CONTENTS

1. ff. 1ʳ–5ʳ: *Flos medicine*; *inc.* '[A]nglorum regi scribit tota scola salerni'; eTK 096A. Ed. Frutos Gonzáles (2010a); accretions to the poem after its composition can be found in the conflated texts in De Renzi i. 445–516, v. 1–104.

2. ff. 5ᵛ–13ᵛ: Expanded Version of *The Dome of Uryne*; *inc.* 'In the byginnyng thow schalt take heede to 4'. **Text I below.** (There are many eVK2 item numbers for the components of *The Dome of Uryne*, omitted here for reasons of space but listed in 'Guide', item 2.2.)

3. f. 14ʳ: Latin prognostic tests for which spouse will die sooner and the sex of an unborn child; *inc.* 'Computa nomina eorum per numeros literarum'.

4. f. 14ʳᵛ: Verse prologue to next item; *inc.* 'That man that wole of leche lere'; eVK2 0644.50, 5039.00, 6902.00–6912.00, 6941.00, 6593.00–6594.00, 7929.00, 8221.00; Manual 10: 3655, 3840; *NIMEV* 3422; Keiser 2003.

5. ff. 14ᵛ–59ᵛ: English medical recipes; *inc.* 'Tak strong vinegre of white wyn and anoyte [*sic*] eche day'; eVK2 6002.00–6011.00. Recipes are numbered up to 200, ending on f. 48ʳ. An explicit on f. 59ᵛ titles the

preceding remedies 'Notule practice gloriosissimi principis Ypocratis et Galeni'. Charms in this and the following text have been heavily cancelled, although their titles often remain unmarred. The recipes in this and the following item are a version of the 'BL MS Add. 33996 remedybook' (ed. Heinrich 1896), though with significant divergences (Keiser 2003; Manual 10: 3655, 3839).

6. ff. 59^v–85^v: English medical recipes; *inc.* 'Take consoude and lete hit not touche the erthe'; eVK2 5246.00. Besides the Latin material in the charms in items 5–6, a few Latin and French recipes are embedded among the other remedies (e.g. 58^v–59^v (Lat.) and 85^r (Fr.)).

7. ff. 85^v–86^r: Latin/French/English herbal synonymy; *inc.* 'Pulegium puliole mountayne hilwort'. Non-alphabetical; probably incomplete: the indexer's numbering on recto pages jumps from 82 on f. 85^r to 90 on f. 86^r. The index contains no cross-references to material in the synonymy or later. On f. 86^r: 'Explicit liber m'e'dicinarum', perhaps referring to items 4–7 as a unit.

8. ff. 86^v–91^v: *Tractus Curie*; *inc.* 'Take blaunchid almaundis and bray hem wel'; eVK2 5161.00; Manual 10: 3679, 3888. Breaks off incomplete in last recipe (as found in Sloane 468).

9. ff. 92^r–93^v: Acephalous Latin phlebotomy; *inc.* 'quia mali In noua luna non debet fac*ere* fleobotomia'.

10. ff. 93^v–94^v: *Dieta generalis Ypocratis et Galieni*; *inc.* 'Ad conseruandum in rigimine sanitatis de sex rebus neccessarijs'. A brief regimen of health dealing mainly with foods to eat or avoid, and to a lesser degree with air, drink, inanition, repletion, and exercise. Despite a similar incipit, this text does not appear to be materially related to the *Tacuinum sanitatis*. On f. 94^v, 'Explicit liber iste de Curia', perhaps referring to items 8–10 as a unit.

11. f. 94^v: Heavily cancelled Latin recipe (presumably a charm) in a later hand, in originally blank space below explicit of item 10.

12. f. 95^{rv}: English medical recipe 'ffor alle aches'; *inc.* 'Take sou*p*erwode an handful wormod an handful'; eVK2 5987.00.

13. ff. 96^r–98^r: s. xvi index to the volume, on heavy vellum, in a hand and black ink similar to that of occasional corrections and running heads in *The Dome of Uryne*, some corrections and glosses elsewhere in the manuscript, and possibly the cancellation of charms.

COLLATION: 1^{16} 2$^{?16}$ (–8, –9?) 3^{16}4^{16}(–1, –2) 5^{16} 6^{16}(–10 to –16) 7$^{?12}$ (–7, –8?) 8^4 (–1?).

Beginning with '1' on f. 6^r (*Dome of Uryne*) and ending with '90' on

f. 86^r (herbal synonymy), recto leaves are numbered in the centre upper margin by the s. xvi hand that writes the index on ff. 96^r–98^r. In this numbering system, two leaves numbered 42 and 43 have been lost between modern f. 46 and f. 47. This loss is confirmed by a catchword that begins with *s* (possibly *shold*) on 46^v and *myth* as the first word on f. 47^r (recipes on either side of the page transition are difficult to read because of cancellations by a later reader, possibly the indexer). No index entries refer to the leaves numbered 42 or 43, and the parallel passage in BL Add. 33996 contains only charms, so it seems likely that they were censored by the indexer. Another gap occurs between modern ff. 85 and 86 (in the herbal synonymy), indicated by a seven-leaf jump in the older foliation from 82 to 90.

Two other textual gaps occur without corroboration from the older foliation, between modern leaves 23 and 24 (in quire 2; numbered 18 and 19 by the indexer) and between modern leaves 91 and 92 (in quire 7; unnumbered by the indexer).

LANGUAGE: Central Midland, around eastern Staffordshire or Warwickshire or western Derbyshire, Leicestershire, or Northamptonshire. Minor divergences of forms between texts, possibly due to dialect differences between exemplars.

TEXTUAL PRESENTATION: Single column, in brown ink, with organizational structure indicated by marginal notes and numbering of selected series (e.g. uroscopic tokens, recipes) by the main scribe. No rubrication; no paraphs. Mainly one-line initial capitals, occasional two- to three-line dropped capitals. Initials are minimally or not decorated.

In *The Dome of Uryne*, the headings are in Latin; in the recipe collection, in English. Headings, explicits, and catchwords are underlined or boxed; some catchwords and explicits are boxed with a crown-shaped design. 'Of Vrines' is written in the upper margin on ff. 5^v–6^r, by a later hand, but there are no other running heads.

PROVENANCE, OWNERSHIP, OTHER NAMES AND DATES: Previously owned by Dr Francis Bernard; donated by Hans Sloane to the British Museum.

DESCRIPTIONS: *Sloane Cat.*: i. 61; Hieatt and Butler 1985: 19 (brief mention).

S42: London, British Library, MS Sloane 3542

s. xv–xvi. Paper, with parchment leaves on the outside of quires 1, 2, and 3 (ff. 1, 16–17, 32–4, 43–4). Ff. iii+74+iv. F. 2 almost entirely torn away; lower third of f. 31 torn away; outer margin of f. 63 is largely torn away, though with minimal loss of text; parchment leaves slightly smaller than paper leaves.

The manuscript has three systems of foliation: the most recent in pencil, continuous from 1 to 74 and followed below; a second, older system of neat small figures in a reddish brown ink, running from 41 to 112, now cancelled (omitting the fragmentary second leaf from the sequence and doubling modern ff. 25–6 as 64 and 64*); a third and oldest system with larger numbers, running from 1 to 79, but skipping 9–10 (possibly a lost centre bifolium in quire 1; see item 1 below), 47–8 (after quire 3), and 50 (after modern f. 45) in its foliation sequence.

DIMENSIONS: *c.*210–12 × 143–5 mm; writing area: manuscript unruled, writing area varies, *c.*150–75 mm × 100–20 mm. LINES/PAGE: variable, 24–32, depending on the hand.

HANDS: Several different hands and inks throughout the manuscript, all relatively informal and possibly added over a significant period of time (note the varied paper-stocks used in the different quires). The first quire is in an anglicana hand, which shifts in subsequent quires to looser anglicana hands with an admixture of secretary forms and other differently shaped letters (*d*, *f*, *r*, *þ*, etc.). Some individual recipes and other short texts may be later additions.

WATERMARKS: Variable from quire to quire, of dates tending towards the third quarter of the fifteenth century; some not recorded in major reference works and none visible in quires 5 and 7: Quire 1: a five-pronged flower or crown with an ovoid base, not in Heawood, Piccard, or Briquet; Quire 2: bunch of grapes with no visible stem, similar but not identical to Heawood, fig. 49 (with looped stem; *c.*1435–56, 1454–60); cf. Piccard 128748–9 (with unlooped stems; 1476, 1541) and 128754–912 (with looped stems; 1437–78); Briquet 13034–43 (with looped stems), esp. 13037 (1441–99) and 13041 (1473–1502); Quire 3: circular design with two ?prongs in middle, possibly a buckle but not a design found in Heawood, Piccard, or Briquet; Quire 4: spray of four leaves with two opposing pairs on a fine stem, somewhat similar to five-leaf sprays ('Bough with several twigs') in Piccard 127273–96 (1589–1603); not in Heawood or Briquet; Quire 6: crowned column, similar to Heawood, fig. 24 (1478–79); cf. Piccard 100192–221 (1422–57); Briquet 4398–4412, esp. 4401–2 (1456, 1477); Quires 8–9: crown with demi-fleurons and a central cross with spearhead arms, similar to Heawood, fig. 27 (1436–77); cf. Piccard 51376 (1482); Briquet 4636–46, esp. 4641 (1444), and to a lesser extent 4636 (1423/7) and 4645 (1459/69).

CONTENTS

1. ff. 1ʳ–31ᵛ: About 200 recipes and charms, mostly medical, in English and Latin; *inc.* 'Radix [*sic*] ob of piper Idem of lang stered peper'; eVK2 4245.00, 8143.00, 7956.00. Possible lacuna between ff. 8 and 9, with a complete recipe for pin and web ending at the foot of f. 8ᵛ, jumping to what appears to be a recipe for Gratia Dei on f. 9ʳ but without a heading, corresponding to the jump in the oldest foliation sequence from 8 to 11.

2. f. 32ʳ: Latin lunary for bloodletting (incomplete, ending after day 22); *inc.* 'Luna prima ˋtotaˊ die bona est / Luna ijᵃ non est bona'; eTK 0838N.

3. ff. 32ᵛ–33ʳ: *Urina Rufa*; *inc.* 'Vryne colourd as gold and clere it signefiud good degestyon and hele'; eVK2 7759.00; Manual 10: 3662, 3852–3; 'Guide' 3.2.2. Cf. eTK 1610B and **Text B below**.

4. ff. 33ʳ–34ᵛ: About twenty medical recipes, in English and Latin; *inc.* 'Who so drynkyth an vnce of þe jus of betonie & ij vnce of þe jus of weybrede ymelled togeder'; eVK2 8122.00.

5. ff. 34ᵛ–38ᵛ: *De virtutibus herbarum* (in English); *inc.* 'Sauge is hote & drye in two degre'; eVK2 4415.00. About sixteen herbs, five recipes, and one charm.

6. ff. 38ᵛ–40ᵛ: Miscellaneous charms and recipes (medical, fishing, against theft, artisanal, etc.), in English and Latin; *inc.* 'Tocsica sunt capta si dicas ananisaptata . . . Whan that crist on Croyse was don'; eVK2 7999.00.

7. f. 41ᵛ: Breviary readings (*historie*) and Matins responsories for the weeks from Trinity Sunday to the beginning of Advent; *inc.* 'Quinto kalend' Augusti incipiatur istoria in principio'. See Hughes 1995: 10–12, 22–3, 189–92 (§§107, 202, 835–8).

8. ff. 41ᵛ–42ᵛ: Two alphabetical Latin lists of dream interpretations, A–Z, C–Z; *inc.* 'Si quis sompniauerit querat librum qualemcunque' (prol.), 'A significat prosperum & veterem' (text). Cf. eTK 0005A.

9. ff. 43ʳ–44ᵛ: *Sompnia Danielis*, Latin, incomplete (A–D); *inc.* 'Ab imperatore se videre osculari gaudium s[ignificat]'; eTK 0007B. Followed by six faint lines of Latin in a later hand and the name 'Thomas' in display script and pen trials, probably s. xvi.

10. f. 45ʳᵛ: About nine Latin and English medical recipes, copied over two pages already lined in a rectangular grid for some other purpose; *inc.* 'R. bibe ?suscum fumitorij & cum succo vnge corpus'; eVK2 4160.00.

11. f. 46ʳ: Vein man with English phlebotomy instructions; *inc.* 'The vayne in the mydyst of the fforhed'; eVK2 7072.00.

12. f. 46ᵛ: Latin knife charm with diagram; *inc.* 'Dum infiguntur cultelli

& cauilla in pane'. Followed by a rectangular charm with sacred names (evangelists and names of Jesus) written outside and inside its perimeter.

13. f. 47^r: Phlebotomy instructions in English; *inc.* 'Ho so do lete him blode in þe ij day of Marche'; eVK2 8121.00.

14. ff. 47^v–58^r: About ninety medical recipes, charms, and a few other items (virtues of herbs, aqua vitae, writing on steel, etc.), in different hands and inks and with different styles of heading, in English and Latin; *inc.* 'Tak a playster on þe rygth syde of barly mele'; eVK2 4787.00, 6462.00, 5905.00, 5519.00, 4867.00.

15. ff. 58^v–59^r: Sphere of Life and Death diagram (f. 58^v) and two sets of Latin instructions for using it (ff. 58^v, 59^r); *inc.* 'Si dies dominica fuerit addes 13'. Cf. the Middle English version of the Pythagorean Sphere in Gc4 item 7, W12 item 5.

16. ff. 59^v–65^r: About thirty-eight medical and other recipes and charms, in English and Latin; *inc.* 'R. crinem capitis [muli(e)ris *in reverse spelling*] & fil"; eVK2 6522.00, 4288.00, 5054.00, 4183.00, 6159.00

17. ff. 65^v–67^r: ps.-Galen, *Regimen by Months*, in English and Latin; *inc.* 'Januarius Isto mense whit wyn ffastyng is gode'; eVK2 3266.00; Manual 10: 3659, 3849–50. See Cc item 5, Gc4 item 31, Ld item 13.

18. ff. 67^r–74^v: About fifty medical recipes and charms in English and Latin, virtues of seven herbs in Latin (f. 67^v); *inc.* 'Take piper & white wyne eysel & flour of whete'; eVK2 5815.00. Ends incomplete.

19. ff. 69^v–70^v: *Urine White and Red* (embedded in recipes), English; *inc.* 'Hyt is for to wete in iiij partys of þe body ys yschewyd' (prol.), 'Iff a mannys vryne be whyt at morwe & rede byfore mete & whyt after mete' (text); eVK2 2568.00; 'Guide' 4.2.1. **Text D below.**

COLLATION: 1–2^{16} 3^{12} 4^8 (–2) 5^4 (–1) 6^{10} (–5?) 7^2 8^6 (–1) 9^4. Quire 1 may originally have had 18 leaves, losing its centre bifolium sometime between the oldest and second-oldest foliation systems. The last page of quire 1 (f. 16^v) is stained with a faint but large smear of red ink.

LANGUAGE: Despite accommodation to relatively standardized spellings, a few signs of westerly origins survive in the sampled folio-runs (ff. 32^v–40^v, 67^r–74^v), possibly from the area around Herefordshire and Gloucestershire.

TEXTUAL PRESENTATION: Variable, with generally modest to minimal ornamentation. Centred headings for recipes and for the herbs in item 5. Occasional red underlining or outlining of words and phrases, red touching on capitals and paraphs in quires 1–2, all-red headings, display script headings, boxed headings, and red dropped initials.

ILLUSTRATIONS: drawing of an ?eye associated with charm for finding stolen objects (f. 19ʳ), vein man (f. 46ʳ), rectangular diagram for knife charm (f. 46ᵛ), Spheres of Life and Death (f. 58ᵛ).

PROVENANCE, OWNERSHIP, OTHER NAMES AND DATES: Donated by Hans Sloane to the British Museum. Other names: 'Thomas' on f. 44ᵛ, written in display script under the lines added below the Latin dream text; 'By me John bethell | Audit' & | & ?Comp" (f. 63ʳ), in a s. xvi hand, below a s. xvi recipe for taking hares in a very similar hand.

DESCRIPTION. *Sloane Cat.*: xv. 5–6.

W12: London, Wellcome Library, MS 8004

s. xv^med (*c.*1454). Vellum. Ff. i+100+i. Leaf 40 is torn across the bottom margin, causing loss of about half a line of text on f. 40ᵛ; small original holes in leaf 66. (The Wellcome Library has preserved the previous binding and paper flyleaves, 3 front and 2 rear leaves.)

DIMENSIONS: 204×143 mm; writing area *c.*165–70×102–13 mm. LINES/PAGE: 25–8.

HAND: One scribe, writing a fluent anglicana. Display script in bastard anglicana.

CONTENTS

1. f. 1ʳ: Remarks on the falsity of astrology and an ownership note by Thomas Hill, dated 10 June 1759.

2. f. 1ᵛ: Six female heads and one full female figure by an amateur, post-medieval artist.

ff. 2–4 blank.

3. ff. 5ʳ–17ʳ: Calendar, dated 1454, in English and Latin; *inc.* 'þis calender is compyled and mad aftyre dyuers calenders'; eVK2 7368.50, 1993.50.

f. 17ᵛ blank.

4. f. 18ʳ: Phlebotomy text, with coloured vein man illustration; *inc.* 'The vayne cardiacul or of þe harte es opynd'; eVK2 7058.00.

5. ff. 18ᵛ–19ʳ: Sphere of Death and Life, Sphere of Pythagoras, with diagrams; *inc.* 'Cownte all þe lettyrs pertenyng to þe name of þe seke'; eVK2 1447.50; Manual 10: 3625–6, 3786. Incomplete. Cf. Gc4 item 7, S42 item 15.

6. ff. 19ᵛ–22ʳ: Table and explanation of calculating the date of Easter,

II. DESCRIPTIONS OF BASE MANUSCRIPTS

dominical letters, movable feasts, leap year; *inc.* 'Thys tabule forto know þe fallynge of pasch day' (prol.), 'The tabull abowue wrytyne is callyd þe tabule of þe day of pasch' (text); eVK2 7477.00, 7042.50.

7. f. 22ʳ: Paragraph on the Ember Days; *inc.* 'Imbrynge days fall allway þe nexte wenysday hafter askwedyns day'; eVK2 1530.50.

8. f. 22ᵛ: Table of squares and cubes for 2 through 40; *inc.* 'Thys tabull benythe for mownteplykacyon es ryghte nedfull'; eVK2 7473.00.

f. 23ʳ blank.

9. ff. 23ᵛ–24ʳ: Computistical table; *inc.* 'Numeri tabularis The dominecal letteris The wekes fro yol to septuagesem'; eVK2 6668.50.

10. ff. 24ᵛ–27ʳ: Astronomical tables in Latin; *inc.* 'Aries ascencionis Arietis in circulo directo'.

11. f. 27ᵛ: Table of planetary hours in English and Latin; *inc.* 'This tabul is for to know by for cuciy howie of þe day or nyght'; eVK2 7479.00.

12. f. 28ʳ: Multiplication table through 10×10; *inc.* 'þis is þe planeste begynynge 2 tymys 2 þat es 4'; eVK 7442.50.

13. f. 28ʳ: Table of axial precession from 1385 to 1469; *inc.* 'Thys tabull ys of contenwance of þe mewyng of þe son'; eVK2 7480.00, 2424.50.

14. f. 28ᵛ: Table for ?measuring land, with index columns running from 10 to 60; *inc.* 'Thys tabull benyth in awgrem yt es ffor metyng of akerys'; eVK2 7472.00.

15. f. 29ʳ: Tables of lunar eclipses from June 1444 to 1481 (two nineteen-year cycles), in Latin with illustration (twenty-five darkened lunar disks); *inc.* 'Eclipsis lune per .iº. ciclo . Duracio . ffigure . eclipsis'.

16. f. 29ᵛ: Incomplete tables of lunar eclipses for cycles 3 and 4; *inc.* 'Ciclus lune per .3. ciclo . Duracio ffigure eclipsis'.

17. f. 30ʳ: Table of planetary hours, in Latin; *inc.* 'Tabula docens quis planetarum regnat omni die'; cf. eTK 0675C.

18. f. 30ᵛ: Table of lunar movement through the zodiac, in Latin and English; *inc.* 'Tabula lune ad sciendum eius signum omni die'; cf. eTK 0602B, 0674N, eVK2 6570.60.

19. f. 31ʳ: Lunar table, in Latin; *inc.* 'Tabula lune ad sciendum eius gradum omni die'.

20. f. 31ᵛ: *Hours of the Day and of the Night*; *inc.* 'Whane þou knawys þe owres of þe day & of þe ny3te'; eVK2 8066.00.

21. f. 31ᵛ: *The Conjunctions*; *inc.* 'Towe [Thou] schall fynd coniunccyons with þe goldyne nowmbre'; eVK2 7508.00.

22. ff. 31ᵛ–34ᵛ: Richard of Wallingford, *Declarations upon the Calendar of the Queen*; *inc.* 'If þer be a questyone mad of þe byrth of manne'; eVK2 2686.50. See Gc4 items 2 and 32.

23. ff. 34ᵛ–36ʳ: *The Properties of the Planets*; *inc.* 'Ther ar .7. planettes þat is to say Saturne Jubiter'; eVK2 7125.00.

24. ff. 36ᵛ–42ʳ: *The Exposition of the Twelve Signs*, with full-page zodiac man (f. 40ʳ); *inc.* 'It profyttys mych to knaw in qwatt syne þe mone es ilk day'; eVK2 3255.00.

25. f. 42ʳᵛ: Short list of biblical and historical dates including English events from 11[70] to 1415 and a tally of churches, knights' fees, etc.; *inc.* 'In the 15. 3ere of þe warld wasse Caym borne'; eVK2 3044.00.

26. ff. 42ᵛ–44ᵛ: *Of Many Great Battles* (list of English battles from 1066 to 1424); *inc.* 'Bott þe fyrste wasse done be for þe conqueste .4. myle frome Beuyrley'.

27. ff. 44ᵛ–46ᵛ: *Of Bloodletting*; *inc.* 'Lattynge of blod is to be consydyrid on two wyse'; eVK2 3363.00.

28. ff. 46ᵛ–49ᵛ: *Of the Hours and Planets* (on natal influences of the planets); *inc.* 'Her it es to note of þe horws of þe planets'; eVK2 2360.00. See also eTK 1149M, 1399I, 1400D.

29. ff. 49ᵛ–50ʳ: *To Know What Shall Be the Prime*; *inc.* 'And þou wold knawe þe pryme 20 3er to cum'; eVK2 1015.00.

30. f. 50ʳ: *To Know How High It Is from the Earth to the Firmament*; *inc.* 'Fro þe eryth to þe mone is þus many lekys 15825', followed by a tally of churches, knights' fees, etc.; eVK2 1991.00.

31. f. 50ʳ: *To Know the Dominical Letters*; *inc.* 'Þo .5. lettyr be neth þe dominicall lettre þat nowe is'; eVK2 6816.00.

32. ff. 50ᵛ–54ʳ: On horological and astronomical calculations; *inc.* 'Tho quantitys of comun artificyall days & of þe twyly3t'; eVK2 6991.00, 2578.00, 7944.00, 7945.00, 7940.00.

33. ff. 54ʳ–55ʳ: *The Humours of Man*; *inc.* 'For aftyr þe sentaunce of Tholome in hys exposycioun Haly proposicione .56.'; eVK2 1829.00.

34. ff. 55ʳ–57ʳ: *To Give a Medicine*; *inc.* 'For to knaw qwatt tyme houyth to be gyuene a medcyne laxatyue'; eVK2 1920.00, 3610.00, 3203.00.

35. ff. 57ʳ–58ᵛ: *The Hour of Diverse Sickness*; *inc.* 'If any manne haue almanake & will acced'; eVK2 2580.00.

36. ff. 58ᵛ–61ʳ: *Twenty Jordans*; *inc.* 'Here aftur foluth vrynalls dyuyrse and þer colourse of þer watyrs' (prol.), 'Karapos The dropcy a wynd vndyr þe

syd þe stone heuy ach' (text); eVK2 2403.00, 3291.50; Manual 10: 3662, 3852; 'Guide' 1.1.1.

37. ff. 61ʳ–62ʳ: *Urine White and Brown* (Phlegm variant); *inc.* 'Her may þou knawe howe þou sall kenne & dysscryue all maner of seknesse' (prol.), 'Uryne whyte by þe morne & browne aftyr mete' (text); eVK2 7847.00; 'Guide' 5.2.2. **Text F below.**

38. ff. 62ʳ–64ʳ: *Urina Rufa*; *inc.* 'Here foloys a nodyr tretys of vryns & tokyns of þem' (prol.), 'Fyrste if an vryne be coulourd as gold gud' (text); eVK2 1648.00; Manual 10: 3662, 3852–3; 'Guide' 3.2.1b. Cf. **Text B below.**

39. f. 64ʳᵛ: *Cleansing of Blood*; *inc.* 'All vryn es a clensynge of blod'; Manual 10: 3662, 3852–3; 'Guide' 3.3.1c. Cf.**Text C below.**

40. ff. 65ʳ–68ᵛ: *The Chapter of Ill Days and Forbidden Days*; *inc.* 'Thys sewynge chapitur schuys & declarys qwylk are þe ill days' (prol.), 'Wytt þou þat ilke a moneth ar .a. dysmel days' (text); eVK2 7395.00, 8175.50, 7119.50, 1380.50, 1992.00, 1816.00, 2793.00, 1184.00, 1178.00, 1235.00, 0749.00; Manual 10: 3624, 3780. From this text to item 44 below, the manuscript shares material with the astromedical compendium in Sloane 213, S10 item 18 (chs. [1–3], [8]). This text is ch. [3].

41. f. 68ᵛ: On the nature of Saturn; *inc.* 'Note þou þat Saturne is þe hyeste planett'; eVK2 3696.00; cf. eVK2 3136.50, 8177.75; Manual 10: 3617, 3768–9. See also Ad2 item 24, Gc4 item 20, S10 item 18 (astromedical compendium, end of ch. [1]).

42. ff. 68ᵛ–70ʳ: Prognostics by New Year's Day; *inc.* 'Thies nexste chapit-ure foloynge schewys howe all þe 3er is rewlyd' (prol.), 'If þe fyrste day of Janiver be onne Sononday' (text); eVK2 7453.00, 2645.50; Manual 10: 3624, 3782–3. Ch. [1] in Sloane 213 Compendium. See also Ad2 item 23.

43. f. 70ʳᵛ: Prognostics by Thunder; *inc.* 'This chapitur nexst foloynge declaris qwat thundur betokyns' (prol.), 'Thundyr in Janiver be'to'kyns grete wynd' (text); eVK2 7559.00; Manual 10: 3624, 3783–4. Ch. [2] in Sloane 213 Compendium.

44. ff. 70ᵛ–72ᵛ: Onomastic prognostics; *inc.* 'Her schews a calkelacioune to knawe' (prol.), 'Take two namys of þo menne' (text); eVK2 6198.00. Ch. [8] in Sloane 213 Compendium.

45. f. 73ʳ: *Table of the Dignities of the Planets*, in Latin and English; *inc.* 'Lordys of þe howse of synes Lordys of þe exaltacioun'; eVK2 4648.00.

ff. 74–5 blank except for lining in writing area on 74ʳ.

46. ff. 76^r–84^v: *Pilgrimage to the Holy Land*; *inc*. 'Who that wyll to Jerusalem gon'.

47. ff. 84^v–85^v: Excerpts from John Lydgate, *Dietary*; *inc*. 'For helth of body couer for cold þi hed'; eVK2 1848.00; Manual 6: 1827–8, 2092–4; *NIMEV* 824.

48. ff. 86^r–99^r: *Thirty Days of the Moon*; *inc*. '[G]od þat all þis warld hath wroghte'; eVK2 6729.50, *NIMEV* 970.

f. 99^v blank.

COLLATION: 1^4 2^{12} 3^4 4–5^2 6^4 7^{12} (–1) 8^{12} 9–10^{10} 11^4 12^{10} 13^{10} (–1, –2) 14^8(–7). Ff. 1–4 and 100 originally blank, possibly serving as flyleaves.

LANGUAGE: Nottinghamshire or Lincolnshire.

TEXTUAL PRESENTATION: Texts in long lines; no running heads. From 5^r to 68^r, two- and a few one-line gold-leaf initials with red and blue decoration including floral sprays touched with gold. From 68^v to 83^v, mainly two-line blue initials with red pen flourishing and one-line alternating red and blue initials with no decoration. From 86^r (item 48), one- and two-line red initials and seven- to nine-line red initial *I/J*s along left edge of text, with no decoration.

ILLUSTRATIONS: Vein man (f. 18^r), sphere of life and death, sphere of Pythagoras (ff. 18^v–19^r), lunar eclipses in blue and gold (f. 29^r), planetary spheres (f. 34^v), zodiac man (f. 40^r), flasks next to colours in *Twenty Jordans* (ff. 58^v–61^r). Dragon in red ink in lower margin of f. 5^r.

PROVENANCE, OWNERSHIP, OTHER NAMES AND DATES: Possibly 'commissioned either by a provincial su[r]geon or a layman with medical interests' (Wellcome Online Catalogue). Ownership note and critical remarks on astrology by Thomas Hill, dated 10 June 1759 (f. 1^r). Later owned by the Dukes of Newcastle and sold in 1938; bookplate of Sir Alan Lubbock (1897–1990) on inside front cover of old leather binding preserved with the manuscript. Sold by Christie's in 1999 and by Sam Fogg Rare Books (to the Wellcome Library) in 2002.

DESCRIPTIONS: Wellcome Library Online Catalogue, n.d.; Robinson 2003: i. 102; Voigts 2004: 202, 204–5.

III. SOURCES AND GENERAL CONTENT

Medieval uroscopy, at least as it survives in written texts, was a learned art, founded on academic treatises. Although the urine flask is the standard attribute of the physician in medieval art, it is not uncommon for physicians in medical illustrations to be depicted holding a flask in one hand while gazing or pointing at a book. Writers of long vernacular urine treatises, like the fourteenth-century author of *Barton's Urines*, Henry Daniel (fl. 1379), and John Arderon (an early fifteenth-century commentator on Giles of Corbeil), were quick to cite learned predecessors at the openings of their works.[7]

Although the academic roots and ramifications of uroscopic knowledge are not highly visible in the short practical uroscopies with which this volume is concerned, it is important to remember that the underpinnings and authority of these late medieval vernacular texts were still fundamentally bookish.[8] The ultimate origins of the texts edited here may be traced back to the scattered but highly influential uroscopic *dicta* of Hippocrates and Galen and the more specialized treatises *de urinis* by Theophilus Protospatharius (*c.* 7th c.?) and Isaac Israeli (*c.*850–*c.*950?),[9] which were in turn developed and organized into more manageable presentations in the twelfth century by Maurus of Salerno and Giles of Corbeil. Theophilus's treatise was one of the earliest texts in the *Ars medicine* anthology of works essential to medieval medical education, later known as the *Articella*. Isaac's *De urinis* and Giles's *Carmen de urinis* were themselves included in a number of *Articella* manuscripts and were already generating commentaries by the mid-thirteenth century.[10]

While these canonical sources for the texts in this volume should be kept in mind, and will be selectively illustrated in the medical commentary below, more direct sources exist for six of the nine treatises, sources in which the learned tradition had already been digested into shorter and simpler formats, as the following section will show.

[7] On Daniel and Arderon, see the forthcoming editions by Harvey, Tavormina, et al. and by Calle-Martín.

[8] For good general overviews of Latin and vernacular uroscopy in the medieval West, see Moulinier-Brogi 2008, 2010, and 2012. Professional medical criticism of uroscopy began to appear in the early modern period (Fisman 1993; Stolberg 2007), usually targeting non-professional practitioners. However, some learned physicians continued to develop the theory and diagnostic use of uroscopy, well into the later 18th or early 19th c. (Shackelford 2008; Stolberg 2009; Stolberg 2015).

[9] Dates for Isaac from Collins 2015: 1; older sources suggest *c.*832–*c.*932 and similar ranges.

[10] Two of the most important commentaries on Giles are those by Gilbertus Anglicus (*inc.* 'Sicut dicit Constantinus in Pantegni') and an anonymous 13th-c. author (*inc.* 'Liber iste quem legendum proponimus est novelle institutionis'; often misattributed to Gentile da Foligno. Further analysis of these commentaries is provided by McVaugh 2010: 302–5 (on Gilbertus's commentary, which McVaugh suggests may date to the 1230s, early in Gilbertus's career) and Sudhoff 1929 (attributing the 'Liber iste' commentary to Giles himself or someone under his supervision; T. Hunt also suggests Giles as the probable author (2011: 25 n. 4)).

Texts A–C: The Vade Mecum Suite

A. *Twenty Colours by Digestion Groups*
B. *Urina Rufa*
C. *Cleansing of Blood*

The first three texts in this volume often appear as a group, both in English and in Latin. Two of the Latin texts are related to a widely dispersed and frequently reworked treatise with Salernitan roots, sometimes referred to as the 'kurzer Harntraktat' (Kadner 1919; Keil 1969; Keil 1970), illustrated with a urine wheel that presents twenty colours of urine classified according to the stage of digestion that they reflect. A number of fourteenth- and fifteenth-century English medical manuscripts contain the Latin group combined with astrological, bloodletting, and calendric texts; these manuscripts are often illustrated with zodiac men, vein men, and volvelles as well as the urine wheel, and sometimes appear in booklet form, sometimes as folding almanacs or girdle books.[11] Following C. H. Talbot's description (1961) of one of these Latin almanacs as a 'mediaeval physician's vade mecum', I refer to texts A, B, and C collectively as the Vade Mecum suite.[12]

The first text edited below, *Twenty Colours by Digestion Groups*, translates the Latin captions of the urine wheel, either with or without the accompanying diagram. These captions present what had come to be a relatively standardized number and list of names for urines, thanks to the canonizing influence of Giles of Corbeil's *Carmen de urinis*, probably composed in the late twelfth century.[13] Around the same time, but perhaps somewhat later than Giles's poem, the colours were being grouped according to six or seven different stages of digestion or coction: 'indigestion' (the

[11] See e.g. Bodl. MSS Ashmole 391, Part V, and Ashmole 789, Part VIII; TCC, MS R.1.86; Cambridge, Magdalene College, Pepys Library, MS 1662; Philadelphia, The Rosenbach Museum and Library, MS 1004/29; and the Dickson Wright manuscript or 'physician's vade mecum' edited by Talbot (1961). BL, MS Harley 5311, a folding almanac, contains similar astronomical and medical diagrams and a variant of the urine wheel laid out in a rectangular table (reproduced in Jones 1998: 54, fig. 46). The combination of the wheel and the Latin versions of texts B and C saw print in the *Fasciculus medicinae* of Johannes Kirchheimer (Ketham), published first in Venice (1491), with several reprints and occasional recopying in manuscripts during the 16th c. (facsimile edn. Sudhoff and Singer 1924). Folding calendars, almanacs, and other folded books are discussed in detail by Gumbert (2016), with the substantial category of English almanacs at pp. 121–206.

[12] Discussed further in Tavormina 2014, under items 3.1–3.3.

[13] The most recent editor of Giles's work notes the limited evidence for most past claims about his life and literary output (Ausécache 2017: 11–15, 'Une biographie incertaine'). Although a precise date for the *Carmen de urinis* cannot be given, it appears to be his earliest work, preceding other poems that probably belong to the 1190s to the early 1220s (pp. 16–18).

complete lack of coction), the beginning of digestion, mediate digestion
(sometimes omitted), perfect digestion, excessive digestion (seen as a kind
of overheating or overcooking), intense adustion or burning, and finally
mortification.[14] Viewed along this spectrum, the colours of urine ran from
the clear and light colours caused by no or weak digestion, through the
yellows and reds of more or less healthy digestion, to the purplish, green-
ish, leaden, and black colours of serious to fatal overheating or extinction
of bodily heat.

The Latin diagrams that present this theoretical association of colour
and metabolism in a single wheel almost always have the same basic layout.
The chromatic arc from clear ('Albus') urine through pale, yellow, and red
to dark urines normally begins at the bottom of the wheel and runs clockwise, as does the metabolic sequence from indigestion to mortification.
The wheels (also called rings, *rotae*, and circular charts by modern scholars) provide a logical and readily comprehensible mnemonic image, and
it is not surprising that one of the earliest examples occurs in a thirteenth-
century *Articella* from Italy, as a full facing-page illustration to the *De urinis*
of Theophilus (Vatican City, Biblioteca Apostolica Vaticana, Pal. lat. 1238,
f. 32ᵛ; with glosses in a fourteenth-century English cursive).[15]

When Latin urine wheels showing twenty colours and seven digestion
groups begin appearing in England in the later fourteenth century (see
Appendix I), they are usually accompanied by a pair of short Latin uroscopic texts already in European circulation, not always connected to the
wheel diagram. One of these texts (*inc.* 'Urina rufa significat salutem et
bonam dispositionem'; ME 'Urina rufa signefieth helthe and gode disposicioun') is a list of some forty to fifty uroscopic *regulae*, giving diagnoses and
occasional prognoses for various combinations of colour and content; the
second (*inc.* 'Omnis urina est colamentum sanguinis'; ME 'Every/All/Ech

[14] In his expanded version of the *Flos medicine* (also known as the *Regimen sanitatis Salernitanum*), De Renzi offers three variant texts on the stages of digestion (lines 2388–406; v. 68–9),
the first with seven stages, the second with six, and the third, possibly defective, passage with
five. On the limitations of De Renzi's editions and on unanswered questions about the work,
see Nicoud 2007. Virginia de Frutos González has since published a critical edition of the *Flos
medicine* (2010a) and a separate edition of a long version of the text in Sloane 351 (2010b), but
De Renzi's texts remain useful as a storehouse of versified medieval medical lore, whether or
not that lore is part of the original *Flos/Regimen*. (The metabolic 'digestion groups' used to
classify the uroscopic colours should not be confused with the three physiological stages of
digestion, occurring in the stomach, the liver and kidneys, and the limbs.)
[15] Schuba 1981: 258. For the manuscript tradition leading up to the urine wheel in the *Fasciculus medicinae*, see Sudhoff and Singer (Kirchheimer facs. edn., 1924: 46–8). The checklist
of medical miniatures in MacKinney 1965 includes at least seventeen 'circular charts' of uroscopy flasks (items 2.2, 20.3, 27.3, 51.1, 57.2, 66.7, 80.10, 80.11, 80.14, 86.51, 86.60, 94.5,
94.22, 124.5, 124.8, 124.27, 172.1).

urine is a clensing of blode') is a brief schematic overview of basic uroscopic theory.

Continental versions of these texts can be found in manuscripts from the twelfth century on. As Gundolf Keil has shown, their transmission in Latin and the European vernaculars often involved significant rearrangement, abridgement, expansion, and conflation with other materials.[16] The Latin versions in English manuscripts share enough material with the versions examined by Keil to be identified as related texts, but they have clearly diverged from the earlier textual traditions on which Keil focuses most of his discussion.[17] They are, however, quite close to the Latin uroscopies published in the late fifteenth-century *Fasciculus medicinae* of Johannes Kirchheimer (Venice 1491 and later reprints), texts that circulated across Europe in the fourteenth and fifteenth centuries.[18] In the English tradition, the form of the two Latin texts is relatively stable, and most of the Middle English translations appear to originate from identical or very similar Latin versions.

The content of *Urina Rufa* is a relatively unstructured series of uroscopic signs or tokens, though a certain amount of clustering and progression can be found within the series; several tokens unique to this text also permit one to identify abridgements and fragments of the text with reasonable confidence.[19] The first few tokens deal with red and citrine colours, ranging from simple colours to reds mixed with green or black; these are followed by a cluster of light or pale colours. About halfway through the list, the signs begin to include consistency and contents (thick, thin, tur-

[16] Keil 1969. See also Keil 1963: 438–55, and 1970: 137–49, 153–4. Keil regularly links the 'kurzer Harntraktat' to the Latin *Urina rufa* and *Omnis urina est colamentum* texts found in the Dickson Wright manuscript and edited by Talbot in 1961 (Keil 1963: 444–5 n. 5; 1969: 18–19 n. 55, 32 n. 75, 33 n. 77).

[17] The earlier forms of the text typically place the general overview *before* the list of *regulae*, usually beginning that overview with 'Sciendum est quod urina duarum rerum proprie est significativa', the second sentence of the *Omnis urina est colamentum* text. Only about fifteen to twenty of the signs in the earlier forms of the 'kurzer Harntraktat' are retained in *Urina rufa*, mainly in the second half of the latter text.

[18] Sudhoff and Singer (Kirchheimer facs. edn., 1924) report late 14th- to early 15th-c. Heidelberg and Paris manuscripts containing the *Fasciculus medicinae* texts and some of the companion illustrations (p. 46). For additional studies and illustrations of versions of the 'kurzer Harntraktat' and the *Fasciculus medicinae*, see Sudhoff 1909 and Sudhoff 1912. Another late manuscript witness of the *Urina rufa* and *Omnis urina*, written in England, occurs in the Notebook of Thomas Betson, librarian of Syon Abbey (d. 1516), preserved in Cambridge, St John's College, MS E.6, ff. 84^r–86^r; the manuscript has been partially transcribed in Adams and Forbes 2015. More recent codicological and bibliographic references related to the *Fasciculus*, and particularly its later print and vernacular histories, may be found in Herrera 1990, Pesenti 2001, Coppens 2009, and Zaun 2011.

[19] For characteristic tokens in *Urina Rufa*, see Tavormina 2014: Appendix D.

bid; Foam, Scales, Pus, Motes, etc.) as well as colours. Near the end of
the series is another cluster of pale urines, followed by some ten to twelve
urines that reveal whether a woman is pregnant, virginal, bearing a dead
child, menstruating, and other reproductive and sexual matters. Among
the 'touchstone' signs in *Urina Rufa* are the 'laudable' or 'praisable' colour
Citrine; the sanguine plethora ('excess of blood') signified by the colour
Rubea 'as blood in a glass', which requires immediate blood-letting, except
on the perilous days when the moon is in the middle of Gemini; the trembling Circle that indicates a flux of humours from the head to the lower
members; and the foamy urine in women signifying gas in the stomach
or a burning from the navel to the throat and great thirst. The order of
the signs is seldom seriously disturbed by scribes, aside from occasional
omissions and minor transpositions of individual signs.

In contrast with the *Urina Rufa* series, the short text (*Urine is a*) *Cleansing of Blood* is highly structured, primarily by the humoral, qualitative,
and anatomical correspondences of urine, to the extent that many scribal
errors are easy to correct based on the appropriate correspondence. *Cleansing* sometimes appears in truncated forms, usually breaking off at natural
transitions, but in its most common full form, it contains short paragraphs
on the following topics:

1. Definition of urine;
2. Four things to consider in judging urine: substance, colour, regions, contents;
3. Four qualities in urine: heat, dryness, cold, moisture; associated colours, consistencies;
4. Four parts of urine: circle, body of air, perforation, ground (a couple of witnesses end after this section);
5. Three regions of urine: nethermost, middle, overmost (with one or two signs of disease for each region; several witnesses end after this section);
6. Contents in the regions of urines: foam, circle, white cloud, gravel, black sediment.

Like *Urina Rufa* and its immediate Latin source, *Cleansing* and its Latin
original are similar but not identical to a section in the earlier forms of the
'kurzer Harntraktat'. As remarked above,[20] the earlier texts often begin
with the *second* sentence in the source for the Middle English *Cleansing*
text, '(Urina) duarum rerum est significativa', omitting the opening definition, 'Urina est colamentum sanguinis', found in later copies and in

[20] See above, n. 17.

numerous uroscopic authorities from Theophilus and Isaac Israeli and their commentators to the Salernitans to Bernard de Gordon. The earlier and later versions often diverge further after the discussion of the prime qualities and urinary colour and consistency (section 3 in the outline above). Instead of turning to the four parts and three regions of urine, the earlier versions frequently proceed to discuss urinary symptoms of humoral dominance, followed by a set of *regulae* on headaches and fevers beginning with some form of the line 'Sed quoniam caput est radix omnium membrorum, incipiendum est ab ipso'. Finally, after the signs for headache and fever, the earlier versions move on to a series of uroscopic *regulae* that share a number of signs with *Urina Rufa*.[21] In contrast to these earlier forms, the *Urina est colamentum* text found in the late fifteenth-century *Fasciculus medicinae* closely matches the Anglo-Latin *Urina est colamentum* texts throughout, reflecting the fact that these texts were not purely insular productions.[22]

Whether in Latin or English, the three texts function well as a group: they provide the practitioner with a miniature uroscopic compendium, combining a brief mnemonic catalogue of colours and their general digestive etiologies, more specific diagnostic indicators for particular illnesses, and general theoretical principles of uroscopy. When one or two of the texts occur without the other(s), it is not uncommon to find similar material replacing the omitted text(s)—e.g. a list of colours, series of diagnostic tokens, or description of humoral theory—presumably reflecting the preferences of a scribe or commissioner of a particular manuscript. Latin versions of all three texts are reproduced in Appendix I, from Bodleian Library, Ashmole 391, Part V, ff. 2ᵛ–3ᵛ and 10ʳ.

---

[21] See e.g. Kadner 1919: 51–2 (Breslau, Stadtbibliothek, MS 1302, now lost; *c.*1200); Pfeffer 1891: 15–17 (Erfurt, Wissenschaftliche Bibliothek, MS Amplonianus Q.178, a version sometimes attributed to Walter Agilon and also found in English manuscripts; 14th c.¹ᐟ²); Wentzlau 1923: 22–3, 25–6 (Erfurt, Ampl. Q.368, 14th c.ᵐᵉᵈ; Vienna, Cpv 2532, 12th c.). These forms of the 'kurzer Harntraktat' also have reflexes in the English vernacular tradition: three English variants of *Cleansing of Blood* include a passage that justifies beginning at the head as the 'rote of alle the body membres', or the 'pryncipall' or 'heyest' member (Di2b, Add3, T2); two late copies treat urines signifying dominance of one or another humour (T7, Ry1).

[22] In addition to the late 14th- to early 15th-c. Paris and Heidelberg manuscript copies of the *Fasciculus medicinae* uroscopies noted by Sudhoff and Singer (see above, nn. 15 and 18), the texts also appear in Vatican City, Biblioteca Apostolica Vaticana, Pal. lat. 1323, ff. 8ʳ, 9ᵛ– 10ʳ (1407; written in southern Germany); Pal. lat. 1229, ff. 3ʳᵛ, 5ʳ(15th c.ᵐᵉᵈ.; written around Montpellier or northern Spain).

Texts D–F: White–Red and White–Brown Token Lists

D. *Urine White and Red*

E. *Urine White and Brown* (Woman variant)

F. *Urine White and Brown* (Phlegm variant)

Texts D through F are all derived from the uroscopy section of a thirteenth-century Anglo-Norman treatise, also found in Old French, titled *Lettre d'Hippocrate* (**LdH**) by modern editors.[23] The full form of this treatise begins with a prologue attributing the text to Hippocrates, followed by a brief description of the 'humours' (more accurately, the prime qualities hot, cold, wet, and dry) that govern all living creatures, a series of uroscopic *regulae*, and finally a relatively variable collection of medical recipes. The most comprehensive version of the uroscopy section, hitherto unedited, appears in BL, MS Harley 2558 and is reproduced in Appendix II; it contains approximately twenty nine signs and accompanying diagnoses, depending on how one divides or combines some closely related signs. Most versions of the French text have fewer *regulae*: of the fifteen copies of the uroscopy section that I have seen, two contain twenty-six to twenty-nine signs, another ten contain between fourteen and nineteen signs, and three a set of five or six. The earliest copies, dating from the second half of the thirteenth century, all fall into the medium-length category; the principal difference between them and the two long versions (both fourteenth-century) consists of some eight or nine roughly similar signs in the long versions following the last sign of the medium-length texts. If the long version was an expansion of a medium-length original, the expansion probably occurred by the late thirteenth century, given that the *shortest* version includes two signs (black gathering on the side of the urinal; urine of a maiden) from the end of the long version, and is found first in a late thirteenth-century copy (Digby 86).

In Middle English, the **LdH** has at least eight distinct reflexes:

1. The *Letter of Ipocras*, whose full versions retain a sometimes-versified prologue, the brief 'humours' text, a uroscopy section that

---

[23] The *Lettre d'Hippocrate* has been edited or transcribed, usually from single manuscripts, by a number of scholars: Meyer 1911: 536–9; Meyer 1913: 46–7; Wiese 1928; Brunel 1956 (recipes only); Tovar 1970 (not seen); Tovar 1973–4: 177–9; Södergård 1981; T. Hunt 1990: 100–41; T. Hunt 1994–7: ii. 259, 264; T. Hunt 2001: 85–160, esp. 85–93; T. Hunt 2011: 41–5. For other notices of the text in various libraries, see Tavormina 2007: 632 n. 2. Whether the text was originally written in Anglo-Norman or French remains unclear: Tovar (1973–4: 177 n. 1) refers to the *Lettre* as 'ce texte anglo-normand', but Hunt (2011: 17–18) is more cautious.

normally contains only six signs or tokens (**ST**; the same six found in the short **LdH** version), and a recipe collection.[24]

2. *Fifteen Discretions of Urine* (**15D**), a series of fifteen tokens that begins with the first five signs in the short **LdH** version.[25]

3. *Urine White and Red* (**WR**; text D below), a relatively close translation of the uroscopy section in the **LdH**, retaining nineteen of the first twenty signs found in the full **LdH**; most similar to the form of the *Lettre* found in TCC O.1.20, which ends at the same point and also contains nineteen of the first twenty signs, though with a different sign omitted.

4. *Urine White and Brown* (Woman variant; **WBw**; text E below), a slightly freer adaptation of the **LdH** uroscopy, the fullest versions of which contain twenty-four signs, of which five are not found in the Anglo-Norman and French tradition or in **WR**.

5. *Urine White and Brown* (Phlegm variant; **WBp**; text F below), a more thoroughly revised derivative of **LdH**, containing about twenty-one signs, of which only eleven match items in the French text and its other ME offspring.

6. *Judicium Perfectum Omnium Urinarum* (**JP**), a component of the *Dome of Uryne* (text I below) with twenty-six tokens, of which seven can be matched to signs in **LdH** or its other ME descendants.

7. *Urina Mulieris* (**UMul**) in the *Dome of Uryne* (text I below), incorporating five gynaecological signs from the **LdH** or its ME reflexes.

8. *Eleven Manners of Urine for a Woman*, which combines seven signs on women's urines from the **LdH** tradition in French or English with four signs from the Latin or English versions of *Urina Rufa*. The text appears to be unique, surviving only in Gc4.

Despite their vernacular status, the *Lettre d'Hippocrate* and a few witnesses to the ME *Letter of Ipocras* are included in Pearl Kibre's repertory of medieval Latin Hippocratic writings (1985: 225–6), as the sole examples of what she calls the *Regimen Sanitatis ad Caesarem*. Although she labels the French and English texts a translation and tentatively suggests that a Latin original 'presumably' lies behind them, later scholars have come to view the treatise as 'an essentially vernacular work' (T. Hunt 1990: 101). However, the text remains rooted in learned medicine at a number of points: several of the uroscopic signs in the first half of the *Lettre* are clear borrowings from the Hippocratic *Aphorisms* (for details, see medical commentary to

---

[24] *The Letter of Ipocras* (excluding the recipes) is edited in Tavormina 2007: 632–43.
[25] Ed. ibid. 644–6.

text D), and another four signs at the end of the fullest version of the **LdH** correspond to items at the end of the Latin *Urina Rufa*.

In the French tradition, both Anglo-Norman and Continental versions of the **LdH** are extant, including several copies from northern France, with a concentration in Picardy. The majority of these witnesses occur in manuscripts dating from the second half of the thirteenth century to the first quarter of the fourteenth. The text continued to be copied through the fourteenth and fifteenth centuries, and was translated from prose to verse in the fifteenth. It seems likely that the Middle English texts are derived from one or more thirteenth- and fourteenth-century Anglo-Norman or northern French versions. The earliest English version of the **LdH** is a copy of *Urine White and Brown* (Woman) in CCCC 388, dated to 1320–30 by Hunt and Benskin (T. Hunt 2001: 85); as Benskin notes, the types of scribal errors seen in the English texts of this manuscript suggest that it is already 'at some remove from the original compositions' (p. 193).

In all but one of the medium-length French versions that I have seen (those with fourteen to nineteen signs), the text ends with the twentieth sign in Harley 2558, on women's urine like flax (*lin*), which is also the last sign from the **LdH** to appear in *Urine White and Red* and in *Urine White and Brown* (Woman), though the latter text adds one to three new signs after the **LdH** material. In *Urine White and Brown* (Phlegm), most of the signs taken over from the **LdH** occur in the first half of the English text, while most of the unique new signs occur at the end of the text, replacing almost all of the **LdH** tokens for women's urines. The more scattered contributions from **LdH** to the two components in the *Dome of Uryne* (text I below), *Judicium Perfectum* and *Urina Mulieris*, are noted in the medical commentary.

Texts D through F, like *Urina Rufa* (text B), are relatively unstructured in comparison to uroscopies organized around the Aegidian colours and contents or placed within a humoral or other conceptual framework (e.g. texts G–I). As with *Urina Rufa*, however, a certain degree of 'thematic' clustering can be discerned within the three token-lists. Most obvious is the attention to women's urines at the end of each text, another parallel with *Urina Rufa* (and other uroscopies). Signs 13–19 in **WR**, signs 15–23 in **WBw**, and signs 14–21 in **WBp** are all gynaecological in focus, with diagnoses that include pregnancy or its absence, death of the fetus, menstrual disorders, diseases of the uterus, desire for men, headache, painful urination, liver ailments, fevers, and terminal illness.

The earlier portions of the texts also contain clusters of related signs: they always begin with healthy urine and move on to urines with or without turbidity; the two **WB** texts include among the turbidity signs one or two signs concerning the colour at the top of the sample. After these tokens, there follow one to three signs about urines associated with fevers, then three to five signs on bladder and kidney ailments (plus dropsy in the **WB** texts), and finally one sign in **WR** on prolonged illness (moved to the end of the text in **WBw** and omitted in **WBp**) or three signs in the **WB** texts relating to the heart, lungs, liver, and body as a whole, followed in **WBp** only by a sign for failure of digestion and another for the stone. Although uroscopic colours are mentioned in many of the signs, the texts follow their source in paying at least as much attention to substance (turbidity vs. clarity, thickness vs. thinness, heaviness), content (Fat, Froth, Blood, floating or falling contents, and fleshy, powdery, or sandy particulates), and non-visual or extra-urinary symptoms (odor, loss of appetite, abdominal swelling, spitting of blood).

The similarities among opening lines and between other signs within the texts can make quick identification of a particular Middle English descendant of the **LdH** difficult, but careful attention to the 'touchstone' signs unique to individual texts will usually allow readers to determine which of the several white-and-red and white-and-brown token lists they are dealing with (for these signs, see Tavormina 2014: Appendix D). The eponymous touchstones for the Woman and Phlegm variants of *Urine White and Brown* are the fourth sign in **WBw** (thin black urine signifies *talent to womman*) and the second in **WBp** (fat, turbid urine signifies *fleume* in the bowels).

Finally, it is worth noting that texts D, E, and F tend to occur in somewhat different manuscript contexts, suggesting different scribal and readerly intentions towards the texts. The fourteen witnesses to *Urine White and Red* are often embedded in recipe collections (S42Ra3A9Ad1S40), though only rarely are those collections the same as the recipes that follow the uroscopy sections in **LdH** and the *Letter of Ipocras*, which usually begin with a remedy for headache involving puliol or hillwort boiled in vinegar. When not bracketed by recipes, **WR** also appears in compendia of two to six uroscopic texts (HtS29S6Cu3Add3Ro3A8), sometimes with the other urine texts appearing on both sides of the token list (HtS29Ro3) and sometimes only before the list, which is then followed by recipes (S6Cu3A8). The association with recipe collections underscores the practical and therapeutic aspects of uroscopy: in such contexts, diagnosis is a relatively brief means to a much lengthier therapeutic end. In contrast, only one copy of *Urine White and Brown* (Phlegm) is contiguous to a series of contemporary recipes (S2, followed by recipes), and all nine witnesses have anywhere from two to four English or Latin urine texts

either preceding, following, or on both sides of the text. The most frequently attested companion uroscopies for **WBp** are *Cleansing of Blood*
(English or Latin; six times), *Urina Rufa* (English or Latin; five times),
and the Twenty-Jordan Series (six times), though other urine texts also
occur. In contexts like these, diagnosis and the conceptual frameworks
that justify diagnostic judgments are the central focus, not the remedies to
be applied. Of the three texts under consideration here, *Urine White and
Brown* (Woman) is the most variable in its manuscript environments, no
doubt partly because it occurs in a large number of manuscripts (twenty-
four) copied over some two centuries. Ten witnesses, in seven manuscripts
(CcS24A9Ro2T14Ro1A8), are embedded in collections of recipes. Most
copies, however, are surrounded by other uroscopic texts, mainly in English but sometimes also in Latin. These companion texts include several
of the most widely disseminated Middle English uroscopies, such as the
Twenty-Jordan Series, some or all components of the Vade Mecum Suite
in English or Latin, full or partial copies of the *Dome of Uryne*, and some
or all components of the *Letter of Ipocras*, as well as 'The Doom of Urine
Thou Shalt Cast in Four', *Three Manners of Inspecting Urine*, *Urine White
and Red*, *Fifteen Discretions of Urine*, and single instances of *Ten Cold Ten
Hot*, *Knowing of Twenty Colours*, Bernard de Gordon's *De urinis* (in Latin),
and others.

Text G: *Rufus Subrufus*

The last three texts in this edition appear to be English productions,
though with roots in the Latin and French traditions. Text G, *Rufus
Subrufus*, begins by listing the twenty Aegidian colours, grouped in most
witnesses according to the stages of digestion they reflect. As in many
copies of *Twenty Colours by Digestion Groups*, the seven stages begin with
perfect digestion, then move through excess of digestion, adustion, death
(the mortification group), and conclude with indigestion, beginning of
digestion, and mediate digestion. After this summary listing, the treatise
continues with a series of approximately twenty remedies for illnesses signalled by five of the digestion groups, after explicitly excluding the urines
of perfect digestion on the ground that they require no medicine and the
urines of death on the ground that medicine can do no good for them.
Connections between the specific ailments described and the digestion
group under which they appear are not always self-evident, and at the end
of the remedies, the text offers several prescriptions for women's illnesses,

which appear to be independent of the digestion headings, as can be seen in Table 1.

TABLE 1. *Rufus Subrufus*: digestion groups, illnesses, and remedies

Digestion group	Illnesses	Remedies
Excess of digestion	Headache	Vervain, betony, wormwood plaster bound to the head with a kerchief 'garland', voluper, and cap
	Purging the head; fixing the teeth	Chewing peleter root
	Vanity of the head	Ointment made from juice of walwort, salt, honey, wax, and incense, applied to the head and temples
	Yellow jaundice	An apple stuffed with saffron and ivory shavings, cooked and eaten
Adustion	Hot ague	Powder made from spinagre, columbine, tormentil, matfeloun, and seeds of fumeter and marigold; potion made from mustard, vinegar, and triacle
	The access	Potion made from rue, wormwood, herb bennet, white wine; drink with prayers
Indigestion	Indigestion	Vert sauce made from sage, mint, calamint, parsley, avens, sour bread, pepper, ginger, and wine or ale
	Hernia	Plaster made of powdered cumin, linseed, anise, and fennel, bound to the sore place with a leather and linen bandage; potion of matfeloun, comfrey, daisy, and osmond in ale; avoid 'goutous' food and drink, labour, stews and potage
Beginning of digestion	Straitness of the breast; 'glet' or aposteme around the heart	Potion of spigernel, harts-tongue, and 'turmentine' in ale

	Straitness of breath	Strained potion made from horehound buds and milfoil roots in ale
	Faintness in all the body	Suffumigation with the patient's urine mixed with cumin, heated on a hot tile, followed by warm bed rest in newly washed sheets
Mediate digestion	Aposteme in the stomach; swelling in the stomach; corruptions between skin and flesh	Decoction of powdered galingale, grains of paradise, cloves, nutmeg, ginger in wine; potage of parsley, borage, mint, marigold, avens, betony, violets, and langdebef. Both good for many sicknesses
Women's urines	*(introduced by five purely diagnostic signs from* Urina Rufa, *with no recipes)*	
White urine	The stone in men, pregnancy in women	
White and clear with white sediment	With child for one to three months	
White and clear with great white sediment	With child four months or more	
Reflection of woman in urine as in a mirror	Conception	
Clear and yellow	A virgin	
Red as blood	Excess menstrual flow	A plaster of comfrey boiled in wine applied to the navel and reins
		A plaster of sheep dung applied to the womb and reins
	Amenorrhoea	Suffumigation with gladden roots boiled in vinegar or wine

Suffocatio matricis	Inhalation of smoke from old shoes cast on the fire; suffumigation with smoke from burning cloves, incense, and other sweet-smelling things

As Table 1 shows, despite the stated association with the digestion groups, the remedy list could also be read as being grouped more or less anatomically: complaints of the head, fevers, abdominal pains, respiratory problems, abdominal and other swellings, and women's reproductive health. This dual or hybrid structure probably stems from the conflation of the uroscopic framework and therapeutic content, given the loosely head-to-toe organization of many recipe collections. Although the specific combination of remedies in *Rufus Subrufus* seems to be unique, several individual prescriptions occur in other Middle English *receptaria* (see medical commentary below).

From one perspective, the treatise can be viewed as reducing the focus of some uroscopies on diagnostics and humoral/physiological theory to incorporate therapeutic content. On the other hand, it could equally well be taken as an 'essential remedies' collection enhanced with a quasi-theoretical, uroscopic scaffolding: an English analogue to the full *Lettre d'Hippocrate*, with a somewhat more scholarly uroscopic introduction and the remedies restricted to only a handful for each of six general *loci* of illness.

As §V will show in more detail, the eighteen witnesses to *Rufus Subrufus* can be divided into five groups, distinguished primarily by their prologues or lack thereof. Four texts are acephalous and thus give no evidence as to a possible prologue; the other fourteen fall into four groups, each with a different prologue. One of those prologues—that used in the base manuscript for text G below, which I label the 'Royal' prologue—attributes the production of the treatise to 'þe wisest clerkis of phisik of Ynglond & itranslatid out of Latyn into Englisch bi þe preier of king Henri þe fourþe [*varr.*: the king; þe kyng & of oþer lordis (*marg.*: kyng hary the v)]'. Another prologue invokes the authority of Hippocrates/Ipocras, Galen, Giles, Maurus, and 'al doctours' who treat of uroscopy; a third simply cites generic 'doctours and auctours' who declare the existence of twenty colours in urine; and a fourth limits itself to noting that the twenty colours can be shown in a circle. These prologues are reproduced in Appendix III below.

A secondary variation among witnesses occurs only in the 'Ipocras' prologue text, which reorganizes and modifies the series of illnesses and remedies in the second part of the text, adding some physiological explanations and more signs from *Urina Rufa* and additional remedies to the text. This variant series is also reproduced in Appendix III.

Text H: *Ten Cold Ten Hot*

Like many medieval syntheses of general knowledge, scientific and otherwise, the anonymous *Ten Cold Ten Hot* has many sources but may itself be an original compilation, not directly translated or adapted from any single text or small set of texts, though its content is thoroughly conventional. As Carrie Griffin has observed about the *Wise Book of Philosophy and Astronomy*, texts like these are 'product[s] of the textual melting pot of the later Middle Ages despite the absence of any one obvious Latin source . . . product[s] of a tradition of writing and learning as opposed to having distinct connections with any one Latin text' (2013: 1).

Just as the *Secreta secretorum* provides the most important but not the sole parallel tradition for the *Wise Book*, so Giles of Corbeil's twenty colours and eighteen contents,[26] Ptolemaic astronomical models, and the broad humoral theory and humoral/cosmological correspondences behind Galenic medicine provide the most important parallel traditions for *Ten Cold Ten Hot*. We have already seen the twenty-colour list in texts A and G above, humoral theory in text C, and will encounter the Aegidian colours and contents and Galenic humoral theory again in text I. *Ten Cold* also retails the correspondences between the principal parts of the body and the parts or regions of the urine flask, a correspondence noted by Giles and traceable to Giles's teacher Maurus of Salerno.[27] Similar material is readily located in other encyclopedic or summary texts, including the *Flos medicine* (Frutos Gonzáles 2010a: 312–20, lines 1338–1405; expanded versions in De Renzi i. 491–3 and v. 65–70, lines 1409–73, 2262–2464 and Frutos González 2010b: 161, lines 975–85), Bartholomaeus Anglicus's *De*

---

[26] Giles actually lists nineteen contents: 'Circulus, ampulla, granum, nubecula, spuma, / Pus, pinguedo, chymus, sanguis, arena, pilus, / Furfura, crimnoïdes, squamae, partes atomosae, / Sperma, cinis, sedimen, spiritus alta petens' (*De urinis*, lines 216–19; ed. Choulant 1826: 13; Vieillard 1903: 288–9), but the final item (vapour rising from the urine, which is not quite a content in any case) was usually omitted from vernacular lists. Vieillard's text is based on Choulant's critical edition, but with the addition of a useful French translation of Giles's sometimes cryptic verse. For that reason, further citations of the *Carmen de urinis* will be to Vieillard.

[27] The four-region correspondence that commonly appears in later medieval uroscopies seems to have been introduced by Giles's teacher, Maurus of Salerno, although Giles himself distinguishes three regions in the urinal (lines 97–102: *summa*, *media/mediana*, and *ima/infima*) and the body, following Galen; see Moulinier 2007: 268. For further discussion of the regions as an analytical category in uroscopy texts, see Tavormina 2014: 69–72 (item 9.0).

proprietatibus rerum 5.45, 'De vrina' (ed. Hanna in Seymour 1975–88: i. 256–8), Johannes Mirfield's *Breviarium Bartholomei* (15.10, 'Tractatus de vrinis'; BL, MS Harley 3, ff. 299ra–301vb); Sir Thomas Elyot's *Castel of Helth* 4.9–10, 'Of vrines' and 'The substance of the vrine' (rev. edn. 1541: sigs. a1^r–a3^v), as well as occurring in more specialized treatises, whether medical or scientific.

Ten Cold Ten Hot also exemplifies the modularity and plasticity of uroscopic compendia, even relatively compact ones, and the difficulty of absolutely defining their beginnings and endings. In this edition and in my taxonomic guide to Middle English uroscopies (2014), for pragmatic reasons of space and focus, I have restricted the content of the text to six sections, with the following topics:

(a) qualities, elements, the concentric cosmos, and complexions;
(b) quarters of the year, day, world, and four ages of man;
(c) four parts of the body; four parts of the urine sample; substances, quantities, and tastes of urine;
(d) ten cold and ten hot colours of urine;
(e) eighteen contents in urine;
(f) four principal parts of the body.

However, as indicated in the taxonomic article just cited, at least half of the fourteen witnesses to the text are embedded within a variety of larger compendia, generally including more astromedical and sometimes physiognomic and onomantic material. Only three manuscript witnesses contain all six of the selected sections (S10S32Cu4); the last of these reorders the sections to *defabc*.[28] Four witnesses contain five sections, *abcde* and *abc-e-cd* in H5 and S1, *bcdef* in Co3Ra6; the remaining witnesses each contain two to four of the sections chosen for this edition, always including at least two of the uroscopic sections *cde*, though not always in that order and occasionally interrupted by other texts.[29] Of all the texts in this edition, *Ten Cold Ten Hot* most clearly raises the question of what constitutes a discrete uroscopic text, and the textual boundaries and the title assigned here should be seen as contingent and practical rather than absolute. An edition of, say, astromedical compendia from

---

[28] One imperfect manuscript, the collection of medical and prognosticatory texts copied in 1586 by Robert Denham from several printed books, derives its acephalous copy of *Ten Cold Ten Hot* from Robert Wyer's *Boke of Knowledge of Thynges Vnknowen* (?1554; ?1556), which contains all six sections (sigs. G1–H4), preceded by some of the astromedical chapters of the Sloane 213 (S10) compendium and analogous content.

[29] For a full listing of the section orders in all fourteen witnesses, see Tavormina 2014: 48–9.

the same witnesses might define the beginnings, endings, and relevant components of its texts differently, depending on its own needs and criteria of inclusion.[30]

Although the section-order of *Ten Cold Ten Hot* is somewhat mutable, the text of the individual components remains generally stable, no doubt aided by the brevity and formulaic nature of the summary lists offered by those components—elements, ages of man, complexions, tastes, colours, contents, and so on. However, the treatise is set apart from other Middle English uroscopies by a number of unique terms and descriptive similes, such as Glaucus colour like leaves (fallow, sallow, or ripe) falling from trees instead of the usual 'bright horn', Karapos like grey russet in addition to the more usual camel's hair or skin, Citrine like yellow (or sallow) flowers or 'pome syter' instead of the more common *pome d'orange* and citrine or yellow apple, and others. Broadly speaking, *Ten Cold Ten Hot* leans slightly more towards everyday similes than do most Middle English renditions of Latin uroscopic terminology.

Text I: *The Dome of Uryne*

The final text edited in this volume, and the source of its title, stands out from the preceding texts in several ways. Though still relatively compact, it is significantly longer than the other texts in this collection, its fullest representatives being nearly two and a half times as long as the nearest competitors, texts G and H. If one includes substantially incomplete or excerpted witnesses, it is the second most widely disseminated Middle English uroscopy, second only to the *Twenty Jordans* series (ed. Tavormina 2005).[31] It continued to circulate in print, as part of the frequently reprinted *Seynge of Uryns* (1525; STC2 22153) and the later *Judgement of All Urynes* (1555; STC2 14834; a different form of the text). Three of its component texts remained of sufficient interest to English readers to be incorporated in a late seventeenth-century almanac, *The Country-Man's Kalender* (attributed to William Dade, a gentleman-physician and almanac writer of the early 1600s); surviving copies of the later almanac with the urine texts date from 1686 to 1708.[32] Finally, it has a complex textual

[30] New Haven, Yale Medical Library, MS 47, and Cambridge, Gonville and Caius College, MS 457/392, for instance, contain section *b* and part of section *a* of the text edited below, plus some of the astromedical and physiognomic chapters from the Sloane 213 compendium, but none of the uroscopic material, and have therefore been omitted from the list of witnesses to *Ten Cold Ten Hot* in this volume.

[31] For a tally of Middle English uroscopies with more than five witnesses, in roughly descending frequency order, see Tavormina 2014: Appendix C.

[32] Wing nos. A1527–33, A1531A, A1535–6, A1537–8, A1540; ESTC T190502, T231423,

history, with four distinctive recensions, containing from six to seventeen separate components; besides these relatively coherent versions, there are also more than two dozen peculiar or fragmentary versions and one- or two-component extracts. Even in the four main versions, the components are often rearranged, added, or omitted, further complicating the textual relationships.

As will be seen in more detail below, the general content of the *Dome of Uryne* is grounded mainly in the Latin tradition, including the Aegidian colours and contents, humoral theory, and short Latin component texts in some witnesses. This Latinate material is enriched with uroscopic signs from the *Lettre d'Hippocrate* tradition (see texts D–F above) and other content that appears to be unique to the *Dome*.

The four principal recensions of the compendium can be distinguished by the selection and arrangement of their component texts: they may be classified as a Core Version, an Expanded Version, an Abbreviated Version, or a Hybridized Version. For more detail on the versions and their arrangements, see §V below.

At the heart of all of these versions is a set of six texts that treat '4 [things] that longeth to the doome of vryne', namely substance, colour, regions, and contents. Included in these texts is a list of ten urines that signify impending death; the explicit of this list in the Core Version (see §V, pp. cv–cvi below) implies that it was originally included as an instance of colours and substances. The headings, incipits, and explicits of these six components suggest that they were composed as a unit, and they remain, with some modification, a recognizable nucleus in all four recensions and in some of the peculiar and fragmentary witnesses to the *Dome*.

Very early in the history of the text, however, seven other short items on related uroscopic topics were added to this nucleus.[33] These items deal with urine and humoral theory; ways to distinguish human from animal urine, male from female urine, and urines passed at different times of day; a White–Brown token list related to but distinct from Texts D–F; and women's urines generally and during pregnancy. At some later stage, four more sections were added, focused on the pulse; the ratios of contrary elements in the first through the fourth degrees of heat, cold, etc. (neces-

T190836. The reprinted segments are the JUDICIUM PERFECTUM token-series and the texts on urines of death and women's urines. The two earliest editions of *The Country-Man's Kalender* (1684, 1685) do not contain the urine texts.

[33] Only two copies of the *Dome of Uryne* are limited to items from the six-text 'nucleus', and each of them breaks off incomplete, so some or all of the added uroscopic segments may have been planned from the beginning, though their location with respect to the rest of the text varies across the tradition, even within versions.

sary knowledge for compounding medicines); and the age of the moon and the stability or mobility of the zodiacal signs (information useful for administering medicines or performing medical procedures). Aside from the paragraph on the pulse, the non-uroscopic add-ons are usually in Latin, except in Ad4 and A14 (for the English translations, see Appendix IV).

Despite its relative length in comparison to other texts in this volume, the *Dome of Uryne* remains a summary treatise, an aggregation of ready-reference lists rather than in-depth explanations. Its copyists clearly felt free to adapt it to their own uses, not merely by rearranging its components, but also by plundering it for individual items. Among the most popular targets of that plundering were the texts on the urines of death (*inc.* 'Urine in a hot access') and the variant White–Brown token list, perhaps because of its promising title, *Judicium Perfectum Omnium Urinarum*, and the familiarity of its incipit, 'Vrine white at morwyn & broun after mete tokneth helthe.'

IV. AUTHORS AND DATES

All texts edited in this volume are anonymous. Copies of each of them commonly appear in manuscripts dated from the first half to the middle of the fifteenth century and later, while some copies appear in manuscripts from the first quarter of the century and a small number come from the fourteenth century. Texts A, B, and C—the Vade Mecum suite—may have been translated near the end of the fourteenth century, soon after the Latin physician's handbooks (some of which include a copy of John Somer's Oxford *Kalendarium*, composed 1380)[34] began to appear.

One of the earliest versions of the *Urine White and Brown* text (in the Woman variant) appears in Corpus Christi College, Cambridge, MS 388, which has been dated to approximately 1320–30. It thus earns the distinction of being the earliest surviving Middle English uroscopy, and, like the other English texts in CCCC 388, is highly precocious as an instance of English medical writing (as Michael Benskin observes, these texts 'are the earliest of their kind, and by a good two generations or more').[35] Interestingly, the closest English rendering of the *Lettre d'Hippocrate* uroscopy section, *Urine White and Red*, survives only in manuscripts that are either dated broadly to the fifteenth century or more narrowly to the second half

---

[34] On Somer's *Kalendarium*, see Eisner 1980: 8–9.

[35] In T. Hunt 2001: 85, 193, 222. A version of the French uroscopy on which the English text is based occurs earlier in the manuscript as well (ff. 2ᵛᵃ–3ʳᵃ), as part of the *Lettre d'Hippocrate* (92–3).

of the fifteenth or the sixteenth century, with more than half of the witnesses being substantially abridged. The earliest witness for the Phlegm variant to *Urine White and Brown* appears to be the second copy in Gonville and Caius College, Cambridge, MS 84/166, in a section of the manuscript dated by James as early fifteenth century. However, this copy already shows signs of revision from the mainstream textual tradition for the work, which may imply that the original Phlegm variant was already circulating *c.* 1400 or earlier.

Some copies of text G, *Rufus Subrufus*, have a prologue that describes it as having been 'translated' by the 'wisest clerkis of physik of Ynglond' at the behest of nobles and the king, identified variously as Henry IV and Henry V, so it may date from the early fifteenth century. One of the manuscripts of the 'Ipocras' prologue version of *Rufus Subrufus* (Digby 29) was copied mainly by Richard Stapulton, Master of Balliol *c.* 1430, who appears in Oxford records from 1411 to 1433, and who donated the volume to his college (*BRUO* iii. 1766; Hunt and Watson 1999: 18).

The fourteen manuscripts containing *Ten Cold Ten Hot* (text H) are mostly dated to the fifteenth century or later, although some recent scholars date a couple of the manuscripts to the early fifteenth or the fourteenth century (Harley 1612; CUL Dd.10.44).[36]

The Dome of Uryne is harder to date precisely, thanks in part to its nature as a compendium of various components and several versions. The best complete witness to the Core Version (which must precede the other three versions because of its unified Contents section, which is dismembered in other versions) is the late fifteenth- to early sixteenth-century copy in Magdalen 221, but an incomplete copy can be found as early as Digby 29, the manuscript copied by Richard Stapulton (see above). One witness to the Expanded Version, Wellcome 409, is dated by its cataloguers as late fourteenth to early fifteenth century (Wellcome Online Catalogue, repeating the dating in Moorat 1962: 277), though this dating may be slightly too early. The earliest witness to the Abbreviated Version appears to be Pepys 1307, of the second quarter of the fifteenth century (McKitterick and Beadle 1992: 14–15). All but one witness to the Hybrid Version, which incorporates elements of the Twenty-Jordan Series in the *Dome*'s own colour list, are late fifteenth- to sixteenth-century copies; the one exception, Sloane 382 (S16), is dated 1450–75 by Keiser (Manual 10: 3840).

Excerpts from the *Dome of Uryne* also shed some light on dating the compendium: in Harley 2558, a compilation of thirteenth- to fifteenth-

[36] Harley 1612: 'early 15th cent.' (BL online catalogue); CUL Dd.10.44: dated to the 14th c. in T. Hunt 1990: 106.

century booklets made and added to by Thomas Fayreford (15th c.[2/4]; see Jones 2008: 3–4), signs from half a dozen *Dome of Uryne* components are scattered across ff. 168[v]–172[r], leaves written by Fayreford, suggesting that some form of the compendium was available to him for excerpting. Finally, two of the component texts (on substance and urines of death, both available in the earliest version of **DU**) are incorporated into John Arderon's commentary on Giles of Corbeil, in Glasgow, University Library, MS Hunter 328, a treatise whose prologue describes the author/compiler as a physician of Henry IV, though the apparently excerpted components could have pre-dated the compendium proper, while the manuscript itself may be from the end of the fifteenth century.[37] Future study of the *Dome of Uryne* and its several versions (discussed more fully in the next section) may permit a better estimate of the dating or at least the relative chronology of the versions.

V. TEXTUAL RELATIONSHIPS

The discussion and diagrams below are designed primarily to illustrate groupings of more and less similar witnesses, without necessarily making strong genetic claims, though some genetic inferences may be drawn for the tighter textual groups and subgroups. Given the large number of witnesses to several of the texts, the likelihood that many more have been lost over the years (especially in heavily used small manuscripts or by way of lost leaves in surviving manuscripts), the potential for independent translations of the Latin and French sources (themselves found in variant forms), and the general plasticity of short practical texts,[38] attempting full-fledged *stemmata* for these uroscopies seems both impractical and most likely unilluminating.

The principal criteria used in defining the groupings laid out below are twofold: first, broad structural similarities and differences, and second,

[37] Dating of Hunter 328 by A. I. Doyle, in a 1954 personal communication to Glasgow University Library Special Collections, according to the online manuscripts catalogue, followed by Cross (2004: 26). In his forthcoming edition of the Arderon text, Calle-Martín argues for an early 15th-c. date on palaeographic grounds.

[38] The plasticity of uroscopic texts, even short ones like those edited here, is not as extreme as the variability of recipe texts, recently noted by Clarke 2016: xlii–xlvii and nn. 52–3, perhaps because the uroscopies are more deeply indebted to the book than the bench. Nonetheless, they remain distinctly more malleable than most literary, devotional, and historical writings; along with other 'Traktaten des Gebrauchsschrifttums', uroscopic texts 'sind nicht nur "zerschrieben", sondern auch überarbeitet, umgeformt, in fremde Gliederungsschemata gepreßt und durch neue Erkenntnisse erweitert worden' (Keil 1969: 8). For a striking demonstration of the variability of recipes, see Hargreaves 1981: 101–8.

selected verbal patterns, especially in the translation of particular phrases or retention of notable errors.[39] Even after applying these criteria, a significant number of witnesses cannot be readily associated with otherwise identifiable groups (especially in texts A–D and I) and have been classified simply as idiosyncratics. In the case of the eponymous *Dome of Uryne* itself, the large number of witnesses, the modular nature of the text, and the substantial number of imperfect, idiosyncratic, or excerpted copies make even the limited groupings offered for texts A–H difficult to emulate, and I have restricted the diagram for text I to a simple depiction of the four major structural types.

A. *Twenty Colours by Digestion Groups*

The Middle English *Twenty Colours* text is based on the urine wheel that sometimes accompanies the Latin 'Urina rufa significat salutem' and 'Omnis urina est colamentum' treatises. The Middle English version appears in four principal formats: single wheels, normally of twenty colours (see Pl. 1), similar to the Latin diagrams; a three-wheel variant of six, seven, and seven colours each;[40] tabular lists (often as figures of division, with or without brackets from the digestions to their associated colours); and run-in prose.[41] Although the wheels are the most visually arresting presentation of the text, in Middle English they are not as common as the tabular and run-in layouts, no doubt for reasons of space. Four manuscripts of the English version provide single wheels; two present the smaller, three-wheel sets. In contrast, the tabular and run-in formats (including occasional

---

[39] It is important to observe that certain recurring turns of phrase may have arisen independently, bringing otherwise separate witnesses together (e.g. the choice of *alle/every/each* as a translation for *omnis* in the opening line of text C or the choice of forms of *token(en)* vs. forms of *signe(fien)* to translate Latin *significare/signare* and French *signefier* in several texts). Where possible, I have tried to use additional words and phrases as a cross-check against this kind of parallel evolution.

[40] Reproduced from Digby 29, ff. 129ʳ, 130ʳ in Gunther 1925: 25–6; available in colour at https://digital.bodleian.ox.ac.uk/(search "digby 29"). Other urine wheels that have been digitized and published online include BL Royal 18 A.vi (English: https://www.bl.uk/catalogues/illuminatedmanuscripts/searchMSNo.asp); TCC R.1.86 (Latin: https://mss-cat.trin.cam.ac.uk/search.php); the Rosenbach almanac, MS 1004/29 (Latin: https://rosenbach.org/collection-highlight/tabula-festorum-mobilium-cum-canone/); Aberystwyth, National Library of Wales, MS 3026C, p. 28 (Welsh: https://commons.wikimedia.org/wiki/File: P._28_a_chart_showing_urine_colours_and_their_meaning.jpg), and others. Further examples are listed in MacKinney's checklist of medical images (1965): see n. 15 above.

[41] For sigla and shelfmarks of the manuscripts, see the list of manuscript sigla (pp. xv–xxi) and §II above.

combinations of the two) occur in more than twenty manuscripts, more or less evenly divided between the two formats.[42]

These different layouts do not affect the substantive content of the text, although there are some lexical variants that appear to be linked with one or the other format: for instance, the descriptions of Rufus and Subrufus urines as being like burnished and unburnished gold occur mainly in association with urine wheels. Most variation is a matter of differences among the descriptions of the colours and, to a lesser extent, in the colour labels, which are usually left in Latin, but are sometimes more fully naturalized.[43] Also salient, in most texts, is the digestion group with which each witness begins, a decision required by the conversion from circular to linear organization. Whereas the single-wheel texts follow their Latin models in placing the colour Albus at the bottom and moving clockwise around the circle in the metabolic and chromatic arcs described above (pp. lx–lxi), most of the remaining witnesses suggest that their Middle English translators assumed that the beginning point of the circle was at the top, with the colours of 'excess' or 'perfect' digestion, ignoring or overriding the physiological logic of moving from one metabolic extreme through temperance to the opposite extreme. (That logic is visible in the verses from the *Flos medicine* on the stages of digestion and the associated colours: all three variants given by De Renzi begin with the clear and pale colours of indigestion and carry on to the yellows, reds, green, livid, and black.[44])

This organizational choice thus provides a preliminary, partial test for grouping the *Twenty Colours* texts into families, and has further intrinsic interest in the light it sheds on how English translators and scribes read the urine wheels they encountered. Nine of the unillustrated texts (LdS35H10 W8Di2Cu5T11S6 W4a) begin with the group of four colours that signify 'excess of digestioun'—Rubeus, Subrubeus, Rubicundus, and Subrubicundus—though the order within the group may vary from one manuscript to the next. These texts then move clockwise through the other digestion groups, concluding with the two colours of 'perfect digestion', Rufus and Subrufus, or, in three instances, reversing the order of the 'mediate' and 'perfect' digestion groups but otherwise following

---

[42] One manuscript, Wellcome 404, contains both a run-in and wheel version of the text, but the two are on adjacent folios and essentially present the same incomplete text, with sixteen colours and five digestion groups. The tabular version found in Sloane 1388 appears to be a direct copy of the text in a wheel diagram, judging from its heading and language (see below).

[43] On Latin labels in otherwise English-language uroscopy texts and other aspects of language switching in medical and scientific texts, see Honkapohja 2017: ch. 5, esp. 130–6.

[44] See n. 14 above.

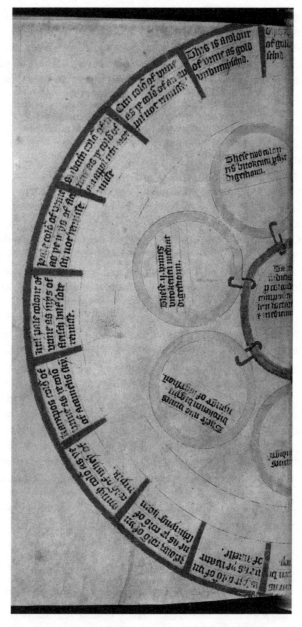

PLATE I. *Twenty Colours by Digestion Groups* (wheel diagram).
Cambridge, Gonville & Caius College, MS 336/725, ff. 77ᵛ–78ʳ

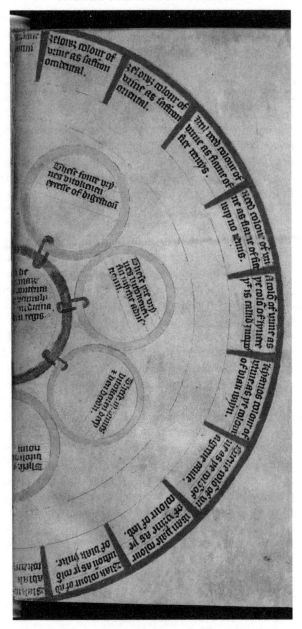

Reproduced by permission of the Master and
Fellows of Gonville and Caius College, Cambridge

the normal sequence.[45] Two acephalous texts (Gc7S21) also belong with this group, based on their parallelisms with the two possible conclusions ('perfect' or 'mediate' digestion) to the sequence. Another two witnesses (Ra6H8) begin with the Perfect Digestion colours, just to the left of the Excess Digestion group on the single-wheel diagram, and then carry on clockwise in the same order, concluding with the Citrine and Subcitrine colours for Mediate Digestion.

Only five unillustrated texts clearly exhibit organizational choices that diverge from the 'clockwise from the top' pattern described in the preceding paragraph. Three move from Indigestion clockwise around to Mortification (the 'metabolic' sequence: Pe3, the closely related W6, and the late copy in T13). S9 begins with the Perfect Digestion colour 'ruffe' and moves *counter*-clockwise through the digestion groups, ending with 'Subred lyke sad saffroun' (i.e. Subrubeus).[46] Finally, the translator or scribe responsible for the text in T7 seems to have read more or less from left to right, with Beginning of Digestion and Mediate Digestion first, then Perfect Digestion and Indigestion (roughly the top and bottom of a single-wheel diagram), and then Excess Digestion and Adustion; the prologue promises to conclude with urines of 'mortyfycacyon or deth', but the text as it stands ends with the colours of Adustion.

The three-wheel diagrams in Ro6Di1 put the Perfect and Excess Digestion groups in their first wheel, followed by 'Too Much Adustion' and 'Death' in the second, and 'Indigestion', 'Begin(ning) to Digest', and 'Mediate (Digestion)' in the third, again as though reading clockwise from the top of a single-wheel original. The circular diagram in A7, though it lacks concentric rings with the names and descriptions of the colours, nonetheless arranges the digestion-group roundels in the same circular pattern as that used in complete twenty-colour *rotae*. Interestingly, however, the later hand that added Latin colour terms and numbered the flasks drawn for each digestion roundel wrote '1' next to the Perfect Digestion colours at the top of the diagram, and continued clockwise with '2' to '7' for the remaining groups, similar to most of the linear and partially linear versions of the text. The captions in the urine wheel in W4 match the prose text on the preceding leaf, so it seems likely that readers would have

[45] This variation is not as uroscopically significant as it might appear, as it was not uncommon to combine mediate and perfect digestion, treating both citrine and rufous hues as signs of health and temperate digestion.

[46] The nineteen colour descriptions in S9 (which omits Subruffe) do not include the names of the digestion groups, but are immediately preceded by another list, with fifteen colour names but no similes and a modified set of five digestion groups, running counter-clockwise from the colour Black and the digestion group 'signat mortem' respectively.

read the diagram as beginning with the Excess Digestion group at the top of the wheel, parallel to the accompanying prose text. The last two urine wheels, in Gc4 and Yo, are the closest in appearance to the Latin *rotae urinarum*, and remain open to reading clockwise from the bottom, but their users and possibly also their creators may have read them from the top as well.

In the incomplete, roughly tabular text in S29, the list of colours is preceded by a heading similar to the central roundels of a number of Latin and English twenty-colour wheels: 'Tabula de judicijs vrinarum per colores & contenta composita per venerabilem doctorem in medicina medicum domini regis approbatum per omnes medicos tangentes de vrinis in vniuersitate oxonie'). The colour list then begins with the Perfect Digestion group and moves clockwise through the remaining groups, albeit with some possibly inadvertent omissions of individual colours and group labels.

Although the order in which the digestion groups are presented can suggest possible groupings among different versions of the text, it is not sufficient in itself as an indicator of textual relationships, since independent translators could have chosen similar organizations easily enough. Closer examination of the language used in the different versions reveals more precise relationships among ten of the unillustrated witnesses on the one hand and among five of the six wheel texts and two related but unillustrated texts on the other. These relationships suggest at least three separate textual families, two unillustrated, one illustrated, possibly descending from separate translations of very similar Latin exemplars.

The relationships within the first two textual families are determined by distinctive descriptions for the colours Rubeus/Subrubeus (at the beginning of the sequence) and Citrinus/Subcitrinus and Rufus/Subrufus (from the end of the sequence). These relationships are represented graphically in Fig. 1, along the unillustrated *a1* branch, and the identifying variants of the two families (α and β) and four subfamilies are summarized in Table 2. The mysterious term 'saffron belyng(er)' (see textual commentary) is unusual enough to support a claim of common ancestry for the seven manuscripts in the β family (including Cu5 and the acephalous S21, which share their Rufus/Subrufus and Citrina/Subcitrina descriptions with other 'saffron belyng(er)' witnesses). Whether a common English ancestor intervenes between a Latin original Ax and the α and β families (as assumed in Fig. 1) or the two families represent distinct translations would be hard to prove or disprove with certainty, given the formulaic quality of the text. The items shared by the manuscript groups in these two families are generally natural English equivalents for the Latin originals and could well have arisen independently: e.g. 'like lead', 'as black wine', 'like water of the well' for 'ut plumbum', 'ut vinum nigrum', and 'ut aqua fontis'.

TABLE 2. Identifying features in *Twenty Colours* textual groups α and β

Group	MSS and identifying variants

α	Rubeus/Subrubeus: 'as crocus oriental(is)/crocus occidental(is)'
	1. Laud misc. 553 (Ld), Sloane 2584 (S35):
	    Citrina/Subcitrina: 'colour of a pome not put out/a citrine pome putous [*sic*]'
	    Rufus/Subrufus: 'as pure gold not put out/pure gold put out'
	2. Harley 3383 (H10), Gonville & Caius 457/395 (Gc7; aceph.):
	    Citrina/Subcitrina: 'colour of a pome orange/the juice of pome orange (put out)'
	    Rufus/Subrufus: 'as pure gold/gold put out'

β	Rubeus/Subrubeus: 'as saffron d'orte ["of the garden"]/saffron belyng(er)'
	1. Wellcome 537 (W8), Digby 75 (Di2); Sloane 3160 (S36; lacks Rufus/Subrufus); CUL Ee.1.15 (Cu5; no similes for Rubeus/Subrubeus):
	    Citrina/Subcitrina: 'as pome orange/(juice of) pome orange' (Wellcome 537: 'appel of orynge' and 'orynge appel' for 'pome orange')
	    Rufus/Subrufus: 'as pure(d) gold/as gold and silver meddled'
	2. TCC R.14.32 (T11), Sloane 121 (S6), Sloane 706 (S21; aceph.):
	    Rufus/Subrufus: 'as pured gold/white gold' (placed before citrine colours)
	    Citrina/Subcitrina: 'as a pome orange/not so high of colour'

The third family (γ) comprises the texts accompanying five of the six extant wheel diagrams, and two unillustrated texts that are verbally close to captions in one or another of the wheels (S29 and the unillustrated text W4a, which corresponds to W4b, its accompanying wheel). The relationships among the seven members of this family are depicted in the γ sub-branch of Fig. 1, with asterisks denoting the unillustrated texts that are closely related to one or more of the wheels.

Five of these texts (Gc4 DiRo6 W4a*W4b) agree that the urines of mortification '(be)token death and be deadly'. Ashmole 1413 (A7), where the

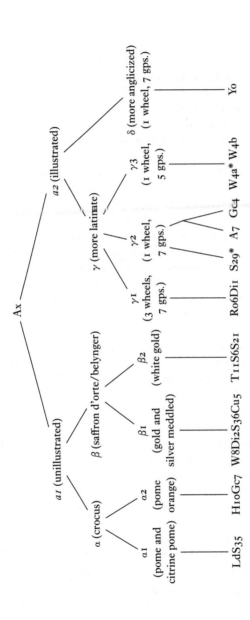

Fig. 1. Textual relationships of Text A, *Twenty Colours by Digestion Groups*

word after 'death and be' is too rubbed to read anymore, should probably
be counted with the group on this feature. The imperfect S29* skips the
group label for Livid and Black urines, though other features link it to
A7 and Gc4. In contrast, the excluded Yo says merely that these urines
betoken death. Six members of the family—all but A7, which omits colour
descriptions entirely—characterize the colours Rufus and Subrufus as
being like 'gold (well) burnished' and 'gold unburnished' (translating 'ut
aurum purum' and 'ut aurum remissum'). The outlier Yo, on the other
hand, describes them as 'Redych colour of a cler gold' and 'Redysche
colour of vryne as puryd gold'.

Three of the witnesses in this group provide a title for the text, either
in a central roundel (Gc4 and A7) or in a heading (S29*). These titles all
expand on the rubric that usually appears in the Latin wheels: where the
Latin rubric typically reads simply 'Tabula de iudiciis (*or* io) vrinarum per
colores', the English manuscripts add an erroneous reference to the urinary contents and an attribution of the information to a royal physician:
'Tabula de iudicijs vrinarum per colores et contenta composita per venirabilem doctorem in medicina & medicum domini regis [Gc4; illustrissimi
principis henrici sexti a conquestu regni anglie cuius anime propicietur
deus Amen Amen *add.* A7; approbatum per omnes medicos tangentes
de vrinis in vniuersitate oxonie *add.* S29*]'. The existence of prior and
subsequent Latin versions, including Continental ones,[47] with no such
attribution in their titles makes the literal truth of the attributions in the
Middle English texts doubtful. It seems more likely to be an instance of
good advertising, parallel to other claims of royal commission and approbation for vernacular medical texts (compare the 'Royal' prologue to *Rufus
Subrufus*, text G below).

None of the other urine wheels has a title in a central roundel, but other
features make it possible to refine their textual relationships somewhat further. Not surprisingly, the two three-wheel variants in the Royal and Digby
manuscripts are close to each other in language as well as in layout: both
use the unusual form 'Kyanops' for 'Kyanos' and translate the 'Sub-' prefix of several colours as 'lyhtt/lite' (rather than 'litil' or 'las' in the other
members of the γ family). The version in Wellcome 404, both illustrated
and unillustrated, diverges from other *Twenty Colour* texts in its intended
or unintended omission of four colours (Lacteus, Karopos, Pallidus, Citrinus) and its combination of the three digestion groups that would have
contained those and four other colours (Albus, Glaucus, Subpallidus, Sub-

---

[47] E.g. Ashmole 391, Part V, f. 10ʳ; Ashmole 789, Part VIII, f. 364ᵛ; TCC O.7.20, I, f. 33ʳ;
Fasciculus medicinae (Kirchheimer 1491), f. 1ᵛ. See also above, n. 11, and Appendix I, n. 2.

citrinus) into a single group, labelled 'indeiestioun withinforth'. A7 stands slightly apart in omitting the colour descriptions, despite being linked through its title to Gc4 and S29.

The remaining unillustrated witnesses (Pe3W6 Ra6H8 S9T13T7 H2Eg3S13) and Yo vary sufficiently from each other and from the three larger groups to suggest that, whether or not they share organizational structures, they may represent several independent translations of their Latin original(s). Some of their translation choices may reflect Latin exemplars that differ in minor details from those behind the main families (e.g. 'fowll blood corruptyd' or 'purpure blak' instead of 'black wine' for Kyanos in H8Pe3W6, variants also found in the Latin tradition[48]); others may reflect a deliberate turn to more native terminology, as seems to be strongly the case in the Yo urine wheel, to a lesser extent in the other wheel texts, and also in S9. In T7, *Twenty Colours* is conflated with *Urina Rufa Signifies Health and Good Disposition*, in ways that make it difficult to see if the writer is starting from scratch or adapting previous translations; the outcome, in any event, is an unusual combination of materials that may have been unique from its very creation.

B. *Urina Rufa*

In the English physician's handbooks containing Latin versions of texts A–C, the two uroscopies in running prose usually occur a few leaves away from the wheel of urines, though typically with a cross-reference to the diagram. The first uroscopic prose text is normally a list of diagnostic and prognostic *regulae*, beginning 'Urina rufa significat salutem et bonam dispositionem humani corporis'. The Middle English reflex of this text typically begins 'Urine/Urina rufa signefieth helthe/hele and gode disposicioun of mannes body'; in this edition, it is titled *Urina Rufa*.

The witnesses to the Middle English *Urina Rufa* text can be grouped into four principal families, three of them with subfamilies, along with seven idiosyncratic texts, as depicted in Fig. 2.

The first distinguishing feature among the witnesses in Fig. 2 is the wording of their incipits, with a group of four texts (δ) offering the phrase 'good digestion' (or, in the macaronic Di1 text, 'bonam digestionem') in place of 'good disposition of man's body', either as a mistranslation of *bonam dispositionem corporis humani* or reflecting a deliberate variant to the

---

[48] E.g. 'ut purpura' (Bodl., MS Ashmole 1438, Part I, p. 165), 'purpureus' (Bodl., MS Rawlinson D.1221, f. 15ʳ), 'sanguis purpureus' (Paris, Bibliothèque nationale de France, MS lat. 11229, f. 19ᵛ), 'sanguis putrefactus' (Leipzig, University Library, MS 1177, f. 28ʳ; Vatican City, Biblioteca Apostolica Vaticana, Pal. lat., MSS 1229, f. 5ʳ, and 1323, f. 8ʳ).

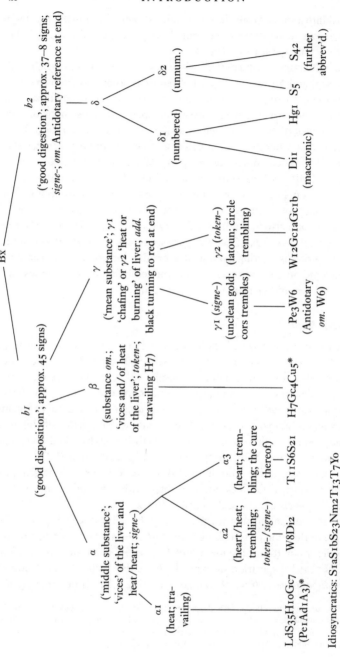

Idiosyncratics: S1aS1bS23Nm2T13T7Yo

* Pe1Ad1A3 are acephalous texts that correspond to the α1 group in later signs; Gc4 and Cu5 are abridged and atelous respectively but agree with H7 otherwise.

Fig. 2. Textual relationships of Text B, *Urina Rufa*

main Latin tradition. In addition to other shared readings, these four texts also abridge the normal forty-five or so uroscopic signs to thirty-seven or thirty-eight signs, with further abbreviation in S42 to about thirty signs; the omitted material includes a citation of the 'Antidotary' (in various spellings and phrasings) at the end of all but one (W6) of the complete witnesses to the other three main families. It is possible, though not certain, that the Middle English members of the δ family all descend from the macaronic text in Digby 29, a manuscript written by Richard Stapulton (Master of Balliol College, c. 1430), who could have adapted the more familiar Latin form of the text as part of his collection of urinological treatises on ff. 73ʳ–116ʳ and 125ʳ–141ᵛ in the manuscript.

The texts that have some form of the phrase 'good disposition of man's body' in their opening line can be differentiated first by the phrasing of their third token: for the Latin 'Urina citrina . . . cum substancia mediocri', one family of witnesses (α) translates *cum substancia mediocri* 'with a middle substance', while another (γ) uses 'with a mean substance', and a third (β) drops the reference to substance. Another distinction between these groups lies in their treatment of the ninth token (red urine somewhat mixed with blackness), which signifies *calefactionem epatis*: the γ family is closest to the Latin original, with either 'chafing of the liver' (γ1) or the slightly more anglicized 'heat or burning of the liver' (γ2); the β family reads 'vices and/of heat of the liver'; for this sign, the α family is farthest from the original, diagnosing either 'vices of the liver and heat' or the understandable but slightly mistaken variant 'vices of the liver and heart'. Among other identifying readings, the γ family describes the colour Subrufa either 'as unclean gold' (γ1) or 'as latoun' (γ2), and adds a final sign concerning black urine that turns towards redness upon some form of stirring or other motion, which signifies the release of the menses.

The α family can be further divided into three subfamilial groups. The first (α1) consistently uses the 'vices of the liver and heat' diagnosis for the ninth token; witnesses in this subfamily also translate a phrase concerning a 'circulus nullo quiescente tremulus' (in sign 24) as 'circle of the urine not resting but travailing (*varr.* draveling, troubling)'. In contrast, groups α2, α3, and γ2 speak of the 'circle . . . trembling', and group γ1 has variants of the mistranslation 'cors of urine in resting trembles'. (This sign is omitted in the δ family.) All three of the witnesses in the α3 group have the 'vices of the liver and heart' variant for the ninth token, as well as changing the concluding citation of 'the Antidotary' to 'the cure thereof'; in α2, one manuscript reads 'vices of the liver and heat' (Di2) and the other 'evil of the liver and heart' (W8).

C. *Cleansing of Blood*

As noted in §III above, the third text in this edition, *Cleansing of Blood*, offers a basic overview of uroscopic and humoral principles, translated from a Latin text very similar to that found in the illustrated physicians' handbooks (see Appendix I). Witnesses to the Middle English text often follow *Urina Rufa* or *Rufus Subrufus* in their manuscripts. In some instances, however, *Cleansing* occurs by itself or with uroscopies unrelated to those in the physicians' handbooks; occasionally, it is positioned before *Urina Rufa*, perhaps reflecting a scribe's decision to put general principles before specific diagnostic and prognostic rules.

The forty-one witnesses to the Middle English *Cleansing of Blood* can be grouped into three principal families and an omnibus group of idiosyncratics, based partially on the modifier for 'urine' in the opening words of the text. Two of the three principal branches ($c1$, $c3$) can be linked to the α and γ families of the *Urina Rufa* text. Relationships among the three principal branches of non-idiosyncratic *Cleansing* texts are represented in Fig. 3.

Nine witnesses (the α1 and α2 groups=LdS35 H10Gc7Pe1 A3 W8T11S6) translate the Latin original's 'omnis urina' as 'each urine', render derivatives of 'significare' with forms of the Latinate 'signefien', and are generally relatively literal in their handling of the source text. An acephalous tenth witness (Ad1) is textually close to Pe1. Fourteen witnesses (groups αβ and β1–β2–β3=Gc4bDi2a A8 JeS29Di1 A10Gc4aW1W10OmNm1 Nm2T15) begin with 'every urine', render 'signific-' with forms of the native words '(be)tokenen' or 'token' (with two exceptions, Gc4bDi2a), and are generally freer and more anglicizing in their translation, along with a fifteenth witness (Ro6) that omits the adjective but is otherwise close to the rest of the group. The three β groups (but not group αβ) truncate and abridge the *Cleansing* text at various points (see Tavormina 2014: 34, item 3.3.2, and textual notes on C/18, 22 below).[49] Four members of the γ family (Pe3 W12Gc1aGc1b) begin with 'all urine', and are also somewhat freer in their translation, though Pe3 uses *signefien* where W12Gc1aGc1b use forms of *(be)token*; a fifth witness, W6, omits the adjective but is otherwise quite similar to Pe3. Eleven witnesses (H7S20 Add3Di2b Yo S1Cu5Ry1 T2T7T13) are acephalous (H7T7T13) or idiosyncratic in their openings and their general handling of the text, though most of those idiosyncrasies have little effect on its substantive meaning.

Within these groupings, some subgroups can be identified: for example,

---

[49] As the exceptions just noted suggest, Gc4bDi2aA8 (αβ) tend to side with the α-group, despite the similarity of their incipits to the β family.

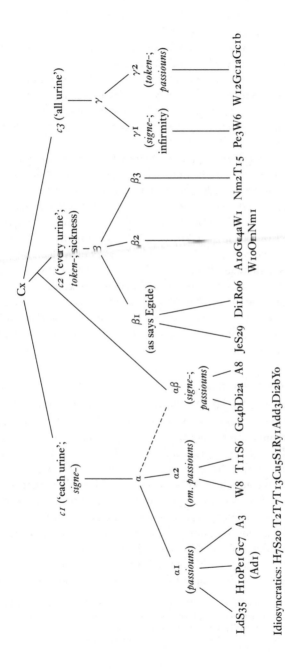

Fig. 3. Textual relationships of Text C, *Cleansing of Blood*

the β1 witnesses insert the phrase 'as says Egide' after the definition of urine; two of these witnesses (Di1Ro6) are also linked by their shared use of the three-wheel version of the *Twenty Colours* text. In some sub-groups, *passiones* in the opening paragraph is translated with the latinate *passioun(es)* (a1 texts LdS35 H10Gc7Pe1 A3; aβ texts Gc4bDi2a A8; γ2 texts W12Gc1aGc1b; and the idiosyncratics Yo S20 H7 Di2b Add3), but in others it is rendered as *sickness* (groups β1–β2–β3), *infirmity* (group γ1), or omitted (a2 subgroup W8T11S6 and the idiosyncratics S1Cu5Ry1 T2T7T13).

Given the apparent popularity, brevity, and relative simplicity of the Latin originals of all three Vade Mecum texts, it would not be surprising if the Middle English versions reflect several separate translations of their Latin sources, including the macaronic text of *Urina Rufa* written and possibly translated by Richard Stapulton in Digby 29 (Di1); the lexically distinctive texts in York Minster XVI.E.32 (Yo); the version of *Twenty Colours* in Wellcome 408 (W6; possibly the work of William Bokynham, a monk of Norwich) and Pepys 1661 (Pe3); the quirky and sometimes confused versions of all three texts as well as other uroscopic items in Sloane 5 (S1; written for or acquired by Richard Dod, London barber-surgeon, *c.*1460);[50] the conflation of *Twenty Colours* with *Urina Rufa* in Trinity O.7.20, II (T7); and others. At least some of the idiosyncratic versions may be one-off productions.

D. *Urine White and Red*

Urine White and Red (**WR**) is the closest ME translation of the uroscopy section in the medium-length versions of the French *Lettre d'Hippocrate* (**LdH**), although it is not normally preceded by the prologue and humoral text found in the French text and in the ME *Letter of Ipocras*. However, many copies of **WR** do retain the association of the **LdH** and *Letter of Ipocras* with recipe collections, situating the text within or near to English receptaria, and occasionally in proximity to texts on regimen, bloodletting, pestilence, other uroscopies, and similar practical medical advice.

Textual relationships among the fourteen witnesses to **WR** begin with a group of seven copies that include a short prologue listing the four parts of the body in which health and sickness 'dwell': head, womb/stomach, liver, bladder. The uroscopic tokens in the text proper are introduced

---

[50] Folio 157[rb]: 'Iste liber constat Richardo Dod de London Barbor Sorior'. Dod appears in London legal documents dated 1460 (Jenks 1985: 224); besides Sloane 5, he probably owned Huntington Library, MS 505, a copy of Henry Daniel's *Liber Uricrisiarum* dated by Hanna to the third quarter of the 15th c. (1994: 192), which also contains his name.

as a means by which to 'hear and learn' about those parts. (For a visual representation of the textual groupings described here, see Fig. 4.) One of these seven witnesses, Nw1, has a compressed and somewhat corrupt form of this prologue, and tends to preserve eccentric readings elsewhere in the text, but the other six (S42Ad1Ra3A9HtS29) present the full prologue accurately. These witnesses also often agree against the readings of other copies. Within this group of six, HtS29 sometimes forms a subgroup against S42Ad1Ra3A9, which in turn sometimes splits into the two pairs S42Ad1 (up to sign 11, where Ad1 ends) and Ra3A9.

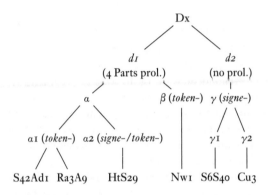

Idiosyncratics (*token-*): Add3Ro3T12   Idiosyncratic (*signe-*): A8

F I G. 4. Textual relationships of Text D, *Urine White and Red*

The other seven witnesses to **WR** are a more varied lot, all with missing signs and some rearranged or interspersed with signs from other texts. Three of them (S6S40Cu3) agree on a number of readings, such as using forms of *signe* (*signefien*, *is signe of*, etc.) to represent the semiotic link between a urine and its diagnosis and a stripped-down first sign, unique to this subgroup, that mentions only red urine instead of white, red, and white urine again. Within this group, S6S40 are particularly close textually, including their common omission of signs 5–9, 11–12, 15, and 18–20. Cu3 often agrees in individual readings with S6S40, but omits a different set of signs: 9 and 11 to 20; like HtS29, it breaks off before the urines of women section, possibly because most of the **WR** gynaecological signs are incorporated into another text later in the manuscript (titled *The Content of Women's Urine* by the Cu3 scribe).[51]

Two versions of **WR**—Add3 and Ro3—are rearranged in different

---

[51] 'Guide', item 7.2.6.

ways, with the first moving the women's urines section to the beginning of the text and the second rearranging about half the signs and interspersing them with signs from other uroscopies. The last two witnesses, A8 and T12, are both acephalous.

Of the fourteen witnesses to **WR**, only three—S42Ra3A9—contain the full complement of twenty signs. Among the incomplete witnesses, several appear to have been truncated so as to omit the section on the urines of women (signs 13–20): Cu3, Ad1, and HtS29. In contrast, A8 omits the signs up to 13 to create a purely gynaecological uroscopy.

E. *Urine White and Brown* (Woman Variant)

The witnesses to **WBw** can be grouped into textual families based on their inclusion or exclusion of selected signs (especially 3, 5, 9, 22, 24, and 25)[52] and by the use, or preponderant use, of the words *signe* and its derivatives (*signifien*, *is signe of*, etc.) or *token* and its derivatives (*tokeneth*, *betokeneth*, *is token of*, etc.) to translate *signefie* in the French original. Other variants also follow these general groupings, with a good deal of individual divergence among witnesses. (For a visual representation of the textual groupings described here, see Fig. 5.)

The first node from which **WBw** copies descend is defined by the choice of derivatives of *signe-* (branch *e1*) or *token-* (branch *e2*) as the preferred link between symptoms and diagnoses. Members of the *e1* branch omit— or do not add—signs 24 and 25 (on urines reflecting disease on the right and left side), while complete and nearly complete members of the *e2* branch include them; these signs are probably additions made in English, as I have not seen them in the French tradition nor do they appear in **WR**. Another distinction between branch *e1* and *e2* occurs in the word order of sign 1: in branch *e1*, the colours of healthy urine are given before the time at which they are observed (urine *white* on the morrow, *brown* after meat), whereas in *e2*, the time of observation precedes the colour (urine *on the morrow* white, *after meat* brown). As with the texts A–C, it is difficult to be sure whether these differences represent two separate translations from the original text, or whether the more naturalized branch *e2* (with *token-* forms for *signefie* and the added signs 24 and 25) was a reworking of a text from *e1*, but the fact that both branches change the usual French

---

[52] 3: thin green or *blo* urine signifying cold complexion or phthisic; 5: urine like ass's piss signifying headache; 9: fat fleshy and turbid urine signifying cold dropsy; 22: women's urine with a frothy surface signifying long sickness; 24 and 25: urines reflecting disease on the right and left side of the body.

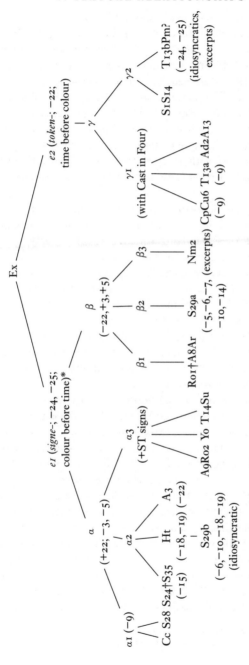

Fig. 5. Textual relationships of Text E, *Urine White and Brown* (Woman variant)

* In Figs. 5 and 6, numbers preceded by + or − indicate the included or omitted signs, as numbered in the edited texts.

† Ro1 contains 3 copies of the same version of **WBw**; S24 contains 2 copies of its version of the text.

sign of healthy urine from three observations (morning, before eating, after eating) to two may tilt the balance towards the second possibility.[53]

The *e1* branch can be divided further into an α family (CcS28 S24S35HtS29b A9Ro2Yo) that omits signs 3 and 5 but keeps sign 22 and a β family (Ro1A8Ar S29aNm2) that keeps signs 3 and 5 but omits sign 22. Two more witnesses, the closely related T14Su, also omit signs 3 and 5 but then end after sign 13, followed by sign 5 from the 'Six Token' list (**ST**, itself an abridgement of *Urine White and Red*); they can thus be assigned to the α group as well. One witness, A3, omits signs 3, 5, *and* 22, but its readings agree with S24S35HtS29b more than with other copies, and it seems likely that the omission of sign 22 is a secondary loss in an α text.

The α family can be further differentiated. One pair of close relatives has already been mentioned (T14Su). Two witnesses (CcS28; group α1), including the earliest surviving English version of **WBw** and a mid-sixteenth-century version, omit sign 9 (urine signifying cold dropsy) as well as 3, 5, 24, and 25; Cc and S28 are not as close to each other as T14Su, but this could reflect the temporal gap between them. Three witnesses add two or three signs from the 'Six Token' list: Yo (**ST** signs 1, 5, and 6) and A9Ro2 (**ST** signs 5 and 6); **ST** signs 1, 2, 3, and 4 are already included in **WBw** as signs 1, 8, 16, and 18 (healthy urine, bloody urine, and women's urines like silver and gold). A9Ro2, but not Yo, omit signs 14 and 15 and frequently share other individual textual variants. Together, A9Ro2Yo T14Su comprise subgroup α3.

The last α group to be noted (α2) includes two closely related texts, S24 and S35, and two others (HtA3) that often, though not always, read together with S24S35. S24S35 agree in omitting sign 15, which is retained in HtA3 and, in a modified version, in the rearranged and idiosyncratic witness S29b. Finally, Ht and S29b agree in omitting signs 18–19; these two manuscripts share several other closely related texts.

The β family of **WBw** texts (Ro1A8Ar S29aNm2) agrees with the α family in its preference for *signe-*, the omission of signs 24 and 25, and the colour-before-time word order in sign 1. However, in their retention of signs 3 and 5 and omission of sign 22, the β texts agree with the *e2* branch (= γ family). S29a and Nm2 are incomplete and disordered copies embedded in collections of other uroscopic texts. Nm2 ends after **WBw** sign 4, but agrees with Ro1A8Ar in using *signe-* forms and in signs 1 and 3. S29a does likewise, but continues—with omission and rearrangement of

---

[53] This shift from three observations to two may reflect a reinterpretation of syntactic boundaries, as discussed in the textual note to E.1/2.

several signs along the way—to the end of the text where, like Ro1A8Ar, it omits signs 22, 24, and 25.

The third family of **WBw** texts (γ) is defined by its preference for forms of *token* to translate *signefie*, the omission of sign 22 and inclusion of signs 3, 5, 24, and 25, and the word order of sign 1 (time before colour). This family can be split into copies that are preceded by the brief text titled 'The Doom of Urine Thou Shalt Cast in Four' (γ1) and those that are not (γ2).[54] Complete and nearly complete members of γ1 are Ad2A13CpT13a. A truncated witness, Cu6, which ends after sign 14, matches this group in all features except those pertaining to signs 22, 24, and 25. Three witnesses are united by their omission of sign 9 (the same sign lost from subgroup α1): CpCu6 and the late T13a.

The γ2 group contains four idiosyncratic or significantly incomplete witnesses, but may belong to this family. S1 is eccentric in several ways (inserted signs, some reordering of signs, some unusual translations), but it includes signs 3, 5, 9, 24, and 25 and puts time before colour in sign 1; it is more or less evenly split in its use of *signe-* vs. *token-* forms. Three significantly incomplete witnesses may also be associated with this group: Pm (three signs, all using *token-* forms), S14 (thirteen signs, all but one with *token-*; and including 24 and 25), and possibly the late witness T13b (nine signs, five with *token-* and four with *signe-*; omissions include signs 1, 3, 5, 22, 24, and 25).

As a result of the omissions in all groups, Ad2A13 are the fullest witnesses to **WBw**, losing only sign 22 from the maximal series of twenty-five signs. The particular patterns of omission, together with the word order of sign 1, mean that none of the three families (α, β, γ) can be ancestral to either of the others.

F. *Urine White and Brown* (Phlegm Variant)

Text F, the 'phlegm' variant of *Urine White and Brown*, diverges quite sharply from the **LdH** tradition, with half of its signs unique among the progeny of **LdH**. However, the eight distinct witnesses to this text are much more consistent in their readings than witnesses to **WR** and **WBw**, which may indicate a shorter time-span between the original compilation of the text (possibly mid-fifteenth century) and its latest witnesses, the late fifteenth-century Eg3 and the sixteenth-century Nw2 and significantly incomplete A14. (For a visual representation of the textual groupings described here, see Fig. 6.)

---

[54] See 'Guide', items 5.2.1, 7.4, 11.3.

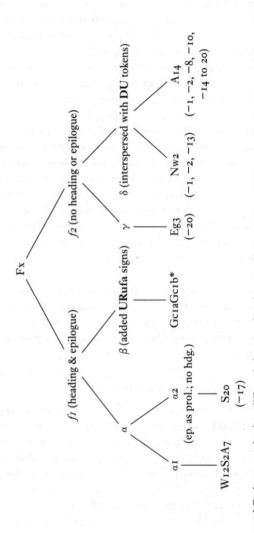

Fx

f1 (heading & epilogue)   f2 (no heading or epilogue)

α   β (added URufa signs)   γ   δ (interspersed with DU tokens)

α1   α2   Gc1aGc1b*   Eg3   Nw2   A14
          (ep. as prol.; no hdg.)   (−20)   (−1, −2, −13)   (−1, −2, −8, −10, −14 to 20)

W12S2A7   S20
          (−17)

* Gc1a and Gc1b arrange the signs differently, but are otherwise textually equivalent, aside from the omission of the epilogue in Gc1b due to its rearrangement of signs.

FIG. 6. Textual relationships of Text F, *Urine White and Brown* (Phlegm variant)

Considered structurally, four of the witnesses (W12S2A7Gc1a) are closely connected by their shared framing texts: the heading 'Here may thou know how thou shall ken and describe all manner of sickness within mans body or womens by the sight of his water' and the short concluding text on the *Four Regions and Four Parts*. The heading also appears within the rearranged Gc1b text and the *Four Regions and Four Parts* epilogue precedes **WBp** in S20.

Full word-for-word collation yields a slightly different picture of textual relationships among the witnesses. From that perspective, W12S2A7S20 are generally very consistent with each other, each witness differing from the others on specific readings, but not in any regular pattern. The other copies of the text (Eg3Nw2A14 and Gc1aGc1b=Gc1)[55] show more deviation from majority readings. Gc1 adds three women's urines from **URufa** at the end of the text, just before the epilogue (the rearranged copy drops the epilogue but keeps the three added signs) Among Gc1Eg3A14Nw2, Eg3 most often omits little words and short phrases independent of other witnesses. To a lesser extent, Gc1 also independently omits small pieces of text as well as substituting more or less synonymous phrasing.

G. *Rufus Subrufus*

The witnesses for *Rufus Subrufus*, with its combination of colour descriptions and remedies, can be grouped initially in accord with the content of their prologues. One prologue attributes the commissioning of the text to the king (identified as Henry IV, Henry V, or left unnamed) and his nobles (Gc4W10OmNm1); a second justifies the subsequent text by citing 'declarations' of 'doctors and authors' (T15W11Nm2). A third prologue begins the text with a brief mention of a circular colour diagram, 'as is showed hereafter in a circle', though with differences in the number of colours actually named in the prologue (A8A10); a fourth invokes the approving authority of Ipocras, Galen, Egide (i.e. Giles of Corbeil), and Maurus (Di1Ro6JeS29). In one witness (Ra2), the prologue seems to be related to the 'doctors and authors' group, although at some distance: the defining phrase for the group is absent, but derivatives of the verb 'declare' do appear, which is not the case in the three other prologues.

---

[55] Based on their nearly identical texts, Gc1a and Gc1b are not independent witnesses, though Gc1b appears to be an earlier copy, which rearranges the signs in **WBp** so as to put the gynaecological signs first (see James 1907–14: i. 80–1, dating the parts containing Gc1a and Gc1b as 15th c. and early 15th c. respectively). If Gc1a was copied from Gc1b, the later scribe must have recognized the rearrangement and returned the text to its normal order.

One of the four prologue-defined groups or families is further distinguished from the other three groups in its choice of signs and remedies: the witnesses with the 'Ipocras' prologue all add a couple of brief paragraphs on physiological theory and a number of uroscopic tokens from *Urina Rufa* (in addition to the *Urina Rufa* signs of pregnancy, excessive menses, and virginity already incorporated in other versions of *Rufus Subrufus*). The 'Ipocras' group also omits some of the remedies found in the other three groups, inserts several remedies not found in the other groups, and orders the remedies shared with the other groups differently. Within the 'Ipocras' group, Di1Ro6 tend to agree against JeS29. In the editions below, the base text chosen for *Rufus Subrufus* belongs to the 'Royal' family of texts, but the three other prologues and the variant series of remedies in the Ipocras texts are given in Appendix III.

Aside from their distinctive prologues, the 'Royal' (α), 'Doctors' (β), and 'Circle' (γ) families have very similar main texts, with the same colours and remedies occurring across all three groups. Variation among the witnesses is relatively minor; within these three groups, the $\alpha\gamma$ families tend to agree against β, as in the readings *voliper* vs. *towaille* in the remedy for headache, the number of doses needed for the saffron-stuffed apple remedy for jaundice (four times in four days vs. five times in five days), *virgin* vs. *maid(en)* in the sign that reveals a woman's sexual inexperience, and others.

Four texts (W1A7Ad6Ro3) are acephalous; A7 and Ad6 are atelous as well. All four agree with the *g1* branch of the text in their surviving signs and remedies. The variants noted above allow a partial association between these acephalous witnesses and the $\alpha\beta\gamma$ families: W1A7Ad6 share readings with the $\alpha\gamma$ groups, Ro3 is of indeterminate allegiance.

The broad textual groupings described above are represented graphically in Fig. 7. Although the labelling of the diagram places δ (the presumed ancestor for the 'Ipocras' family) and $\alpha\beta\gamma$ (the presumed common ancestor for the main text in the remaining families) on the same level, an argument can be made for the priority of $\alpha\beta\gamma$ on the grounds of its descendants' greater structural coherence. The inserted theoretical paragraphs in the 'Ipocras' group appear to be *ad hoc* observations, one pertaining to the causes of headache and the other to the second digestion, rather than an attempt to provide a complete conceptual framework. The 'Ipocras' group disperses the women's urine signs from *Urina Rufa* from their position together at the end of the text among the other groups, moving two of them into the middle of the text and leaving two others at the end. It also removes the sentences that classify ailments under the digestion group to

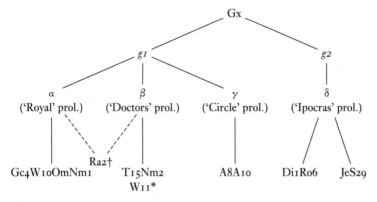

Acephalous: W1A7Ad6 Ro3

* W11 contains several texts that appear to be lineal descendants of texts in T15.
† Ra2 has mixed allegiances to the α and β families, but appears to be somewhat closer to β.

FIG. 7. Textual relationships of Text G, *Rufus Subrufus*

which their uroscopic sign belongs, a classification that provides a unifying structure in other versions of the text.

Whether the 'Royal' group (α) has temporal priority within αβγ remains an open question, despite—or even because of—the tempting attraction of its claim of royal and roughly datable authority for 'translating' the text. More detailed studies of the textual relationships between the witnesses to *Rufus Subrufus* and of its manuscripts may allow questions of precedence among the αβγ families to be answered, but they are beyond the scope of the present edition.

H. *Ten Cold Ten Hot*

The witnesses to *Ten Cold Ten Hot* can be divided first into those that are accompanied by some or most of the astromedical, physiognomic, and onomantic material in Sloane 213 and those that are not so accompanied (see Fig. 8). The first branch (*h1*) includes Sloane 213 itself (S10, the base manuscript for this edition), S32 (John Eames's book, copied in 1530, but textually close to S10 aside from some linguistic modernization), H5 (John Crophill's book), Co3 (which contains the compendium's physiognomic chapter), and *K* (Robert Wyer's *Boke of Knowledge of Thynges Vnknowen*, which includes most of the Sloane 213 compendium and all six sections of *Ten Cold*). Nm3 probably also belongs here, since its imperfect version of *Ten Cold* is copied from *K*.

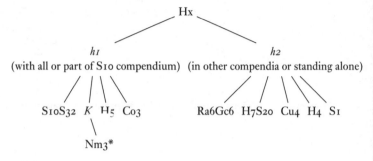

Brief excerpts: H1Cu3

* Nm3 is an acephalous manuscript copy based on *K*, Wyer's ?1554 *Boke of Knowledge of Thynges Vnknowen* or its slightly later reprint (?1556).

F I G. 8. Textual relationships of Text H, *Ten Cold Ten Hot*

The second branch (*h2*) is more of a catch-all group than a coherent set of genetically related texts, aside from two pairs of textually related witnesses. It includes three full or nearly full copies of the text, Cu4, Ra6, and the verbally idiosyncratic S1 (each with six or five sections; see 'Guide' item 6.3 for details). This branch also contains the shorter but still continuous texts in H4Gc6H7S20 (four or three sections each).

Within the omnibus branch *h2*, two pairs of closely related texts can be identified, Ra6Gc6 (both of which are followed by a text on Circles in urine) and H7S20 (both followed by a short text on the governance of limbs by zodiacal signs). Besides the similarities in their accompanying texts, each pair shares distinctive internal verbal features, a few of which are reported in the textual commentary.

I. *The Dome of Uryne*

The textual relationships among all fifty-plus manuscript witnesses are too complex to be analysed in this volume, but the following discussion provides a general overview of the broad development of the four principal versions. The general relationships and approximate dates of the versions are sketched in Fig. 9.

The foundation of the Core Version[56] is a six-segment cluster that fulfils the opening sentence: 'In the [b]egynnyng þou schalt take hede to iiij þat longyt to þe dome of vryne: to þe substance, to þe coloure, to þe

[56] For the manuscripts that belong to each of the versions, see 'Guide', item 2.0, updated as indicated in n. 2 above.

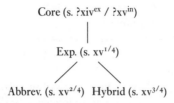

Versions only; dates are approximate at best.

FIG. 9. Textual relationships of Text I, *The Dome of Uryne*

regiones, & to þe content.'[57] This edition uses the following titles for these six sections:

Preamble (with Substance): *Four Things that Belong to the Doom of Urine* (**4Th**)
The Twenty Colours (**20C**)
Urina Mortis tam Hominum quam Mulierum (**UMort**)
The Third Knowledge of Urines: The Regions (**3Reg**)
On the [Four] Contents of Urines (**4Con**)
Urine that Has Great Contents (**GrCon**)

The defining feature of the Core Version is that the two content texts, **4Con** and **GrCon**, are treated as a single unit, describing fifteen contents moving more or less from top to bottom of the urinal, based on but not exactly identical to the Aegidian content list found in *Ten Cold Ten Hot*. The contents covered in the *Dome of Uryne* are Froth, Sky, Circle, Grains (**4Con**); Pus, Blood, Humour, Fat, Bran, Gravel, Motes, Hairs, Sperm, Ashes, and Ypostasis (**GrCon**).

The organization of these segments is well marked by incipits, headings, and explicits:

1. Substance (included in **4Th**): 'Fyrst loke to þe substance . . .'
2. Colour (**20C**): *inc.* 'The secund þat þou schald tak hede to i[s] þe color of þe vryne . . .'
   (**UMort**): *expl.* 'And þis for knowyng of þe substaunce & of þe colors of vrynys suffyseth'
3. Regions (**3Reg**): *hdg./inc.*: '*Tercia cognicio vrinarum que dicitur*

---

[57] Core Version passages are quoted from Ashmole 1447 (A11), a slightly imperfect copy whose scribe occasionally confuses the letters *þ* and *w*, but whose local readings tend to be closer to other witnesses than the complete but late copy in Magdalen 221 (e.g. A11's 'take hede' vs. Om's 'tak atendment').

regionum. þou schalt vnderstande þat in þe vryne whan it is in þe vrynal þer ben iij regionis'

4. Contents (**4Con**): *hdg./inc.*: '*De contentis vrinarum*. Nowe y woll schewe the 4 [i.e. the fourth thing] þat longys to vryn & þe [b]hen these contentes'
(**GrCon**): *expl.*: 'Now haue I schewyd þe substance of þe vryne þe color þe regions & þe content þat longen to þe dom off vryn. *Explicit*'

The incorporation of **UMort** directly after **20C** probably arises from the conclusion of the colour list, which runs from White (i.e. clear) to two kinds of Black, the first indicating relief from a quartan fever and the second signifying death. Judging from its explicit, the compiler saw his ten 'urines of death'—a token list that addresses colour, cloudiness and dregs, odor, and patient behaviour as signs of impending death—as an application of both colour and substance.

These six components thus offer a coherent, four-topic urine treatise, but it usually occurs in combination with other brief uroscopic texts: two on humoral theory; two on qualities of urine based on species and gender and on the time of production; a White–Brown token list; and two token lists on women's urines. Titles used in this edition for these segments are:

The Complexions of Urine (**CplU**)
Where the Complexions Are Generated (**CplG**)
The Urines of Man, Woman, and Beast (**MWB**)
The First and Second Urines (**1&2U**)
Judicium Perfectum Omnium Urinarum (**JP**)
Urina Mulieris (**UMul**)
Ad Cognoscendum Pregnantes (**CogPr**)

The position of these added texts in the Core Version is less stable than the series **4Th-20C-UMort-3Reg-4Con-GrCon**. All or some of them may appear directly after **GrCon** (5×) or partly before and partly after the main series (3×); twice they are inserted *between* **20C** and **UMort**, and three of them appear several leaves in advance of **4Th** in one witness. However, a couple of the segments possess 'organizational' incipits or explicits that are similar in style to those in the substance-colours-regions-contents cluster, which may mean that they were intended as a part of the original compendium, or that they were added by a second compiler who wanted to integrate his new material smoothly into the original:

Complexions (**CplU, CplG**): *hdg./inc.* '*De complexionibus*. Nowe afture þy colors of þy vryne loke ȝyff þyn vryn be þyk & rede'

Kinds of Urine (**MWB, 1&2U**): *expl.* 'Nowe haue I tolde þe knowyng of
þe substaunce of vrines with þe colours & complexions and to knowe
mannys vryn from wommans & beste womans with childe from cowes
with calff'

Whether the seven additional segments belonged to the Core Version from
the beginning or not, scribes evidently felt free to rearrange or selectively
omit them.

The three remaining recensions all involve a textual dislocation that
disturbs the medical coherence of the text as a whole and implies that they
must be later developments from the Core Version. The first development
in the text was probably the version edited in this volume, which I have
labelled the Expanded Version (Exp.). For reasons that are less than
clear, but may have to do with confusion about the phrase '4 that longeth
to vrynys' in **4Con** (misinterpreted as 'four specific contents in urine'
instead of contents as the fourth thing to be considered), the Expanded
Version detaches the **GrCon** segment from the four contents with which
it should begin (**4Con**) and shifts it to a position just after **20C**. The
UMort-3Reg-4Con subcluster remains together, but is transposed with
the **CplU-CplG-MWB-1&2U-JP-UMul-CogPr** series, so that the
Expanded Version usually ends with **UMort-3Reg-4Con**. In addition, in
five of the nine Expanded Version witnesses, three or four of the following
short texts are inserted between **GrCon** and **CplU**:

De gradibus (*gra*)
De etate lune (*lun*)
De signis (*sig*)
To Know the Pulse (**pul**)

These are not uroscopic texts per se, but an explanation of taking the pulse
is a natural diagnostic enhancement to uroscopy, and the paragraphs (usually in Latin) on degrees of heat, cold, etc., the age of the moon, and
the fixed, movable, or neutral qualities of the zodiacal signs would have
been helpful to anyone wishing to make medicines or undertake medical
procedures.

Again, other arrangements occur, though less frequently: two witnesses
place the Latin texts before or after the main uroscopy series; another loc-
ates the two complexions texts before **4Th**. The Latin components *gra*,
lun, and *sig* are translated into English in Ad4; a different English translation of the three texts and the pulse text is added before the Core Version
in the late witness A14 (for the English translations, see Appendix IV).

The two remaining versions modify the Expanded Version in relatively simple ways. The Hybrid Version conflates (4×) or replaces (1×) the **20C** colour list with elements from the *Twenty Jordans* series. In the Abbreviated Version, whose witnesses tend to be textually close, the entire first half of the Expanded Version from **4Th** to **CplG** is dropped, leaving only the transposed second half (**MWB-1&2U-JP-UMul-CogPr-UMort-3Reg-4Con**).

VI. LANGUAGE

Ad2: Text E.2, the second version of *Urine White and Brown* (Woman), is based on the copy in **London, British Library, MS Add. 4898,** which can be situated in West Norfolk, with a mixture of more standard forms, based on such features as *xal(t)* (along with *shal-* forms), *qw-* beside *wh-* for OE *hw-*, *tende* for TENTH, *che* for SHE (with *sche*), *werk* sb, *arn* (with *ben*), *ilk*, *mechel* for MUCH, and the almost universal use of *y* for *þ*.

Cc: Michael Benskin identifies the dialects of the English texts in **Cambridge, Corpus Christi College, MS 388,** the base manuscript for text E.1, *Urine White and Brown* (Woman), as 'belong[ing] to the borders of the East Midlands and East Anglia', with local origins in 'a small area in Ely and West Norfolk', and with some traces of south Lincolnshire language. Support for this localization includes such forms as *qw-* for OE *hw-*, *deid* for DEATH, *os* (beside *as*) for AS, *-un* for pl. pr. ind., *-et* (beside less frequent *-it*, *-ut*, *-ud*) for 3 sg. pr., and *wer(c)k* for WORK.[58]

Gc4: For texts A.2, the wheel form of *Twenty Colours by Digestions*, and G, *Rufus Subrufus*, the base manuscript (**Cambridge, Gonville and Caius College, MS 336/725, part I**) is written in broadly East Midland language. Inventories of forms from the first five leaves of the Guy de Chauliac translation (ff. 1^r–5^v), the first five leaves of the Seventeen-Chapter Abridgement of Henry Daniel (ff. 80^r–84^v), and the complete text of *Rufus Subrufus* and the *Twenty Colours* wheel (ff. 69^r–72^r, 77^v–78^r) reveal a scribe whose repertory of forms and spellings is strikingly consistent across the manuscript and avoids almost all narrowly regional markers.[59]

[58] Benskin in T. Hunt 2001: 201–7, 228.

[59] In his edition of the Chauliac translation, Wallner concludes that the 'central part of the (S)EMidl. is a reasonable location for [the MS]' (1970: xv); more recently, discussing the Wallingford *Declaraciouns*, Voigts characterizes the manuscript's dialect as 'not distinctive', though the book itself has 'London associations' related to the Sloane Group texts in part II of the manuscript (2004: 200–1).

Differences between the four sampled texts, which might reflect different dialects in

One possible item that may narrow the analysis further is the spelling *fleisch* for FLESH: based on the user-defined maps of the *eLALME* website, this spelling clusters most strongly in Bedfordshire, Huntingdonshire, and eastern Northamptonshire, with scattered nearby instances in Cambridgeshire, south-east Lincolnshire, Hertfordshire, and Buckinghamshire.

The scribe may have deliberately normalized some of his forms in the direction of Samuels's 'Type I' or 'Central Midland standard' variety of Middle English (1963: 84–7 *et passim*; *LALME* i. 40).[60] Gc4 includes a number of the characteristic Type I forms: *sich(e)*, *ony*, *myche*, *ȝouen*, *silf*, and *lijf* for SUCH, ANY, MUCH, GIVEN, SELF, and LIFE (also the frequent *lijk* for LIKE, though Samuels does not include this form among his identifying features). Samuels describes 'Type I' as being based on the language of Northamptonshire, Huntingdonshire, and Bedfordshire, but as appearing across a much wider area and 'surviv[ing] in written form unchanged until the later fifteenth century' (1963: 85). More recently, Taavitsainen has argued that 'Central Midland spellings were widely disseminated in scientific writing and continued in use in the late fifteenth century' (2000: 131), and Gc4, part I, may be a further example of her thesis.

Ld: The base manuscript for texts A.1, B, and C, **Oxford, Bodleian Library, MS Laud misc. 553**, is analysed in *LALME* (LPs 7310 and 7211, for ff. 7ᵛ–19ʳ (Hand A; Herefordshire) and 31ʳ–74ʳ (Hands C and D alternating)). The latter profile includes all of texts A.1 and BC, and is localized by *LALME* to Gloucestershire, near modern Newnham (i. 150; iii. 149; Key Map 5, ii. 387). Forms that contribute to this identification include *he* for SHE, *hure* for HER, *hy* for THEY, *ham* and *hem* for THEM, *buþ* for ARE, along with *fuyr*, *whoche*, *swich*, *tweyne*, and words in other texts by the same two scribes, such as *seluer*, *schulle(þ)* pl., etc.

S10: Text H, *Ten Cold Ten Hot*, is edited from **British Library, MS Sloane 213**; *LALME* analyses the hand in which the text is written ('Hand A'; ff. 91ʳ–109ᵛ, 111ʳ–124ʳ) as from Nottinghamshire (LP 504, with a grid reference near Newark-upon-Trent; *LALME* iii. 403–4).

the scribe's exemplars, are extremely minor: e.g. *Rufus Subrufus* prefers *whiche* to *which* for WHICH (but uses both) and *call-* to *clep-* for CALL (again using both), while the Seventeen-Chapter Abridgement uses only *which* and *clep-* forms in the sampled section. In general, the scribe of Gc4 (part I) seems to have been a very careful 'translator' of source to target forms.

[60] Labelling this variety of Central Midland language as a 'standard' has come to be seen as unsatisfactory for a number of reasons, most recently discussed by Hudson 2017, but it does appear to remain a recognizable variety of written Middle English. Taavitsainen suggests the label 'Central Midland spelling system' and restricts her analysis to scientific texts (2000: 131). For the language of Gc4, part II, see Honkapohja 2017: 173–8, 192–4, localizing its forms within Samuels's Types III and IV of London English.

Characteristic forms include *swilk*, *whilk*, *ilk(e)*, and *ilkone* for SUCH, WHICH, and EACH, *es* (beside *is*) for IS, *ere* (beside *are*, *ben*, and rare *ar*, *bes*, *be*) for ARE, *yem* and *yeir(e)* for THEM and THEIR, *mekil* and other *-kVl-* forms for MUCH, *sall* and *suld* for SHALL sg. and SHOULD sg., both *clepe* and *calle* for CALL, *-es* for 3 sg. pr., and *o* for OE/ON ā. Hand B (ff. 135ᵛᵇ–159ʳᵇ) is described in *LALME* as a 'mixture of elements from N and S Lincs' (i. 115).

S15: The English texts in **British Library, MS Sloane 374**, including text I, *The Dome of Uryne*, can be traced broadly to the Central Midland region, roughly the area around eastern Staffordshire or Warwickshire or western Derbyshire, Leicestershire, Northamptonshire. Support for the localization includes a general lack of strongly Northern, East Anglian, West Midland, or Southern features,⁶¹ and more specifically *man* for MAN, *mekel*/*mykel* for MUCH, *ben*/*arn* for ARE, *hit* for IT, *hure* for THEIR (1×), *ʒif* (beside *if*) for IF, *o* for OE/ON ā, *-th* endings for 3 sg. pr., *clep-* (beside *cal-* 1×) for CALL. Inventories of forms from the English recipe collections (tallied fully from ff. 14ʳ–27ᵛ and scanned from ff. 59ᵛ–69ʳ) and the *Tractus Curie* (ff. 86ᵛ–91ᵛ) display minor divergences from the forms in *The Dome of Uryne*, suggesting that the manuscript's scribe left some dialect differences among his exemplars untranslated.

S42: Text D (*Urine White and Red*) is edited from **British Library, MS Sloane 3542**, a miscellany from the latter half of the fifteenth century. The language in the manuscript shows signs of accommodation to a relatively standard spelling system, but it still retains a few characteristically western forms, based on inventories of forms for ff. 32ᵛ–40ᵛand 67ʳ–74ᵛ, folio-runs that include the two English uroscopies in the manuscript.⁶² Most notable are the forms for ARE (*buth* 4×, *but* 2×, next to *ben* 1×, *bene* 1×) and THEM (*hᵃm* 90×, *hem* 8×). The abbreviated form *hᵃm* is quite rare in *LALME* records, appearing in only three manuscripts (from Devonshire, Gloucestershire, and Herefordshire), though other forms of *ham* are common enough in the south and south-west.⁶³ Other words that reinforce the westerly origin of the analysed hand(s) are HER (*hure* 12×, *hur* 1×) and FIRE

---

⁶¹ One exception may be *nouʒ* NOT, common in both *The Dome of Uryne* and the recipe collections, alongside other forms including *nouʒt*; *LALME* only records examples of this unusual spelling in Norfolk (four LPs), Suffolk (one LP), and Bedfordshire (one LP). *Nouʒt*, on the other hand, occurs in nearly all counties.

⁶² These two passages, in similar anglicana scripts but with a greater use of secretary *a* in the second, may have been written by the same scribe at different times, given their generally consistent spelling systems. Other folio runs in more obviously distinct hands contain different forms (e.g. *them* and *hem* in the recipes on ff. 47ᵛ–58ʳ).

⁶³ Though it is not used by the S42 scribe(s) in the analysed folios, another abbreviated form of THEM, *hā*, is especially frequent in Herefordshire and Gloucestershire.

(*fure* 2× in 32^v–40^v; *fyre* 1× in 67^r–74^v may reflect the untranslated but familiar spelling of an exemplar). In both analysed passages, UPON appears as *apon* (8×), a spelling found more commonly further north, but well attested in the Herefordshire manuscript Sloane 5, which also uses several forms of *ham* including *h^{a}m*.

W12: **London, Wellcome Library, MS 8004**, the base manuscript for text F, *Urine White and Brown* (Phlegm), comes from the north-east Midlands, probably Nottinghamshire or Lincolnshire, based on forms such as *pies(e)*, *sall*, *os* (beside less common *as*), *es* (besides more common *is*), *such(e)*, *ilk(e)*, instances of *qw-* for WH- (OE *hw-*), *þem* and *þer* for THEM and THEIR, a mix of *o* and *a* reflexes of OE/ON *ā* and of *-s* and *-th* endings for 3 sg. pr. Text F's language is very close to that of Wallingford's 'Declarations' on ff. 31^v–34^v, identified by Margaret Laing as belonging to East Nottinghamshire or central west Lincolnshire (Voigts 2004: 204). The most similar *LALME* linguistic profiles appear to be LPs 225 and 16. The Calendar that opens the manuscript adds the Feast of St Hugh of Lincoln (17 Nov.; f. 15^v).

VII. EDITORIAL PRINCIPLES AND PRACTICE

General Plan

Manuscript copies of the texts edited in this volume are characterized by an interesting and sometimes frustrating blend of flexibility and consistency. Translators, adaptors, and scribes were open to modifications of technical vocabulary and description, presumably for purposes of clarification; to differing arrangements of material within the texts; to omitting or including particular sections of compendious texts; and, on rare occasions, to the interweaving of multiple texts. However, they also appear to have valued general fidelity to the basic medical content of the texts and parts of texts that they transmitted, even when they modified the structure or diction of those texts. Although the different texts do not always completely agree on the diagnoses for specific symptoms, contamination or correction between texts that reflect those disagreements is rare; scribes occasionally hybridize texts, but usually by accumulating information rather than correcting it. Nor do the textual variants suggest much adaptation based on individual practitioners' experience, a contrast to the practice of adding attributed recipes, details of successful cures, corrections, and statements of approbation or criticism to medical recipe collections.

Because of the large number of witnesses to the texts edited here, the substantive consistency of their medical content, and the very extensive *non*-substantive variation among them, the editions presented below do not seek to provide a full—or even a restricted—critical apparatus of the kind normally undertaken in EETS editions.[64] They are conceived instead as 'reading editions', inspired by but with an even more restricted apparatus than those in the recent EETS texts of the *Speculum Vitae* and *The Prick of Conscience* (Hanna 2008; Hanna and Wood 2013), and analogous in other ways to the Society's edition of cookery texts in *Curye on Inglysch* (Hieatt and Butler 1985). The textual apparatus restricts itself entirely to support for emendations of the base texts, and normally reports only a few witnesses to that end (typically from four to seven manuscripts), usually chosen to represent principal textual groups among all known witnesses, with only very occasional and highly selective reporting of other witnesses where such reporting may aid emendation.[65] The goal has been to make these texts available to scholars of Middle English medical writing and accessible to historians of medieval medicine more generally, in full and readable versions, with sufficient ancillary material to support further study of the works and their textual traditions.

The selection of the base text for each work is determined by the combined criteria of completeness, relative accuracy and legibility, and (if possible) earlier rather than later date. Witnesses are chosen for reporting in the apparatus on the basis of similar criteria, especially as to relative completeness and accuracy, subject to the constraint of representing all or most of the major textual groups for a given work. The base text should thus be seen as *a* 'best text', in terms of presenting its uroscopic content, though not necessarily a perfect text or *the* 'best text'.

A select number of illuminating and otherwise interesting variants from manuscripts not collated in the textual apparatus—including variants that

---

[64] In trial critical editions of the relatively formulaic texts A and C, limited to 7 (of 29) and 10 (of 41) witnesses respectively and even with generous definitions of what counts as non-substantive variation, these texts of about 30 lines each generated preliminary textual apparatuses of 45 and 75 lines respectively. As Hieatt and Butler say of the culinary texts edited in *Curye on Inglisch*, giving a full set of substantive variants would be 'expensive, and extremely tedious for the reader' (1985: 32).

[65] One exception should be noted: *The Dome of Uryne* is edited only from the Expanded Version, and the five collated manuscripts are chosen for relative completeness and reasonable accuracy, but not for representativeness across the several versions of the compendium. Both the length of the overall text and the substantial structural changes among the several versions of *The Dome of Uryne* would create an excessively unwieldy apparatus, even after restricting the apparatus to emendations. However, an edition of the longest version of the text will give future students of the text and its development a starting point for comparison, despite the organizational flaws in the Expanded Version and the fact that it cannot be the oldest version of the text.

suggest alternative understandings of unemended terms or phrases, or possibly independent translations of Latin or French originals—is reported in the textual commentary. A second, medically oriented commentary explains the medical content and identifies sources and selected analogues in Latin, French, and English medical literature.

In addition to the textual and medical commentaries, a series of appendices complements the editions by giving Latin and French source materials for texts A–C and D–F, the variant forms of the prologue and remedies in text G, and English versions of the Latin components in text I:

- I. The Latin Vade Mecum Suite
- II. Uroscopy Text from the *Lettre d'Hippocrate*
- III. *Rufus Subrufus*: Variant Prologues and Remedies
- IV. *The Dome of Uryne*: English Versions of Latin Component Texts

Base Texts of the Individual Editions

Because text A is brief and appears in two distinct formats, both with and without diagrammatic support, it is edited here twice, first from the non-illustrated Bodleian Library, MS Laud misc. 553 (Ld), and secondly from Gonville and Caius College, MS 336/725 (Gc4), the clearest of the urine wheels. Ld is an early (late fourteenth to early fifteenth century) and generally careful representative of the α family; like other members of that family, it offers a relatively close translation of the likely Latin source. It is collated against S35, H10, W8, and T11 (representing the α1, β1, and β2 groups respectively); the idiosyncratic Pe3; and a Latin text close to the original (see Appendix I). Gc4 (Part I: mid-fifteenth century) is collated with all five other urine wheels, and with the non-diagrammatic texts in Wellcome 404 and Sloane 1388, which are either clearly or probably derived from an English urine wheel.

Texts B and C, *Urina Rufa* and *Cleansing of Blood*, are also edited from Ld, again because of its comparatively early date, legibility, and relative fidelity to the Latin versions of the *Urina Rufa* and *Cleansing* texts. Although there are a few omissions and mistranscriptions in Ld's versions of these two texts, they are easily emended by comparison with other witnesses, especially other complete copies in its subfamily, and with Latin versions of the texts. For *Urina Rufa*, Ld has been collated against the following representative witnesses: S35, W8 (from the *Urina Rufa* α group); Pe3 (*Urina Rufa* γ group); and Hg1 (*Urina Rufa* δ group); and selectively against S6 and Di1 (α and δ groups) and a Latin text close to the original. For *Cleansing of Blood*, Ld has been collated with S35, W8

(*Cleansing* α group); Gc4b (*Cleansing* β group); Pe3 (*Cleansing* γ group); and a Latin text close to the original.

Text D, *Urine White and Red*, is edited from British Library, MS Sloane 3542 (S42), collated against Ra3A9Nw1S6Add3Ro3 and selected thirteenth- and fourteenth-century Anglo-Norman and French copies of the *Lettre d'Hippocrate*. The choice of a base manuscript for text D is significantly restricted by abridgements in the majority of witnesses (detailed in items 4.2.1 and 4.2.2 in Tavormina 2014); only S42 and Ra3 contain the full series of nineteen signs in the original **LdH** order, though Add3 has the full series in a rearranged order and A9 and Nw1 are nearly complete, missing one and four signs respectively. None of the witnesses, whether complete or not, appears to be particularly early, but watermark evidence (§II above) may place S42 in the third quarter of the fifteenth century, at least for the leaves containing *Urine White and Red*. The manuscripts selected for collation represent subgroups α1, β, γ1, and two idiosyncratic copies.

For text E, *Urine White and Brown* (Woman variant), I provide two texts, primarily because of the intrinsic interest of the first of them, despite its omissions of some signs, and the near-completeness of the second. Text E.1 is edited solely from Cambridge, Corpus Christi College, MS 388 (Cc), a closely dated and localized compendium of Anglo-Norman, Latin, English, and mixed-language texts that has been edited by Tony Hunt (though the edition omits the English uroscopy), with detailed Middle English dialect analysis by Michael Benskin (see T. Hunt 2001). The very specific dating (*c.* 1320–30) and dialect identification (west Norfolk into Ely) makes this a particularly important example of Middle English medical writing, and indeed, the earliest surviving Middle English uroscopy, worth presentation and study for both those features and the trilingual environment from which it springs. I edit text E.2 from British Library, MS Add. 4898 (Ad2), a carefully written, fifteenth-century manuscript that gives one of the most complete witnesses to the text, omitting only one sign (which can be supplied from other witnesses). Despite the general accuracy and near-completeness of the text, minor omissions and misapprehensions require emendation, which is based on the readings of A13Ro1A8S35A9A3, with occasional citation of other witnesses and of readings in the French tradition that shed light on the English text. A13 is closely related to Ad2 (both in the γ1 group); Ro1A8 are among the better witnesses to the β family (both from the β1 group); S35, A9, and A3 represent different subgroups in the α2 and α3 groups. For the last two signs in the text, which appear only in members of the γ family, Ad2 has been collated with other representative members of that family, A13CpS1S14.

Text F, the Phlegm variant of *Urine White and Brown*, has only nine witnesses. The fullest texts are those with a heading and epilogue (the *f1* branch, containing the α and β groups). Among these, the most carefully written manuscript is arguably London, Wellcome Library, MS 8004 (W12), the 'Physician's Handbook' dated *c.*1454.[66] Because the number of witnesses is relatively small, all have been collated in the edition below.

Complete copies of *Rufus Subrufus*, text G, occur in fourteen manuscripts representing four textual groups. The base manuscript Gc4 (part I, mid-fifteenth century, also used for text A.2) may not be the oldest member of its group (α), but it is one of the most carefully written and elaborately produced. Collated witnesses include one each from groups β (T15, third quarter of the fifteenth century), γ (A8, fifteenth century; probably earlier than its fellow group member A10, from the end of the century), and δ (Di1, first third of the fifteenth century, possibly before *c.*1425 given the career arc of its scribe Richard Stapulton[67]). An additional member of the α group (W10, mid-fifteenth century) has been collated as a closer check on the readings in Gc4; it is a much smaller and less elaborate manuscript than Gc4, but generally well written and similarly dedicated to medical texts.

Text H, *Ten Cold Ten Hot*, is edited here from British Library, MS Sloane 213 (S10), a large and carefully written volume possibly of the early fifteenth century, collated with other witnesses containing at least five of the six components in the text (see comments in §III above on the blurry edges of the term 'text' applied to *Ten Cold Ten Hot*, which is often embedded in larger compendia of medical and astromedical works). Those witnesses are S32 (textually very close to S10, despite its sixteenth-century date of 1530) and Cu4, both with all six components, along with H5 and Co3, with five components each.

Sloane 374 (S15), the base manuscript for *The Dome of Uryne* (Expanded Version), is a clearly written copy dated to the second quarter of the fifteenth century, accompanied by helpful marginalia by the main

---

[66] The earliest copy of text F may be Gc1b, of the early 15th c., but it and its close sibling Gc1a diverge in several significant ways from all other witnesses, including the insertion of three women's urines from *Urina Rufa*, the substitution of *lyghtys* 'lungs' for *bowells* in sign 2 (diverging from all other White–Brown texts), and several small additions of phrases with less substantive effect. These variations make the two Gc1 witnesses less useful as a base text, though interesting in their own right as evidence of a possible early revision of the text.

[67] Stapulton appears in records dating from 1411, when he took major orders, to at least 1433, by which time he was Master of Balliol (*BRUO* iii. 1766).

scribe, highlighting topics and numbering signs. Of the eight other witnesses to the text, three (H7SeRa4) are excluded as incomplete and another (A6) for its mid-sixteenth century date, though H7 and Se are worthy of note as otherwise good copies. The remaining witnesses are collated: Ad4 (textually very close to S15, including most of the marginalia), Ad7 (relatively careful in presentation, with some marginalia and headings, but slightly less accurate than S15Ad4), and Sj3 and W7 (both possibly earlier than S15, but not as well laid out and somewhat less reliable textually).

Editorial Practice

In all texts edited in this volume, word-division, punctuation, capitalization, and paragraphing follow modern conventions. Abbreviations are expanded silently, following the preponderance of spelled-out forms where available, with three exceptions: the ampersand (*&*) represents scribal symbols for *and/et*; *i.* (*id est/þat is*) and *s.* (*scilicet/namely*) are left in their abbreviated forms. Curls on medial and final *r* are usually expanded as *-re*, but other small final tags and flourishes on letters are normally ignored, as are bars on *ll* except where they serve as an abbreviation for *-es*, as in *elles* and *bowelles* and on final *l* in the abbreviation for *-is* in Latin words. In W12, the base manuscript for text F, the scribe often uses nasal suspensions and other abbreviation marks redundantly (e.g. *urẏne*, *wẏn*, *graveĺĺ*, etc.), and these are ignored in that text.

At the beginning of a sentence or a proper noun, *ff* is transcribed as *F*, but left unchanged elsewhere. Manuscript use of the letters *u/v* and *i/j* is retained, but for hands in which *y/þ* or *ʒ/z* are represented by the same character, those characters are transcribed according to their phonetic intention, primarily for ease of reading. The capital *I/J* character, for which all hands use the same letter form, is transcribed as *I* or *i*, depending on modern capitalization conventions.[68]

The following abbreviations are used in the textual apparatus: *add.* 'adds, added'; *canc.* 'cancels, cancelled'; *char(s).* 'character(s)'; *corr.* 'corrects, corrected, correction'; *foll.* 'followed'; *illeg.* 'illegible'; *ins.* 'inserts, inserted, insertion' (also indicated by ` ´ in the text); *marg.* 'margin, marginal, in the margin'; *om.* 'omits, omitted, omission'; *poss.* 'possible, possibly'; *prec.* 'preceded'; *prob.* 'probable, probably'; *Lat.* 'Latin'; *Fr.*

[68] The use of an initial *i-* where modern readers would expect *j-* is relatively rare in the texts edited below, mainly affecting the words *iaundys/iauneys* and their variants ('jaundice'), *iuys* ('juice, sap, broth'), *ioyntis* ('joints'), and the months *Ianyuer*, *Iuny*, and *Iuly* ('January', 'June', and 'July').

'French'. Angle brackets (⟨ ⟩) around a word or phrase indicate text supplied by the editor, usually because of inaccessibility in tight bindings or damage to the manuscript; supplied text is normally based on context or other witnesses. When it is impossible to determine a plausible reading of the damaged, inaccessible, or lost material, angle brackets around an ellipsis (⟨. . .⟩) signal the unreadable text. A preceding question mark on a single word indicates an uncertain reading. Textual variants are cited, insofar as possible, in order of increasing distance from the lemma; Latin or French parallels are given last, if helpful for establishing the reading.

Emendations are spelled in the orthography of the base text. Interlinear notes and corrections by original scribes are indicated by forward and reverse primes (ʽ ʼ); marginal notes by original scribes are indicated by curly brackets ({ }) in the text. In the several series of uroscopic tokens that are not already numbered by their scribes (*Urina Rufa*, the descendants of the *Lettre d'Hippocrate*, and some components of the *Dome of Uryne*), numbering has been added in square brackets for ease of reference.

BIBLIOGRAPHY

Entries preceded by an asterisk (*) contain editions of Middle English uroscopy texts, including texts not specifically cited in this volume.

Adams, J., and S. Forbes, eds. (2015). *The Syon Abbey Herbal: The Last Monastic Herbal in England, c. AD 1517, from St John's College, Cambridge, MS 109 (E.6)* (London).

Adams, Robert (2013a). *Langland and the Rokele Family: The Gentry Background to Piers Plowman* (Dublin).

—— (2013b). 'Langland as a Proto-Protestant: Was Thomas Fuller Right?', in M. A. Calabrese and S. H. A. Shepherd (eds.), *Yee? Baw for Bokes: Essays on Medieval Manuscripts and Poetics in Honor of Hoyt N. Duggan* (Los Angeles), 245–66.

—— (2014). *The Piers Plowman Electronic Archive*, vol. 7: London, British Library, MS Lansdowne 398 and Oxford, Bodleian Library, MS Rawlinson Poetry 38. SEENET Series A.10, Web Edition. http://piers.chass.ncsu.edu/texts/R.

Alonso Guardo, A. (ed.) (1997). *Bernardi de Gordonio Tractatus de crisi et de diebus creticis*, Tesis Doctoral, University of Valladolid.

Ausécache, M. (ed.) (2017). *Gilles de Corbeil, Liber de uirtutibus et laudibus compositorum medicaminum: Édition et commentaire* (Florence).

Avicenna (1486). *Canon medicinae* (Venice).

*Ayoub, L. J. (ed.) (1994). 'John Crophill's Books: An Edition of British Library MS Harley 1735' (Ph.D. thesis, University of Toronto).

Barragán Nieto, J. P. (ed.) (2012). *El De secretis mulierum atribuido a Alberto Magno: Estudio, edición crítica y traducción* (Porto).

Beck, L. Y. (trans.) (2005). *Pedanius Dioscorides: De materia medica*, Altertumswissenschaftliche Texte und Studien, 38 (Hildesheim).

Bernard de Gordon (1574). *Lilium medicinae* (Lyons).

Biggam, C. P. (2006). 'Political Upheaval and a Disturbance in the Colour Vocabulary of Early English', in C. P. Biggam, C. Kay, and N. Pitchford (eds.), *Progress in Colour Studies*, i (Amsterdam), 159–79.

The Boke of Knowledge of Thynges Vnknowen Aperteynynge to Astronomye (?1554, ?1556). STC 11930.7, STC2 11931 (London: Robert Wyer).

British Library (1977). *Catalogue of Additions to the Manuscripts 1756–1782: Additional Manuscripts 4101–5017* (London).

Brodin, G. (ed.) (1950). *Agnus Castus: A Middle English Herbal Reconstructed from Various Manuscripts* (Uppsala).

Brunel, C. (1956). *Recettes médicales alchimiques et astrologiques du XVe siècle en langue vulgaire des Pyrénées*, Bibliothèque Méridionale, ser. 1, 30 (Toulouse).

*Calle-Martín, J. (ed.) (2012). 'A Late Middle English Version of the *Doom of Urines* in Oxford, MS Rawlinson C.81, ff. 6r–12v', *Analecta Malacitana* (Universidad de Málaga), 35, nos. 1–2, pp. 243–73.

*——— (ed.) (2015). 'The Late Middle English Version of *Practica Urinarum* in London, Wellcome Library, MS 537 (ff. 15r–40v)', in P. Shaw, B. Erman, et al. (eds.), *From Clerks to Corpora: Essays on the English Language Yesterday and Today. Essays in Honour of Nils-Lennart Johannesson* (Stockholm), 35–52.

*——— (ed.) (forthcoming). *The English Vernacular Versions of Gilles of Corbeil's Treatise of Urines in MSS GUL Hunter 328 and MUL Rylands 1310* (Liverpool). [Edition of John Arderon's Commentary on Giles of Corbeil's *Carmen de urinis*]

Choulant, L. (ed.) (1826). *Liber de urinis metrice compositus*, in *Aegidii Corboliensis Carmina medica* (Leipzig), 1–18. [Also in Vieillard, *L'Urologie*, 1903, with French translation, 267–301]

Clarke, M. (ed.) (2016). *The Crafte of Lymmyng and The Maner of Steynyng: Middle English Recipes for Painters, Stainers, Scribes, and Illuminators*, EETS, os 347 (Oxford).

Collins, K. E. (2015). 'Isaac Israeli: An Introduction', in K. E. Collins, S. Kottek, et al. (eds.), *Isaac Israeli: The Philosopher Physician* (Jerusalem), 1–14.

Constantine the African (1515). *Viaticum* (trans. of Ibn al-Jazzar's *Zād al-Musāfir*), in *Omnia opera Ysaac*, 2 vols. (Lyons), ii. 144rb–171vb.

Coppens, C. (2009). *De vele levens van een boek: De 'Fasciculus medicinae' opnieuw bekeken* (Brussels).

Cotgrave, R. (1611). *A Dictionarie of the French and English Tongues* (London).

Coxe, H. O. (1852). *Catalogus codicum mss. qui in collegiis aulisque oxoniensibus hodie adservantur*, 2 vols. (Oxford).

Cross, R. (2004). *A Handlist of Manuscripts containing English in the Hunterian Collection, Glasgow University Library* (Glasgow).

Dase, S. (ed.) (1999). *Liber urinarum a uoce Theophili: Edition einer Übersetzung des 12. Jahrhunderts mit ausführlichem Glossar* (Ph.D. thesis, Osnabrück, 1997), Edition Wissenschaft, Reihe Sprachwissenschaft, 20 (Marburg).

Dawson, W. R. (ed.) (1934). *A Leechbook or Collection of Medical Recipes of the Fifteenth Century: The Text of MS. No. 136 of the Medical Society of London, together with a Transcript into Modern Spelling* (London).

Dean, R. J. (1999). *Anglo-Norman Literature: A Guide to Texts and Manuscripts*, ANTS Occ. Pub. Ser. 3 (London).

Dickinson, F. H. (ed.) (1861–83). *Missale ad Usum Insignis et Præclarae Ecclesiæ Sarum* (Burntisland).

Donden, Y. (1986). *Health through Balance: An Introduction to Tibetan Medicine*, ed. and trans. J. Hopkins, L. Rabgay, A. Wallace (Ithaca, NY).

*Edmar, D. (ed.) (1967). 'MS. Wellcome 405: A Middle English Leech-Book' (Lic.Phil. thesis, Stockholm).

Eisner, S. (ed.) (1980). *The Kalendarium of Nicholas of Lynn*, The Chaucer Library (Athens, Ga.).

Elyot, T. (1541). *Castel of Helth*, corr. and augm. edn., STC2 7644 (London: Berthelet).

*Esteban-Segura, L. (ed.) (2012). *System of Physic (GUL MS Hunter 509, ff. 1r–167v): A Compendium of Mediaeval Medicine including the Middle English Gilbertus Anglicus*, Late Middle English Texts, 3 (Bern).

Fisman, D. (1993). 'Pisse-Prophets and Puritans: Thomas Brian, Uroscopy, and Seventeenth-Century English Medicine', *The Pharos*, 56, pp. 6–11.

Frisk, G. (ed.) (1949). *A Middle English Translation of Macer Floridus De viribus herbarum*, Essays and Studies on English Language and Literature, 3 (Uppsala).

Frutos González, V. de (ed.) (2010a). *Flos medicine (Regimen sanitatis Salernitanum): Estudio, edición crítica y traducción* (Valladolid).

—— (ed.) (2010b). 'Edición crítica del *Regimen sanitatis Salernitanum* transmitido por los manuscritos Add. 12190 y Sloane 351 de la British Library de Londres', *Minerva*, 23, pp. 143–95.

Gaddesden, John of (1502). *Rosa anglica* (Venice).

Getz, F. (1990). 'Medical Practitioners in Medieval England', *Social History of Medicine*, 3, pp. 245–83. [Supplement to Talbot and Hammond]

Giles of Corbeil. See Choulant; Vieillard.

Grant, E. (1996). *Planets, Stars, and Orbs: The Medieval Cosmos, 1200–1687* (Cambridge).

Green, M. H. (2011). 'Making Motherhood in Medieval England: The Evidence from Medicine', in C. Leyser and L. Smith (eds.), *Motherhood, Religion, and Society in Medieval Europe, 400–1400: Essays Presented to Henrietta Leyser* (Farnham), 173–203.

—— and L. R. Mooney (eds.) (2006). 'The Sickness of Women', in M. T.

Tavormina (ed.), *Sex, Aging, and Death in a Medieval Medical Compendium: Trinity College Cambridge, MS R.14.52, its Texts, Scribe, and Language* (Tempe, Ariz.), ii. 455–568.

Griffin, C. (ed.) (2013). *The Middle English* Wise Book of Philosophy and Astronomy: *A Parallel-Text Edition*, Middle English Texts, 47 (Heidelberg).

Gumbert, J. P. (2016). *Bat Books: A Catalogue of Folded Manuscripts containing Almanacs or Other Texts*, Bibliologia, 41 (Turnhout).

Gunther, R. T. (1925). *Early Science in Oxford*, iii: *The Biological Sciences; The Biological Collections* (Oxford).

Guthrie, D. W., and S. S. Humphreys (1988). 'Diabetes Urine Testing: An Historical Perspective', *The Diabetes Educator*, 14, pp. 521–5.

Hanna, R. (1993). *William Langland* (Aldershot).

*—— (ed.) (1994). 'Henry Daniel's *Liber Uricrisiarum* (Excerpt)', in L. M. Matheson (ed.), *Popular and Practical Science in Medieval England* (East Lansing, Mich.), 185–218. [Book 1, chapters 1–3]

—— (ed.) (2008). Speculum Vitae: *A Reading Edition*, 2 vols., EETS 331–2 (Oxford).

—— and S. Wood (eds.) (2013). *Richard Morris's* Prick of Conscience: *A Corrected and Amplified Reading Text*, EETS OS 342 (Oxford).

Hargreaves, H. (1981). 'Some Problems in Indexing Middle English Recipes', in A. S. G. Edwards and D. Pearsall (eds.), *Middle English Prose: Essays on Bibliographical Problems* (New York), 91–113.

*Harley, M. P. (ed.) (1985 for 1982). 'The Middle English Contents of a Fifteenth-Century Medical Handbook', *Mediaevalia*, 8, pp. 171–88. [Edition of the Twenty-Jordan Series from Harvard MS Countway 19]

*Harvey, E. R., M. T. Tavormina, et al. (eds.) (forthcoming). *Henry Daniel, Liber Uricrisiarum: A Reading Edition* (Toronto). [Edition of the earlier, 'alpha' version of the *Liber Uricrisiarum*]

Heawood, E. (1929–30). 'Sources of Early English Paper-Supply', *The Library*, ser. 4, 10, pp. 282–307, 427–54.

—— (1950). *Watermarks, Mainly of the 17th and 18th Centuries* (Hilversum).

Heffernan, C. F. (ed.) (1993). '*The Wyse Boke of Maystyr Peers of Salerne*: Edition and Study of a Fourteenth-Century Treatise of Popular Medicine', *Manuscripta*, 37, pp. 290–321.

Heinrich, F. (ed.) (1896). *Ein mittelenglische Medizinbuch* (Halle).

Henslow, G. (ed.) (1899). *Medical Works of the Fourteenth Century, together with a List of Plants Recorded in Contemporary Writings, with their Identifications* (London).

cxxii BIBLIOGRAPHY

Herrera, M. T. (ed.) (1990). *Compendio de la Humana Salud* (Madrid). [Spanish translation of *Fasciculus medicinae*, 1494]

Hieatt, C. B., and S. Butler (eds.) (1985). *Curye on Inglysch: English Culinary Manuscripts of the Fourteenth Century (including the Forme of Cury)*, EETS, ss 8 (London).

Hippocrates (1931). *Aphorisms*, ed. and trans. W. H. S. Jones, Loeb Classical Library, 150=Hippocrates, *Works*, vol. 4 (Cambridge, Mass.), 97–221.

Honkapohja, A. (2017). *Alchemy, Medicine, and Commercial Book Production: A Codicological and Linguistic Study of the Voigts-Sloane Manuscript Group* (Turnhout).

Hudson, A. (2017). 'Observations on the "Wycliffite Orthography"', in S. Horobin and A. Nafde (eds.), *Pursuing Middle English Manuscripts and their Texts: Essays in Honour of Ralph Hanna* (Turnhout), 77–98.

Hughes, A. (1995). *Medieval Manuscripts for Mass and Office: A Guide to their Organization and Terminology* (Toronto).

Hunt, R. W., and A. G. Watson (1999). 'Notes on Macray's Descriptions of the Manuscripts', Part 2 in W. D. Macray, *Digby Manuscripts*, facs. repr. (Oxford). [1883 Quarto Catalogue IX, with added notes and appendix]

Hunt, T. (1987). 'The "Novele cirurgerie" in MS London, British Library Harley 2558', *Zeitschrift für romanische Philologie* 103, pp. 271–99.

—— (ed.) (1990). *Popular Medicine in Thirteenth-Century England: Introduction and Texts* (Cambridge).

—— (ed.) (1994–7). *Anglo-Norman Medicine*, 2 vols. (Cambridge).

—— (ed.), with M. Benskin (2001). *Three Receptaria from Medieval England: The Languages of Medicine in the Fourteenth Century*, Medium Ævum Monographs, NS 21 (Oxford).

—— (ed.) (2011). *Old French Medical Texts* (Paris).

Jacquart, D. (1979). *Dictionnaire biographique des médecins en France au moyen âge: Supplément* (Geneva). See also Wickersheimer.

James, M. R. (1907–14). *A Descriptive Catalogue of the Manuscripts in the Library of Gonville and Caius College*, 3 vols. incl. Supplement (Cambridge).

—— (1909–13). *A Descriptive Catalogue of the Manuscripts in the Library of Corpus Christi College, Cambridge*, 2 vols. (Cambridge).

*Jasin, J. (ed.) (1983). 'A Critical Edition of the Middle English *Liber Uricrisiarum* in Wellcome MS 225' (Ph.D. thesis, Tulane).

Jenks, S. (1985). 'Medizinische Fachkräfte in England zur Zeit Heinrichs VI. (1428/29–1460/61), *Sudhoffs Archiv*, 69, pp. 214–27.

*Johannessen, T. A. (ed.) (2005). 'The Liber Uricrisiarum in Gonville and
    Caius College, Cambridge, MS 336/725' (M.A. thesis, Oslo), https://
    www.duo.uio.no/handle/10852/25409.
Jones, P. M. (1994). 'Information and Science', in R. Horrox (ed.),
    *Fifteenth-Century Attitudes: Perceptions of Society in Late Medieval
    England* (Cambridge), 97–111.
—— (1995). 'Harley MS 2558: A Fifteenth-Century Medical Common-
    place Book', in M. R. Schleissner (ed.), *Manuscript Sources of Medieval
    Medicine: A Book of Essays* (New York), 35–54.
—— (1998). *Medieval Medicine in Illuminated Manuscripts*, rev. edn. (Lon-
    don).
—— (2008). 'Witnesses to Medieval Medical Practice in the Harley
    Collection', *eBLJ*, Article 8, http://www.bl.uk/eblj/2008articles/
    article8.html (London).
Jones, W. H. S. See Hippocrates.
The Judgement of All Urynes (?1555). STC2 14834 (London: Robert Wyer).
Kadner, A. (ed.) (1919). *Ein Liber de urinis des Breslauer Codex Salernitanus*
    (Med. Inaug.-Diss., Leipzig).
Keil, G. (1963). 'Die mittellateinische Übersetzung vom Harntraktat des
    "Bartholomäus": Untersuchungen zur Wirkung der frühen deutschen
    Rezeptliteratur', *Sudhoffs Archiv*, 47, pp. 417–55.
—— (1969). 'Der "kurze Harntraktat" des Breslauer "Codex Salernita-
    nus" und seine Sippe' (Inaug.-Diss., Rheinische Friedrich-Wilhelms-
    Universität, Bonn).
—— (1970). *Die urognostische Praxis in vor- und frühsalernitanischer Zeit*
    (Habilitationsschrift, Freiburg-im-Breisgau).
*Keiser, G. R. (2003). 'Verse Introductions to Middle English Medical
    Treatises', *English Studies*, 84, pp. 301–17.
—— (2004). 'Scientific, Medical, and Utilitarian Prose', in A. S. G.
    Edwards (ed.), *A Companion to Middle English Prose* (Cambridge),
    231–47.
—— (2005). 'Robert Thornton's *Liber de Diversis Medicinis*: Text, Vocabu-
    lary, and Scribal Confusion', in N. Ritt and H. Schendl (eds.), *Rethink-
    ing Middle English: Linguistic and Literary Approaches* (Frankfurt am
    Main), 30–41.
Kibre, P. (1985). *Hippocrates Latinus*, rev. edn. (New York).
Kirchheimer, J. [Johannes de Ketham] (1491; facs. repr. 1924). *The Fa-
    sciculus medicinae of Johannes de Ketham Alemanus*, facs. of Venice 1491
    edn., introd. by K. Sudhoff, trans. and adapted by C. Singer, Monu-
    menta Medica, 1 (Milan).

Macaulay, G. C. (ed.) (1899–1902). *The Complete Works of John Gower*, 4 vols. (Oxford).

MacKinney, L. (1965). *Medical Illustrations in Medieval Manuscripts* (Berkeley, Calif.).

The MacKinney Collection of Medieval Medical Illustrations. University of North Carolina Digital Collections. https://dc.lib.unc.edu/cdm/landingpage/collection/mackinney.

McKitterick, R., and R. Beadle (1992). *Catalogue of the Pepys Library at Magdalene College, Cambridge*, vol. v, part 1: Manuscripts, Medieval (Cambridge).

Macray, W. D. (1883; repr. 1999). *Digby Manuscripts*, facs. repr. of the 1883 catalogue (Oxford). See also Hunt and Watson.

McVaugh, M. R. (1969). 'Quantified Medical Theory and Practice at Fourteenth-Century Montpellier', *Bulletin of the History of Medicine*, 43, pp. 397–413.

—— (1974). 'The "Humidum radicale" in Thirteenth-Century Medicine', *Traditio*, 30, pp. 259–83.

—— (ed.) (1975a). *Aphorismi de gradibus*, Arnaldi de Villanova Opera Medica Omnia, 2 (Granada).

—— (1975b). 'An Early Discussion of Medicinal Degrees at Montpellier by Henry of Winchester', *Bulletin of the History of Medicine*, 49, pp. 57–71.

—— (1997). 'Bedside Manners in the Middle Ages', The 1996 Fielding H. Garrison Lecture, *Bulletin of the History of Medicine*, 71, pp. 201–23.

—— (2010). 'Who Was Gilbert the Englishman?', in G. H. Brown and L. E. Voigts (eds.), *The Study of Medieval Manuscripts of England: Festschrift in Honor of Richard W. Pfaff*, Arizona Studies in the Middle Ages and Renaissance, 35 (Tempe, Ariz.), 295–324.

Madan, F., R. W. Hunt, et al. (1895–1953). *A Summary Catalogue of Western Manuscripts in the Bodleian Library at Oxford*, 7 vols. (Oxford).

Malcolm, N. (2002). 'Pierre de Cardonnel (1614–1667), Merchant, Printer, Poet, and Reader of Hobbes', in his *Aspects of Hobbes* (Oxford), 259–316.

Manzalaoui, M. A. (ed.) (1977). *Secretum Secretorum: Nine English Versions*, EETS, os 276 (Oxford).

Martin, C. T. (2016). 'Butts, Sir William (*c.*1485–1545)', rev. R. E. Davies, *Oxford Dictionary of National Biography*, online edn. at https://doi.org/10.1093/ref:odnb/4241.

Martínez Gázquez, J., M. R. McVaugh, and A. Labarta (eds.) (2004).

Translatio Libri Albuzale de medicinis simplicibus; Kitāb al-adwiya al-mufrada, Arnaldi de Villanova Opera Medica Omnia, 17 (Barcelona).

Maurach, G. (ed.) (1978). 'Johannicius: Isagoge ad Techne Galieni', *Sudhoff's Archiv*, 62.2, pp. 148–74.

Meyer, P. (1911). 'Notice du ms. Sloane 1611 du Musée britannique', *Romania*, 40, pp. 532–58.

—— (1913). 'Notice du ms. Sloane 2412 du Musée britannique', *Bulletin de la Société des anciens textes français*, 39, pp. 45–56.

Mirfield, J. *Breviarium Bartholomei* (London, British Library, MS Harley 3).

Mooney, L. R. (ed.) (1994). 'Diet and Bloodletting: A Monthly Regimen', in L. M. Matheson (ed.), *Popular and Practical Science of Medieval England* (East Lansing, Mich.), 245–61.

Moorat, S. A. J. (1962). *Catalogue of Western Manuscripts on Medicine and Science in the Wellcome Historical Medical Library*, vol. 1, Mss. Written before 1650 A.D. (London).

Moulinier, L. (2007). 'La Science des urines de Maurus de Salerne et les *Sinthomata Magistri Mauri* inédits', in D. Jacquart and A. Paravicini Bagliani (eds.), *La scuola medica salernitana: Gli autori e i testi* (Florence), 261–81.

Moulinier-Brogi, L. (2008). 'L'Uroscopie en vulgaire dans l'Occident médiévale: Un tour d'horizon', in M. Goyens, P. De Leemans, and A. Smets (eds.), *Science Translated: Latin and Vernacular Translations of Scientific Treatises in Medieval Europe* (Leuven), 221–41.

—— (2010). 'Un flacon en point de mire: La science des urines, un enjeu culturel dans la société médiévale (xiiie–xve siècles)', *Annales: Histoire, Sciences Sociales*, 65, pp. 11–37.

—— (2012). *L'Uroscopie au Moyen Âge: Lire dans un verre la nature de l'homme* (Paris).

Müller, G. (ed.) (1929). *Aus mittelenglischen Medizintexten: Die Prosarezepte des Stockholmer Miszellankodex X.90*, Kölner anglistische Arbeiten, 10 (Leipzig).

Nasmith, J. (1777). *Catalogus librorum manuscriptorum quos Collegio Corporis Christi et B. Mariae Virginis in Academia Cantabrigiensi legavit Reverendissimus in Christo Pater Matthaeus Parker, Archiepiscopus Cantuariensis* (Cambridge).

Nicoud, M. (2007). 'Il *Regimen sanitatis Salernitanum*: Premessa ad un'edizione critica', in D. Jacquart and A. Paravicini Bagliani (eds.), *La scuola medica Salernitana: Gli autori e i testi* (Florence), 365–84.

Norri, J. (2016). *Dictionary of Medical Vocabulary in English, 1375–*

1500: Body Parts, Sicknesses, Instruments, and Medicinal Preparations, 2 vols. (Abingdon).

O'Boyle, C. (1991). *Medieval Prognosis and Astrology: A Working Edition of* Aggregationes de crisi et creticis diebus, *with Introduction and English Summary* (Cambridge).

Ogden, M. S. (ed.) (1938). *The* Liber de Diversis Medicinis *in the Thornton Manuscript (MS Lincoln Cathedral A.5.2)*, EETS os 207 (London).

Ogilvie-Thomson, S. J. (2000). *Manuscripts in the Laudian Collection, Bodleian Library, Oxford*, Index of Middle English Prose, 16 (Cambridge).

Pannier, L. (ed.) (1882). *Les Lapidaires français du moyen âge des XIIᵉ, XIIIᵉ et XIVᵉ siècles* (Paris).

Peine, J. (ed.) (1919). *Die Harnschrift des Isaac Judaeus* (Ph.D. thesis, Borna-Leipzig). Repr. in F. Sezgin (ed.) (1996), *Ishāq ibn Sulaymān al-Isrā'īlī (d. c. 325/935): Texts and Studies*, Islamic Medicine, 35 (Frankfurt am Main), 41–121.

Pesenti, T. (2001). *Fasiculo de Medicina in Volgare*, facs. and study, 2 vols. (Treviso). [Italian translation of *Fasciculus medicinae*, Venice, 1494.]

Pfeffer, J. (ed.) (1891). *Das Compendium urinarum des Gualterus Agulinus (XIII. Jahrhundert)* (Med. Inaug.-Diss., Berlin).

Rand, K. A. (2009). *Manuscripts in the Library of Corpus Christi College, Cambridge*, Index of Middle English Prose, 20 (Woodbridge).

Rand Schmidt, K. A. (2001). *Manuscripts in the Library of Gonville and Caius College, Cambridge*, Index of Middle English Prose, 17 (Woodbridge).

Rapgay, L. (2005). *The Tibetan Book of Healing* (Twin Lakes, Wis.).

Robinson, P. R. (2003). *Catalogue of Dated and Datable Manuscripts c. 888-1600 in London Libraries*, 2 vols. (London).

Roper, J. (2006). 'Personal and Place Names in English Verbal Charms', *Il Nome nel testo: Rivista internazionale di onomastica letteraria*, 8, pp. 65–75.

Samuels, M. L. (1963). 'Some Applications of Middle English Dialectology', *English Studies*, 44, pp. 81–94.

Schuba, L. (1981). *Die medizinischen Handschriften der Codices Palatini Latini in der Vatikanischen Bibliothek* (Wiesbaden).

Seymour, M. C. (gen. ed.) (1975–88). *On the Properties of Things: John Trevisa's Translation of Bartholomaeus Anglicus* De Proprietatibus Rerum, 3 vols. (Oxford).

The Seynge of Uryns (1525). STC2 22153 (London: J. Rastell for Richard Banckes). With multiple reprints until 1575.

Shackelford, J. (2008). 'Paracelsian Uroscopy and German Chemiatric Medicine in the Medicina Pensylvania of George de Benneville', in J. Helm and R. Wilson (eds.), *Medical Theory and Therapeutic Practice in the Eighteenth Century: A Transatlantic Perspective* (Stuttgart), 13–35.

Simek, R. (1996). *Heaven and Earth in the Middle Ages: The Physical World before Columbus*, trans. A. Hall (Woodbridge).

Södergård, Ö. (ed.) (1981). *Une lettre d'Hippocrate d'après un manuscrit inédit*, Acta Universitatis Lundensis, I/35 (Stockholm).

Steer, F. W. (1946). 'The Butts Family of Norfolk', *Norfolk Archaeology*, 29, pp. 181–200.

Stolberg, M. (2007). 'The Decline of Uroscopy in Early Modern Learned Medicine (1500–1650)', *Early Science and Medicine*, 12, pp. 313–36.

—— (2009). *Die Harnschau: Eine Kultur- und Alltagsgeschichte* (Cologne).

—— (2015). *Uroscopy in Early Modern Europe* (rev. trans. of Stolberg 2009), trans. L. Kennedy and L. Unglaub (Farnham).

Sudhoff, K. (1909). 'Eine Pariser "Ketham"-Handschrift aus der Zeit König Karls VI. (1380–1422)', *Archiv für Geschichte der Medizin*, 2, pp. 84–100 and Tafel IV.

—— (1912). 'Neue Beiträge zur Vorgeschichte des "Ketham"', *Archiv für Geschichte der Medizin*, 5, pp. 280–301 and Tafel III–VI.

—— (1929). 'Commentatoren der Harnverse des Gilles de Corbeil', *Archeion* (Rome), 11, pp. 129–35.

—— and C. J. Singer. See Kirchheimer.

Taavitsainen, I. (1988). *Middle English Lunaries: A Study of the Genre* (Helsinki).

—— (2000). 'Scientific Language and Spelling Standardisation 1375–1550', in L. Wright (ed.), *The Development of Standard English 1300–1800: Theories, Descriptions, Conflicts* (Cambridge), 131–54.

Talbot, C. H. (ed.) (1961). 'A Mediaeval Physician's Vade Mecum', *Journal of the History of Medicine and Allied Sciences*, 16, pp. 213–33.

—— and E. A. Hammond (1965). *The Medical Practitioners in Medieval England: A Biographical Register* (London).

Tavormina, M. T. (2014). 'Uroscopy in Middle English: A Guide to the Texts and Manuscripts', *Studies in Medieval and Renaissance History*, ser. 3, 11, pp. 1–154. Also cited as 'Guide'.

*—— (ed.) (2005). 'The Twenty-Jordan Series: An Illustrated Middle English Uroscopy Text', *ANQ* 18/3, pp. 40–64.

*——— (ed.) (2007). 'The Middle English *Letter of Ipocras*', *English Studies*, 88, pp. 632–52.

*——— (ed.) (2010). 'Three Middle English Verse Uroscopies', *English Studies*, 91, pp. 591–622.

Thorndike, L. (1955). 'Unde Versus', *Traditio*, 11, pp. 163–93.

Tovar, C. de (1970). *La Lettre d'Hippocrate à César* (Th. 3ᵉ cyc., Strasbourg) [not seen].

——— (1973–4). 'Contamination, interférences et tentatives de systématisation dans la tradition manuscrite des réceptaires médicaux français: Le réceptaire de Jean Sauvage', *Revue d'histoire des textes*, 3, pp. 115–91; 4, pp. 239–88.

Trotter, D. A. (1987). 'The Influence of Bible Commentaries on Old French Bible Translations', *Medium Ævum*, 56/2, pp. 257–75.

Ussery, H. E. (1971). *Chaucer's Physician: Medicine and Literature in Fourteenth-Century England*, Tulane Studies in English, 19 (New Orleans).

Veit, R. (2015). 'Isaac Israeli: His Treatise on Urine (*De Urinis*) and its Reception in the Latin World', in K. E. Collins, S. Kottek, et al. (eds.), *Isaac Israeli: The Philosopher Physician* (Jerusalem), 77–113.

Vieillard, C. (1903). *L'Urologie et les médecins urologues dans la médecine ancienne: Gilles de Corbeil, sa vie, ses œuvres, son poème des urines* (Paris).

Visi, T. (2015). 'Tradition and Innovation: Isaac Israeli's Classification of the Colors of Urines', in K. E. Collins, S. Kottek, et al. (eds.), *Isaac Israeli: The Philosopher Physician* (Jerusalem), 39–66.

Voigts, L. E. (1990). 'The "Sloane Group": Related Scientific and Medical Manuscripts from the Fifteenth Century in the Sloane Collection', *British Library Journal*, 16, pp. 26–57.

——— (1994). 'The Golden Table of Pythagoras', in L. M. Matheson (ed.), *Popular and Practical Science of Medieval England* (East Lansing, Mich.), 123–39.

——— (2004). 'The *Declaracions* of Richard of Wallingford: A Case Study of a Middle English Astrological Treatise', in I. Taavitsainen and P. Pahta (eds.), *Medical and Scientific Writing in Late Medieval English* (Cambridge), 197–208 and plates 7–8 (ff. 33ᵛ, 34ᵛ).

Wallner, B. (ed.) (1970). *A Middle English Version of the Introduction to Guy de Chauliac's 'Chirurgia Magna'*, Acta Universitatis Lundensis, I/12 (Lund).

Weisser, C. (1982). *Studien zum mittelalterlichen Krankheitslunar: Ein Beitrag zur Geschichte laienastrologischer Fachprosa*, Würzburger medizinhistorische Forschungen, 21 (Ph.D. thesis, Würzburg, 1981) (Patten-sen/Han.: H. Wellm).

Wellcome Library. Western Manuscripts and Archives Catalogue (on line), http://archives.wellcome.ac.uk. [Wellcome Online Catalogue.]

Wentzlau, K. (ed.) (1923). *Frühmittelalterliche und salernitanische Harntraktate* (Med. Inaug.-Diss., Leipzig) (Eilenburg).

Wickersheimer, E. (1936; repr. 1979). *Dictionnaire biographique des méde-cins en France au moyen âge*, 2 vols. (Geneva). See also Jacquart.

Wiese, L. (ed.) (1928). 'Recettes médicales en français', in *Mélanges de lin-guistique et de littérature offerts à M. Alfred Jeanroy par ses élèves et ses amis* (Paris), 663–71.

Wilkins, N. (1993). *Catalogue des manuscrits français de la bibliothèque Par-ker (Parker Library), Corpus Christi College, Cambridge* (Cambridge).

Young, Sidney (1890). *The Annals of the Barber-Surgeons of London* (Lon-don).

Zaun, S. (2011). 'Die Harnfarbbezeichnungen im *Fasciculus medicine* und ihre italienischen und spanischen Übersetzungen', in I. Bennewitz and A. Schindler (eds.), *Farbe im Mittelalter: Materialität — Medialität — Semantik*, 2 vols. (Berlin), ii. 969–85.

TEXTS

THE VADE MECUM SUITE
(TEXTS A–C)

A. *TWENTY COLOURS BY DIGESTION GROUPS*

1. Unillustrated Text

Oxford, Bodleian Library, MS Laud misc. 553, ff. 30ᵛ–31ʳ
Reporting LdS35 H10 W8 T11 Pe3; Lat. (from Ashmole 391, Part V: see App. I)

Vrina subrubea as *crocus occidentalis.*   f. 30ᵛ
Vrina rubea as *crocus orientalis.*
Subrubicunda as flame of fuyr ysend out.
Rubicunda as flamme of fuyr noȝt ysend out.
  þes iiij vreynes signefieþ excesse of degestion.   5
Ynopos as þe colour of lyuer.
Kianos as blak wyn.
Greyne colour as of | cawle.   f. 31ʳ
  þes þre vreynes syngnefieþ to myche adustion.
Lyuidus colour as colour of led.   10
Blak colour of adustion as yn[ke].
Blak colour of mortificacion as blak horn.
  þes iij vrynes signefieþ deþ.
Albus colour as water of wel.
[*Glau*]*cus* colour as schynyng horn.   15
Lacteus color as whey of mylk.
Karapos colour as þe flessh of a camele.
  þes iiij vrines signefieth yndygestyon.
Vrina subpallida as þe iuys of flessh half sode yput out.
Pallidus as þe iuys of flessh half sode noȝt yput out.   20
  þis tweyne signefieth þe bygynnyng of digestion.
Subcitrinus color as þe colour of a c[i]trine pomme put ou[t].

11 ynke] H10T11W8, ynekes LdS35, fethere of a crowe Pe3; *Lat.* incaustum
15 Glaucus colour] H10T11, Calcus colour LdS35, Vryn þat is W8, ȝelowe Pe3; *Lat.*
Glaucus color   22 of a citrine pomme] of a ctrine pomme Ld, of an ?attrine appul
S35, of þe juce of pome orenge (an orynge appel W8) H10W8, *om.* T11, *om.* Pe3; *Lat.* pomi
citrini   put out] H10, put ous LdS35, *om.* W8, *om.* (*simile changed to* not so hye of colour)
T11, *om.* (*simile changed to* as þe colour of fistulet) Pe3; *Lat.* remissa

Citrinus as þe colour of a pomme nouȝt put out.

þes ij vrynes signefieþ myddel degestion.

25 *Subrufus color vrine* as pure gold put out.

Rufus color vrine as pure gold noȝt put out.

þes ij vrines signefieth parfit degestion.

2. *Ring of Urines* (Illustrated)

Cambridge, Gonville and Caius College, MS 336/725, ff. 77ᵛ–78ʳ (see Pl. 1 at pp. lxxxii–lxxxiii above)

Reporting all witnesses: Gc4A7S29 Ro6Di1 W4 (=W4aW4b) Yo

ff. 77ᵛ–78ʳ *Tabu⟨la⟩ de iudicijs ⟨v⟩rinarum per colores ⟨&⟩ contenta composita ⟨per⟩ venirabilem doctore⟨m in⟩ medicina & medicum ⟨domini⟩ regis*

f. 77ᵛ   Whiȝt colour of vrine as þe watir of a welle.

ȝelowȝ colour of vrine as þe colour of schinyng horn.

Milky colour as þe colour of whey of mylk.

Karapos colour of vrine as þe colour of a camelis skyn.

5   These 4 vrines bitoken⟨en⟩ indigestioun.

Litil pale colour of vrine as iuys of fleisch half sode remisse.

Pale colour of vrine as þe iuys of fleisch not remisse.

These two vrines bitokenen bigynnynge of digestioun.

Subcitrin colour of vrine as þe colour of an appil citrin [re]misse.

10   Citrin colour of vrine as þe colour of an appil not remisse.

These ij vrines bitokenen mediat digestioun.

This is a colour of vrine as gold vnburnyschid.

This is ⟨as⟩ colour of gold ⟨bu⟩rnisschid.

Text A.2 *Title*: Tabula . . . regis] *supplied letters illeg. in tight binding* Gc4, Tabula de iudicium vrinarum per colores & contenta composita per venerabilem doctorem in medicina & medicum domini Regis illustrissimi principis Henrici sexti a conquestu regni Anglie cuius anime propicietur deus Amen A7, Tabula de judicijs vrinarum per colores & contenta Composita per venerabilem doctorem in medicina medicum domini regis approbatum per omnes medicos tangentes de vrinis in vniuersitate Oxon' S29; *shorter or no titles in other witnesses* 5 These 4 . . . indigestioun] *supplied letters illeg. in tight binding* Gc4, These .3. vryns betokyn indygestioun (*Karapos included in Beginning of Digestion group*) A7, Thes iiij vryns bytokynnyth yndygestyon wythyn S29, þes foure vrynys betokene defying (*lege* vndefying) Yo, Thies iiij betokeneth indeiestioun withinforth W4, thes iiij take indigestion within (the body *add.* Ro6) Ro6Di1   9 remisse] not (*poss. canc.*) misse Gc4, not (ful *add.* Ro6) rype Ro6Di1S29W4, nout cler in þe comp' Yo, *om.* A7; *Lat.* remissa   o oThis is . . . burnisschid] *supplied letters illeg. in tight binding* Gc4, Rufus color vryn as color of gold burnyssyd Ro6Di1, Rufus color vryne as golde & burneschede S29, Rufus as coloure of gold wel burnischid W4, Redych colour of a cler gold Yo, *om.* A7

These two colouris bitokenen parfiȝt digestioun. |

ȝelowȝ colour of vrine as saffron occidental.   f. 78ʳ

ȝelowȝ colour of vrine as saffron oriental.   16

Litil reed colour of vrine as flame of fier remys.

Reed colour of vrine as flame of fier wiþ no remis.

These foure vrynes bitokenen excesse of digestioun.

A colour of vrine as þe colour of lyuere þat is callid Inopos.   20

Kyanos colour of vrine as þe colour of blak wiyn.

Grene colour of vrine as þe colour of a grene caule.

These þre vrynes bitokenen ful myche adustioun.

Wan pale colour of vrine as þe colour of leed.

Blak colour of adustioun as þe colour of blak ynke.   25

Blak colour as a blak horn bitokeneþ deeþ.

These iij vrines bitokenen deeþ & ben deedli.

B. *URINA RUFA*

Oxford, Bodleian Library, MS Laud misc. 553, ff. 31ʳ–32ʳ (see Pl. 2)

Reporting LdS35 W8 Peȝ Hg1; S6 Di1 selectively; Lat. (from Ashmole 391, Part V: for Lat. and Di1, see App. I)

[1] *Vrina rufa* signefieth helþ and gode disposicion of mannes body.   f. 31ʳ

[2] *Vrina subrufa* signefieþ gode helthe but noȝt so parfitliche in alle maner as *rufa*.

[3] *Vrina citrina* when hit is with a myddel substance and whan þe cercle is of þe same colour: hit is [preisable].   5

[4] And also *subcitrina* þow hit be not so parfit as *citrina*.

[5] *Vrina rubea* as a rose signefieth *febrem effimeram* and if he pisse con-tinualliche hit signefieth þe feuere continual.

[6] *Vrina rubea* as blod in glas: hit signefieþ a feuere of to moche blod and þenne he moste be let blod but if þe mone be in the myddel signe of 10 *Geminorum*.

[7] *Vrina viridis* whan hit is pissed after red: hit signefieþ adustion and hit is mortel.

[8] *Vrina rubea* in alle maner remouyd fro clernesse signefieth declynyng of þe yuel.   15

[9] *Vrina rubea* ymellid somwhat with blaknesse: hit signefieþ vices of þe lyuer & hete.

Text B 5 hit is preisable] S35W8, hit is preshable Ld, it is to preysynge Peȝ; the feuer cotidian hit signifiethe Hg1, significat febrem cotidianam Di1; *Lat.* est laudabilis

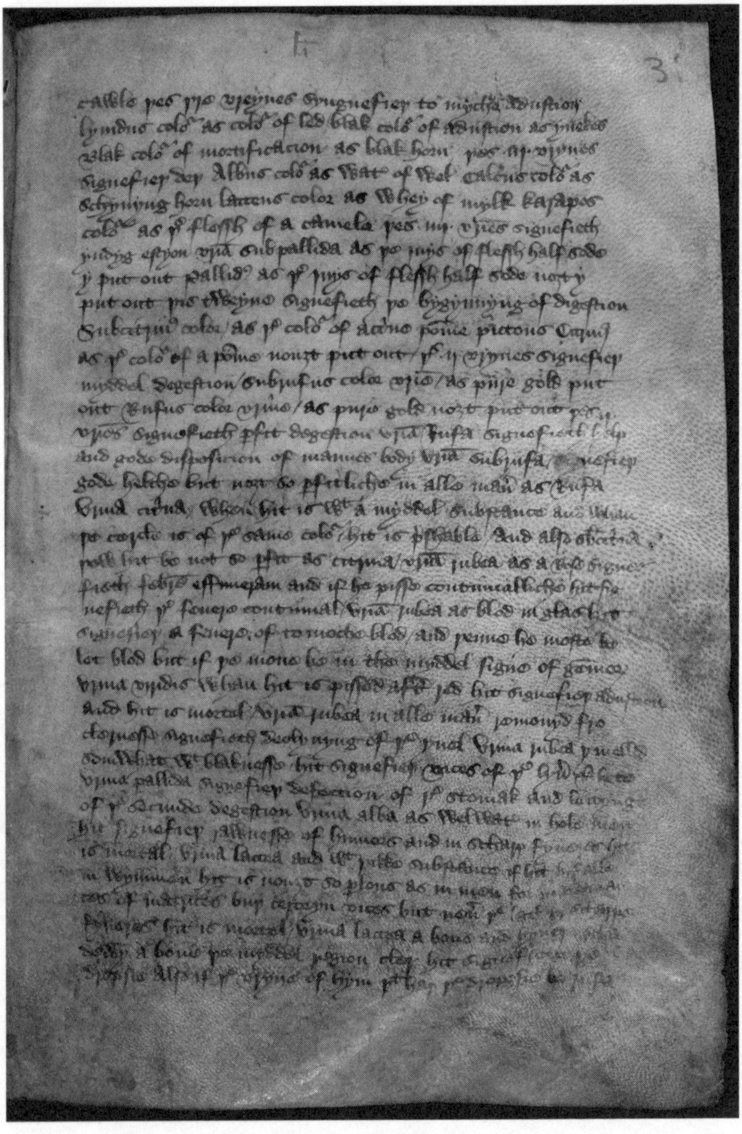

PLATE 2. *Twenty Colours by Digestion Groups* and *Urina Rufa*. Oxford, Bodleian Library, MS Laud misc. 553, f. 31^r

[10] *Vrina pallida* signefieþ defeccion of þe stomak and lettyng of þe secunde degestion.

[11] *Vrina alba* as wel water in hole men: hit signefieþ rawnesse of 20 humors and in scharp fyueres hit is mortal.

[12] *Vrina lactea* and with þikke substance: if hit bifalle in wymmen hit is nouȝt so perlous as in men for inordinances of matrices buþ certayn vices. But neuerþelater in scharpe fyueres hit is mortel.

[13] *Vrina lactea* aboue and byneþ schadewy, abou[t]e þe myddel region 25 cler: hit signefieth þe dropsie.

[14] Also if þe vryne of hym þat haþ þe dropesie be *rufa* | oþer *subrufa*, f. 31ᵛ hit signefieþ deþ.

[15] *Vrina karapos* signefieþ multitude of humours corrupte, as hit bifalleþ *yn flaumatico, ydropico, pedacrito*, and so of oþer. 30

[16] *Vrina nigra* may be of kyndeliche hete yquenchid and þanne hit is mortel. Oþer hit may be for expulcion of venemosy matcres þe whoche buþ ypuł out by viïue veynes and hit signefieþ helþe. *In quartana* forsoþ hit is euermore mortel and yuel.

[17] *Vrina lucida* as an horn signefieþ indisposicions of þe splen and 35 disposicion of þe quartane.

[18] *Vrina crocea* with þikke substance and stynkyng and fom[y]e sygnefieþ þe iaundys.

[19] *Vrina rufa* oþer *subrufa*, hangyng byneþe round resoluciounes & white & aboue sumwhat fat, signefieþ feuere etike. 40

[20] *Vrina* in þe ground of þe vessel and into þe myddel [clere], after þikke and þynne, signefieþ yuel in þe brest.

[21] *Vrina* þat is fomie clere and *subrubea*: hit signefieþ more harm in þe riȝt side þan in þe lift.

[22] [If] þe vryne be whit and fomye, hit signefieþ more harm in þe luft 45 side [þen in þe riȝt] for þe lift side is coldere þan þe riȝt.

[23] Vrine þat is þynne and pale and clere: hit signefieþ *acetosum* [*f*]*lewma*.

[24] If þe cercle of þe vryne be noȝt restyng but trauaylyng, hit signefieþ rennyng *flewma* and of oþer humors by þe hed and by þe nekke after þe 50 hynder parties to þe neþer parties.

25 aboute] W8Pe3, aboue LdS35, *om.* Hg1; *Lat.* circa   29 as hit] Pe3, as Hg1, as as hit Ld, at it S35, whiche W8, and þat S6; *Lat.* sicut   35 lucida] *prec. by* lud *canc.* Ld   37 fomye] W8, fomyng S35Pe3, fome S6, withe fome Hg1, fomþe Ld; *Lat.* spumosa   41 clere] W8Pe3Hg1, *om.* LdS35; *Lat.* clara   45 If] S35W8, Ift Ld, *om.* Pe3Hg1   46 þen . . . þan þe riȝt] *om.* Hg1   þen in þe riȝt] W8Pe3, *om.* LdS35; *Lat.* quam in dextro   47–8 Vrine . . . flewma] *om.* Hg1   48 flewma] W8, flemme S35, flume Pe3, plewma Ld; *Lat.* fleuma

[25] Vrine þicke and ledy and aboute þe myddel region blak: hit signefieþ *paralitism*.

[26] Vrine þicke and mylky and litel and fat byneþe with skalis: hit
55 scheweþ þe ston.

[27] If þe vrine withoute skalis be þikke [& mylky] and litil: hit signefieþ þe flux of þe wombe.

[28] Vrine þicke and mylky & moche dropes in þe ouer partys: hit signefieþ þe goute in membris of þe body.

60 [29] Vrine byneþe pal: in men hit signefieþ harm in þe reynes and in wymmen hit signefieþ vices of þe matrice.

[30] Vryne in þe whoche litel gobettis apereþ: if hit be litel and trubul, hit signefieþ bre[k]yng of a veyne aboute þe reynes and þe bladder.

[31] [Vryne in whoche whitter aperiþ in þe ground of þe vessel betokeneþ
65 rotyng of þe bladder] oþer a postom.

[32] And if hit apere whitter þorw al þe vrine: hit signefieþ rotyng of [al] þe body.

[33] Vrine in whoche frustris apperith litel and brod: hit signefieþ excoriacion of the bladder. |

f. 32ʳ [34] Vrine motie: hit signefieþ by longe tyme þe ston in þe reynes.

71 [35] *Vrina alba* withoute fyuer boþe in men and in wymmen: oþerwhile hit signefieþ harm in þe reynes and oþerwhile inpregnacion of wymmen.

[36] Vrine of hem þat buþ with childe: ȝif he haue oo monthe oþer too oþer þre, hit schal be ful clere and hit shal haue a whit ypostatesie in þe
75 ground.

[37] And if he haue iiij monthes, þe vrine schal be clere and a whit ypostatecis and a þikke in þe ground.

[38] Hit was woned a ymage in þe glasyne vessel as in a mirrour apeire: if þilke vrine be of a womman hit signefieth þe concepcion to be ymade.

80 [39] And if þe ymage of hym þat [scheweþ] apeireþ in þe vrine of þe pacient, hit signefieþ *febres interpollatas* oþer *eppaticam egritudinem* oþer drawyng of lengþe of seknesse.

56–7 If . . . þe wombe] *om*. Hg1   56 & mylky] W8, melkeshe Pe3, and þicke *canc*. Ld, *om*. S35; *Lat*. et lactea   63 brekyng] S6, a breche Hg1, rupture Pe3, brennyng LdS35W8; *Lat*. rupturam   64–5 Vryne . . . of þe bladder] W8Pe3, *om*. LdS35, The 27ᵗⁱ wherein semythe quitter & bollis as of rayne water in the resuduns signifiethe the rotyng of a postom in the kedenys or in the bladder Hg1, 27 vrina in qua apparet putredo vlceris in zedimine significat putrefaccionem apostomatis in rene uel vesica Di1; *Lat*. Urina in qua sanies apparet in fundo uasis contiguam renum & uesice putredinem vel apostema significat 66 al] W8Pe3Hg1, *om*. LdS35; *Lat*. tocius   79 beˡ] *foll. by* ?efi *canc*. Ld   80 þe ymage . . . apeireþ] W8, þe ymage of hym þat apeireþ (*foll. by space of appx. 6–7 chars*. Ld) LdS35, þe ymage of hym þat yowgeþ þe water seme Pe3, semethe owre image Hg1, apparet nostra ymago Di1; *Lat*. ymago iudicantis appareat   vrine of þe] vrin of a W8S6, vrine of Pe3, vrine of þe vrine of þe LdS35, *om*. Hg1

[40] *Vrina* fomie signefieþ ventosite of þe stomak in wymmen oþer hete fro þe nauyl to þe þrote and þriste.

[41] *Vrina* of a maide schal be as *subcitrina*, wherof *vrina liuida* & ful clere 85 declareþ þe maide stedfast.

[42] Vrine troubli in þe whoche sed apeireþ in þe grounde: hit signefieþ þe womman ytake with man.

[43] Vrine of a womman þikke: hit signefieþ hure corrup[te].

[44] þe forsede vryne, namliche trubele in þe whoche þe sed apereþ in 90 þe grounde of þe vessel, if forsoþe swich vryne be in a man, hit declareth hym to haue delit with a womman.

[45] Wymmen þat beþ menstruat makeþ blody vryne.

[46] ʒif þis blod be crodded in þe wymmen, he schal semy with childe til hit be dissolued, as hit scheweþ in *Antioda*. 95

C. CLEANSING OF BLOOD

Oxford, Bodleian Library, MS Laud misc. 553, f. 32^{rv}

Reporting LdS35 W8 Gc4b Pe3; Lat. (from Ashmole 391, Part V: see App. I)

[*Definition of Urine*]

Eche vrine is þe clansyng of blod and hit is properliche of too þynges sig- f. 32^r
nificatif: oþer forsothe hit signefieþ passion of þe lyuer oþer of veynes oþer of þe bladder oþer of þe reynes. Of oþer þynges forsoþe hit is inproperliche significatif.

[*Things to Consider in Urine*]

But in vrine þere buþ to dyuerse þyngis properliche to be ylokid, þat is 5 to wite, substance, coloures, regionys, and þat is conteyned. Anoþer is by cause of substance, anoþer bi cause of coloures, anoþer by cause of residence.

[*Four Qualities in Urine*]

Siþþe forsoþe in a mannes body beþ iiij qualites, s. hete drynesse coldnesse and moistenesse, and hy buþ cause of substance and coloures. Hete is cause 10 of red colour, coldnesse is cause of [white] colour, [drynesse is cause] of þynne substance, moistnesse | is cause of þykke substance. f. 32^v

89 Vrine . . . corrupte] *om.* Pe3Hg1   corrupte] S35W8, corrup Ld; *Lat.* corruptam
Text C 1 properliche] *prec. by* prophie *canc.* Ld   10 moistenesse] *with stroke somewhat like long* s *after* moiste Ld   11 white] W8Gc4Pe3, þynne S35, *om.* Ld; *Lat.* albi
dryenesse is cause] W8Gc4Pe3, *om.* LdS35; *Lat.* siccitas est causa   12 cause of þykke]
W8Pe3, cause of colour of þykke LdGc4b, cause of þicke colour S35

[Four Parts of Urine]

Vrine is dyuydid into iiij parties. þe ouer partie is þe cercle, þe secunde is
body of eir, þe þridde is *perforacio*, þe ferþe is þe grounde. By þe cercle:
15 siknesse of þe hed, of þe brayn; by þe body eir: siknesse of spiritual membris and of þe stomak; by perforacion: of þe lyuer and of þe splen; and [by
þe grounde we shewen accidentes] of þe reynes and of the matrice and of
[þe neþer] membris.

[Three Regions of Urine]

Vrina haþ þre regions, s. þe neþmoste, þe myddel, and þe ouemest. þe
20 neþmest bygyneþ fro þe ground of þe vrynal and dureþ by þe space of too
fyngres. þe myddel region bygynneþ þere as endeþ þe neþere and dureþ
to þe cercle. þe cercle is þe ouemest region.

[Contents in the Regions of Urines]

And whan in þe ouemest region is fome, hit signefieþ ventosite bollyng
vp in þe weyys of vrine or inflacion or oþer vices of þe longon. þe cercle
25 forsoþe þikke signefieþ to moche replecion in þe hed and dolour. In þe
myddel region a white clude is in hole men an yuel signe. But in ham þat
haueþ þe feueres, hit signefieþ degestion of þe mater of þat yuel. In þe
neþemost region buþ oþerwhile grauely litel stones and þanne hit scheweþ
þat þe pacient is ful of litel stones. And oþerwhile þe residence is blak and
30 þanne (but hit be by expulcion of suche vrine of venemos maters) hit is
signe of deþ.

16–17 by þe grounde we shewen accidentes] W8, the ground bitokeneþ yuel Gc4, be þe
bottum we shul dome þe enfremite Pe3, *om.* LdS35; *Lat.* per fundum . . . accidencia iudicamus   17–18 of þe neþer membris] membris benethe Pe3   18 þe neþer] Gc4, þe
priue W8, oþer LdS35; *Lat.* inferiorum   21 þe neþere] S35W8Gc4b, þe neþerre *with
poorly formed* -re (*looks like* -rse) Ld, it Pe3; *Lat.* infima

WHITE–RED AND WHITE–BROWN TOKEN LISTS (TEXTS D–F)

D. *URINE WHITE AND RED*

London, British Library, Sloane MS 3542, ff. 69ᵛ–70ᵛ

Reporting S42 Ra3A9 Nw1 S6 Add3Ro3 and selected s. xiii–xiv Anglo-Norman and French witnesses HVOTYCWS (Fr.; for sigla, see App. II)

Hyt is for to wete in iiij partys of þe bodye ys yschewyd þe dwellyng of f. 69ᵛ
þe helthe and of þo sekenesse. that is, in þe hede & in the wombe, in the
lyuere & þe bladdere. In what maner þou mayste yknowe þe parteys þerof
þou mayste here and lurne.

[1] Iff a mannys vryne be whyt at morwe & rede byfore mete & whyt after 5
mete, he is hole.

[2] And yf his vryne be fatte & þycke & stronge, þat is noȝt gode.

[3] And ȝyf þe vryne be melled þykke, it is gode. |

[4] And ȝyf þe vryne be þykke 'in þe maner' as asse pysse, hit bytokenyȝt f. 70ʳ
hede ache.   10

[5] *Feuerosus* vryne þe vij dayis comyng, vryne þat is ij days rede and iiij
day whyte: hit bytokenyth very helth.

[6] Vryne ffatte, whyte, & moyste bytokenyȝth feuer quartyn.

[7] Vryne þat is blody: it bytokenyth þat þe bladdere ben horte by som
maner of rotyng þat is withinne.   15

[8] Lytel vryne & flesly & fatte bytokenyȝt 'seknes' in þe reynys.

[9] Ho-so pessyth blody withoute sekenesse, he hath a veyne ybroke at
þe raynys.

[10] Vryne that is poudrows bytokenyth þe bladder ben herte.

[11] Vryne that is sumdel blody of sekenysse bytokenyth gret euell in þe 20
body & namlych in þe bladder.

[12] Vryne þat ffallyth be dropys abowe 'ase' at it were bol[n]ys: it
betokenyth longe sekenesse.

3 In] *prec. by* In what 'maner' partys *canc.* S42   6 hole] *prec. by* ?hul *canc.* S42
10 hede] A9Ro3Add3S6, heued Ra3Nw1, hedede S42   22 bolnys] Ra3A9, bolmys
S42, bollys of watyr Ro3, ampulettes Nw1, *sign om.* Add3S6, *Fr.:* ampules HVOTYC,
boulonne W, borboille S

De Muliere

25   [13] Wommanys vryne þat is clere & schynnyng [in] þe vrynal as
siluer, þat woman braketh moche, & yf sche hath no talent to mete, and
bytokenyth þat sche ys with chylde. |

f. 70ᵛ   [14] Womannys vryne þat is whyt & stronge & styngyng bytokenyth sekenesse of þe raynys and [hure reseyith is] ful of euell & of sekenesse of hure
30   sy⟨lf⟩.

[15] Womanys water þat is blody above & clere as water vnderenethe: het
bytokeneth hed ache.

[16] Wommanys vryne þat is leche of colour to golde and clere and mythy
bytokeny3t hure to haue kynde of man.

35   [17] Wommanys vryne þat is stable clensyng betokenyth for to haue þe
feuer quarteyn & sche scholde [dye] þe iij day.

[18] Wommanys vryne þat is p[ey]s & of colour lede, yf sche be with
chylde, it is dede withinne. And 3yf sche be no3t wyth childe, hure reseyith
is rotet & so þe vryn ys sty[n]kyng.

40   [19] Wommanys 'vryne' þat is lyche flaxe betokenyth þe woman to ben
bolle & for to 'haue' þe colde menson. And sche schal neuer ben hole.

E. *URINE WHITE AND BROWN* (WOMAN VARIANT)

1. The Earliest Middle English Uroscopy (*c.*1320–1330)

Cambridge, Corpus Christi College, MS 388, ff. 53ᵛ–54ʳ (see Pl. 3)

Reporting only Cc

f. 53ᵛᵇ   He[r] mayst þou knowen vrins be coloures.

[1] Vrine qwyt at morwen and brown at afteremete: þat is singne of god
hele.

25 schynnyng] schenyng *above line in similar hand* S42   in] Ra3A9Ro3Nw1, as S6, *om.*
S42; in þe vrynal *om.* Add3   26 sche] *prec. by* 3e ?*canc.* S42   29 hure reseyith
is] here recept is Ra3, here resseppet ys stoppyd & Ro3, her receate Add3, sche is reseuyd
(fall *canc.*) S42, þe matrice S6, þe marewe Nw1, *om.* A9; *Fr.*: le matriz HO, vis V, le maris
YCWS, la marcie T   29–30 & of sekenesse of hure sylf] of syckenes of her sellfe
Add3, & of sekenesse of hure sy (lf *illeg. in tight binding*) S42, of sekenes of colde Nw1,
engendryd of colde S6, *om.* Ra3A9Ro3; *Fr:* enfermeté de (e T) froit VOTYCW, enferte S,
om. H   31 Womanys] *prec. by* Womanys water þat is bl blody *canc.* S42   36 dye]
A9S6Add3Nw1, deyn Ra3, day S42; *sign om.* Ro3   iij] *preceded by* iij *canc.* S42   37 peys
&] pays and of þe wei3t Nw1, pers S42, pers Add3, partie Ra3A9; *sign om.* Ro3S6; *Fr.*: de (del
Y, sicum C) peys HYC, de poi V, qui mult poise WS, de pois semblanz O, pesante T   yf sche]
prec. by yf sche *canc.* S42   38 reseyith] *prec. by unfinished descender* S42   39 ys
stynkyng] ys stykyng S42, be stynkynge Nw1, stynketh Ra3A9, stynkes Add3, *sign om.* S6Ro3
Text E.1   1 Her] He

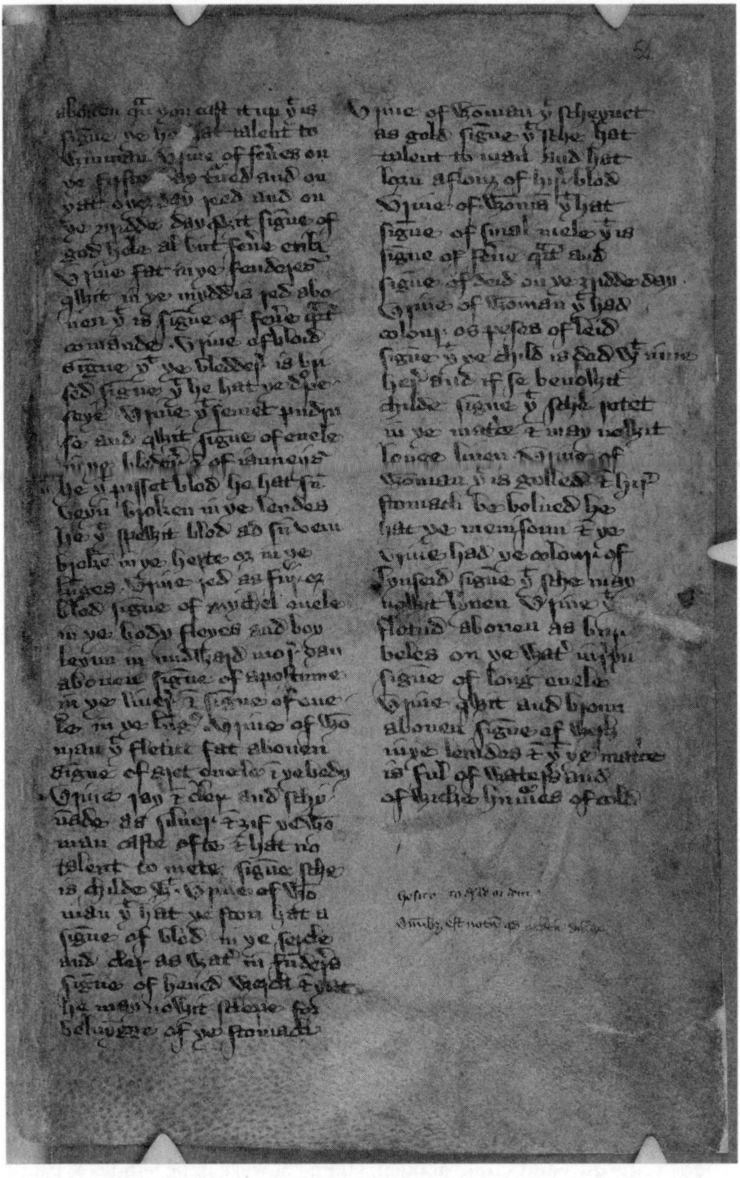

PLATE 3. *Urine White and Brown* (Woman variant).
Cambridge, Corpus Christi College, MS 388, f. 54ʳ
Reproduced by permission of The Parker Library, Corpus Christi College, Cambridge

[2] Vrine fat & truble: þat is singne of no god hele, singne of water in þe
5 boweles.

f. 54ra   [3] Vrine blac | abouen quan þou cast it up: þat is singne þe he hat talent
to wmman.

[4] Vrine of feueres on þe firste day turned and on þat oþer day reed and
on þe þridde day qwit: singne of god hele, al but feuere etik.

10   [5] Vrine fat in þe fenderes, qwit in þe myddis, red abouen: þat is singne
of feuere quart' comande.

[6] Vrine of bloid: singne þat þe bleddere is brised, singne þat he hat þe
dropeseye.

[7] Vrine þat semet pudruse and qwit: singne of euele in þe bledere & of
15 iauneys.

[8] He þat pisset blod he hat sum veyn broken in þe lendes.

[9] He þat spewit blod ad sum vein broken in þe herte or in þe lunges.

[10] Vrine red as fiir or blod: singne of mychel euele in þe body.

[11] Fleyes and boyleyun in midward more þan abouen: singne of apos-
20 tume in þe liuere & singne of euele in þe lunges.

[12] Vrine of womman þat fletut fat abouen: singne of gret euele in þe
body.

[13] Vrine ray & cler and schynande as siluer & 3if þe womman caste ofte
& hat no talent to mete: singne sche is [with childe].

25   [14] Vrine of womman þat hat [scom] hat a singne of blod in þe sercle
and cler as water in funderes: singne of heued werck & þat he may nowit
sclepe for bolnyngge of þe stomack. |

f. 54rb   [15] Vrine of womman þat scheynet as gold: singne þat sche hat talent
to man and hat lorn a flour of hire blod.

30   [16] Vrine of womman þat hat signe of smal mele: þat is singne of feuere
quart' and singne of deid on þe 3ridde day.

[17] Vrine of woman þat had colour os peses of leid: singne þat þe child
is ded withinne here. And if se be nowit [with] childe: singne þat sche rotet
in þe matrice & may nowit longe liuen.

35   [18] Vrine of womman þat is golled & hire stomack be bolned, he hat þe
menisoun & þe vrine had þe colour of lynseid: singne þat sche may nowit
lyuen.

[19] Vrine þat flotud abouen as burbeles on þe water in reyn: singne of
long euele.

40   [20] Vrine qwit and broun abouen: singne of werk in þe leindes & þat þe
matrice is ful of wateres and of wicke humures of cold.

24 with childe] childe with *marked for transposition*   25 scom] þe ston, *Fr.* escume
V   33 with] *om.*

TABLE 3. Table of variants of *Urine White and Brown* in E.1, E.2, F*

Urine White and Brown (Woman variant), lines E.1/19, E.2/26–7

	Fleyes and boil in midward	more than above	Cc
Urine that	*fleyth* and boileth in the midward	and thin above	A3
Urine that falleth as rain	*flepes* and boileth in the midward	thin above	S24
Urine that falleth as rain	*fleres* and boileth in the midward	thin above	S35
That falleth with rain	?*flyches* and boileth in the midward	thin above	S28
Urine that falls with drovy ('turbid')	*fleihes*/*fleghes* boils in (the) midward	thin above	Ro1A8
Urine that falleth white in the drovy	*fleys*/*flyx* and boileth in the midward/middle (and)	thin above	HtS29b
Urine that falls wide down	*fleghes* and boils in midward	thin above	Yo
Water that falleth down with drovy	bolles ('bubbles') in the midward	and skim ('foam') above	Ar
Urine drobly red as raw flesh	and boileth in the midward	and thin above	Cp
Urine drovy as is the water that raw flesh is washen in	in the myddys	and thin above	Ad2
Urine drowry red as the water that raw flesh is washen in	in the midward	and thin above	Cu6
Urine through red as water that raw flesh is washen	in the midward	and thick above	Ar3

Urine White and Brown (Phlegm variant), line F/22

Urine that	*fleyeth* and boileth in the midward	and thin above	W12S2A7Gc1S20
Urine that	*fletteth* and boileth in the midward	and thin above	Nw2
Urine that	*flowmys* (?*flowm ys*) in the midward	and thin above	Eg3

* Spelling has been normalized except for forms of *flien* and its reflexes.

2. The Fullest Copy of the Text

London, British Library, Add. MS 4898, ff. 116ᵛ–117ʳ

Lines 1–44: reporting Ad2A13 Ro1A8 S35 A3 A9, with selective citation of other witnesses in line 10; lines 50–3: reporting Ad2A13 Cp S1 S14, on maladies on the right and left sides

f. 116ᵛ [1] Vrine at morwe whiȝt and aftyr mete broun is tokene of good hele.

[2] Vrine fat & turble is tokene of [no good hele, but it is token of water] in þe bowelys.

[3] Vrine thinne and grene aboue is tokene of cold conpleccioun. And ȝif
5 þou castys and it be bloo abouyn as botonys of leed þat is toke[n] of ptysyk.

[4] Vryne thenne and blak abouyn qwan þou castis þat, þe vrine tokeneth þat þe man hath talent to womman.

[5] Vrine of feuerouse þat is drubled as þe pisse of an asse þat tokenyth heued werk.

10 [6] Vrine of feuerouse on þe ferste day [turned], and on þe toþir day reed, & thridde day whyȝt is tokene of good hele of alle eueles saue of þe feuere etyk.

[7] Vrine fat in þe botme and whiȝt in þe myddys and reed abouen: þat is toke[n] of þe feuere quarteyn þat is comande.

15 [8] Vrine blody of þe man tokenyth þat hys bladdere is b'r'osed. & ȝif it be nowt brosed, þanne tokeneth it þat he is in þe hote dropesye.

[9] Vrine fat & flessh[y] & in þe founsse [be drubly] as schauyngges: þat synefyeth þe colde dropesye.

f. 117ʳ [10] Vrine þat semeth pouderouse and whiȝt bemeneth e|ueles of þe
20 bladdere and of þe iaunys.

[11] And he þat pisseth blood hath a veine brokyn in þe lendes.

[12] And he þat spittyth blood hath a veine brokyn in þe herte [or] þe lungge.

[13] Vrine reed as pesyn broth þat is tokene of mechel euel in þe body of
25 þe menysoun.

2 no good hele] A13Ro1A8S35A9, no god help A3, *om. at line break* Ad2   but . . . water] A13, (and A9) syn of water A8A9, it is signe of water S35, but of water Ro1, for þer is a water A3, *om. at line break* Ad2   5 is token] A13, signifiet Ro1, signe A8, is toke Ad2, *sign om.* S35A9A3   10 turned . . . toþir day] YoS28T14Su, termyned on þat oþer day S35, termun hit on þe oþer day Ro1, turnnes on þat oþer day A8A9, turnyng & on þat oþer day A3, and on þe toþir day turned (turneth A13) in Ad2A13; *Fr.* termine . . . & al secunde jur H   14 token] A13, toke Ad2, signe Ro1A8S35A9A3   17 flesshy] A13, flesshly A13, fatt of fleshe (fleres S35) A8S35, fat as flesche A9A3, flessh+us *curl* Ad2   be drubly] A13, drouy Ro1, drobly A8, trouble S35A9, by drabily Ad2, *om.* A3   22 or] A13Ro1A8S35, oþer A3, of Ad2, *sign om.* A9

[14] Vrine drouie as is þe water þat raw flessh is wasschen inne in þe myddys and þinne abouen signifieth þat he hath a postume in þe lyu[ere] & euel in þe longges.

[15] Vrine of womman þat fletyth fat aboue is signe of gallades.

[16] Vrine of womman þat is [raie &] ʻclerʼ & scynend and whiȝt as mer- 30
curye and heuy, and ȝif che casteth ofte and hath no talent to mete, þat is signe þat che is wyth childe.

[17] Vrine þat hath scom of blood in þe sercle and [cler is] in þe botme: þat is signe of heued werk and þat sche ne may etyn ne drynken ne slepyn for bolnyng of þe stomak. 35

[18] Vrine of womman þat schineth as gold is signe þat che hath talent to man.

[19] Vrine of womman þat hath þe colour of [s]mal mele þat hath þe feuere quarteyn is signe of deeth wythinne þe þridde day.

[20] Vrine of womman þat hath þe colour of peses of leed and sche be 40
wyth childe: þat is tokene þat þe child is deed in hyre body. *Et si non sit inpregnata signum est mortis sue.*

[21] Vryne of womman þat is gulle, & ȝif here stomak be bolnyd and [hath] þe menysoun and þe vrine haue colour of lynsed, che ne may not lyuen. 45

[22] [Vryne of a womman þat fleteth aboue as burbles on þe water whan it rayneth: it is signe of longe euel.]

[23] Vrine whiȝt benethe and broun aboue: þat is tokene of febelenesse of lendes of man and womman also and þat hire matrice is vicious.

[24] Vrine þat is reed, thikke or thenne: þou xal demyn þe euele is on þe 50
ryȝte syde, for þere liȝth þe lyuere.

[25] Vrine þat is whyth, thikke or thenne: þou xalt demyn þat þe euele is on þe left syde, for there ly⟨ȝt⟩h þe splen.

27 lyuere] A13Ro1A8S35A3, lyueu*ere* Ad2, *sign om.* A9 30 raie &] Ro1A8S35A3, & ray (*after* clere) A9, *om.* Ad2A13 33 and cler is in þe botme] Ro1, & cleer in the fonce (fundirs A8) A13A8, (and S35A9) cler as watur in þe grounde (foundres A9A3) S35A9A3, and (*line end*) in þe botme Ad2 38 smal] A13Ro1A8S35A3, smlle A9, spmal Ad2 40 of peses of leed] Ro1, as pese of lede A8, liche pecis of leed S35, as peses of blode A9, as knottis of lede A3, of peses or of leed Ad2A13 44 hath] A13Ro1A8S35A9, sche haue A3, *om.* Ad2 46–7 Vryne . . . longe euel] S35, *with minor variants in* A9A3; *om.* Ad2A13Ro1A8 50 thikke] A13CpS1S14, thikke thikke Ad2 53 lyȝth] ȝt *under water damage* Ad2, is A13CpS1S14

F. *URINE WHITE AND BROWN* (PHLEGM VARIANT)

London, Wellcome Library, MS 8004, ff. 61ʳ–62ʳ (see Pl. 4)

Reporting all witnesses: W12S2A7 S20 Gc1aGc1b Eg3Nw2A14

f. 61ʳ   Her may þou knawe howe þou sall kenne & dysscryue all maner of seknesse within mannys body or womens by þe syȝte of hys watyr.

[1] Uryne whyte by þe morne & browne aftyr mete: it betokyns gud hele.

[2] Uryne fatt & trobele: þat is syne þat þer is flwme emonge hys bowells
5   and a begenynge of a dygestioun.

[3] Uryne thynne os watyr vndyr þe cercule: þat is tokyne of a stomake feuyr and schuld brake all þat is in hys stomake.

[4] Uryne þat schewys a grete cercule & changes colours os grene or blew or blake: þat betokyns hed ache for þe watyr þat es bytwene þe fylmyne &
10   þe brane.

[5] Uryn blake in þe founderel, whyte in þe mydys, red above: þat is tokyne of a fyuyr quartayne.

[6] Uryn red as blod: þat betokyns þat þe bleddyr is brystyne & þe begynynge of þe dropsy.

f. 61ᵛ   [7] Uryne red os watyr | þat flesch is waschyne in & fatt abowue: þat
16   betokyns þe cold dropsy & it betokyns deth.

[8] Uryne þat semysse ponderouse & white: þat is syne of blod in þe bleddyr.

[9] & if he spytt blod, þat betokyns þat he has a posteme in hys lunges.

20   [10] Uryne þat semys red lyke old wyn & fatt abowue: þat is a syne þat hys lyuyr is stuft.

[11] Uryn þat fleyeth & bolyth in þe mydword & thynne abowue: þat is syne of a postem in þe lyuyr.

[12] Uryn þat schynys lyk a lanterne horne betokyns þat he has no dyges-
25   tioun for þe stomake is ingleymyd.

[13] Uryn of a mane þat hath þe stone sall haue small grauell in þe ground of þe vrynall.

[14] Uryne of a womane þat semysse gold: þat is syne þat sche hath gud hele & lykynge to mane.

30   [15] Uryne of a womane þat is lyke wheye & þer be a cloud in þe bothome of þe vrynall with whyte flourynges: it betokyns þat sche is with chyld.

[16] Uryne of a womane þat is red lyk blod: þat is syne þat hyr flourys be to heuy on hyr.

31 flourynges] r *poorly formed, appearing like* p *or* þ W12

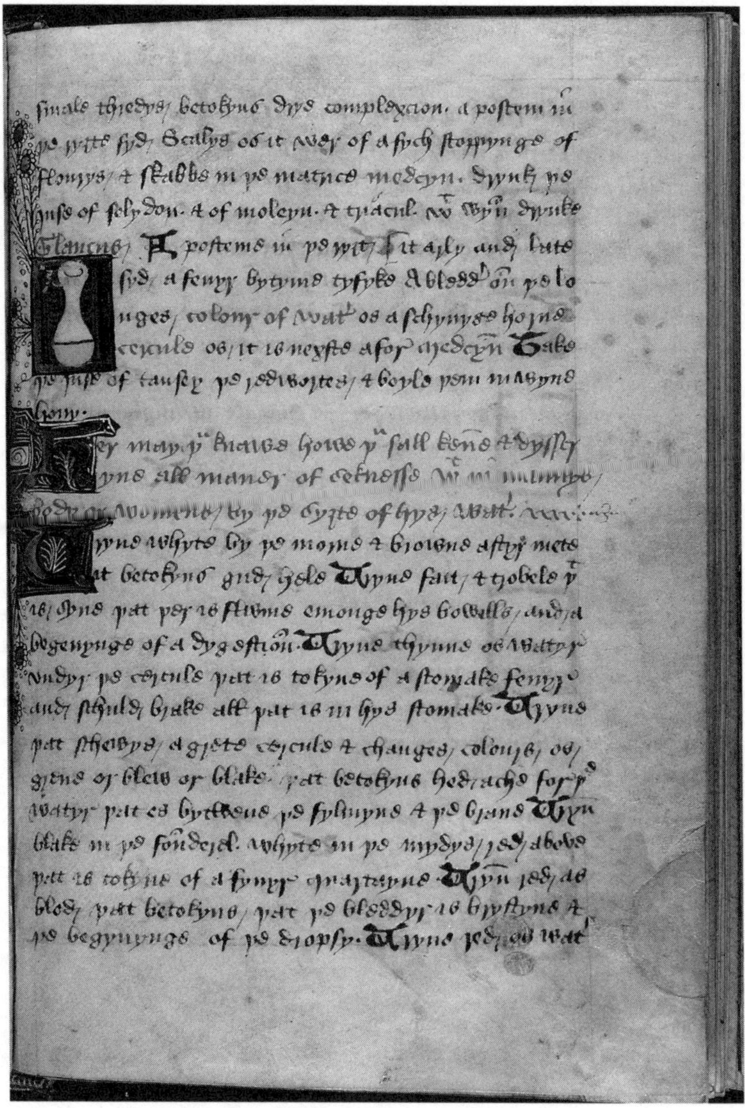

PLATE 4. *Urine White and Brown* (Phlegm variant).
London, Wellcome Library, MS 8004, f. 61ʳ

[17] Uryne of a womane þat has blake flourys in hyr watyr in þe ground
35 of þe vrynall with blak matyr: þat betokyns þat sche has þe ma[r]es.

[18] Uryn of a womane þat has þe colour of led: þat betokyns þat sche is
with ded chyld.

[19] Uryne of a womane þat has smale grauell in hyr watyr: þat is syne
of þe chawd pysse & greuaunce in hyr renysse.

f. 62ʳ   [20] Uryn of a womane þat semys thynne vndyr þe cerkyll & | lytyll sub-
41 staunce of watyr: þat is syne of a wastyng stomak for þar is a feuyr in hyr
stomake.

[21] Uryne of a womane þat semys aumbre: þat betokyns þat hyr lyuyr
es stoffyd and hase a stronge fyuyr our all hyr body.

45 The dyscrecyoun of þies waters moste be knawne by þe 4 regyouns of hys
body & by þe 4 partyes of his body watyr. þe cercule longes to þe hed.
A nynch vndyr longes to þe herte. The medel longes to þe stomake, the
ground to þe kydneys & to þe membris. And whych of þies ʻ4ʼ be moste
trobulyd, þat is most greuyd.

35 mares] maris S2A7Eg3Nw2, mayes W12Gc1aGc1b, *cropped* S20, *om.* A14   40 &]
& (*page break*) and W12   44 es] e *poorly formed, appearing like* o W12   49 þat]
A7S20, þat at W12, that parti of man S2, and (*foll. by* most grevyd moste be consideryd)
Gc1a, *epilogue om.* Gc1bEg3Nw2A14

TEXTS OF LIKELY
ENGLISH ORIGIN
(TEXTS G–I)

G. *RUFUS SUBRUFUS*

Cambridge, Gonville and Caius College, MS 336/725, ff. 69ʳ–72ʳ

Reporting Gc4W10 Di1 T15 A8

Here bigynneþ a tretice of a mannys or of a wommans vrine or watir, þat we   f. 69ʳ
take for oon, icontryued & maad bi þe wisest clerkis of phisik of Ynglond
& itranslatid out of Latyn into Englisch bi þe preier of king Henri þe
fourþe.

    And first 3e schulen vndirstonde þat þer ben xx diuers colouris of man- 5
nis watir as it schal be schewid here suynge. þat is to wite, *Rufus, Subrufus*,
whiche bitokenen parfi3t digestioun: but fewe men han þis watir & þerfore
it nediþ not to 3eue hem medicyn.

    Also þer ben foure þat bitokenen excesse of digestioun, whiche ben þese
foure: *Subrubeus, Rubeus, Subrubicundus, Rubicundus*. And þese foure nediþ 10
medicynes and þo schulen be schewid heraftir.

    And aftirward þer ben þre whiche ben icallid *Ynopos, Kyanos, Viridis
color*. And þese þre bitokenen myche brennynge wiþinne. |

    Thanne aftir þer ben þre of oþir colour: a wan pale colour as led, anoþir f. 69ᵛ
blak colour as enke, anoþir blak colour as blak horn. And þese þre bitokenen 15
deeþ and þerfore þer is no medicyne yordeyned for hem. [*Cum dicitur:
Contra vim mortis non est medicamen in ortis.*] But oþirwhile blak colour
bitokeneþ deeþ and oþirwhile it bitokeneþ þe venemous matere goinge out
bi þe watir weies & þanne þat bitokeneþ heelþe.

    And aftir þer ben foure watris þat bitokenen indigestioun, þat is, whi3t 20
watir as welle watir, and 3elow3 colour as 3elow3 horn, mylk colour as whey,
and Karapos as þe colour of camels fleisch.

    Thanne beþ þer oþir tweyne: oon a litil pale as fleisch not ful soden and
anoþir pale as þe iuys of fleisch half soden. þese two bitokenen bigynnyng
of digestioun. 25

    Aftirward þer is citryn colour as þe colour of a citryn appil remysch,

---

16–17 Cum dicitur . . . ortis] (*with minor variations*) W10T15A8, *om.* Gc4Di1

anoþir colour as þe colour of a citryne appil not mysse. And þese ij watris bitokenen mediat digestioun.

{heed ache} Now go we to þe foure firste & I wole discryue hem & aftir
30 telle medicyns for hem. The firste is callid *Subrubeus* & if it be wiþ a greet blak sercle aboue þat bitokeneth heed ache.

And þerfore is a fair medicyne & a liȝt: take verueyne & seþe it & biteyne & wormod & þerwiþ waische þe sijk heed. & þanne make a plastre on þe molde on þis maner: take þe same eerbis whanne þei be soden & wrynge
35 hem & grynde hem smal in a morter and tempere hem aȝen wiþ þe same licour. And do þerto whete bran for to holde in þe same licour. & make a gerlond of a kerchir & bynde þe sike heed & leie þe plastre on þe molde wiþinne þe garlond as hoot as þe sike may suffre. & bynde þe heed wiþ a voliper & sette a cappe aboue. & do þus but þre tymes & þe sike schal be
f. 70ʳ hool on warantise of ony sijk | nesse engendrid wiþinne þe heed.
41 Anoþir medicyne for clensynge of þe heed: take peletre of Spayne & chewe þe roote þre daies a good quantite & it wole purge þe heed & do awey þe ache & fastne þe teeþ in þe gomes.

A good medicyne for vanite of þe heed: take the iuys of walwort & salt &
45 hony & wax & encense & boile hem weel togidere ouer þe fier and þerwiþ anoynte weel þin heed & þi templis & it schal heele þin heed.

{iaundise} If þe watir of vrine be ȝelowȝ as saffron: it bitokeneþ þe ȝelowȝ yuel, as þe iaundise.

A fair medicyn aȝens þat: take an appil & kitte awei at þe stalke a litil
50 gobet and þanne kutte awey al þe core. And fille þe appil þere þe core satt wiþ saffron & wiþ þe schauynge of yuery & stoppe it vp aȝen wiþ þe same pese & sette þe appil in hoot emeris. & whanne it is tendre ynowȝ, þanne ȝeue it to þe pacient for to ete it as hoot as he may suffre it. & on warantise þe pacient schal be hool wiþinne foure tymes asaiynge wiþinne iiij daies.
55 {þe hoote agu} Ther ben þre oþere colouris of vrine þat bitokeneþ miche adustioun or brennynge of vnkyndely heete in þe bodi, and þat is tokene of an hoot agu in þe bodi.

Aȝens þat here is a fair medicyne proued: take spinagre, columbine, turmentille, matfeloun, þe seed of fumiter, þe seed of golde; of ech of þese
60 herbis & of þese seedis take an handful & drie hem weel out of þe sunne. And make þerof poudre & þat schal heele him.

Here is anoþir medicyne proued for þe same: take mustard a quantite & vynegre euene porcioun & triacle as miche as a bene & alle ymedlid togideris. Drinke þerof þries & wiþouten doute þou schalt be hool.
65 {For þe axcesse} For þe axesse a fair medicyne: take rue, wormod, eerbe benet, and whiȝt wiyn; take of ech an handful & staumpe in a morter and |

wringe out þe iuys. And putte þerto a pynte of þe forseid wiyn & drinke it   f. 70ᵛ
twies or þries [& sey v Pater Noster & v Aue Maria & Credo *pro animabus*
patris & matris archidriclini & animabus omnium fidelium defunctorum. &
eris sanus sine dubio.]   70

   Ther ben foure oþere colouris of vrine whiche bitokenen indigestioun. A
fair medicyne for þe firste þat is colourid as whiȝt as welle watir: take sauge,
mynte, calamynte, perseli, auence, euene porcioun. & take sour breed &
tempere it wiþ wiyn or stale ale & poudir of pepir & gyngeuer & make
þerof verte sauce & vse þis. þis medicyne is proued.   75

   {indigestioun} Ther is anoþir vrine þat bitokeneþ indigestioun, which is
whiȝt as whey. {a man þat is brosten wiþinne} & þat is a tokene þat a man
is tobroste wiþinne þat hise bowelis goon doun into his cod.

   Aȝens þat take rosyn, wex, frankencense, mastik, swynys grese, oile of
olyue & medle alle togidere. & take poudre of comyn, of lynseed, poudir of   80
anise, poudre of fenel & caste þerto & medle alle togidere. & take leþir &
make a plastre & leie alle þis þing þeron. & take lynnen clooþ & leie þervpon
& powne it weel togidere & leie it to þe soor place. & take matfeloun &
comferie & putte þerto consoud, i. daies yȝe, and osmond. Staumpe alle
togidere & ȝeue it him to drinke in stale ale eerly at morowe & at euen last. 85
& lete him absteyne him from alle goutous metis & drinkis, þat is to wite,
oynouns, garleek, sour breed, rie breed, ne traueile not ne ete no potage ne
no sewis. And þis schal saue him & heele him. Turne vp.

   {streitnesse of þe brest} Next aftir þer ben þre þat bitokenen bigynynge
of digestioun. & if þis be wiþ a þicke substaunce in þe myddil & þat   90
bitokeneþ streitnesse of þe brest.

   & aȝens þat here is a fair medicyne & aȝens glet aboute þe herte & for
þe postyme aboute þe herte: take a porcioun of lyuerwort & as myche of
spigirnel & as myche of her|tis tunge & as miche of turmentyne. & boile   f. 71ʳ
alle þese eerbis in good stale ale to þe þriddendel. & drinke þerof first a   95
morowe & last an euen & þou schalt be hool on warantise. *Probatum est.*

   {For streit breeþ} Here is a fair medicyne for a streit breeþ & schort:
take croppis of horhowne, þe rootis of mylfoil, & braie hem in a morter.
And putte þerto leuk ale & drawe it þoruȝ a clene lynnen clooþ & ȝeue it
þries fastynge.   100

   And if þat vrine be whiȝt & þinne substaunce in þe myddil, þanne it
bitokeneþ feyntnesse in al his body.

   And þeraȝen here is a fair medicyn: take a quart of his pisse & seþe it &
putte þerto a sponful of comyn. And take an hoot tijl þat is weel hoot in þe

────────────────────────────────────

68–70 & sey . . . sine dubio] (*with minor variations*) W10A8, *heavily canc.* T15, & he schal
be hool Gc4, *om.* Di1

105 fier & leye þeron a sponful of comyn & lete him sitte or stonde þerouer al
cloos al aboute, hise leggis weel keuerid wiþ clooþis, til he swete for heete.
& aftir lete him go to bedde þat is maad wiþ newe waischen schetis & hile
him warme.

{apostym in a mannys stomac} Thanne aftirward þer ben two dyuers
110 colouris in mannys watir whiche bitokenen apostym in a mannys stomak &
swellynge in a mannys stomak.

Here bigynneþ a fair medicyne aȝens alle sijknesse & alle corrupciouns
bitwixe þe skyn & þe fleisch, be it watir or what it euere be, and for yuel
drynke: take a galoun or a potel of whiȝt wiyn (or reed for nede) & seþe
115 it into half. & þanne take þerto poudre of galyngale, of greynes, clowis,
notemuge, euene porcioun. & whanne þe wiyn is soden into þe half, þanne
putte yn þe forseid poudris. & whanne þe greete heete þerof is ouerpassid,
þanne putte þerto poudre of gynger. & lete him vse þis & he schal be hool
of manye sijknessis.

120 Here bigynneþ a potage for þe same yuel: take persely, borage, mynte,
f. 71ᵛ golde, auence, biteyne, violet, | & langdebeef. Of alle þese make potage
and þis schal preserue þee fro manie dyuers sijknessis.

{a whiȝt watir in a man} A whiȝt watir in a man bitokeneþ sijknesse in
þe reynes wiþ [reed] grauel stoonys and in a womman it bitokeneþ þat sche
125 is wiþ childe.

{a womman with childe} A watir of a womman þat is wiþ childe, if sche
haþ goon with childe a moneþe or two or þre, hir watir schal be whiȝt &
weel cleer and a whiȝt substaunce in þe botme. And if sche haþ goon foure
moneþis or more, hir watir schal haue a greet whiȝt matere in þe botme.
130 And if sche mai se hir silf in þe vrinal as in a mirrour, þat bitokeneþ þat
sche haþ conseyued a child.

The vrine of a virgyne schal be cleer and ȝelowȝ.

{flouris} Wommen þat han to miche of her flouris maken watir as reed
as blood.

135 {Medicyne} A fair medicyne aȝens þat, for [to] lesse hem faire and weel
and soone: take confi[r]ie and waische it and staumpe it and seþe it in wiyn
and make a plastre to hir nauele & to hir reynes.

Anoþir for þe same: take scheepis tirdlis & staumpe hem weel togideris
and make a plastre to þe wombe and to þe reynes & þat schal helpe hir faire
140 & weel.

{distried hir flouris} And if a womman haue distried hir flouris, to haue

124 reed] W10T15A8, greete Gc4, _om._ Di1   135 for to lesse] for to 'lasse' W10, to
lessen Di1, to sesse A8, to cease T15, for lesse Gc4   136 confirie] confyry A8, confery
Di1, confrey T15, comfery W10, confilie Gc4

hem a3en faire and weel: take þe roote of gladen and seþe it in vinegre or
in wiyn, and whanne it is soden, sette it on þe grounde and lete hir stride
þerouer so þat þer mai noon heete awey but vp to hir priuy membre. þis
medicyne failiþ neuere, but loke þat sche be not wiþ childe.   145

Ther is anoþir infirmitee þat greueþ wymmen greetly and clerkis callen
it *suffocacio matricis*, þat is, whanne it goiþ in þe bodi vp to þe herte and it
semeþ þat wymmen schulden die þeron or ben aprest.

{Medicyne} A fair medicyn þer | a3ens: take oold schoon & stynkynge &   f. 72ʳ
caste into þe fier & lete hir take a sauour þerof vp into hir þrote. & also lete   150
hir haue a fier of coolis & caste þerinne clowis & greynes & frankencense
& swete smellyng þing þat þe sauour þerof may goon vp into hir priuitee.
& lete hir cloþis close yn þe eir & þe goode sauour. & þis schal make þe
modir þat is clepid *matrix* goon doun into his naturel place & so sche schal
be hool.   155

H. *TEN COLD TEN HOT*

London, British Library, MS Sloane 213, ff. 117ʳᵃ–118ᵛᵃ (see Pl. 5)
Reporting S10S32 Cu4; H5 (lines 1–146); Co3 (lines 60–154)

Here sues descripcion of þe 4 elementes and of þe 4 complexiones. And   f. 117ʳᵃ
wite þou þat in ilk man and ilk womman regnes ilk planet and ilk signe of
þe zodiak and ilk pryme qualite and ilk elemente and ilk compleccion but
noght in ilkone elike. For in summe man regnes one more and summe man
anoþer. And þerfore men are of dyuerse maneres. Wherfore gode es þat we   5
se schortly þe kyndes of þise prime qualitees and so furth of þe oþer.

Foure prime qualitees þere are, þat es to say, moystnes, hotnes, drynes,
coldnes. Moystnes & drynes are tuo contraries | and þerfor þei may noght   f. 117ʳᵇ
negh togidere withouten a mene. For þe hotenes on þat one side byndes
þem togidere & coldnes on þat oþer. Also hotenes and coldenes are tuo   10
contraries and þerfor þei may noght negh togidere withouten a mene.
For þe moystnes on þat one side byndes þem togidere and drynes on þat
oþer. Moystnes es cause of ilk thik substaunce and of ilke swete taste.
And þereagayne drynes es cause of ilk thyn substaunce & of ilk soure and
stynkyng taste. Also hotenes es cause of ilk rede culour and large quantite. 15
þereageyne coldnes es cause of ilk white culoure & litel quantite.

Combyne (þat es to say, knytte) þise foure prime qualites after þeire
foure combynaciones (þat es to say, knyttynges) and þan þei wille 3elde
foure elementes: þat es to say, ayre moyste and hote, fyre hote and drye,

11 negh] e *poorly formed, appearing like* o? S10

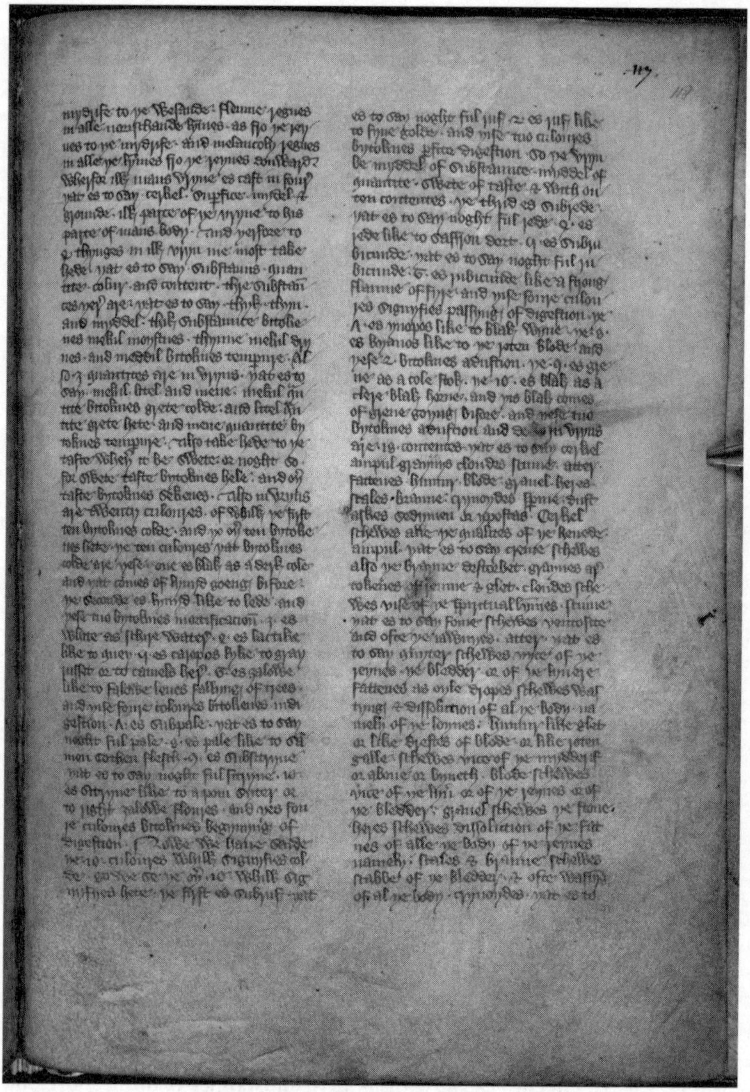

PLATE 5. *Ten Cold Ten Hot*. London,
British Library, MS Sloane 213, f. 118^r
© The British Library Board

erthe dry and colde, water colde and moyste. þe ayre and þe erthe are tuo 20
contraries and þerfor þei may noght negh bot as þe fyre byndes þem on þat
one side bitwene þem and þe water on þat oþer side bytwene þem. Also fyre
and water are tuo contraries and þerfore þei may noght negh bot as þe ayre
bitwene byndes þem on þat one side and þe erthe bitwene þem byndes þem
togidere on þat oþer side. þe fyre es scharpe, sotel, & meueable. þe ayre 25
es sotel, meueable, & corpulente, þat es to say, thik. þe watere es meuable,
corpulent, and dulle. þe erthe es corpulent, dull, and vnmeuable. Right as
in an ey þe schelle vmgos a thynne skynne, and þat skyn vmgos þe white, þe
white vmgos þe 30lke, and in þe myddel of þe 30lk es a litel tendire hole, so
þe fire vmgos þe ayre ten sithes more and ten sithes thynnere þan þe ayre. 30
þe ayre vmgos þe water ten sithes | more and ten sithes thynnere þen þat f. 117va
water. þe water vmgos þe erthe ten sithes more and ten sithes thynnere þan
þat erthe. In þe herte of þe erth es þe center of þe werlde, þat es to say þe
medil poynte, and in þat ilk center es hello. And percageyne abouen þe fyre
are þe sternes and abouen þem es heuene cristallyne, þat es to say waters 35
of al blisse, departed in nyne ordres of aungels. þan es heuene in þe hyest,
roumest, and largest, and þereageynes helle es in þe lowest, narowest, &
straytest.

Right as þere are 4 elementes, so þere are foure complecciones acordyng
in al maner qualites to þise 4 elementes. þe first es sanguyne, þat es to say 40
blode, gendred in þe lyuer[e], thynne & like to þe ayre. þe seconde es coler,
gendred in þe galle & lyke þerto & hit is acordyng to þe fyre. þe thrid es
melancoly, gendred in þe my[l]te and like to drestes of blode and it acordes
to þe erthe. þe ferthe es fleume, gendred in þe longes, like to glet, and it
acordes to þe watere. 45

A sangwyn man mekil may & mekil coueytes for he es moyste & hote.
A colerike man mekil coueytes and litel may for he es hote and dry.
A melancolyus man litel may & litel coueytes for he es drye and colde.
A fleumatyke man litel coueytes and mekil may for he es colde & moyste.
A sangwyne man es large, louyng, glad of chere, lagheng, and rody of 50
    coloure;
    stedfast, fleschy, right hardy, manerly, gentil, & wele norischede.
A coleryk man es gylefull, fals & wrathfull, tretrus & right hardy;
    queynte, smalle, drye & blak of culoure.
A melancolius man es envius, sory, couetus, hard & fast holdynge; 55
    gylefull, dredefull, sleuthfull, and claye of culour.

40 say] y *corr. from illeg. char.* S10   41 lyuere] Cu4, lyuers S10S32H5
43 mylte] S32Cu4H5, mynte S10

f. 117vb   A fleumatike man | es slomery, slepy, slowe, sleuthfull, and mekil
             spittyng;
             dul & harde of witte, fatte visage, and white of culoure.

60   In þe ȝere are foure quarters reuled by þise 4 complecciones, þat es to
       say, ver, somer, heruest, & wynter. Ver has 3 monethes, þat es to say,
       Marche, Auerel, and May, and it es sangwyne complecion. Somer has
       also thre monethes, þat es to say, Iuny, Iuly, and August, and þis quarter es
       colerike complecion. Heruest also has 3 monethes, þat es to say, Septem-
65   ber, October, and Nouember, and þis quarter es melancolius complec-
       cion. Wynter has also 3 monethes, þat es to say, December, Ianyuer, and
       Feuerȝere, and þis quartere es fleumatik complecion.

       Ilk day also þise foure complecions regnes. þat es to say, fro thre
       aftere mydnyght vnto nyne regnes sangwyne. And fro 9 aftere mydnyghte
70   to thre aftere mydday regnes coler. And fro thre aftere mydday to nyne
       aftere mydday regnes melancoly. & fro nyne aftere mydday to thre aftere
       mydnyght regnes fleume.

       Also in þe foure quarters of þe werlde regnes þise foure complecciones,
       þat es to say, sanguyn in þe est, coler in þe southe, melancoly in þe west,
75   and fleume in þe northe.

       Also þise 4 complecciones regnes in þe 4 ages of man, þat es to say, coler
       in childhede, sanguyn in manhede, fleume in age, and melancoly in elde.
       Childhode es fro þe birthe to fourtene ȝere ful done, manhede fro þethen
       to thritty ȝere, age fro þethen to fifty ȝere, and elde fro þethen to eghteth
80   ȝere, and so furth to þe ded.

       Also þise foure complecciones regnes in 4 parties of mans body. Coler
       regnes in alle souled lymmes, as fro þe breste vpward. Sangwyn regnes in
f. 118ra alle spirituale lymmes, as fro þe | mydrife to þe wesande. Fleume regnes
       in alle norischande lymmes, as fro þe reynes to þe mydrife. And melancoly
85   regnes in alle þe lymmes fro þe reynes donward.

       Wherfor ilk mans vryne es cast in foure, þat es to say, cerkel, superfice,
       mydel, & grounde, ilk parte of þe vryne to his parte of mans body. And
       þerfore to 4 thynges in ilk vryn me most take hede, þat es to say, substauns,
       quantite, colur, and content.

90   Thre substaunces þere are, þat es to say, thyk, thyn, and myddel. Thik
       substaunce bitokenes mekil moystnes, thynne mekil drynes, and meddil
       bitoknes temperure.

       Also 3 quantites are in vryns, þat es to say, mekil, litel, and mene.
       Mekil quantite bitoknes grete colde and litel quantite grete hete and mene
95   quantite bytoknes temperure.

Also take hede to þe taste, wheþer it be swete or noght so. For swete taste bytoknes hele and oþer taste bytoknes sekenes.

Also in vryns are twenty culoures of whilk þe first ten bytoknes colde and þo oþer ten bytokenes hete. Þe ten culoures þat bytoknes colde are þese: One es blak as a derk cole and þat comes of lyuyd goeng bifore. Þe seconde es lyuyd like to lede. And þese tuo bytoknes mortificacioun. 3 es white as schire watere. 4 es lactike like to quey. 5 es caropos lyke to gray russet or to camels here. 6 es ȝalowe like to falowe leues fallyng of trees. And þise foure coloures bitokenes indigestion. 7 es subpale, þat es to say, noght ful pale. 8 es pale like to sammen sothen flesch. 9 es subsitryne, þat es to say, noght ful sitryne. 10 es sitryne like to a pom syter or to right ȝalowe floures. And þes foure culoures bitoknes begynyng of digestion.

Nowe we haue saide þe 10 culoures whilk signyfies colde, go we se þe oþer 10 whilk signyfyes hete. Þe first es subruf, þat | es to say, noght ful ruf. 2 es ruf like to fyne golde. And þise tuo culoures bytoknes parfite diges- tion, so þe vryn be myddel of substaunce, myddel of quantite, swete of taste, & withouten contentes. Þe thrid es subrede, þat es to say, noght ful rede. 4 es rede like to saffron d'ort. 5 es subrubicunde, þat es to say, noght ful rubicunde. 6 es rubicunde like a strong flaume of fyre. And þise foure culoures signyfies passyng of digestion. Þe 7 es ynopos like to blak wyne. Þe 8 es kyanos like to þe roten blode. And þese 2 bitoknes adustion. Þe 9 es grene as a cole stok. Þe 10 es blak as a clere blak horne and þis blak comes of grene goyng bifore. And þese tuo bytoknes adustion and dede.

In vryns are 18 contentes, þat es to say, cerkel, ampul, graynys, cloudes, scume, atter, fattenes, humur, blode, grauel, heres, scales, branne, crynoydes, sperme, dust, askes, sedymen or ypostas.

Cerkel schewes alle þe qualites of þe heuede.

Ampul, þat es to say creme, schewes also þe brayne destorbet.

Graynes are tokenes of reume & glet.

Cloudes schewes vise of þe spiritual lymmes.

Scume, þat es to say fome, schewes ventosite and ofte þe iawnyes.

Atter, þat es to say quyter, schewes vyce of þe reynes, þe bledder, or of þe lyuere.

Fattenes as oyle dropes schewes wastyng & dissolution of al þe body, namely of þe loynes.

Humur like glet or like drestes of blode or like roten galle schewes vice of þe mydderif or aboue or byneth.

Blode schewes vice of þe lyuer or of þe reynes or of þe bledder.

Grauel schewes þe stone.

135 Heres schewes dissolution of þe fatnes of alle þe body, of þe reynes
namely.

Scales & branne schewes scabbe of þe bledder & ofte wastyng of al þe
body.

f. 118ᵛᵃ Crynoydes, þat es to | say resolucions gratter þen branne, schewes þe
140 thrid spice of þe feuyre etike, incurable.

Sperme, þat es to say man kynde, schewes to mykel liccherie.

Dust schewes þe goute or a womman conceyued.

Askes schewes þe preuy harnes to be greued.

Sedymen, þat es to say cloddes in þe grounde of þe vryn or brekyng vp
145 toward þe cerkel, es called ypostas, þat es to say, þe grounde. And it has
moste significacions of alle & namely of þe lowere parties.

Of ilk mans bodye are 4 principale lymmes, þat es to say, souled
lymmes, spirituale lymmes, norischand lymmes, & gendryng lymmes.
Sowled lymmes are þe braynes and alle þat es þereaboute doune to þe
150 wesand. Spiritual lymmes are þe herte & þe longes and alle þat are aboute
þem bitwene þe wesande and þe mydrife. Norischand lymmes are þe lyuer,
my[l]t, galle, guttes, and alle þat are aboute þem bytwene þe mydrife and
þe raynes. Gendryng lymmes are þe raynes, bleddir, priuy harnes, and
alle þe lemes aboute þem fro þe raynes donward.

I. *THE DOME OF URYNE*, EXPANDED VERSION

London, British Library, MS Sloane 374, ff. 5ᵛ–13ᵛ (see Frontispiece)

Reporting S15Ad4 Ad7 Sj3 W7; in sidenotes with damaged or lost characters, supplied text is based on context in S15 and parallel readings (when available) in Ad4,
which is textually close to S15 and the only other copy with extensive structural
marginalia in the hand of its own scribe

f. 5ᵛ In the byginnyng thow schalt take heede to 4 that longeth to the doome of
vryne: to the substance, to the colours, to the regions, and to the contentis.

{*Nota* ⟨. . .⟩} Furst lok to the substance, whether hit is thikke or thynne
other bytwene bothe. Yf the vryne b[e thynne], thanne schalt thow see
5 thourgh the vryne the ioyntis of thi fyngers and that thynnehed bytokeneth a bad splen and a badde stomake & water in the bowelles. And yf hit
be thykke that thow may nout3 see thourgh, hit bytokeneth wynd in the
stomake & in the hed and in the bowelles. And yf hit be bytwyxt thikke
and thynne, hit tokeneth swellyng of the galle.

152 mylt] S32Cu4Co3, mynt S10   Text I 4 be thynne] Ad4Ad7Sj3, by twyne *corr.*
in later hand to be thinn S15, Yf . . . thynne *om.* W7

The secunde that thow schalt take heed to ys colour of the vryne: as seyn   10
these maisters, ther ben 20 colouris in the vrine.

{*Col⟨or albus⟩*} The firste colour ys whyt as cler water of the welle. This
colour bytokeneth indigest'i'oun, as a badde stomake & a badde lyuer. And
yf thow see in this vryne manye shynyng bemys, hit bytokeneth a postem
in the mylte.   15

{*Col⟨or lacteus⟩*} The secunde colour ys white as whey. Yf this vryne
be droubli, thyk, and litel in quantite whyth white contentis, hit tokeneth
the flux.

{*Colo⟨r glaucus⟩*} The thrydde colour ys white 3olw a[s] bryth horn of a
lanterne. This vryne litel in quantite & ofte made tokeneth that the seek   20
may nout3 kepen his vryne. And this colour ys neuere knyt wyth thykke
substance.

{*Col⟨or karopos⟩*} The ferthe colour ys a whit russet. This vryne, 3yf hit
be thyke in substance wythoute grauel in the bottoum, hit tokeneth *colica
passio*.   25

{*Sub⟨pallidus⟩*} The fifte colour ys as broth of flesh that ys half sothyn.
This vryne, yf hit be litel in quantite | and fat as oylle & frothi abovyn, hit   f. 6ʳ
tokeneth a waistyng.

{*Pallidus*} The syxte colour ys as broth of flessh wel sothyn. This vryn,
3yf hit be thynne in substaunce, hit bytokeneth a cotydyan feuer that   30
cometh of fleume. And all these 6 colours afornseid bytokeneth badde
digestioun.

{*Subcitrinus*} The 7 colour ys nout3 fully so 3elow as a 3elew appel.
This vryne, yf hit be oueral thynne in hervest and wynter, hit tokeneth
a quarteyn. And 3yf hit be thynne in the tastyng wythouten sauour, hit   35
tokeneth a tercian.

{*Citrinus*} The 8 colour ys 3elow as a 3elew appel. This vryne with a
thynne substaunce & a salt sauour tokeneth a double tercian that cometh
of malencolie. And 3yf hit be a childis vryne, hit tokeneth a cotidian.

{*Subrubeus*} The 9 colour ys ney as yelow as saffroun d'oort. This vryne,   40
3yf hit be thynne in substaunce & shadwyd oueral aboute, more thykke
abovyn than bynethen, hit tokeneth a tercian. And 3yf colour appere in
haruest & in vynter, hy[t] tokeneth a quarteyn.

{*Rubeus*} The 10 colour is as reed as ony saffroun. This vryne, 3yf hit
haue a 3elow froth abovyn, hit tokeneth the iavndes.   45

{*Subrufus*} The 11 colour ys as qwhit gold. 3yf this vrine be thynne in

19 as] Ad4Ad7Sj3W7, a S15   24 thyke] *preceded by* tyke *canc.* S15   43 hyt]
Ad4Ad7Sj3W7, hy S15

sustaunce in a child, hit bytokneth a cotidian; in a ʒong man a tercian; in a
hold man a double tercian; in a woman a quartayn.

{*Rufus*} The 12 colour is as reed gold. This vryne, ʒyf hit be thykke
50 in substaunce & shadwyd abovyn wythouten eny wanhed, hit tokneth a
lastyng cotidian.

{*Subrubicundus*} The 13 colour is [a]s reed as a rose. This vryne, yf he
be more thikke than thynne, hit tokeneth of a brynyng feuere.

f. 6ᵛ   {*Rubicundus*} The 14 colour ys reed as brennyng cole. This | vryne,
55 yf hit be in the by[gi]nnyng thyn, afterward reed and thikke and colourid
abovyn sumwat as leed, and ʒyf the vryne stynke noutʒ, hit tokeneth a
feuere of excesse of blood that ys cleped *sinocha inflati*[*u*]*a*. And ʒyf the
vryne stynke, than hit ys clepid *sinecha putrida*. In these feuers these arn
the toknes: [a] rody face, greet thurst, a drye tounge and a shaarp, noo
60 reste at al, greet euel in the heued, a gret pulse withoute ordre & euermore
moor seke.

{*Ino⟨pos⟩*} The 15 colour is reed suart as the liuere of a best. This vryne
with a ʒelow froth abovyn bytokeneth þe iawnd and a postim of the lyuere.
Also this vryne, ʒyf hit be [dresty] in battoum, hit tokeneth the floures.

65 {*Kay⟨nos⟩*} The 16 colour is as blak wyn or rootyn blood. This vryne in
a lestyngg feuere tokneth deth yf hit be drubli, fetty, & stynkyng. And ʒyf
the vryne tofoorn was reed as fuyre coole and ʒyf this vryne appere in an
hoil body, hit tokeneth brestyng of a veyn in the reyns of skyppyngg or of
ly[f]tyngg.

70 {*Lyu⟨idus⟩*} The 17 colour ys waan as leed. ʒyf this vryne be bloo al
abowtyn so that no residens in the vryne may doon awey the bloohed, hit
tokeneth deth.

The 18 colour ys grene as woorts. This vrine, ʒyf hit be litel in quantite,
hit tokeneth deth.

75 {*Ni⟨ger⟩ ut p⟨ena⟩*} The 19 is blaak shynyng as a rafnys fether. This
vryne mykel in quantite & thyne in substaunce bytokeneth delyuryng of
the quarteyn.

{*Nig⟨er ut⟩ car⟨bo⟩*} The 20 colour ys blak as coole. This vryne in a ague,
f. 7ʳ lytel, fetti, and stynkand, ʒyf thou see thi face therinne hit | tokeneth deth.
80 {*De contentis vri⟨narum⟩*} Vryne that hath grete contentis as hit were
quytour after the vryne is cast, ʒyf the vryne stynke more than hit scholde

52 as] W7, ys S15, *om.* Ad4Ad7Sj3   55 byginnyng] Ad4Ad7Sj3, bygynnyng(*line
end*)nyng W7, bynnyng S15   57 inflatiua] Ad4Ad7Sj3, inflatia *with nasal suspension
over* - ia S15, ynflacyam W7   59 a¹] Ad4Ad7, and S15W7, of Sj3   64 dresty]
Ad4Ad7Sj3W7, destry S15   tokeneth] *preceded by* toke *canc.* S15   68–9 skyppyngg
or of lyftyngg] lepyngge or lyftyngge W7, skyppyngg or of lystyngg S15Ad4, skyppyng oþer
of lepynge Ad7, skyppyng or by lepyng Sj3

doo of kynde, bytokeneth peyne in the reynys and in the spleen. And ʒyf
this quytour stynke noutʒ, hit tokeneth peyne of the lyuere and badde
digestion.

{*6 Sanguis*} Blood and hit be cler & pure bytokeneth of brekynge of a   85
vayne in the lyuere. ʒyf hit be thykke and litel wyth a strong sauour and ly
on gobettes in the bottoum, hit cometh fro the bladdere. ʒyf hit be spotti,
as bloo & reed, thanne the peyne ys in the reynes and in the schoore. ʒyf
hit be cleer and blakyssh, thanne the peyne ys in the baak, in the schoore,
and aboute the bladdere.   90

{*Humoures*} Raw humouris ys a content of the vryne the wych thow
schalt k[no]w thus: ʒyf the vryne after hys castyng fleete ful of smal motis,
the wiche come of residens of the battoum or in the myd regioun, than in
vryne arn raw humouris. ʒyf thes raw humouris be on the ouer partie of
the water, hit bytokeneth streythede in the breste, schorthede of breth, &   95
nyppyng of the splene. ʒyf they appere in the myddys, grynddyngg in the
body & crullyng in the guttes and wynde in the stomake. Al this cometh of
excess of mete and drynke. ʒyf they be in the bottoum, payne in the reyns
& sumtyme in the cod.

{*8ᵐ*} Fathed wythoute access tokeneth wastyng of grees | aboute neeris.   f. 7ᵛ
ʒyf hit be wyth an access, hit tokeneth wastyng of the body.   101

{⟨*Prima*⟩ *species etice*} In the firste spice of etyk, the fathed hovyth aboven
by parties as hit were of fat broth.

{⟨*Secunda*⟩ *species etice*} The secunde spice hit wryeth the vryne aboven
and hit is lyk the webbe of an erayn.   105

{⟨*Tercia*⟩ *species etice*} The 3 spice: the vryne ys fat oueral aboute as oyle
and ʒyf hit be cast on a ston of marbyl, hit sowneth as oylle. And this spice
hit ys incurable.

{*9*} Brenny contentis hit ben like bren, sumtyme rownd lyk skalis of
fissh. ʒyf this apperen wyth an access, hit tokeneth the firste spice of etyk.   110
And the secunde of the etyk they appere lyk bran that hath a litel of the
flour wyth hym. In the 3 spice of etik, there appere contentis lyk this two
first, but hit ben grettere & thanne they ben al whyte.

{*de lapide* 10} Grauel reed tokeneth the stone in the reyns. ʒyf the grauel
be whyte or blak and hard & gret, hit tokeneth the ston in the bladdere. ʒyf   115
they be reed and nessch, brend blode in the lyuere.

{⟨11⟩} Motis that ben whyt & smal & rounde tokneth the goute bothe in
man & womman. ʒyf they appere in the bottoum, hit tokneth goute in the
reyns. ʒyf they appere in the myd region, hit tokneth the rewmatik goute

91 of the] *preceded by* of the *canc.* S15   92 know] Ad4Ad7Sj3W7, konw S15

120 [bothe] in the stomak [&] the rewmatik goute at the brest. 3yf they gadere
thanne togedere in a gobet round & lyen thykke in the botthum or onder
f. 8ʳ the cercle, 3yf they | ben redyssh & round, hit tokeneth a knawe child. 3yf
they be whyt or bloo & thynne as skalys, hit tokneth a mayde chi[l]d.

{*Crines*} Heres that ben auelong & smal, 3yf they schewe wyth an access,
125 hit tokeneth wastyng of the body. And 3yf wyth an access be a flux & these
heris appere, hit ys deth.

{*Sperma*} Spermatik resolucions, 3yf they apperyn fletyngg abowte in
the vryne and the vryne be raw in colour, hit tokneth passyng of kynde
wythoute lykyngg. 3yf they appere in the vryne [and 3yf the vryne] be hy
130 of colour, hit tokneth that hit was mad *post suppositum.*

{*Cineres*} Askis, 3yf they appere in the vryne & [the vryne be] low of
colour wyth resoluciouns blak and bloo beyng in the bothum, hit tokneth
the emorodis. And hure contentis ben blak or bloo or purpure with a low
colour, hit tokneth stoppyng of floures.

135   {*Ypostasis*} The laste content is cleped *ypostasis* in Latyn, in Englyssh
'that stondeth in the bothum', brod bynethen & scharp vpward. 3yf this
content be whit & brood in the bothum & scharp vpward wythoute brekyng
and long lestyng, hit tokneth that the seeke is warsschid. 3yf hit be broken
& hoofe in myddis or ellis abowte in the parties, hit tokneth that the seke
140 lyuer ys cold & may nout3 defye. 3yf hit be in the myddis than hit ys cald
f. 8ᵛ *nefilis*: hit tokneth badde digestion in the stomake. | 3yf this *ypostasis* be
reed, hit tokneth badde digestion & longhed of syknesse. 3yf hit be blak,
hit tokneth distrucioun of kynde & deth.

Now have Y schewed the substance of the vryne, the colouris, the
145 regions, & the contentis that longeth too the doome of vryne. *Explicit.*

Ad sciendum gradus siccitatis & caliditatis.

*Prim[u]s gradus caliditatis est cum aliqua res habeat vnam porcionem frigi-
ditatis & duas caliditatis. Tunc res illa dic[i]tur esse calida in primo gradu.
Secundus est quando habeat vnam porcionem frigiditatis & 4 caliditatis. Tunc*
150 `dicitur' esse calida in 2° gradu. Tercius gradus est quando habeat vnam partem*

---

120 bothe] Ad4, botym S15, bothe . . . rewmatik goute *om.* Ad7Sj3W7   &] in S15Ad4,
phrase om. Ad7Sj3W7   122 ben] *prec. by* gadere thanne *canc.* S15   123 child]
Ad4Ad7Sj3W7, chid S15   129 and 3yf the vryne] Sj3, þat þey W7, *om.* S15Ad4,
and 3yf . . . suppositum *om.* Ad7 (hygh of Collour . . . suppositum *added in later hand*
Ad7)   131 the vryne be] Ad4Ad7Sj3, in the vrynele S15, yn þe secund yuylle W7
147 Primus] Ad7W7Sj3, Primis S15, *in English* Ad4 (*see App. IV*), *sections on degrees, moon,
signs, and pulse occur later in MS* Ad7   148 dicitur] Ad7Sj3, dicietur S15, decetur W7
149 Tunc] *foll. by* dn *or* du *with nasal suspension, canc.* S15

*frigiditatis & octo caliditatis tunc [dicitur] esse calida in 3° gradu. Quartus est
quando habeat vnam porcionem frigiditatis & 16 caliditatis. Tunc dicitur esse
calida in 4 gradu.*

De etate lune quando est sicca vel calida

Prima etas lune calida est & humida; 2ᵃ calida & sicca; 3ᵃ frigida & humida; 155
4 frigida & sicca.

De signis mobilibus & fixis & eorum condicionibus

*In signis fixis debet incipi opus quod multum durare debet, vt edificia. In mobi-
libus, mobilia, vt vendere & emere & cetera.*

Item nota si in principio egritudinis luna fuerit in signo mobili: tunc est va- 160
*riabilis egritudo. Si in signo fixo vel stabili, infirmitas erit in vno statu. Si in
signo mediocri se | habebit mediocriter. Item egritudo in augmento lune sepius* f. 9ʳ
terminatur ad bonum & econtra ei in defectu sepius terminatur ad malum.

{*Versus*}   *Mobilis est Aries, Cancer, Capricorn quoque Libra;*
           Sed Leo sunt stabiles & Taurus, Scorpio, Limpha;   165
           Virgo, Sagit, Pisces bipartita sunt Geminisque.

Ad cognoscendum pulsum alicuius

To knowe the puls, lay thy foure fyngeris on the puls. Yf the puls vnder
the litel fynger be febel in smytyng, vnder the leche hit be strongere, and
vnder the myddel fyngere more strong, & so goyng vpward, hit toketh 170
goode. Yf hit be the contra[r]ye, hit ys wyk and toketh deth. And thus:
yf the puls be feble vnder the firste fynger, & vnder the secunde fynger
more feble, and so goynge vpward, hit toketh deth. Also yf the puls be
felt vnder foure fyngeris til he come to 10 strokis and he faille in the 11
strok to telle agayn fro the hed, thanne yf he faille in the 11 strok, hit ys 175
good. And yf hit be contrarie, hit ys token of deth. As yf the defaute come
of the 11 strok and be febel & more febil in the 10, and more fibel in the
[9], and so goyng donward, this toketh deth. {*Hic ?venᵗ ⟨?v . . .⟩*}

151 caliditatis] Sj3W7, calidi Ad7, caliditatatis S15, of ho⟨otnysse⟩ Ad4 (*see App. IV*)
dicitur] Ad7Sj3W7, dn *or* du *with nasal suspension* S15, *MS damaged* Ad4 (*see App. IV*)
169 in smytyng] yn (þe W7) smytyng Sj3W7, *preceded by* & snytyng *canc.* S15, & snytyng
& smytyng Ad4, & smytyng & smytyng Ad7   171 contrarye] Ad4Ad7Sj3W7, contraye
S15   ys wyk] Ad4, wyk *corr. in darker ink and later hand to* wek S15, ys wykkyd Ad7,
betokenyth (þe W7) ewell Sj3W7   174 11] Ad4Ad7Sj3, *second* 1 *erroneously altered to* j,
in darker ink by later hand, with dots added over 1s (*to read* ij) S15, *sentence om.* W7   176 ys
token] Ad7Sj3, is tokeneþ Ad4, ys token, *with* en *in darker ink by a later hand, foll. by 2 erased
chars., prob. corr. from* ys tokneth S15, *sentence om.* W7   178 9] Ad4Ad7, 19 S15, 3 Sj3,
sentence om. W7

De complexionibus

180 Now after thi colouris of thyn vryne be thykke & reed, than hit bytokneth
f. 9ᵛ [b]lood. 3yf hit be reed and thynne, | than hit tokneth colore. And 3yf be
whyte & thykke, hit tokneth flewme. 3yf hit be white and thynne, than hit
tokneth malencolie.

And 3yf thow wilt knowe the complexiouns by the tast of the vryne, loke
185 yf hit be suete, hit tokneth blood. 3yf be sowre, hit tokneth colore. 3yf
hit be whithouten sauour as water, hit tokneth flewme. 3yf hit be salt, hit
tokneth malencolie.

Ad sciendum vbi complexiones generantur

{⟨C⟩olera} 3yf thou wolt knowe whe[re] these complexciouns arn ygendred
190 in mannes body, I saye that colore [ys] ygendred in the lyuere and his
duellyng place ys in the coffre of the galle.

{⟨S⟩anguis} Blod ys ygendred in the lyuere and his duellyng ys in the
vayns.

{⟨F⟩lewme} Flewme also that ys naturell ys gendred in the lyuere and
195 hit nath non propre duellyng place. And therefore ys he melled wyth the
blod to make the blod rennyng.

Malencolie ys ygendred in the lyuere and his propre duellyng place ys
in the spleen. And malencolie & flewme kepyn the bothum of the vryne.

Ad discernendum vrinam humanam ab vrina muliebri et vrinam bestie ab
200   vrinam humana vel muliebri

Thou schalt vnderstonde that 3yf there be eny drublihede in mannys
f. 10ʳ vryne that drublyhed schewyth in | the myddes of the vryne. And in the
womannes water hit doth nout3 soo.

Another ys this: the froth aftir the castyng of a mans vryne schal ben
205 auelon[g] and in a womannys vryne after the castyng hit schal be round.
This too laste toknes saith Avicen.

Now bestes water fro manns water ys the saltere and the simplere
of complexioun. And also the bestis water smylleth more raw than the
mannys. Another: medle the vryne of the best with vyn & that on schal
210 partie fro that other.

3yf hit be a cowis water that ys wyth calf, hit ys eth to knowe fro a
womanns water that ys wyth child, [for] the drestes or the contentis of the

---

181 blood] Ad7Sj3W7, lood S15Ad4   189 where] Ad4Ad7W7, whetre S15, 3yf...
ygendred *om.* Sj3   190 ys] Ad4Ad7Sj3W7, *om.* S15   205 auelong] Ad4Ad7,
euelong W7, auelond S15, well longe Sj3   212 for] Ad7W7, fro S15Ad4, that ys
wyth . . . womanns water *om.* Sj3

cowis water schal be mykke grettere than of the womanns water, in as mekel
as the cow ys mekel more beste than a woman and foulere of complexioun.

Ad cognescendum primam aquam et secundam   215

[Take] good hede of that oweth the water, whether he lyve in gret etynk &
drynkyng & thanne the firste water is grettere in quantite and lesse tynkt
than the secunde. Or ellis that he lyueth mesurable & thanne the firste
schal be more tynkt than the secunde.

Now Y haue told the knowyng of the substance of vrynys with the co-   220
louris and complexions, and to knowe | manys vryne fro womanns and   f. 10ᵛ
bestes, womanns with child from cowis wyth calf.

Iudicium perfectum omnium vrinarum

First I begynne at vryne of man or womann that tokneth helthe.

{1ᵃ} Vrine white at morwyn & broun after mete tokneth helthe.   225
{2ᵃ} Vryne fat and drubly tokneth water in the bowelles.
{3ᵃ} Vryne that ys ry3t reed and cler tokneth a brennyng feuere that ys
of colre.
{4ᵃ} Vryne reed and thykke oueral wyth a blak sercle: hit tokneth syknesse oueral aboute. And bute the pacient may swete, he schal deye.   230
{5ᵃ} Vryn that ys white and thynne and a litel dym tokneth cold in the
body.
{6ᵃ} Vryne cler wyth a blak cercle tokneth that syke schal ben *tysicus*.
{7ᵃ} Vryne thynne sumwhat reed & cler wyth a bry3t cercle tokneth a
badde stomake.   235
{8ᵃ} Vryne thynne and grene abovyn ys tokyn of cold comple`x´ioun.
And 3yf in the castyng hit schewe blew abovyn, hit tokneth tisyk.
{9ᵃ} Vryne thynne & blak abovyn in the castyng tokneth greet lust of
kynde.
{10ᵃ} Vryne thykke and drubly as hors pisse tokneth heued werk.   240
{11ᵃ} Vryne fat in the bothum, whit in the myddis, reed abovyn tokneth
of a quarteyn.
{12ᵃ} Vryne fat & flesshy and hath drest in the bothum as schaddyng: |
hit tokneth the cold dropesye. Also 3yf hit be as whey aboven, cler in the f. 11ʳ
myddis, & schadwyd beneth`e´n, hit tokneth the cold dropesy.   245
{13ᵃ} Vryne that hath blak drestes in the bothum lyke `gobettis´ of colys,
3yf the be partid asunder and nout3 to grete, hit tokneth wormes in the
body.

216 Take] Ad4Ad7Sj3W7, The S15   221 knowe] *prec. by* kowe *canc.* S15   and³]
W7, manes and S15Ad4Ad7, and womannys from Sj3   246 gobettis] *ins. above* botys
canc. S15

{14ᵃ} Vryne that hath blak contentis smal as mootis in the myddes of
250 the water hit tokneth a postem vnder the syde.

{15ᵃ} Vryne that hath in the bothum as gobettis of flessh or smal schyvys
or as rasyng of parchymyn tokneth stoppyng of the reyns and of the pipes
epatis.

{16ᵃ} Vryne that ys blak grene wyth long white contentis lyk the kynde
255 of a man: hit tokneth the palseye. And also 'yf' hit be frothy & lyk leed in
the myddys, *paralisis*.

{17ᵃ} Vryne that hath greynes vnder the sercle: hit tokneth a stomak ful
of vmers and also a brennyng atte breste.

{18ᵃ} Vryne that [hath] a sky aboven tokneth hete in the herte, in the
260 loungis, & in the spleen.

{19ᵃ} Vryne that hath contentis whit & blak in the bothum tokneth
costyfnesse.

{[2]oᵃ} Vryne that ys long lestyngg thynne: hit tokneth bolnyngg of the
body & gret rewme.

265 {21ᵃ} Vryne thykke and litel in quantite hit tokneth begynnyng of the
ston.

{22ᵃ} Vryne lytel in quantite & riȝt hye of colour tokneth gret brennyng
in the body.

{23ᵃ} Vryne that ys frothy hit tokneth wynde and peynes vnder the
270 sydes.

f. 11ᵛ   {24ᵃ} Vryne frothy and cler & litel reed tokneth peyne in the | riȝt side.

{25ᵃ} Vryne reed as coole: hit tokneth a postem on the lyuere.

{26ᵃ} Vryne reed as brend gold: ȝyf he be ydropyk, hit tokneth deth.

Vrina mulieris

275 [1] Vryne of woman that ys wyth child: hure water schal haue sum clere
stripis. The most parte schal be drubli and the drublynesse schal be reed-
isch in the manere of thanne. And this tokne schal noutȝ faille as sone as
the child hath lyf.

[2] And ȝyf hit be a knaf child, the drubles schal hove thykkyst above.
280 And ȝyf hit be a mayde child, the drubles schal draven donvard.

[3] Vryne of a woman whit and hevy and stynkand tokneth payne in the
reyns and peyne of the moder and sykenesse of cold.

[4] Vryne of woman colourid as bryȝt gold tokneth talent to man.

[5] Vryne of woman that fletith fat abovyn tokneth peyne in the reyns.

259 hath] Ad4Ad7Sj3W7, *om.* S15   263 20ᵃ (*marg.*)] Ad4, 10ᵃ S15, *marg. numbering*
om. Ad7Sj3W7

[6] Vryne of woman wyth blak contentis in the bothum tokneth fallyng 285
of floures.

[7] Vryne of womman wyth whit contentis in the bothum tokneth mykelhed of floures.

[8] Vryne of woman that ys of the colore & weygth of leed, 3yf sche be
wyth child, hit tokneth that the child ys ded wythin hure. And 3yf sche be 290
nout3 wyth chylde & the water stynke, hit tokneth that the moder ys roten.

[9] Vryne of woman colourid as lynseed, 3yf sche haue the flux, hit
tokneth deth. |

[10] Vryne of woman reed as gold wyth a watery cercle abovyn tokneth f. 12ʳ
that sche ys wyth child. 295

[11] And take heede: 3yf thou see thy face in womans water and sche be
wythouten feueres, hit tokneth that sche ys wyth child.

[12] And 3yf thow see thy face in the vryne of the hoote feuere, hit
tokneth deth

[13] 3yf thou see thi face in mans water that hath non access, hit tokneth 300
longg syeknesse.

Ad cognoscendum prengnantes

[1] [Take] the firste water after that sche hath commyned wyth man. 3yf
that water be cler, sche ys wyth child. 3yf hit be thykke, sche ys nout3
wyth chyld. 305

[2] Another: gyf hure to eete a clowe of leeke whan sche goyth to bedde,
and after hure furste sclep, 3yf sche fele sauour of leek in hure mouth, sche
ys wyth no chyld. & 3yf sche fele nout3, sche ys wyth childe.

[3] And 'a'nother: 3yf hure pulsis beete swythe and sche haue no access,
hit tokneth that sche ys wyth child. And yf the pulse of the ry3t hond beete 310
swythere than the puls of the lyft harm, hit tokneth a knave child. And 3yf
hit be contrarie, hit tokneth a mayde child.

[4] 3yf the child be ded wythin the woman, than arn these the toknes:
hure hond stynkz, sche hath grete peyne aboute hure nauele, sche may
euel goon, euermore ne syttyng stille, hure eyn are small. | 315

Vrina mortis tam hominum quam mulierum f. 12ᵛ

{1} Vrine in an hoot access, in o parti reed, in another blak, in another 317
grene, in another blew, tokneth deth.

{2} Vryne in a hoot access blak & lytel in quantite & fatty & stynkand
tokneth deth. 320

303 Take] Ad4Ad7Sj3W7, That S15   317–33 *Marg. numbering only in* S15, *poss. by*
the main hand but in lighter ink

{3} Vryne oueral colourid as leed tokneth a prolongyng of deth.

{4} Vryne derk abovyn & cleer bynethen tokneth deth.

{5} Vryne that schyneth ri3t bri3t, 3yf the sky in the bothum schyne nout3, hit ys deth.

325 {6} Vryne thynne in substaunce, hauende fletyng abovyn as hit were a derk sky, tokneth deth.

{7} Vryne dresty, stynkand, & derk wyth a blak skye wythinne hym tokneth a prolongyng of deth.

{8} Vryne that ys of the colour of water: 3yf hit haue a derke sky in an 330 access, hit tokneth deth.

{9} Vryne that hath drestes in the bothum medlid wyth blood: hit tokeneth deth.

{10} Vryne blak and thynne: 3yf the syke lothe whan he goth to priuy & spekith ouerthaward or vnderstondeth nou3t ary3t, and 3yf this goo nout3 335 fro hym, hit tokneth deth.

And this for knowyng of the substaunce of vryne.

Tercia cognicio vrinarum que dicitur regionum

Thu schalt vnderstande that in the vryne whan hit is in the vrinal there ben 3 regions: the firste, the secunde, the thrydde. The thrydde region bygyn-
f. 13ʳ neth at the bothum of the vrynal & lastyth the thyknesse of two | fyngeris
341 brede vpward. The secunde regioun bygynneth there the thyrde endyth and lastyth vp al to the cercle. And in ylke of these regions arn diuerse contentis &c.

De contentis vrinarum

345 {*Spuma*} Now Y wolle schewe the 4 that longeth to vrynys & tho ben these contentis. & first I wol begynne at froth. Froth that dwelleth & cleueth to the sercle tokneth indygestioun, as wynd in the stomake, in the bowels, & in the hed. And [3yf] abovyn the froth dwellyn gret bublis, hit tokneth peyne in the reyns. Froth also that dwelleth gret tokneth indigestioun and 350 wynd. And 3yf the froth dwelle smale, hit tokneth brynnyng in the stomak and brend blood in the lyuere. 3yf the froth be ful of greyns, hit tokneth the rewme in the heed and in the breste. 3yf the froth be blak, hit tokneth the blake iawndis. 3yf hit be grene, the iawndys that cometh of brend blood in the lyuere, as of envye & wrethe. & bothe in this spice of iawndys & yke of 355 the blak ys swellyng of the galle. 3yf hit be yelewe, swot. And this cometh of greet heete of blood of the lyuere.

{*Nubes*} A smal sky apperyngg & schaddeuyngg the vryne aboven: 3yf

348 3yf] Ad4Ad7W7, hit S15, *sign om.* Sj3

the vryne be in partie blew, hit tokneth peyne atte herte, schorthed of breth
that cometh of the lunges, and peyne in the brayn. And 3yf the vryne [be]
nout3 | blew and syche a sky schadueth the vryne abovyn, hit tokneth   f. 13ᵛ
chauffyng of the lyuere and specialy & the froth be yelw.   361

{ *Circulus*} Cercle thykke and litel colourid tokneth payne in the braynes.
A cercle thykke colourid or as reed purpill tokneth peyne in the forhed. A
cercle blak or whyt, thynne & litel colourid, tokneth peyne in the lyft syde
of the heued. A cercle thynne & heye of colour, as reed or yelw: hit tokneth   365
peyne in the ri3t syde of the hed. A cercle colourid as leed tokneth epilensie.
A cercle grene tokneth waueryng in the hed and brennyng in the stomak.
A[nd] 3yf hit appere in an hoot access, hit tokneth frenesy that cometh of
colore. A cercle that ys colourid as brith blew: 3yf hit tremell, hit tokneth
deth and namly in an hoot access. A cercle thykke and blak oueral tokneth   370
dethe. A cercle that quaketh: hit tokneth peyne fro the nekke down to the
rygbons ende.

Greyns that dwellyn in the cercle & after castyng of the vryne goon
down & after rysen vp agayn to the sercle tokneth rewme in the heued.
3yf they goon down & tourne nout3 agayn to the scercle, than they tokne   375
rewme in the brest, in the lunges, and 'in' the spleen. And 3yf thow see two
smale greyns in the secunde regioun or moor or lesse knyt to a smal sky,
hit tokneth peyne in the brest of rewme & a wyckyd stomake and a badde
lyuere & a badde lunges &c. *Explicit. Hic intrat.*

359 be] Ad7Sj3W7, *om.* S15Ad4   362 Cercle] Cercle wyth S15Ad4, Item a a serkyll
Sj3, A serkyl 'þat ys' wyth W7, Cercle al whyt wyþ Ad7   368 And] Ad4Ad7Sj3W7, A
S15

APPENDICES

APPENDIX I

THE LATIN VADE MECUM SUITE

Texts

A. *TWENTY COLOURS BY DIGESTION GROUPS*

Ashmole 391, Part V, f. 10^r (A; s. xiv^{ex}, after 1387)

In this illustrated text, the colour descriptions are given in the outer ring of a single-wheel diagram; coloured flasks fill a ring inside the outer ring, with lines drawn to seven interior roundels. The roundels contain the names of the digestion groups and the number of urines in each group; a central roundel contains the title of the text. The colours and digestion-group roundels begin with Albus and Indigestion at the bottom of the wheel and proceed clockwise around the circle.

f. 10^r

Tabula de iudiciis vrinarum per colores

Iste quatuor vrine significant indigestionem.
  Albus color vrine vt aqua fontis.
  Glaucus color vrine ut cornu lucidum.
  Lacteus color vrine ut serum lactis.   5
  Karopos color vrine ut vellus cameli.

Iste due vrine significant principium digestionis.
  S⟨ubpallidus co⟩lor ut succus ⟨car⟩nis semicocte remissus.
  ⟨Pallidus color ut succu⟩s carnis semicocte non remissus.

Iste due vrine significant mediatam digestionem.   10
  Subcitrinus color ut pomi citrini remissus.
  Citrinus ut color pomi citrini non remissus.

 Iste due vrine significant perfectam digestionem.
  Subrufus color vrine ut aurum remissum.
  Rufus color vrine ut aurum purum.   15

Iste quatuor vrine significant excessum digestionis.
  Subrubeus color urine ut crocus occidentalis.

8, 9 *Readings obscured by tight binding*   16 vrine] vri[*line end*]rine

Rubeus color vrine ut crocus orientalis.
Subrubicundus color ut flamma ignis remissa.
20   Rubicundus vt flamma ignis non remissa.

Iste tres vrine significant nimiam adustionem.
Ynopos color vrine ut color epatis.
Kyanos color vrine ut vinum nigrum.
Uiridis color vrine ut caulis.

25   Iste tres vrine significant mortificacionem.
Liuidus color vrine ut plumbum.
Niger color adustionis ut incaustum.
Niger color mortificacionis ut cornu nigrum.

B. *URINA RUFA*

Although this text and the *Cleansing of Blood* text below may occur in either order in their Middle English translations, the Latin versions that accompany urine wheels in English manuscripts usually put the practical diagnostic *Urina Rufa* text first, followed by the more abstract overview in *Cleansing of Blood*, an order followed here. The abbreviation *sig^t* is expanded as 'significat', matching the occasional full spelling; '.s.' in *Cleansing of Blood* is expanded as 'scilicet'; and the 7-shaped symbol for 'et' is expanded as such.

The Latin version from Ashmole 391 is followed by the unique, mixed Latin/English adaptation of the text in Digby 29, a manuscript written mainly by Richard Stapulton, Master of Balliol College *c.*1430 and donor of the manuscript to the college. Stapulton's presence in Oxford is documented from 1411 to 1433. The Digby text is included here for its linguistic interest.[1] Stapulton may have been responsible for the adaptation, though there are some omissions and errors in the text that suggest he was copying, at least partly, rather than composing. His abbreviations *.s.*, *sig^t*, and *v.* are expanded as 'significat' and 'vrina' where appropriate, although in some cases they might have been intended as 'signifieth' and 'vrine'; his +-shaped symbol for 'et' or 'and' is expanded as appropriate for the linguistic context. In a few instances, his forms of the letters *e* and *o* can be difficult to distinguish.

---

[1]   Based on the English texts on ff. 125^r–128^v, 243^v last 6 lines, and 303^v, *LALME* identifies the dialect of the Digby 29 scribe as 'probably of SE Notts' (i. 147). On Stapulton, see *BRUO* iii. 1766, Macray 1999 (1883): 25, and Hunt and Watson 1999: 18.

Ashmole 391, Part V, ff. 2vb–3rb, supplemented with material from Bodley 648, ff. 5^r–6^v (B), a grammatically less accurate but slightly fuller text, written at Canterbury *c.*1465[2]

Restat postea figura de vrin[i]s   f. 2vb

Urina rufa significat salutem et bonam disposicionem corporis humani. Urina subrufa sanitate[m] bonam significat, sed non ita perfecte sicut rufa [omnino *add.* B]. Urina citrina quando est cum substancia mediocri et quando circulus est eiusdem coloris est laudabilis, et eciam 5 subcitrina licet non ita perfecte sicut [omnino *add.* B] citrina. Urina rubea sicut rosa significat febrem effimeram, et si continue mingatur, significat febrem continuam. Urina rubea sicut sanguis in vitro significat febrem ex nimio sanguine, et tunc statim debet fieri minucio, nisi luna fuerit in signo Geminorum. Urina viridis quando mingitur post rubeam 10 significat adustionem, et est mortalis. Urina rubea a claritate omnino remota declinacionem morbi significat. Urina rubea permixta aliquantulum nigredine epatis calefactionem significat. Urina pallida significat defectionem stomachi et impedimentum secunde digestionis. Urina alba sicut aqua fontis [in sanis *add.* B] significat cruditatem humorum, et in 15 acutis febribus est mortalis. Urina lactea et cum spissa substancia—et si accidit in mulieribus non est ita periculosum sicut in viris propter indispociciones matricis—tamen in acutis febribus est mortalis. Item vrina lactea superius et inferius | obumbrata, circa mediam regionem clara, f. 3ra ydropisim significat. Item vrina in ydropico rufa vel subrufa mortem 20 significat. Urina karapos significat multitudinem humorum corruptorum, sicut accidit in fleumatico, ydropico, podagrico, et sic de alijs. Urina nigra

1 vrinis] vrins   3 sanitatem] sanitate   10 signo] medio signi B
16 febribus est] est febribus, *with baseline virgules indicating reordering (and cf. line 18 below)*   22 fleumatico ydropico . . . Urina] fleumatico ydropico and alijs U *written over erasures*

---

[2] Other manuscripts containing the Latin texts of *Urina Rufa* and *Cleansing of Blood* and of likely English origin include the following:

BL: Egerton 2852, 16^v–18^v; Harley 5311, f. I, face Di (folding almanac); Royal 17 C.xxiv, ff. 1^r–4^r; Sloane 7, ff. 60^v–61^v; Sloane 1388, ff. 38^v–39^v.

Bodl.: Ashmole 789, f. 366^{ra-b}; Ashmole 1481, ff. 2^v–3^v, 42^{rv}; Bodley 591, ff. 33^r–34^v; Hatton 29, ff. 75^v–77^v, and 78^r–79^v; Rawlinson D.1221, ff. 9^r–10^v.

Cambridge: CUL Ii.6.17, ff. 42^r–47^r; Gonville and Caius 413/630, ff. 32^r–34^v; Pepys 878, pp. 108–10; St John's E.6, ff. 88^r–90^r (in the Herbal of Thomas Betson, librarian of Syon Abbey, 1516; ed. Adams and Forbes 2014); TCC R.1.86, ff. 1^v–4^r; TCC O.9.31, f. 28^{rv}. Digitized copies of the Trinity manuscripts may be accessed through the online James Catalogue: https://mss-cat.trin.cam.ac.uk/search.php

Philadelphia: Rosenbach Museum MS 1004/29, f. 9, face D (folding almanac).

Current location unknown: the Dickson Wright MS (ed. Talbot 1961; folding almanac, whose more recent ownership history is partially traced in Gumbert 2016: 132).

potest esse ex calore naturali extincto, et tunc est mortalis; uel potest esse
propter expulsionem materie venenose, que expellitur per uias vrinales,
25 et tunc significat salutem. In quartana autem semper est mortalis et mala.
Urina lucida sicut cornu significat indisposiciones splenis et disposiciones
quartane. Urena crocea cum spissa substancia fetida et spumosa ictericiam
significat. Urina rufa vel subrufa inferius habens resoluciones rotundas
et albas, superius aliquantulum pinguis, febrem ethicam significat. Urina
30 a fundo uasis usque ad medietatem clara, postea uero spissa [et tenuis
add. B], grauedinem pectoris significat. Urina spumosa et clara et quasi
subrubea dolorem in dextro [latere add. B] magis quam in sinistro significat. Urina alba et spumosa significat maiorem dolorem in sinistro latere
quam in dextro. Frigidius est enim sinistrum latus quam dexterum. Urina
35 tenuis [et pallida et clara add. B] acetosum fleuma significat. Si circulus
[vrine add. B] nullo quiescente tremulus apparuerit, decursum fleumatis
et aliorum humorum a capite per collum et per posteriora ad inferiora significat. Urina spissa et plumbea, circa mediam regionem nigra, paralasim
significat. Urina spissa et lactea et pauca et crassa inferius cum squamis
40 lapidem demonstrat. Urina sine squamis spissa et lactea et pauca fluxum
ventris significat. Urina spissa et lactea et multa guttam in superioribus
partibus vel in inferioribus membris significat. Urina inferius pallida in
f. 3ʳᵇ uiris dolorem renum, in mu | lieribus uero uicium matricis significat. Urina
in qua frustra apparent, si pauca sit et turbosa, vene rupturam circa renes
45 et uesicam significat. Urina in qua sanies apparet in fundo uasis contiguam
renum et uesice putredinem vel apostema significat. Et si in tota vrina
sanies apparet, tocius corporis putredinem significat. Urina in qua frustra
apparent parua et lata uesice excoriacionem significat. Urina athomosa per
multum tempus lapidem in renibus significat. Urina alba sine febre in viris
50 et in mulieribus aliquando dolorem renum, aliquando imprignacionem
mulierum, significat. Urina pregnancium, si vnum mensem vel duos vel
tres habuerint, debet esse multum clara, et albam ypostosim debet habere
in fundo. Si vero quatuor menses habuerint, vrina debet esse serena et
ypostosis alba et grossa in fundo. Solet ymago in [vase add. B] vrinali
55 tanquam in speculo apparere: si vrina illa sit mulieris, concepcionem
factam significat. Et si ymago iudicantis appareat in urina pacientis, febres
interpollatas vel epaticam egritudinem [vel add. B] prolixitatem morbi significat. Urina spumosa ventositatem stomachi in mulieribus vel ardorem
in vmbilico usque ad guttur et sitim significat. Urina vero virginis quasi
60 subcitrina debet esse, unde vrina liuida et nimis serena uirginem declarat

---

33 et] vel B   36 quiescente] inquiescente B   38–40 Urina spissa et plumbea . . . lapidem demonstrat] *two signs reversed* B   44 frustra] frustula B   turbosa]
turbida B

constantem. Urina [vero *add*. B] turbida in qu[a] semen aparuerit in
fundo mulierem retentam cum viro significat. Urina vero mulieris densa
eam esse corruptam [tunc *add*. B] declarat [predictam *add*. B]. [Urina]
saltem turbida in qua semen apparuerit in fundo vasis, si vero fuerit talis
vrina in viro, eum retentum cum muliere coisse autem declarat. Mulieres 65
menstruate faciunt vrinam sanguineam. Et si iste sanguis sit coagulatus in
muliere, apparebit pregnans donec dissoluatur. [Dissolucio patet in antidodam. Urina multum nigra mulieris superueniet, si mota aliquantulum
ruborem habuerit, solucionem menstruorum significat *add*. B]

Digby 29, ff. 75ᵛ–76ᵛ (s. xvⁱⁿ; anglicana script; mixed Latin and occasional English;
English italicized for visibility)

Hic sequuntur secundum alios nature vrinarum sub compendio.   f. 75ᵛ

Prima vrina colorata ut auɪum significat bonam digestionem et sanitatem
commendandam. 2 *as fadid gold* significat salutem, non tamen tam bonam.
3 Vrina *as fox or no3t so rede*, si circulus sit consimilis coloris, significat
febrem cotidianam. 4 Vrina rubea sicut rosa significat similiter febrem co-   5
tidianam. 5 Vrina rubea ut sanguis significat febres generatas de sanguine
superfluo. 6 Vrina viridis, *3if red as blak go tofore*, significat adustionem et
mortem. 7 Vrina nigra proximo post rubeum mortem significat, si vrina
tam rubea non precedat. 8 *Rede sumdele dyrke* notat infirmitatem et siccitatem epatis propter calorem. 9 Vrina alba sicut aqua in viro significat 10
frigidum stomacum et digestionem debelem; et si febrem habeat, significat mortem. 10 Vrina pallida significat defectum stomachi. xj Vrina *as qwit
as qway and picke is nou3t so perloys in woman as in man, by cheson of þe ma-
ries; neuer þeles* in febribus significat mortem. 12 Vrina *as qwhey picke aboue
and bene þe and clere toknys þe dropesi*. 13 Vrina in viro ydropico sicut au- 15
rum bonum puratum significat mortem. 14 Vrina sicut pellis camely [*blank
space of about 15 chars. or 3–4 words*] et spiss[a] significat congregacionem
malorum humorum, et ydropicum, potagricum, et huiusmodi. 15 Vrina ni-
gra significat mortem, quia calor naturalis con | sumitur, excepto quod in f. 76ʳ
muliere significat purgacionem humorum venenosorum. 16 Vrina *remisse* 20
nigra in febre quartana mortem significat. 17 Vrina splendens ut cornu in
qua sunt splendentes *rowes* significat *infirmite of þe mylte* et ordinacionem
febre quartane. 18 Vrina *3elow* et spiss[a] et fetens cum spuma eiusdem coloris significat ictoriciam. 19 Vrina rubea sicut aurum vstum, infra quam

61 qua] qu   62 retentam] recentem B   63 Urina] B, *om.* A   65 reten-
tum] recentem B   66 faciunt] *text slightly blotted*   **Digby 29** 17 spissa] spiss*us*
22 splendentes] *final* s *poss. added in different ink*   23 spissa] spissu*m*   fetens] *poss.*
corr. from fetons

25 sunt viue parue resoluciones, si pinguedo supernatauerit, significat febrem
cotidianam. 20 Vrina spissa cuius residencia est clara significat dolorem
pectoris. 21 Vrina *remisse* rubea et spumosa significat infirmitatem in latere
dextro. 22 Vrina alba et clara et spumosa significat infirmitatem in sinistra
parte. 23 Vrina spissa et plumbos[a] et nigra in medio significat parali-
30 sim. 24 Vrina alba ut serum spissa et modica et pinguis ad intra significat
fluxum, et si in illa sint parue squame, significat lapidem. 25 Vrina alba ut
serum et spiss[a] in qua sunt plures resoluciones significat guttam. 26 Vrina
sanguinea significat fracturam in renibus cuiusdam vene uel aliter lesuram
vesice. 27 Vrina in qua apparet putredo vlceris in zedimine significat putre-
35 faccionem apostomatis in rene uel vesica. Si totum appareat putrifactum,
significat putrifaccionem tocius corporis. 28 Vrina in qua sunt viue parue
sqwame significat quod vesica est excoriata ad intra. 29 Vrina habens plura
parua scissa in finibus significat lapidem in renibus. 30 Vrina viua in ho-
mine significat infirmitatem in renibus; in muliere quod est consumpta
40 [*error for* concepta]. 31 Vrina mulieris inprignate ij uel iij mensibus est
clara et habet viuam residenciam, et maioris etatis puero maioris residencie
est vrina. 32 Vrina mulieris vbi apparet nostra ymago significat euidentem
concepcionem. Et talis vrina hominis significat febrem uel infirmitatem
epatis et longam perseueranciam in eadem infirmitate. 33 Vrina mulieris
45 spumosa significat infirmitatem stomachi, fistularum et pulmonum, et magnam adustionem ab vmbilico ad guttur et magnam sitim. 34 Vrina vnius
intigre virginis pulcra clara et aliqualiter rubea. 35 Vrina turbida in qua
apparet semen humanum in residencia significat cognicionem seu congricionem viri recentem. 36 Vrina mulieris turbita sicut vrina bestie in qua
50 est *strene* significat infirmitatem uulue *and of þe meryes*. 37 Mulieris nigra
f. 76ᵛ et | in iactura quodammodo rubea significat mundacionem *of þe meryes*.
38 Vrina rubea sicut sanguis per totum significat menstruositatem.

C. *CLEANSING OF BLOOD*

Ashmole 391, Part V, f. 3ᵛᵃ, supplemented with occasional material from Bodley
648

f. 3ᵛᵃ Omnis vrina est colamentum sanguinis et est duarum rerum proprie
significatiua. Aut enim significat passiones epatis et venarum aut vesice et
renum. Aliarum rerum est improprie significatiua.

25, 36, 38, 41 viue, viua, viuam] *apparent errors for forms of* albus (*cf. corresponding readings
in Ashmole 391, Part V*), *possibly by some kind of confusion betwen* qwit *and* quic   27 rubea
et] -a et *written above erasure*   29 plumbosa] plumbos*us*   32 spissa] spiss*um*

In vrina consideranda sunt diuersa, scilicet substancia, colores, regiones, et contenta. [Aliud est causa substancie; aliud causa coloris *add*. B]; 5
aliud causa sediminis.

Cum enim in humano corpore quatuor qualitates, scilicet caliditas, frigiditas, siccitas, et humiditas, sint cause substancie et coloris. Caliditas est
causa coloris rubei; frigiditas [est causa coloris *add*. B] albi; siccitas est
causa tenuis substancie; et humiditas [est causa *add*. B] spisse [substancie 10
add. B].

Urina in quatuor partes diuiditur. Superior est circulus, 2ᵃ corpus aeris,
3ᵃ perforacio, 4ᵃ fundus. Per circulum [egritudo *add*. B] capitis et cerebri,
per corpus aeris [egritudo *add*. B] spiritualium membrorum et stomachi, per perforacionem epatis et splenis, per fundum renum et matricis 15
et inferiorum membrorum accidencia iudicamus.

Urina habet tres regiones, scilicet infimam, mediam, et suppremam. Infima incipit a fundo nasis [vrinalio *add*. B] et durat per spacium duorum
digitorum. Media regio incipit vbi terminatur infima et durat usque ad
circulum, qui circulus est in supprema regione. 20

Et quando in ista supprema regione est spuma, significat ventositatem
ebullientem in vijs vrinalibus uel inflacionem vel aliud vicium pulmonis.
Circulus vero grossus significat nim[i]am replecionem in capite et dolorem. In regione media, quedam nebula est in sanis malum signum, sed
in febricitantibus, significat digestionem materie morbi. In infima regione 25
sunt aliquando quidam lapilli arenosi, et tunc denotat quod paciens est
calculosus. Et aliquando sedimen est nigrum, et tunc nisi fuerit per talem
vrinam expulsio materie venenose, est signu⟨m⟩ mort⟨is⟩.

Translations

A. *TWENTY COLOURS BY DIGESTION GROUPS*

Ashmole 391, Part V, f. 10ʳ

Table of the judgements of urines by colours

These four urines signify a lack of digestion:
   Clear colour of urine like water of a well.
   Glaucus colour of urine like shining horn.
   Milky colour of urine like whey.
   Karopos colour of urine like a camel's pelt.

23 nimiam] nimeam   28 signum mortis] *text slightly rubbed at end*

These two urines signify the beginning of digestion.
    Palish like broth of half-cooked meat, light in colour.
    Pale like the broth of half-cooked meat, not light.

These two urines signify intermediate digestion.
    Pale yellow colour like a yellow fruit, light in colour.
    Yellow like the colour of a yellow fruit, not light.

These two urines signify complete digestion.
    Light reddish colour of urine like pale gold.
    Reddish colour of urine like pure gold.

These four urines signify an excess of digestion.
    Light red colour of urine like western saffron.
    Red colour of urine like eastern saffron.
    Light rubicund colour like a pale flame of fire.
    Rubicund colour like a flame of fire, not pale.

These three urines signify extreme overheating.
    Inopos colour of urine like the colour of liver.
    Kyanos colour of urine like black wine.
    Green colour of urine like kale.

These three urines signify dying.
    Wan colour of urine like lead.
    Black colour of overheating like ink.
    Black colour of dying like black horn.

B. *URINA RUFA*

Ashmole 391, Part V, ff. 2vb–3rb

The diagram of urines appears below.

Reddish urine signifies health and good disposition of the human body.

    Pale reddish urine signifies good health, but not as perfectly as reddish urine does.

    Yellow urine with a moderate thickness and a circle of the same colour is praiseworthy; and so too is pale yellow urine, though not as perfectly as yellow urine.

    Urine that is red as a rose signifies an ephemeral fever; and if it is passed continually, it signifies a continual fever.

Urine that is red as blood in a glass vial signifies a fever from too much blood; in that instance, bloodletting should be done immediately, unless the moon is in the sign of Gemini.

Urine that is green when it is passed and after red signifies overheating and is fatal.

Red urine that is entirely lacking clarity signifies the decline of disease.

Red urine somewhat mixed with blackness signifies heating of the liver.

Pale urine signifies a disorder in the stomach and an inhibition of the second digestion.

Urine that is clear as the water of a well signifies an undigested state of the humours and in acute fevers it is fatal.

If thick milky urine occurs in women it is not as dangerous as in men, on account of disorders of the uterus; in acute fevers, however, it is fatal.

Also, urine that is milky above, shadowed below, and clear in the middle region signifies dropsy.

Also, reddish or pale reddish urine in a dropsical patient signifies death.

Karapos urine signifies many corrupt humours, as happens in patients who suffer from excess phlegm, dropsy, gout, and also other things.

Black urine can be from the quenching of natural heat, and then it is fatal; or it can be caused by the expulsion of poisonous matter through the urinary vessels, and then it signifies health. In a quartan fever, however, it is always fatal and evil.

Urine that is bright as horn signifies disorders of the spleen and tendencies towards the quartan fever.

Thick saffron-coloured urine that is fetid and foamy signifies jaundice.

Reddish or pale reddish urine that has round white precipitates below and is somewhat greasy above signifies hectic fever.

Urine that is clear from the bottom to the middle of the flask and afterwards thick signifies heaviness of the chest.

Urine foamy, clear, and somewhat pale red signifies pain in the right side more than in the left.

Urine clear and foamy signifies greater pain in the left side than in the right, for the left side is colder than the right.

Thin, sour urine signifies phlegm.

If the circle appears tremulous with no resting, it signifies the descent of phlegm and other humours from the head by way of the neck and the posterior parts to the lower parts.

Thick, lead-coloured urine that is black in the middle region signifies palsy [or paralysis].

Urine that is thick, milky, sparse, and heavy below with scales signifies the stone.

Urine that is thick, milky, and sparse without scales signifies a flux of the belly [*or* womb].

Urine that is thick, milky, and plentiful signifies gout in the upper parts or lower members.

Urine that is pale below signifies kidney pain in men, a disease of the uterus in women.

Urine in which small chips appear, if it is sparse and cloudy, signifies a rupture of a vein near the kidneys and bladder.

Urine in which pus appears in the bottom of the flask signifies festering or an abscess near the kidneys and bladder. And if pus appears in the entire urine sample, it signifies rotting of the entire body.

Urine in which small, broad chips appear signifies abrasion of the bladder.

Urine that contains tiny particles for a long time signifies kidney stones.

Clear urine without fever in men and in women sometimes signifies pain in the kidneys and sometimes the impregnation of women.

Urine of pregnant women who have been so for one or two or three months should be very clear and should have a white sediment in the bottom of the flask. If they have been pregnant for four months, the urine should be calm and the sediment white and thick in the bottom of the flask.

An image customarily appears in the urine flask as if in a mirror: if it is a woman's urine, this signifies that conception has occurred; and if the image of the person judging should appear in the urine of the patient, it signifies intermittent fevers or a liver disorder [or] an extended illness.

Foamy urine in women signifies gassiness of the stomach or a burning from the navel to the throat and thirst.

The urine of a virgin should be more or less pale yellow; wan and extremely calm urine declares a constant virgin.

Cloudy urine in which semen appears in the bottom of the flask signifies that the woman was held by a man.

Thick urine of a woman declares her to be corrupt.

Cloudy urine in which seed appears in the bottom of the flask, if such urine should be in a man, it declares that he was held by and had sex with a woman.

Menstruating women make bloody urine. And if that blood should be coagulated in a woman, she will appear pregnant until it is dissolved. [*B adds*: The dissolution is made clear in the *Antidotary*. The very black urine of a woman will follow; if it has some redness when shaken, it signifies the release of the menses.]

Digby 29, ff. 75ᵛ–76ᵛ

Here follow the natures of urine according to some, in brief.

The first urine, coloured like gold, signifies good digestion and health, which is praiseworthy.

The second, like faded gold, signifies health, but not so good.

3. Urine that is fox-coloured or not so red, if the circle is of similar colour, signifies a cotidian fever.

4. Urine red as a rose likewise signifies a cotidian fever.

5. Urine red as blood signifies fevers generated from excess blood.

6. Green urine, if red as black goes before, signifies overheating and death.

7. Black urine, soon after red, signifies death, so long as red urine did not come first.

8. [Urine that is] red, somewhat dark, indicates sickness and dryness of the liver on account of heat.

9. Urine clear as water in a man signifies a cold stomach and weak digestion; and if he has a fever, it signifies death.

10. Pale urine signifies a disorder of the stomach.

11. Urine as white as whey and thick is not so perilous in woman as in man, because of the uterus; nevertheless in fevers it signifies death.

12. Urine like whey, thick above and beneath and clear, betokens the dropsy.

13. Urine like good refined gold in a dropsical man signifies death.

14. Urine like the pelt of a camel [*blank space*] and thick signifies a gathering of evil humours, and a dropsical [or] gouty patient and such like.

15. Black urine signifies death, because the natural heat is consumed, except that in a woman it signifies purging of poisonous humours.

16. Dull black urine in a quartan fever signifies death.

17. Urine shining like horn in which there are shining streaks signifies infirmity of the spleen and the regulation of a quartan fever.

18. Yellow urine, thick and stinking with foam of the same colour, signifies jaundice.

19. Urine red as burnt gold, within which are small lively [*error for* white] precipitates, if grease floats above, signifies a cotidian fever.

20. Thick urine whose sediment is clear signifies pain of the chest.

21. Dull red and foamy urine signifies infirmity in the right side.

22. White, clear, and foamy urine signifies infirmity in the left side.

23. Thick, lead-coloured urine, black in the middle, signifies palsy [*or* paralysis].

24. Urine white as whey, thick and sparse and greasy within signifies a flux; and if there are small scales in it, it signifies the stone.

25. Urine white as whey and thick, in which there is a heavy sediment, signifies gout.

26. Bloody urine signifies a rupture of some vein in the kidneys or else an injury to the bladder.

27. Urine in which pus from a sore appears in the sediment signifies festering of an abscess in the kidney or the bladder. If the whole [sample] appears putrefied, it signifies festering of the whole body.

28. Urine in which there are small, lively [*error for* white] scales signifies that the bladder has been abraded within.

29. Urine having many small bits cut in the ends signifies kidney stones.

30. Lively [*error for* White] urine in man signifies infirmity in the kidneys; in a woman, that she is consumptive [*error for* has conceived].

31. Urine of a woman pregnant for two or three months is clear and has a lively [*error for* white] sediment; and the greater the age of the child, the greater the urine's sediment.

32. Urine of a woman in which our image appears signifies manifest conception; and such urine in a man signifies fever or infirmity of the liver and long continuation in the same infirmity.

33. Foamy urine of a woman signifies infirmity of the stomach, of the airways and of the lungs, and a great burning from the navel to the throat and great thirst.

34. The urine of an untouched virgin is fair, clear, and somewhat red.

35. Cloudy urine in which the seed of man appears in the sediment signifies recent knowledge of or congress with a man.

36. Urine of a woman that is cloudy like the urine of a beast, in which there is sperm, signifies a disorder of the vulva and of the uterus.

37. [Urine] of a woman black and somewhat red upon shaking signifies the cleansing of the uterus.

38. Urine red as blood throughout signifies menstruation.

C. *CLEANSING OF BLOOD*

Ashmole 391, Part V, f. 3va

Every urine is a cleansing of the blood, and it properly signifies two things: either it signifies disorders of the liver and the veins or of the bladder and the kidneys. It signifies other things improperly.

In urine, diverse things should be considered, namely substance, colours, regions, and contents. One thing is the cause of substance, another is the cause of colour, and another is the cause of the sediment.

Since there are four qualities in the human body, namely heat, cold, dryness, and moistness, they are the causes of substance and colour. Heat is the cause of red colour, cold of white, dryness is the cause of thin substance, and moistness of thick.

Urine is divided into four parts. The highest is the circle, the second the body of air, the third the *perforatio*, the fourth the ground. By the circle we judge the circumstances of the head and brain, by the body of air those of the spiritual members and stomach, by the *perforatio* those of the liver and spleen, by the ground those of the kidneys, uterus, and lower members.

Urine has three regions, namely the lowest, the middle, and the highest. The lowest begins with the bottom of the flask and extends for the space of two fingers. The middle region begins where the lowest ends and lasts to the circle, which is in the highest region.

And when there is foam in this highest region, it signifies gassiness boiling into the urinary vessels or distension or some other disorder of the lung. A large circle signifies extreme fullness and pain in the head. In the middle region, a certain cloud is an evil sign in healthy people, but in those suffering from fever, it signifies breaking down of the matter of the illness. In the lowest region, there are sometimes certain little sandy particles, which denotes that the patient suffers from the stone. And sometimes the sediment is black, and unless there is an expulsion of poisonous matter by means of such urine, that is a sign of death.

APPENDIX II

UROSCOPY TEXT FROM THE
LETTRE D'HIPPOCRATE

Harley 2558, f. 175^{rv}

Text

Texts D, E, and F are all derived, more or less closely, from the series of uro-scopic signs incorporated in the French *Lettre d'Hippocrate*, described by Tony Hunt as 'the most influential collection of vernacular medical receipts before 1300' (T. Hunt 1990: 100) and by Claude de Tovar as 'un des textes les plus copiés au Moyen Age' (Tovar 1973–4: 129). That text 'probably . . . first appeared in French', but was disseminated widely in both Anglo-Norman and Continental versions;[1] its length and content vary considerably in its numerous manuscript witnesses. In its fuller versions, the *Lettre* includes a brief prologue invoking the authority of Hippocrates, a short humoral text, a list of urines and their diagnostic significance, and a collection of recipes for ailments from head to toe.[2] The numbers of urines and of recipes in the two latter sections of the *Lettre* are both highly mutable.

The fullest version of the urine text in the *Lettre* is found in BL, MS Harley 2558 (H; this text dated s. xiv[1]),[3] which is edited here, although it includes at least two significant omissions, affecting two pairs of uroscopic signs in a series of twenty-nine (signs 15–16 and 24–5 below). Those omissions are supplied from the next fullest version of the text, a copy made in northern France, Vatican City, Reg. lat. MS 1211 (V; s. xiv; Södergärd 1981). Further variation is reported from the Anglo-Norman copies found in Cambridge, Trinity College MSS O.1.20 (O; s. xiii[2])[4] and O.5.32 (T; s. xiii; T. Hunt 1990); and from two more Continental French copies,

---

[1] T. Hunt 2011: 18; cf. T. Hunt 1990: 101: 'an essentially vernacular work'. Hunt appears to take an agnostic stance as to whether the text originated in an insular or Continental environment, though Tovar speaks of the *Lettre* as 'ce texte anglo-normand' (1973–4: 177 n. 1).

[2] For studies and editions of the *Lettre d'Hippocrate*, see the bibliographic materials reported in T. Hunt 2011: 15–19 nn. and 41 n. 1; Tavormina 2007: 632–3 nn. 2–4.

[3] See T. Hunt 2011: 'one of the fullest and most coherent versions' (p. 18), and similarly described in Tovar 1973–4: 'parmi les copies anciennes anglo-normandes, la plus complète' (p. 136). Harley 2558 was compiled and partially written by Thomas Fayreford, a medical practitioner active in south-west England in the second quarter of the fifteenth century (Jones 1998 and 2008: 3–4). For earlier studies of Harley 2558, see T. Hunt 1987, Jones 1995. A digitized copy of Harley MS 2558 may be found on the British Library website: www.bl.uk/manuscripts/FullDisplay.aspx?ref=Harley_MS_2558.

[4] For a digitized copy of Trinity MS O.1.20, see the online James Catalogue: https://msscat.trin.cam.ac.uk/search.php.

Paris, Bibliothèque nationale de France, MS nouv. acq. fr. 10034 (N; s. xiii; To-var 1973–4: 177–9) and London, Wellcome Library MS 546 (W; *c.*1340; T. Hunt 2011: 42–3). Variants are selective, chosen either to correct errors or for their cor-respondence with one or more Middle English versions of the text. Four more witnesses are cited in the textual commentary and apparatus to the main text but not in the apparatus below: Y=BL, MS Harley 978 (*c.*1240–50); C=Cambridge, Corpus Christi College, MS 388 (*c.* 1320–30); S=BL, MS Sloane 2412 (s. xiv); F= CUL, MS Ff.1.33 (1420).

Curls at the ends of words are normally transcribed as -*e* or -*er*, depending on context; barred final *h* is transcribed as -*he*. Word-initial *Ll*- and *Pp*- are transcribed as *L* and *P* respectively; abbreviations (e.g. for *signefie*, *femme*, etc.) are spelled out. Punctuation, capitalization, and word-division follow modern practice. Token numbers have been added for ease of reference.

[Prologue] Ens quatre parties de le corps la nesaunce de sante & de enfer-   f. 175ʳ
mete est demostre: al le chef, al ventre, al esplen, a la vessie, le quele choses
cuuente issi cunustre.

[1] Ly hume serrat seyn si la vrine est blanche de tut le matin, deuant le
manger ruge, apres manger blanch.   5

[2] Le vrine crase truble & [pouaunt]: cele n'est pas bone.

[3] Le vrine mult tenue & nent trible bon est.

[4] Le vrine qui est feueruse, cele est truble cum vrine de anne, signefie
dolour del chef preceynement auenir.

[5] Le vrine en feures al setime jur termine, si al quarte jur blanche & al   10
secunde jur ruge, cel signefie garisun.

[6] Le vrine crasse & mult blaunche, sicum icele est qui est de moustes
humurs, signefie auenir quartime feuere.

[7] Le vrine qui est sanglente signefie la vessie estre blesse de acune
pourture qui dedeyns i ad.   15

[8] Le vrine petite & charnuse & crase & cum ele fust uelue coe signefie
le mal de les reyns.

[9] Ky sang estale senz mals, si il ad veyne rumpue es reynns.

[10] Le vrine qui semble pudrouse signefie la vessie bleche.

6 pouaunt] puans V, poy hu*m* ad H, poi en i a O, .i. pou W, *om.* TN   8 feueruse] enfievrés V, en feure O, en figures N, *om.* T, *sign om.* W   cele] se ele VON, *om.* T, *sign om.* W   10 en feures] enfievré V, savereuse T, en figures NW, *om.* O   16 uelue] velue V, uelu O, veluye T, voulue N, pleine de pierres W   18 Ky sang . . . reynns]et qu'il a vaine rompue (*added to prec. sign*) V, Qui sanc crache sanz mal si a ueine corrompue es rains W, *om.* OTN   19 pudrouse] poureuse V, poudrouse OT, *sign om.* NW

20   [11] Le vrine sanguente & for mise od peccoies de sang signefie grant
mal dedeyns le corps & meisment en la vessie.

[12] Le vrine qui chet par gutettes & si noe desure cum ampules signefie
long enfermete.

[13] Vrine qui noe desure vn crasse royle angue & lunge enfermete si-
25   gnefie.

[14] Le vrine a femme pure & clere si al vrinal relut cum argent icele
femme suuent vomist & si n'at nul talent de manger signefie la femme estre
enceynte.

[15] Le vrine a femme blanche & puaunte & peisaunte signefie dolour
30   de reyns & le matriz [plain de mal d'enfermete de froit.

[16] Le vrine de femme que a escume de] sang desure, qui est clere cum
euwe, signefie dolure de chef & talent de manger & de dormir pur l'emflure
del estomac aueyr perdu.

[17] Vrina a femme ke est de colours de ore & clere & peysaunte signefie
35   la femme auer talent de auer a fere od humme.

[18] Le vrine a femme qui ait ferine espurgement, si la femme ad la
quartayne feure, signefie ke ele murra al teers jur.

[19] Vrine a femme qui est de peys & de colur de plum, si ele est en-
f. 175ᵛ   ceynte, signefie l'enfauntes | estre mort; & si ele n'est pas enceynte, signe-
40   fie le matriz purrir & si est cele vrine puaunte.

[20] Vrine a femme qui est emfle & qui [ad] la tuse & la menisun se cele
est de colur de lin signefie la femme qui ne peyt pas estre sey[n]e.

[21] De vrines de humme & de femme qui malades sey[e]nt de la dolur del chef, si ert tel sa vrine vn gros cercle auerat eyns blanche v ruge &
45   si li cercles est ruge, ceo signefie qe trop ad abundaunce de sang al chef,
dunt est humme a seyner de la veyne capital. & si ceus est deuaunt la seyne
prendre medecine Paulin v theodoricon v adrian v piles diacosti.

20 peccoies] pieretes V, perettes T, petites gotes (peçotes N) ON, *sign om.* W
21 meisment] meisemement VO, nomément T, malvaisement N, *sign om.* W   24 royle]
sign om. V, ryke (*but with* roielee *ins. in adjacent 'com argent' sign*) O, rouele T, *om.* W, *sign*
om. N   angue] *sign om.* V, ague O, auke T, fieure ague W, *sign om.* N   30 le matriz]
HO, la marcie T, le vis V, *add* porrie et N, *add* estre W   30–1 plain . . . escume de]
VOTNW, *om.* H   32–3 l'emflure del estomac] HVOTN, la froidure du uentrail W
33 aueyr perdu] perdu V, aver (a W) perdu *before* talent TW, le talent avoir perdu *after*
talent de dormir et de mengier N, *om.* O   35 de auer a fere od humme] avoir talent
d'ome VOT, a uolente d'omme W, *sign om.* N   36 qui ait ferine espurgement] se ele
a ferm [*lege* ferin] espurgement V, qui a color de ferrin espurgement (espurgee T) OT, qui
a talent de faire .i. espurgement N, qui e perse W   38 est de peys & de colur] est de
couleur de poi et V, est de pois semblanz & de color O, est pesante e de la colour T, est
de poist et de color N, mult poise qui a coleur W   41 ad] a VOW, eit T, ai N, est
H   42 seyne] garie V, saine ON, seine T, seyme H, (que le) garra (a grant poine) W
43 seyent] soit V, seynt H, *sign om.* OTNW   46 ceus] çou V, *somewhat rubbed or faint*
H, *sign om.* OTNW

[22] Dame qui fet vrine ruge medlee de [neyr] signefie qe mal ad el feye, dunc deit prendre vne medecine qui ad a num dialacusta. & apres seyner sey del destre bras de la veyne de la feye. Pur la dolur de l'oye deyt l'un 50 prendre iceste medecine: auream alexandrina v Paulin freis.

[23] Vrine de humme & de femme qui ad la feure angue qui ad neyre ipostasim, ceo est vn neyre quilette en le vrinal, signefie la mort.

[24] Vrine de humme ou de femme qui est vnkes uerte—[c'est une orine qui est verte en l'ourinail—senefie la mort. 55

[25] Urine d'ome u de feme qui a le fievre] & ad ipostasim petite & verte signefie la mort.

[26] Vrine de mechine seyne ky vnkes compayne de hume ne n'ont: pure & clere & saunz tutes teches.

[27] Vrina de femme qui compayne ad ou humme en jur ou en la nut est 60 truble & la semense du l'humme pert en la vrinal.

[28] Vrine de femme qui est enceynte ankes est clere & ad vne apostasim blanche en funs.

[29] Vrine de femme qui est en se flurs est cum sang.

[Epilogue] Si deuez cunutre par les vrines le mals de corps des hummes. 65 & quant vous les auerez ⟨cun⟩ous, si porrez ver' medecines encuntre che-chun mal. Plusours i at medecines.

Translation

[Prologue] The origin of health and illness is shown in the four parts of the body: the head, the stomach, the spleen, and the bladder, which should be known thus:

[1] That man will be healthy if the urine is white all morning, red before eating, white after eating.

[2] Urine fat, turbid, and stinking: that is not good.

[3] Urine very thin and in no way turbid is good.

[4] Feverous urine that is turbid like the urine of an ass signifies headache about to occur.

[5] Urine in fevers ending on the seventh day, white on the fourth day, and red on the second day, signifies recovery.

[6] Urine fat and very white, like that caused by moist humours, signifies the quartan fever to come.

48 neyr] noir V, veyr H, *sign om.* OTNW   54–6 c'est une orine . . . le fievre] V, *om.* H, *both signs om.* OTNW   56 & verte] en verité V, *sign om.* OTNW   66 cunous] cun *rubbed and indistinct* H, coneuz O

[7] Bloody urine signifies that the bladder is injured with some purulence that is therein.

[8] Urine sparse and fleshy and fat and as if it were velvety, that signifies an illness of the kidneys.

[9] Whoever passes blood without pain has a ruptured vein in the kidneys.

[10] Urine that seems powdery signifies that the bladder is wounded.

[11] Urine that is bloody and produced with pieces [= 'clots'] of blood signifies great infirmity within the body and especially in the bladder.

[12] Urine that falls in droplets and floats above like bubbles signifies long sickness.

[13] Urine that floats above [with] a fat ring signifies ague and long sickness.

[14] Woman's urine pure and clear, if it shines like silver in the flask, the woman vomits often, and if she has no desire to eat, signifies that the woman is pregnant.

[15] Woman's urine white and stinking and heavy signifies pain in the kidneys and that the uterus is full of a cold sickness.

[16] Woman's urine that has a froth of blood above, which is clear like water, signifies headache and that she has lost the desire to eat and to sleep on account of swelling of the stomach.

[17] Woman's urine that is of the colour of gold and clear and heavy signifies that the woman desires to have sex with a man.

[18] Woman's urine that has [colour of] the sifting of meal, if the woman has the quartan fever, signifies that she will die on the third day.

[19] Woman's urine that is of the weight and colour of lead, if she is pregnant, signifies that the child is dead; and if she is not pregnant, it signifies that the uterus is rotting and so the urine is fetid.

[20] Urine of a woman who is swollen and who has the cough and the flux, if it is the colour of linseed [or flax or linen], signifies that the woman cannot be whole.

[21] Urines of man and of woman who are sick with the headache, if their urine should have a large circle that is white or red within and if the circle is red, that signifies too great an abundance of blood in the head, for which a man should have blood let from the cephalic vein. And before the bloodletting, take medicine: *Paulinum* or *Theodoricon* or *Adrianum* or pills of *diacostum*.

[22] A woman who makes red urine mixed with black signifies she has an infirmity of the liver, for which she ought to be given a medicine called *dialacusta*. And afterwards, to be let blood from the right arm from the

hepatic vein. For pain of the ear, one should take this medicine: *aurea alexandrina* or fresh *Paulinum*.

[23] Urine of man and of woman with an acute fever that has a black sediment, that is, a black gathering in the flask, signifies death.

[24] Urine of man or of woman which is always green—that is, a urine that is green in the flask—signifies death.

[25] Urine of man or of woman who has the fever and has a small and green sediment signifies death.

[26] Urine of a healthy maiden who never had the company of man: pure and clear and without any blemishes.

[27] Urine of a woman who has companied with man by day or by night is turbid and the semen of the man appears in the flask.

[28] Urine of a woman who is pregnant is always clear and has a white sediment at the bottom.

[29] Urine of a woman who is menstruating is like blood.

[Epilogue] Thus you should know by the urines the ailments of men's bodies. And when you have known them, you can see the medicines for each ailment. There are many medicines.

APPENDIX III

RUFUS SUBRUFUS: VARIANT PROLOGUES AND REMEDIES

Variant Prologues

One of the principal distinguishing features between the textual families for *Rufus Subrufus* is the prologue provided in different copies of the work. The prologue in the edition above is the one that I label the 'Royal' prologue, because of its reference to the commissioning of the work by the king of England—identified as Henry IV or Henry V or left unnamed—and, in some copies, also by his lords. The 'Royal' prologue appears in Gc4=Cambridge, Gonville and Caius College, MS 336/725, f. 67ʳ; W10=London, Wellcome Library MS 784, f. 1ᵛ; Om=Oxford, Magdalen College, MS 221, f. 63ʳ; and Nm1=Bethesda, National Library of Medicine, MS 4, f. 57ᵛ. Besides the 'Royal' prologue, three other prologues appear at the head of the text in other manuscripts, as follows, quoting from the witnesses used in the textual apparatus above:

'IPOCRAS' PROLOGUE (Ap3a)[1]

Di1=Oxford, Bodleian Library, MS Digby 29, f. 125ʳ

(Also found in Ro6=BL, Royal MS 18.A.6, f. 23ʳ; Je=Cambridge, Jesus College MS 43 (Q.D.1), f. 61ᵛ; S29=BL, Sloane MS 1388, f. 53ʳ)

f. 125ʳ To knaw þe state of man & woman be thare water, se wele þis tretis & ȝow schal know perfetly all hyr infirmytes and al medicynys aȝanys þose infirmites, þe qwyche medycynes ben apruwyd be Ypocras in hys *Afforismis*, be Galyen, be Egide, be Mawrus and al docturus þat tretyn of þis mater.

5   At þe begynnyng ȝe schal vnderstonde þat we take al for one a mannys water, a mannys state, & pisse & a mannys vrine. But for þe more camune and faire word we vse þis word vryne. And ȝe schal vnderstonde þat þare ben xx diuerse colourus of vryne, as wytnys Egedie, qwyche betoknys diuerse sekenes. But tweyne þe fy[r]ste ben klepyd *Rufus* & *Subrufus*, þat is,
10   as burnest gold and vnburnest, token good hele but feu men han þat.

---

2 aȝanys] *foll. by* ham *canc.*

---

[1] The abbreviations Ap3a–Ap3d (and Ap4a–Ap4b in Appendix IV) are assigned to the texts in these two appendices for purposes of Glossary citation.

'DOCTORS' PROLOGUE (Ap3b)

T15 = Cambridge, Trinity College, MS R.14.52, f. 170ᵛ

(Also found in W11 = London, Wellcome MS 7117, f. 122ᵛ; Nm2 = Bethesda, National Library of Medicine MS 30, f. 11ʳ; and possibly in a related form in Oxford, Bodleian Library, Ra2 = Rawlinson MS C.81, f. 1ʳ: the phrase 'doctors and authors' does not appear in this copy, but derivatives of 'declaren' occur twice, along with other similarities to the Trinity, Wellcome, and NLM texts.)

Doctours and auctours declaren ffirst that ther bien xx divers colours f. 170ᵛ
of vrynes as it shal be plenily declared hereafterward. That is to say in
Latin tunge as *Ruphus, Subruphus*, whiche bitokenyth parfite digestioun,
but riȝt fewe men han this vryne. And therfor it nedith nat to yeve hym no
medicyne.   5

'CIRCLE' PROLOGUE (Ap3c)

A8 = Oxford, Bodleian Library, MS Ashmole 1438, I, pp. 150–1

(Also found in A10 = Oxford, Bodleian Library, Ashmole MS 1444, p. 219, abridged but still with the reference to 'showing hereafter in the circle' and to the two colours of perfect digestion. The full list of colour names is unique to A8, which typically expands colour terms and descriptions throughout the text.)

⟨N⟩owe it is to knowe þat þer be 20 diuers colours in a mans or womans p. 150
vryn or water nat contryuid, as it shal be shewyd her afte[r] in a cercle
folowyng, whech be þes: *Subrufus Rufus Subrubeus Rubeus Subrubicundus
Rubicundus Ynops Kyanos Viridis Liuidus Subniger | Niger Albus Glaucus* p. 151
Lacteus Karapos Subpallidus Pallidus Subcitrinus Citrinus. Wherof *Subrufus* 5
& *Rufus* betokyn parfit dygestyoun but fewe men or women have þis water.
& ⟨þer⟩for it nedeth nat to ȝeve hem medycyn. *Subrufus* is a colo⟨ur⟩ of vryn
as goolde vnbornyd; *Rufus* is a colour as goolde bornyd.

Several copies of *Rufus Subrufus* are acephalous, and thus lack a prologue entirely:

   A7 = Ashmole 1413, p. 2
   Ro3 = BL, Royal 17 C.xv, ff. 62ʳ–64ᵛ
   W1 = Wellcome 7, f. 1ʳᵛ
   Ad6 = BL, Add. 19674, f. 68ʳ

Variant Remedies (Ap3d)

As noted in the introduction, the other large structural distinction between the *Rufus Subrufus* textual groupings is the presence of an alternative series of colours, diagnoses, and remedies in the 'Ipocras' group. Although that series shares a few signs and recipes with the more standard text represented in the edition above, it probably reflects an attempt to combine *Rufus Subrufus* with *Urina Rufa* and to add elements of physiological theory to the treatise. Both moves might be seen as tending to make the 'Ipocras' version slightly more academic or Latinate, but the treatise remains solidly practical in its provision of remedies for a range of ailments. On the other hand, by removing the sentences that link particular ailments and remedies with the appropriate digestion groups, the version below loses an important structuring and unifying device found in the other versions of the text. A few signs and remedies in the Ipocras-group series appear to derive from other token lists or recipe collections.

The following version of the alternative series of signs is taken from Di1, which gives the most complete text and may be the earliest copy; each of the other three members of the Ipocras group omits one or two of the paragraphs in the text below. For ease of comparison to the other versions, new material in the Ipocras version transcribed below is indicated by a reduced font.

Di1 = Oxford, Bodleian Library, MS Digby 29, ff. 125^r–126^v

(Also found in Ro6 = BL, Royal MS 18.A.6, ff. 23^r–25^v, 26^v, f. 28^v; Je = Cambridge, Jesus College MS 43 (Q.D.1), ff. 61^v–64^r; S29 = BL, Sloane MS 1388, ff. 53^r–54^v)

f. 125^r But 3e schal vnderstond þat fro þe stomake ascendet vp into þe hede diuerse humours & vapores. & [þorgh] þe coldenes o[f] þe brayne, þat ys cold be way of kynd
(for þare is no best þat has so muche of brayne in comparysoun of hys body as has
man), þilke vapores & humours sum gone to þe ene & bene cause of diuerse sekenes
5   in þe ene and sum go to þe eryn and cause þare diuerse sekenes in þe hede. And
for alle þyse ben diuerse medycynes.

Fyrst for þe hede ache: Rx ueruayne, betayne, wormode & lay hem in
qwythe wyne and þarewith wesche wel þe seke hede & þan make a plaster
& lay it oppon þe mold in þis maner. Take þe same erbis qwan þay bene
10   soþyn and wrynge hem & grynd hem smal in a morter & temper hem with
þe same lycour a3an & do þareto qwete bran for to hold in þe liquour. &
make a garland of a courchef & bynd þe seke hede þarewith & lay þe plaster
on þe mold within þe garland as hote as þe seke may sufer. And bynd þe
hede with a valypere and do a cappe abowe. & do þus bot iij tymes & þe
15   seke schal be hole on warantyse, if hit be curabil—þatt is to say, if syn or
lac of grace lette not kynd to wyrche.

2 þorgh] JeS29, þare Di1, *om.* Ro6   of ^{1}] JeS29, ob Di1, *om.* Ro6

For þe clensyng of þe hede: Rx peleter of Spayne and sethe þe rotis a good quantite iij days and hit schal purge þe hede | and do away þe ache f. 125ᵛ and festen þe te[t]he in þe gomes.

A gode medycyne for þe wanyte of þe hede: Rx jus of walwort & salt & 20 hony & wax & encense & boyle hem wele togeder & þarewith anoynt þe hede & þe templis.

Now for il heryn:[2] Take grene plantes of has and lay þa[m] on þe treuet owre þe fyre & berne hem & kepe þe water þat comes owte of hem at þe endys in a schel & þe jus of syngrene in schelful and a schelful of elys grece and of þe jus of þe neþer 25 endys of lekys with þe rotys a schelful & a schelful of hony. & put þareof hote in þe hole ere of þe seke and lay þe seke on þe toþer syde þat is defe and he schal be hele within nene tymys. & take þe wowle of a blacke schepe vnder þe wombe pluckyd, wete it in þe jus, and lay hit abowe.

A fayre medicine for þe ene: Tak þe gal of a hare, þe gal of a cocke, & þe gal of a 30 kynd ele & hony clarefiyd and mel al þese togeder.[3] & þis schal clere a mannys svȝth be he neuer so olde. & hit wyl destruy þe pyn, þe web. & kepe þe fro þise thyngys contyned in þis vers: *Allia vina venus ventus faba fumus & ignis / Ista nocent oculis sed vigilare magis.*[4] And al þese infirmites ben betokened be þe colours þat Egid callys *Sub[rubius] color vt crocus occidentalis & Rubius ut crocus orientalis* [et] colour 35 *Setrinus & Subcitrinus.*

Forþermore ȝe schal vnderstonde þat þe secunde perfite dygestion is in þe leuere. & þere is separacioun of þe clene fro þe vnclene, as says þe philofer Aristotil. & þat þat is clene gothe to þe harte & to þe vaynes & minsters gode blode to al þe membris, & þat is vnclene gose downe to þe bladder & gothe owte be þe ȝerde. 40

Here is a gode medycyne & a preciouse for al spiritual membris, & for þe tesyke, þe hede, þe harte, stomake & lewer & þe longys: Rx flowre de lyce, smalache, loueache, radiche, licorice, saxifrage, philipend, stanmarche, fenyl, percyl, venyger & hony a quarte, of radyche & of liquoris of yche ij handful, but of yche of þe oþer one handful. And lay hem in vineager a nyȝth and a day or more. But firste stampe 45 hem smal togeder & put alway to a pynt of venigre iij pyntys of water qwan ȝow sethes hit on þe fire. & sethe hit til þe thirde parte be sothyn in. And þan clense hit throw a clothe clene & þan put þareto þy hony and trie it on þe fyre. & drynke it fastyng at morne & at ewyn and ȝow schal be hole for þis is pruuid.

19 tethe] Ro6JeS29, teche Di1   23 þam] Ro6JeS29, þan Di1   29 abowe] to stop the ere *add*. Ro6   35 Subrubius] S29, subrufus Di1Ro6Je   et] Ro6JeS29, *om.* Di1

---

[2] Parallel remedies *for il heryn*: Heinrich 1896: 66, 210; Henslow 1899: 133; Ogden 1938: 6, 7; Müller 1929: 51–2, 110; T. Hunt 2001: 163.

[3] For other gall-based remedies, see Heinrich 1896: 90; Müller 1929: 112; Ogden 1938: 11; T. Hunt 1990: 112; also the archangel Raphael's prescription of fish gall as a cure for blindness in Tobit 11: 1–15.

[4] The lines in this couplet (with some variation) appear in expanded versions of the *Flos medicine*, in sections on things harmful to the eyes. See De Renzi, i. 488, lines 1317, 1320; 1859: v. 55, lines 1923, 1926; Frutos González 2010b: 186, lines 2826, 2829, 2831, 2835; Walther 810.

50   A good potage for þe same ewyl: Rx borage, myntys, goldys, auance,
betayne, violet, langedebefe. & of al þyse make potage, for þis is pruuid.

       A gode medecyne for drynes þat makys a man faynt & oft time to swete:
Rx a quarte of hys owne pisse and sethe hit & put þarein a sponeful comyn
f. 126ʳ & take a hote tele wele hetyd in þe fyre and lay þareon | a sponeful of
55   comyn. & late [hym] stonde or set þareon and cloþid al abowte, his leggys
wele couerid with clothys to he swete for hete. & after late hym go to a
bed made with new waschen schetys & hil hym hote & he schal be hole of
warandise.

       Vryne rede as blode in þe glas betokys fewer of ful mekyl blode & þan he schuld
60   be latyn blode, but þe mone be in þe syne of Geminis.

       Now here is a medicyne for þat fewer and al maner fewer: Rx mustard
a quantite and veniger ewen proporcionde & triakyl as muche as a bene &
mel al togeder. Drynke þerof [þr]iyse & withowten dout þow schalt be hole.

       Vryne grene qwen it is made & afterward rede betokyt byrnyng within & þat is
65   dedely.

       Vryne of a woman þat is with chyld, if sche ha[w] gone a monþe or ij or
iij, hit schal be clere & hit schal hawe a qwyte substance in þe bothem. &
if sche hawe foure monþs go with chyld, þe vryne schal be schynyng with
a qwyte substance with a drope of blode in þe medyl of þe cirkyl abowe.

70   Vryne as qwyte as mylke with a thyke substance: yf hit be of a woman, it is not
so perloce as of a man, for indisposicion of þe moder. But in scha`r´pe feuerys it is
dedely & vncurabil.

       Vrine as milke abowe & benethe dirke & abowte þe medyl cirkyl clere betokyns
þe dropsy.

75   A fayre medycine for þe same dropsy: Rx wormode, pety moryl, fewerfu,
spourge, walwort, þe rotys of yche dj libre, & fenel sede & sauge, smalache,
auance, mentys, wel-cryssys, hore-hofe, endywe, lywerworte, þe medyl barke of
þe eldertre, of iche half a quartron. Wesche clene þe rotys & þyn erbis & grynd
hem wele in a morter & put hem in a new erthyn pot þat was neuer notyd. & do
80   þareto ij galons of qwyte wyne or of wort þat is not changed & sethe it til it com
to a galon. & take it downe & lat it ryn throȝt a here syf into a fare pan. & wesche
clene þi pot & do in þy licours & keuere hit wele & iuste & lete þe seke þareof
hawe a pynt at onys at euen hote, at morne cold. & lat him thre days ete no mete
but brede and potage made of wel-kyrsyn & of qwyte wyne & otemele & he schal
85   be hole.

       Vryne blacke as ynke betokyns dethe and is vncurabil. Or ellys it betokyns þat
þe mater of þe euyl passis away be mannys ȝerde & þan it betokyns hele. But in a
feuer quartane euere more it betokyns dethe.

55 hym] Ro6, it Di1, Rx om. JeS29   60 mone] JeS29, mone must Di1Ro6
63 þriyse] JeS29, Ro6 iij tymys, Di1 .iij thiyse   66 haw gone] g written over w(e) Di1
77 þe] foll. by rotis of the canc. Di1   82 keuere . . . iuste] stop hit fast Ro6, keuer it
clene JeS29

Vrine ʒolwe with a thicke substance and ful of spume abowe betokys þe iaundese.

Medicina: Rx an appil and kut him abowe & take owte al þe cor & put   90
hit ful of saferon and of schawyng of ewery. & lay þe cottyng of þe appyl
abowe on þe appyl qware it was. And þan set þe appyl in þe hote aymers
til hit be | hote. & þan ete þat apil as hote as þow may sufer wele & þow   f. 126ᵛ
schal be hole within sex tymes.

And vse to drynke þe iuse of celydon al þat tyme & þow schal be hole on   95
warandyse.

Vrine þat in þe bothum has smal grauil stonys: qwyte betokyns þe stone in þe
bledder, rede in þe renys.

Medicina: Rx blacke iete & asur & jwe-beris & þe skyn of þe maw of a capon or
of peionys & dry hem to powder. & drynke þis with ale nene tymes & nene days &   100
þow schalt be hole.

Vrine pale & thycke with sqwames in þe bothom betokyns þe *colica* passyoun.

Medicina contra illam: Rx peritori, wormode, sauge or plantayne or reu and
sclitied liem and put hem in a pokyt & venegre and al hote put hem to þe nauil
of þe seke & he schal be hole.   105

A gode medicyne aʒenys a murmale þat is betokenyd accidentali be vrine as it
were raw flesche & colouryd: Rx smalache, mynten, goldys, hundes-tong, waybrede, malwys, orpyn, mercury, fenel & stampe hem with grece & buttyr ryʒth
smal & ley þareto.

Vrine colouryd as þe skyn of camel betokyns þe emorautys.   110

Bo[na] medicina: Rx a morter of lede & a pestil of lede & take a hanful of mulan
& a handful of vnset leke & halfe a hede of a lile rote & stampe al þyse togeder in
þe morter of lede with þe pestil of lede til it coloure of þe lede. & lay it on a clothe
& lay it to þe sore & it schal be stoppyd for ewere more.

Vrine clere coloryd after a ʒonge appil on a tre betokyns in a woman þat she is a   115
clene mayde. But vrine trubule in þe qwyche mannys sede schewys in þe bothom
betokyns þat sche is corrupte.

Vrine of a woman rede as blode betokys þat sche has þe flowres.

Medicina to hyr þat has to muche of þe flowres, to lessen ham fayre and
wele: Rx confery & wasche hit and stampe hit & sethe hit in wyne; & make a   120
playstre to hyr nawyl & to hyr wombe & to hyr r`e´ynes. Sche schal be hole.

To make a woman to hawe flewrys qwan þay ben differyd, þis medisyne
falis neuer, but loke sche be not with chyld: Take þe rote of gladwyne &
sethe it in veniger or in wyne. & qwen it is wele sothyn set it on þe grunde
& lete hyr stride þereowre so þat þare may non are passe away but vp into   125
here priuite.

111 Bona medicina] (Here is Je) a fayr medicyne JeS29, ?Bomeⁿᵃ Di1, *om.* Ro6
120 and] and (*line end*) & Di1   124 in²] *foll. by* ?skyn *canc.* Di1

APPENDIX IV

THE DOME OF URYNE: ENGLISH VERSIONS OF LATIN SEGMENTS

BRITISH LIBRARY, MS Add. 10440, f. 52^{rv} (Ap4a)

f. 52^r For to knowe þe greys huche is drye and hoote.

þe first gree of hottnysse is whanne hany þyng haþ oon porcioun of
cooldnysse and too of hootnysse: þan þat þyng is ycallid hoot in þe first degree. þe secunde gree is whanne a þyng hath oon porcion of cooldnys ⟨and

5 4 of hootnysse: þan he⟩ is ycallid hoot in þe 2 gree. þe 3 ⟨gree is whanne a
þyng hath oon⟩ party of cooldnysse and 8 of ho⟨otnysse: þan he is ycallid
hoot in⟩ þe 3 gree. þe 4 gree is whanne ⟨he hath oon party of cooldnysse⟩
and 16 of hotnysse, þan he is ycal ⟨lid hoot in þe 4 gree⟩. |

f. 52^v þe first age of þe mone is musty & hoot. þe 2 is hot & drye. þe 3 is cold

10 & musty. þe 4 is cold & drye.

Of þe signys þat buþ mevable & onmevabel & of here condicions. In
þe signys vnmevabel þou schal bygynne þi werke þat schal abyde & longe
durye, as makyng of hous & oþer þingys. In mevabel syngnys, bygynne
mevabel þyngys, as sellyng & bychgyng.

15 Also if þe begynyng of sikeness þe mone be in a mevabel signe, þan þe
sikenesse may wel chonge. And if it be in a signe vnmevabel & stabel, þan
þe sikenesse schal abide in on state. And if it be in þ⟨e⟩ meddel betwene
too, in þe mene hit schal durre. Also sikenesse in þe wexyng of þe mone
often hit comyt⟨h⟩ to good & 'þe' contrarie & yvel in þe wanyng.

20 And þes be þe signes þat be mevabel: Aries, Cancer, Capricornus, &
Libra. But þes ben stabel: Leo, Taurus, Scorpio, Aquarius. And þes be
half on half oþer: Virgo, Sagittarius, Pisses, & Gemini.

4–8 *Text supplied for material lost due to large hole in MS, based on phrasing in surviving text
and Latin version in S10*   15–22 a mevable signe . . . & Gemini] *partially written in
margins in order to fit text in four lines above heading for next section* (*on Pulse*)   17 þe] e
hidden by tight binding   19 comyth] h *hidden by tight binding*

BODLEIAN LIBRARY, MS Ashmole 1477, X, f. 17ʳᵛ (Ap4b)

To knowe the degrees which be hot & drye,
cold & drye, hot & moyst, cold & moyst

f. 17ʳ

Ye shall knowe ther be iiijᵒʳ degrees: the first degre is hott, as whan any
thing hath one part of coldnes & ij partes of heat, that that thing is cawled
hot in the first degree.   5

The seconde degre is whan any thing hath one part of coldnes & fowre
partes of heat, ʻthenʼ that part is cawled hott in the second degre.

The therd degre is whan any thing hath one part of coldnes & viij partes
of heat, then that thing is cawled hott in the thirde degree.

The fowrth degree is whan any thing hath one part of coldnes & xvj 10
partes of heat, then that erbe or that man is cawled hott in the iiij degree
& so a lyke proporcioun of all other degrees.

Degrees of the mone

The first age of the mone: that is the first quarter of hym. The first quarter
of the mone is hot & moyst. The second quarter is hott & drye. The therd 15
is cold & moyst. The fowrth is cold & drye.

Nota: in the begynyng of euery sicknes, yf the mone be in a sygne that
is movable, then that sycknes is varyable. & yf the mone be in a signe that
is stedfast, then that sycknes is constant & long holding. & yf the mone
be in a signe that is neyther movable nor constant, then the sycknes is 20
betwixt both.

And yf the sycknes com in the waxing of the mone, that sycknes is most
often torned to good. & yf it come in the wanyng of [the] mone it is often
torned to damag of the bodye. Note theis versys after (*verte*): |

Movable sygnes be theise: Aries, Cancer, Capricorne, & Lybla.
Leo stable, Tawrus, Scorpio.
Mene sygnes: Virgo, Sagittarious, Pisses, Lyber,[1] & Gemyne.

f. 17ᵛ
26

20 neyther] *foll. by* holding *canc.*   23 of the] of of

---

[1] Lybla . . . Lyber: The scribe may have been confused by the similarity of the Latin
words *Libra* and *Limpha* (=Aquarius; see I/165), properly classified as movable/cardinal and
stable/fixed signs respectively. The adjective *bipartita*, modifying the four mixed (modern
'mutable') signs in I/166, has dropped out entirely. As Liber is another name for Bacchus,
Lyber may have been seen as a synonym for Aquarius, perhaps with an eye to the pouring of
wine rather than water.

TEXTUAL COMMENTARY

Witnesses cited in the notes below are listed, as far as possible, in the order and textual groupings given in Figs. 1–9 above. Greek-letter group labels are used where applicable, both to save space and highlight textual relationships. Although there is a certain degree of overlap with the medical notes that follow, the textual notes focus on issues in which variation across witnesses or sources may shed light on how scribes and readers understood the texts, while the medical notes are intended to place the medical terms and concepts of the texts in their intellectual context, including the identification of sources where known. Cross-references to other textual notes are labelled 'n(n.)'; cross-references to notes in the Medical Commentary are labelled 'm.n(n.)'.

TEXTS A–C

Texts A through C are connected by their common descent from a set of three Latin texts that frequently appear together in late fourteenth-century physician's handbooks, often accompanied by calendric, astrological, and bloodletting treatises and diagrams. For a transcript of the three Latin texts in one such handbook (Bodl., MS Ashmole 391, Part V) and of a macaronic Latin/English version of Text B, *Urina Rufa* (from Bodl., MS Digby 29), see App. I.

A. *Twenty Colours by Digestion Groups*

1

Collated witnesses: LdS35 H10 W8 T11 Pe3; **Uncollated:** Gc7 Di2S36Cu5 S6S21 W6 Ra6H8 S9T7T13 H2Eg3S13

3–4 *ysend out . . . no3t ysend out*: 'ysend out' is a hyperliteral rendering of Latin *remissa* 'dull, dim, faded, less intense', often used to describe uroscopic subcolours (Subrubicundus, Subpallidus, etc.; occasionally replaced by *dimissa*, a variant that may be the immediate antecedent for Ld's *ysend out*). Describing the principal colours as 'not sent out', though a bit redundant, derives from *non remissus, -a, -um* in the Latin source (see App. I). Alternatives to *ysend/sent out* are common across Middle English uroscopic treatises: the simple anglicization *remisse*, as well as 'put out', 'sad', 'deep(er)', 'not as high (of colour)', 'not so bright', 'less', 'light', 'not so perfect', the suffix *-ish*, qualitative contrasts with the principal colour (e.g. impure or unburnished vs. pure or burnished gold, watery vs. red blood, etc.), as well as readings that suggest scribal misunderstanding of one or another of these options.

2

Collated witnesses (all): Gc4A7 Ro6Di1 W4b Yo (illustrated), S29W4a (not illustrated)

Captions and visual design in urine-wheel texts: Descriptions of the digestion groups are given in roundels spaced around the central roundel in Gc4A7Yo (for Gc4, see Pl. 1, pp. lxxxii–lxxxiii above); in sections of the space within the 'hub' of each wheel in the three-wheel diagrams in Ro6Di1 (for digitized copies of the Ro6Di1 wheels, see Introduction, n. 40); and in arcs of the third of four concentric rings in W4 (digitized copy available at https://hunter.uma.es/). Coloured flasks are drawn in A7Ro6Di1Yo, but not in Gc4 or W4. S29 has no illustration, but its 'Tabula' heading is related to the central roundel text in Gc4A7, while some of its colour similes appear to be most closely related to those in Ro6Di1.

6–7 *et passim remisse . . . not remisse*: See n. to A.1/3–4 above.

B. *Urina Rufa*

Collated witnesses: LdS35 W8 Pe3 Hg1; S6Di1 selectively; **Uncollated:** H10Gc7Pe1Ad1A3 Di2 T11S21 H7Gc4Cu5 W6 W12Gc1aGc1b S5S42 S1aS1bS23Nm2T13T7Yo

1 *signefieth*: The various textual groups for *Urina Rufa* usually prefer either *signify* and its forms or the anglicized *(be)token* and its forms to translate forms of *significare* and *signare*, although individual witnesses may also include a few uses of the alternative word. *Signify* is the preferred form in groups α1, α3, γ1, δ, and in Di2 (a member of α2) and the idiosyncratic witnesses S1bS23; *(be)token* is preferred in groups β and γ2, and by W8 (a member of α2) and the idiosyncratics Nm2T7T13S1aYo. These preferences in the central verb of *Urina Rufa* are paralleled in *Cleansing of Blood*, where the Latinate term *signifien* appears mainly in the α and γ1 groups of that text, and the native *(be)token(en)* mainly in its β and γ2 groups.

4 *myddel*: The variants for this word help to distinguish families of witnesses, as noted in the introduction and listed here in full: *myddel* (α1, α2, α3); *mene* (γ1, γ2, Nm2T7Yo); *meanly thin* T13; *feeble* S1a; *thin* S1b; word om. (β, δ); sign om. A3S23; text acephalous Pe1Ad1.

8 *feuere continual*: The δ family reads *cotidian* here, perhaps an inadvertent slip reflecting the familiarity of the disease-term *cotidian* (*fever*) in Middle English, or it may derive from a deliberate alteration by Richard Stapulton in Di1. Cf. the *cotidian feuer/feuer eueri day* variants to *feuere etike* in B/40, also found only in δ witnesses.

16–17 *vices of þe lyuer & hete*: Another feature that helps to distinguish families of witnesses. For the α and γ groups, the phrase originates in the Latin *calefac-*

tionem epatis, rendered most closely by the γ group: 'chaffyng (W6; jaffyng Pe3; heete or brynynge γ2) of þe lyuer (*foll. by* and lungis W6)'. The phrase used in the all-English members of the δ group, 'sickenys and (*foll. by* sumdel S42) drynes of the lyuer of (for S5S42) heete', corresponds to the Latin expression in Stapulton's macaronic text in Di1: 'infirmitatem et siccitatem epatis propter calorem'.

20–1 *rawnesse of humors*: Lat. *cruditatem humorum*; *remiscenes* in the α3 group is probably a derivative of the adjective *remisse*, in the humoral sense of 'weak, watery, of low intensity', a state believed to be caused by cold in the body and thus an apposite interpretation of clear urine (*MED*, s.v. *remis(se* (adj.)). The late witness T13 reads *feblenes of all humers*. The variants *jaundis* (S1a) and *iuaundes* (S35) may derive from misreadings of *rawnesse*, rather than alternative translations of *cruditatem*. Yo renders the diagnosis as 'gaderyng of moysture betwen þe felle & þe flesch', possibly indicating a variant in the source text.

23 *inordinances of matrices buþ certayn vices*: The last three words are a gloss on *inordinances*: they have no equivalent in the Latin versions of the text and occur only in LdS35 (with S35 reading *ben* for *buþ*).

35–6 The δ group adds the symptom 'wherin be gletterynge (*varr.* glyderande S5, splendentes Di1) rowes' to this sign, after *horn*. 'Rows' or 'rays' in urine (*urina radiosa* or *virgata/virgulata*; ME *bemy* or *yerded urine*) are commonly associated with obstruction of the spleen, as in Walter Agilon's *Summa medicinalis* and its uroscopic derivatives (see 'Guide', item 16.0), although Agilon links this feature with the colour Albus rather than Glaucus.

49 *cercle*: Although the variant *cors* (γ1 family) diverges from the Latin original (*circulus nullo quiescente tremulus*), the scribes who transmitted it may have understood it as describing a trembling or a disturbance in the body (i.e. central region) of the sample, rather than at or just below the surface or Circle.

54–70 The signs presented in these lines focus mainly on urines with suspended particles or substances: Scales (*squame*), drops (apparently a doubling of *guttam* 'gout', the signified disease for this sign), little *gobettis* or *frustris* (*frusta, frustula* '[little] crumbs'), *whitter* (*sanies* or *pus*), and *motie* urine (*urina athomosa*). While Scales and drops remain generally stable across the texts, the variants for *litel gobetis* and *frustris litel and brod* include *frustis* (α3; W8H7), *lytyll frustes* (Di2), (*small resolucyons & brod*) *lyke shaueynges of flesshe* (T13), *brokelet(t)es* (γ1), *pypes* (Yo; misreading *frustula* as *fistula?*), and *smale lumpes* (S1a). In the δ group, the underlying Latin terms are Di1's 'sanguinea' (for *litel gobetis*) and 'parue squame' (for *frustris litel and brod*), translated respectively as *blody* (Hg1S5S21) and *white small fflawys* (Hg1) or *smalle (brode) whyte flayeres* (S5S21).

The word *whitter* is a back-spelling of *quitter* 'pus', usually Northern according to the *MED*, though Ld's language is from Gloucestershire (*LALME*). Variant readings include forms beginning with both *wh-* and *qu-/qw-* (e.g. *whyttour, quitour/qwetour/qwyttour*, etc.: H10W8; α3; Gc4W6); *rottynnys* and *þe corrupcioune* (γ2); *putredo* (Di1), *quether as it were of a byle* (S5), *quitter of a bowel* (= 'boil') (S42), *quitter & bollis as of rayne water* (Hg1); and the scribal errors *whit/wytth* (Gc7H7), *water* (S1a), *white* (S1b), and *wore* (Di2).

For *vrine motie*, variants include *aperynge full of motys* (γ2; S1a), *athomosa* (γ1), *grauelly* (T13); *plura parua scissa in finibus* (Di1), *that has oftyn tymes small rownde endis* (Hg1), *small round therein* (S5).

78–80 *a ymage in þe glasyne vessel . . . þe ymage of hym þat scheweþ apeireþ*: W8's *schewyþ* 'judges, examines (the urine)' is supported by H10Gc7Di2, and may help explain Yo's *þe ymage of chewyng*, S1a's *þe image be of him hit oweth*, and *the image* (*urine* Nm2) *of him shaketh þe water* in W6 and Nm2. See also *ymago iudicantis* in the Latin *Urina Rufa* (App. I).

87–92 These signs of sexual activity in women and men show an exceptional range of variants, reflecting the delicacy of the topic. For sexual activity in women, the variants to the first sign (B/87–8) include (*y*)*take*(*n*) *with man* (a1; Di2), *to take with man* (H7), *to be* (*hath be*) *with a man late* (W8; a3), *hat3 late be knowe of a man* (W6), *hath be* (*was*) *late swyued* (*& corupte*) (Pe3S5), *late swewenge* (Hg1, in cipher), *cognicionem seu congricionem viri recentem* (Di1), *to haue don letcherye wyth a man noght late gon* (Yo), *haþe layn by a man* (S1a), *to be layne by* (S1b), and (applied to both men and women) *holdyne with Venurys worke* (γ2), translating *retentam* (varr. *recentem, iacentem*) *cum viro*.

For the male sexual activity described in lines 90–2 (Lat. *eum retentum/recenter cum muliere coisse*), the variants include *to haue delit/delyd/deled/dalte/delyte with a* (*menstruate*) *womman* (see n. to B/92 for details), *be holdyn with sume woman* (W12), and *neweleche to haue leyn be a womman* (Yo).

Hg1's use of ciphers appears to be aimed at masking potentially offensive words (*swewenge, cownte,* and *marees* in signs that correspond to B/87–9 and signs 35–6 in Di1; see App. I), although the Hg1 scribe also ciphers *woman* in these lines, a word he normally leaves uncoded.

87, 90 *sed*: Although *sed* is widely used to render Lat. *semen* in these lines, some δ witnesses (S5Di1Hg1) translate with 'manys strene' and 'strene'.

92 *delit*: The spelling of this word in Ld could represent either the sense 'dealt' (pa.p. *delen*) or 'delight'; other witnesses use unambiguous spellings for one or the other sense: *deled* (S35Gc7), *delyd* (H10A3H7), *dalte* (Gc1aGc1b) or *delite, delyte* (a2; a3).

The macaronic version of *Urina Rufa* in Di1 and the fully Englished version in S5 here add a sign not found in the related Hg1 version: '37. mulieris nigra & in iactura quodammodo rubea .s. mundacionem of þe meryes' (Di1) and 'womans vreyn that ys blake & in þe castyng sumdell rede yt signifiet clensynge of þe meryse' (S5). Di1 ends its series of signs with a thirty-eighth, roughly equivalent to line 93 and corresponding to sign thirty-seven in Hg1 but with a more plausible diagnosis: '38 v. rubea sicut sanguis per totum .s. menstruositatem' (Di1), as opposed to 'The 3^{ti}7 vrine red as bloode ouer alle signifiethe menys strene &c.' (Hg1; *sign om.* S5).

Hg1's *menys strene* error for *menstruositatem* (cf. Pe1's *men streynyd*) was probably caused by the earlier correct references to 'manys strene' (i.e. semen; see n. to B/87, 90 above).

95 *Antioda*: A form of the word *antidota* (varr. *antitod(e)* Pe3Gc7Nm2, *antitoda* H10Di2, *antidoda* W8, *antidiare* γ2, *antitatorye* H7, *a tamidar* S1a; also translated as *the cure therof* α3). I have to date found the Latin original of the final phrase, 'as it scheweþ in Antioda', in only two versions of the Latin text, both of English provenance (*dissolucio patet in antidodam*: Oxford, Bodleian Library, MS Bodley 648; Talbot's reading of the Dickson Wright manuscript (1961: 226), *dissolucio patet manticodia*, should be corrected to '. . . in antitodia').

A number of witnesses (the γ group and the idiosyncratic S1a) and some Latin versions (e.g. Bodley 648) add a final sign, roughly equivalent to Di1's sign 37 (see preceding note), about the urine changing from black to red upon stirring or movement, signifying the 'solution of the menstrues' (var.: le launsing menstruorum S1a; Lat. *solutio menstruorum*).

C. *Cleansing of Blood*

Collated witnesses: LdS35 W8 Gc4b Pe3; **Uncollated:** H10Pe1Gc7Ad1 A3 T11S6 Di2aA8 JeS29Di1Ro6 A10Gc4aW1W10OmNm1 Nm2T15 W6W12Gc1a Gc1b H7S20 T2T7T13Cu5H7S1S20Ry1Add3Di2bYo

2 *forsothe*: Here and below, *forsothe* usually represents *enim* or *vero* in its Latin source; the word mainly appears in witnesses from the α group.

2–3 *lyuer . . . veynes . . . bladder . . . reynes*: The most common substantive variation in the four nouns in this phrase is the unsurprising substitution of 'reynes' for 'veynes', usually without a corresponding change of 'reynes' at the end of the phrase (H10Pe1 W8 S29Gc4aNm1; γ1). Unique variants include '⟨blou⟩d' for 'lyuer' (S20), 'braynys' for 'veynes' (A10), and 'bowels' for 'reynes' (Yo); Gc4b changes the entire phrase to 'þe reynes & of þe lyuere'. The phrase is omitted in the idiosyncratic witnesses H7T7T13Cu5S1Ry1.

5 *þere buþ . . . to be ylokid*: Only LdS35 include *to* twice in this phrase, which may be a faulty translation of the Latin *consideranda sunt diuersa*, or a conflation of 'to dyuerse þyngis . . . to loke' and 'diuerse þinges . . . to be loked'. Reading the first *to* as the number 2 seems unlikely given the series of four things that follows, though one witness (Gc7) makes that choice. Other α-family readings include 'buth (*add* ij Gc7) to be lokyd dyuerse thynges' (H10Pe1Gc7), 'bith dyuers þinges to be lokyd' (A3), 'are dyuerse thinges (diuerse þynges be S6) to be consideryd' (T11S6), and several unique phrasings. The β family is more consistent, reading either 'ȝe shal considere diuerse thynges' (β1) or 'ȝe shul considere iiij (conceyue iiij T15) þinges' (β2; β3). The γ group offers word-order variations on passive constructions: 'diverse things are/be to be considered (seen Pe3)', while the idiosyncratic texts vary widely among themselves.

7 *by cause*[1]: In the Latin source, *causa* is in the nominative case, but the Ld translation has interpreted it as an ablative, followed by most other α witnesses (S35H10Pe1Gc7W8) and one αβ witness, Di2a. The large majority of other witnesses translate *causa* as a nominative, while a few witnesses either omit the word *cause* (A3), omit the first two branches of the statement (γ2, possibly following a Latin source similar to Ashmole 391, Ashmole 798, and the second copy in Hatton 29), or drop the statement on causes entirely (A8W10T2Add3Yo).

8 *residence*: This term for the material that settles to the bottom of the urine flask is also translated as 'sodomen/sedemyne þat is þe content (beneth the contentis T15) in the myddel (myddes Nm1)' (A10W1Gc4aOmNm1; β3), 'sedements' (γ2; H7), 'sedemyne liche a cloud of whyt' (T2), 'grownde' (Di2b), 'þe sedimen and residence or þe sede' (γ1), 'mynge(lyng) þat hanggyth in þe bottum' (JeS29), 'þe thycke in þe bottom' (Di1), 'content' (Ro6), 'content in þe myddyl' (W10), 'sondre greis' (S1), and 'wasteyng of complexyoun' (T13). The term is equivalent to *ypostasis* and its variants found in other texts in this volume.

11-12 *white . . . dryenesse is cause . . . cause of þykke substance*: The erroneous omissions and insertions in LdS35Gc4bA10 and some other witnesses can be identified by their faulty humoral theory: heat and cold are properly associated with red and white colour respectively, dryness and moisture with thin and thick substance respectively. Most witnesses do report the correspondences correctly, supporting the emendations here.

13-14 *cercle . . . body of eir . . . perforacio . . . grounde*: The name for the second part of the urine, the *body of (the) air*, occurs in about half (nineteen) of the witnesses, but it also generates many variants, including 'body eir' (C/15 below, in LdS35); 'eirli bodi' in Gc4aW1W10OmNm1 (from the β2 group), 'eyr' A3, 'body' A3W8Ro6Cu5T2, 'erthye body' A10 or 'erthely body' A10Om Nm2T15 (all β-group texts); 'body of eyþer' Gc7H7, 'body of oþer' Gc7Pe1Di2a, 'bodye aydyr' H7, '(erthely Di1) body þat hanges in the vryn' Ro6Di1, and 'body in þat schal schewe eyrys & wynd' T2. T7 retains Latin *corpus aeris*. Alternate translations for *perforacio* include the predictable *perforacioun* (twenty witnesses), *inperforacioun* Gc7, *persyng* in A8, *thurlynge* Yo, (*þe*) *hurlynge* (error for *thurlynge*) Pe3W6, *þorw ?þeroyng* T2, and *vtter parte* T13; Latin *perforacio* is retained in LdS35Di2aT7. *Circulus* and *fundus* were easier to translate, with *circulus* almost always in some form of **cercle** and *fundus* represented by **grounde** (all ten α witnesses, the αβ witnesses Gc4bDi2a, and Cu5H7T2W12Yo), *bottom* (ten of the twelve β witnesses, the γ1 and γ2 witnesses, and A8H7T2T13), *residens* (A8), and *fundus* (T6).

18 *neþer membris*: The β3 group (Nm2T15) ends here.

22 *ouemest region*: The β2 group ends here; several members of the group

(Gc4aW1OmNm1) conclude with a scribal *explicit*. For the varied abridgements and incomplete texts of JeS29Di1Ro6 (β1), see 'Guide', items 3.3.2a, 3.3.2b.

23–4 *fome . . . ventosite bollyng vp*: In addition to the variants *boylynge* and *bulnyng* 'swelling', *bollyng vp* 'boiling/bubbling/swelling upwards' is also rendered as *enbollyng vpe* (Yo), *ventosite vp* (Gc7), *wellynge vp* (S1), and *bollys* 'bubbles' (H7).

24 *weyys of vrine*: This rendering of Lat. *viis urinalibus* (urinary vessels) appears only in LdS35; also translated as *vryn weyes* (γ1) and *vrynall ways* (γ2). Most witnesses translate *viis* as *veynes*, presumably in the sense 'ducts, tubules' (H10Pe1Gc7 T11S6 Gc4bA8 Cu5) or *vaynys off the curse* ('course, *cursus*'?) in T7; W8Di2a render *viis* as *reynes*.

26 *hole men*: A few witnesses (A3S29S1) change *hole men* (Lat. *sanis*) to *olde men*, either through misreading or deliberate alteration on medical grounds.

27–8 *In þe neþemost . . . litel stones*: These *grauely litel stones* (Lat. *lapilli arenosi*) are sandy particulates in urine, read as a sign of kidney or bladder stones. In A8, *litel stones* is followed by 'as it were of þe see sond & þat betokeneth þat þe syke body is castyng oute of wyttes as a man þat begynnyth to rave', with the final sentence of the text omitted.

31 *signe of deþ*: In Ld, uniquely, the end of the text is followed by the transposed conclusion to the Middle English *Letter of Ipocras*: 'þou schalt þis ['thus'] yknowe by vryne alle þe iuelis of mannes body. Whanne þou hast yueles yknowe, here þou my3t se medecynes and charmes for many yuelis' (cf. Tavormina 2007: 641). Ld's copy of the *Letter of Ipocras* itself occurs only two leaves earlier and omits the passage.

TEXTS D–F

These three texts are all derived from the uroscopy section of the French *Lettre d'Hippocrate*, though with increasingly less literal rendition into English. When a given sign or phrase within a sign occurs in more than one of texts D, E, and F, it is annotated in the first text in which it appears, with additional evidence drawn from and cross-references to the other text(s). For the fullest and hitherto unpublished version of the French text (from BL, MS Harley 2558, Thomas Fayreford's commonplace book), with selected variants and manuscript sigla of cited witnesses, see App. II.

D. *Urine White and Red*

Collated witnesses: S42 Ra3A9 Nw1 S6 Add3Ro3; **Uncollated:** Ad1 HtS29 S40 Cu3 T12A8. Sigla and shelfmarks for cited Anglo-Norman and French witnesses are given in App. II.

5–6 *whyt at morwe & rede byfore mete & whyt aftyr mete*: The relative placement of the colour words and the times at which the urine is viewed vary among witnesses, but in **WR**, the preponderance of copies (S42Ad1 Ra3A9 Ht Ro3) gives the colours before their time of inspection, as here: white at (*var*. by) the morrow (*varr*. morn, morrow tide), red before meat, white after meat. Two witnesses (Nw1Add3) change the colour/time order for the second and third inspections: before meat red, after meat white. Four witnesses abridge the sign in different ways to a single colour: by the morrow (and) before meat red (γ1); by the morrow before meat and after meat red (γ2); white after meat (S29). Two acephalous witnesses now lack the sign (A8T12). Whether intentional or not, the alterations in the γ group yield uroscopic symptoms in direct contradiction to the mainstream reading.

7 *fatte & pycke & stronge*: French *crase truble et pouaunt/puans* (see App. II); *pouaunt* is often altered in the French tradition, sometimes to forms of *peu*, sometimes by simple omission, sometimes by omission through eye-skip from *crase truble* to *truble cum vrine* in **LdH** sign 4. On *stronge* for 'stinking', see *MED*, s.v. *strong* (adj.), sense 9(c). In five of the Middle English witnesses (γ; Nw1Add3), *pycke* is replaced by forms of *troubly/troubled*, *stronge* by *white*. No French text that I have seen includes the adjective *blanche* in this sign.

8 *melled pykke*: This sign appears in only eight of the fourteen witnesses; its relation to the French *mult tenue & nent trible* ('very thin and in no way turbid') is closest in the γ group (S6S40Cu3), which reads 'moche þenne & not trowbly' (trobyld Cu3). S42's *melled pykke* may mean 'mingled thick, thickened, congealed' (*MED*, s.v. *medlen* (v.), sense 1b.(e)), either through misreading the French original, perhaps as containing some form of AN *me(d)ler* 'to mix', or by way of an error in the translator's exemplar (e.g. eye-skip or omission of *tenue* or *nent*, all of which are attested among French witnesses). The remaining four Middle English witnesses also suggest some degree of thickness or turbidity: *meneliche thikke* (Ra3A9), *sumwhat thyk* (Ht), and the slightly awkward phrase *lyke trubledde* ('similarly or consistently turbid') in Add3. In **LdH** and most **WR** witnesses, the key point to the sign itself is the contrast of thin or moderately thick good urine with the fat, turbid, and stinking bad urine described in the preceding sign. **WBw**, **WBp**, and **JP** replace these two tokens with a single sign, fat and turbid urine indicating water or phlegm in the bowels.

9 *asse pysse*: Two witnesses render *asse pysse* as *asschys* or *aschyn* (α2); the three γ group witnesses change *pykke in þe maner as asse pysse* to *troubly as it were* (add *reyn* γ1) *water*, probably indicating a bubbly or foamy quality in the urine. Bubbles (*ampullae*) or Foam (*spuma, froth, scum*) are commonly included among the contents of urine; see H/123, H/126, and I/345–56 below.

11–12 *Feuerosus vryne þe vij dayis comyng . . . ij days rede and iiij day whyte*: This sign appears to have presented a range of challenges to translators and scribes, particularly with the words *feuerosus, comyng*, and the numerals *vij, ii*, and *iiij*. In *Urine White and Brown* (Woman), text E below, the difficulties continue. The sign is dropped in text F, *Urine White and Brown* (Phlegm).

The original **LdH** token is essentially a prognosis related to the critical days of an illness, based on the Hippocratic *Aphorisms* 4.71 (see m.n. on D/11-12): for the French text, in a fever that ends on the seventh day, good health can be expected if the urine has been white on the fourth day and red on the second. But the French *en feures* and *enfievré* were sometimes misunderstood even in their original language (see apparatus in App. II), and Middle English scribes had occasional difficulties with it, sometimes punctuating the word as belonging with the preceding sign (HtAdd3) or rendering it *enfugurid* (Nw1; cf. the French variant *en figures*).

French *termine*, translated as *comyng* in S42, tends to be heavily abbreviated in the manuscripts and may have suffered from some confusion between the letters *t* and *c*; it is misunderstood by almost all English translators. In **WR**, beside S42's *comyng* (possibly an attempt to make sense of the next variant), it is rendered *crem(y)/cremynge* in Ad1Ra3A9, as well as *grene* (Ht), *fowle* (Add3), and *þe twelfe day* (Nw1). Cu3 drops the reference to fever and instead highlights the technique of judging the urine over time, altering the first half of the sign to read 'Vrine 7 dayes holden to se it diuerse'. Witnesses to **WBw** approach *termine* a little more closely, usually with forms of the verb *turnen* or (once) *chaungen*. In three cases, witnesses to **WBw** reflect the original relatively accurately: S35Ar translate *termine* as *termynyd* and Ro1 reads *termun hit*, most likely an aural misapprehension or miscue for the correct word. (Ht's *mynd* could be a scribal error for *termynd*.) However, most **WBw** texts opt for forms of *turnen*, and it is those readings that I have provided in texts E.1 and E.2.

Finally, the numbers for the seventh, second, and fourth days in the French text are often garbled in the **WR** versions of the sign and are radically simplified to first, second, and third in **WBw**, significantly changing the sign's meaning (see n. to E.1/8-9).

19 *poudrows*: Of five copies of **LdH** that I have found which include this sign, four read *pudrouse* (HTOY) while the fifth has *poureuse* 'fearful' (V), probably in error. However, the evidence of the English texts suggests that some scribes interpreted ME *pouderous* (a likely initial translation of *pudrouse*) as *ponderous* 'heavy'. 'Powdery' is a rare descriptor for urine, whereas 'heavy' occurs somewhat more often and heaviness may have seemed a more familiar medical concept in general.

Thus, in text D, the word transcribed here as *poudrows* 'powdery' could have been intended as *pondrows* 'heavy', with indistinguishable scribal *n* and *u*, in three witnesses (S42Ad1Cu3); five witnesses render it as *heuy* (S6S40) or *heuy as leed* (Ra3A9Ro3), while in Add3 it appears as *pōderus*, and in Nw1, whose scribe distinguishes *n* and *u*, as *ponderos*. In **WBw**, ambiguous *n/u* spellings occur in eleven to fourteen witnesses (Ad2A13CpCu6Ro1S35 T14ArS28S14S1 and possibly HtSuRo2), derivatives of *pouder* in five (*pudruse* Cc, *powderows* S24, *pewdres* A9, *poudred* A8Yo), with *heuy & troblyd* in only one (A3). In **WBp**, on the other hand, five witnesses have ambiguous *n/u* letters (W12S2A7Gc1aNw2) and three read *pōderowse* (Gc1bS20Eg3). Many Middle English readers would have had to decide for themselves which sense was intended in the text they encountered.

20–1 *Vryne that is sumdel blody . . . bladder*: A sign that evolves dramatically across the Middle English posterity of **LdH**, beginning with *Le vrine sanguente / sanglente & for mise od peccoies* (varr.: *pieretes, perettes, pecotes, petites gotes*, etc.) *de sang signifie grant mal dedeyns le corps & meisment en la vessie*. In **WR**, the reading of the base manuscript S42 is repeated with only minor variations in the other α1 witnesses; Add3 and Ht abridge the sentence in different ways, while Nw1 adds *myd litil tachez of blode*, retaining the idea of *peccoies de sang*.

The **WBw** texts retain the diagnosis *much evil in the body*, usually (though not in E.1) adding *of the menisoun*. Several witnesses further specify the location or nature of the evil (see n. to E.2/24–5). However, the signifying symptom varies significantly across the manuscripts, with some retaining the comparison to blood or to spots or pieces of blood, while others compare the urine to fire, pease broth, pease blooms, and the mysterious 'prosper (?) broth'.

In **WBp**, the sign is modified almost beyond recognition, aside from its position in the list of signs: *Uryne þat semys red like old wyn & fatt abowue: þat is a syne þat hys lyuyr is stuft* (F/20–1). None of the *regulae* in **JP** appears to derive from this **LdH** sign.

29 *reseyith*: 'Uterus, womb', a specialized application of the sense 'receptacle, vessel' (*MED*, s.v. *receit(e* (n.), sense 3(b)), translating *matriz* in **LdH**. The scribe of S42 misinterpreted the word here as the past participle of *receiven* ('sche is reseuyd'), though he understands it correctly a few lines later ('here reseyith is rotet'). Three witnesses (γ1; A8) replace the term with the more common *matrice*, while Nw1 substitutes *marewe* 'marrow', either in error or used figuratively for 'core, center, interior'. The sign is omitted in **WBw** and **WBp**, but recurs in **UMul** in **DU**.

33 *mythy*: Translating OF *peysaunte* 'heavy', as suggested by the variants *perwith hevy* (S6S40) and *hevy as lede* (A8); applied to urine, the French term may also mean 'oppressive, stale, rank' (*AND*, s.v. *peisant*[1], a., sense 5).

34 *kynde of man*: S42's reading here is unique, though comparison with other French and English versions makes the sense 'desire for man' clear: *talent d'omme* (VTO), *talent de auer a fere od humme* (H), *uolente d'omme* (W), *tallent de compaignie d'omme* (F), *mestier d'oume* (S); *talent to man* (Ra3A8); *(great) lust to man* (γ1; A9Add3). In texts E.1 and E.2, the analogous sign reads *talent to man* in all witnesses; in F, the phrase is rendered *lykynge to* (most witnesses) or *lof to* (Eg3) *man*. The specific sense '(sexual) desire' for *kynde* is not recorded in the *MED*, but would be an easy extension of the sense 'natural instincts, desires, or feelings within man or animal' (s.v. *kinde* (n.), sense 5a), especially given the several sexually oriented definitions under sense 14a. (Cf. *OED*, s.v. *kind*, n., senses 5a, 6a, and 15a–b.)

35 *stable clensyng*: S42's reading *stable clensyng* (also found in Ra3A9Add3; *stedefaste [s]purgyng* in γ1 and A8) is corrupt. Only Nw1's reading *mele spurgynge* accurately reflects **LdH**. The original French sign refers to urine that has a colour like sifted meal, albeit in phrasings that sometimes only make sense after comparison to other variants: *colour de ferine espurgee* (T), *colour de ferine espurgement* (O), *ferine espurgement* (HV), *talent de faire .i. espurgement* (N), etc.; some French versions change the symptom to *perse* 'livid' (WFS). An early English translator of text D may have read *ferine* as *ferme*, and interpreted it as 'firm, steadfast, stable'.

Most witnesses to texts E.1 and E.2 read *colour* (or occasionally *signe*) *of smal mele*, which captures the sense of *ferine* and may interpret *espurgee* or one of its variants to mean finely sifted (hence 'smal'). Text F drops the sign.

37 *peys & of colour lede*: The French witnesses to this sign consistently refer to urine of the weight and colour of lead, though their phrasing varies somewhat (e.g. *de peys/pois, pesante, moult poise*, etc.). Most Middle English versions of **WR** that include the sign appear to derive from a translation that interpreted *peis* as *pers* 'livid' or *pars* 'parts', yielding *pers* in Add3 and (with *er/ar* curl) S42, *partie* in Ra3A9. Only Nw1 keeps the original sense with 'of þe pays and of þe weiȝt'. Most copies of **WBw** translate *peys* with forms of *peses* 'pieces' (Ad0A13 R01A1 S35HtS20b A9Ro2Yo S29a) or *pese* (A8S24); in S1 and A3, one finds *pesyn* 'peas' and *knottis* 'lumps'. In **WBp**, the sign is simplified by omitting *de peys &* entirely (all witnesses). See also I/289–91 for incorporation of this sign into the **UMul** component of the *Dome of Uryne*.

40 The colour or other quality of urine implied by the comparison to flax is not entirely clear: of a flaxen colour (i.e. *OED*, s.v. *flaxen*, adj. 'colour of dressed flax'; perhaps like the modern urinary descriptor 'straw-coloured'); the colour of linseed (either light brown or golden); or perhaps the golden colour of linseed oil? A flaxen colour seems possible for the French texts, which agree on the phrase *colur de lin*, and for **WR**, whose variants include *flaxe* (S42 Ra3A9 T12), *colour of flex* (A8), and *coloure of lyn* (Nw1). However, in the **WBw** texts, the translator(s) interpret *lin* as linseed across the board: E.1 reads *colour of lynseid*; E.2 variants are all forms of *lynsed* or *colour of lynsed*. The only quasi-outlier is S1, which specifies the colour further: 'a browne hewe rede after lonsyd'. **WBp** omits this sign.

E. *Urine White and Brown* (Woman Variant)

1

Witness: Cc. The earliest extant copy of **WBw**, which survives in a manuscript that also contains an Anglo-Norman copy of **LdH** (T. Hunt 2001), though the Middle English text is not a direct translation of the **LdH** version earlier in the manuscript.

2 *brown at afteremete*: The most notable and diagnostically problematic variation between the White–Red(–White) and White–Brown reflexes of **LdH** lies in the time at which healthy urine should be more intense in colour: *before* eating in the white–red versions and *after* eating in the white–brown versions (including **JP** in the *Dome of Uryne* as well as the two **WB** texts).

Witnesses to the whole class of white–brown texts are quite consistent in defining healthy urine as white in the morning and brown 'at aftermeat', with no third colour stage given. This variation on the **LdH** original and the Middle English White–Red texts may derive from a misinterpretation of the syntactic boundaries in the sign, from 'white in the morning, before eating red, after eating white signifies health' to 'white in the morning before eating, red after eating, white signifies health'. Such a change may have been preceded by an inadvertent omission of the second 'white' or followed by its deletion as no longer meaningful in the sentence.

Although most French witnesses to **LdH** agree with the text in Harley 2558 (*blanche de tut le matin, deuant le manger ruge, apres manger blanch*), at least two show such omissions and/or syntactic redivision: most significantly, CCCC 388 (the multilingual English manuscript that also contains the earliest witness to *Urine White and Brown*), with 'Si le urine seyt blanche de tut le matyn e ruge aprés manger, signefiet sainté' (T. Hunt 2001: 92), and TCC O.1.20, reading 'L'ome iert sains si sa urine est blanche dou tot le matin deuant mangier roge apres mangier' (f. 54ʳ). Similar though not identical are the variations on the sign in **WR** described in the n. to D/5–6 above.

7 *wmman*: An alternate spelling of *wumman*, with the letter *w* = *uu*. Similar spellings for words like *wnde* 'wound', *walwrt* 'walwort', *wlgariter* = *vulgariter*, *wlnera* = *vulnera* are sporadically attested in Cc (T. Hunt 2001: 87, 113, 180, 211–12) and elsewhere in early Middle English (*MED* cites the forms *wman* and *wmmone* from before 1275 and *c.*1300).

8–9 *Vrine of feueres . . . firste day . . . þat oþer day . . . þridde day . . . etik*: The **LdH** version of this sign (see n. to D/11–12 and App. II) undergoes substantial revision in **WBw**: where the French text highlights the seventh, fourth, and second days of a fever, **WBw** simplifies the chronology to the first, second, and third; the generally positive prognosis is qualified by the exception of hectic fever; and, as noted above, the original French participle *termine* is usually translated as *turned*. Some of these changes can be explained as scribal misunderstandings: for example, *vii* 'seven' may have been read as *vn* 'one'; as suggested in the n. to D/11–12, *turned* is probably a response to an abbreviated form of *termine*, and a fever that 'terminates' on the first day instead of the seventh would no longer make sense. Other alterations may have been seen as medical improvements, clarifying the chronology of febrile symptoms and nuancing the prognosis. The sign is dropped in **WBp** and **JP**.

10 *fenderes*: Suspended matter, sediment, or dregs in a liquid (< AN *fundril*, *fundriz*; cf. *MED*, s.v. *foundres* (n. pl.)), used here as an equivalent to the *fundus* or lowest region in a urine sample. For English variants on *fundus* in E.1/E.2, see n. to E.2/13–18 below.

Both versions of **WB** revise the diagnostic details of this sign in **LdH** and **WR**, changing the characteristics from fat, white, and moist (D/13, **LdH** sign 6) to fat (**WBw**) or black (**WBp**) in the lowest region of the sample, white in the middle, and red in the uppermost region. All texts in both languages read the attributes as indicators of an impending or occasionally a present quartan fever.

17 *spewit blod*: Spitting or coughing up blood is a natural enough expansion on the preceding sign (pissing blood), which is found in both variants of **WB** (texts E and F), though it does not appear in **WR** or in most versions of **LdH**. However, the copy of **LdH** in Wellcome 546 (*c.*1340) replaces the sign of blood in the urine with one for spitting blood: 'Qui sanc crache sanz mal si a ueine corrompue es rains' ('He who spits blood without pain has a vein ruptured in the kidneys'; T. Hunt 2011: 42). The English texts (E.1, E.2, F) seem more anatomically plausible than Wellcome 546, associating bloody expectoration with a broken vein in the heart or lungs rather than the kidneys or loins; perhaps Wellcome 546 conflated two signs here.

18 *Vrine red as fur . . . in þe body*: See ill. to E.2/24, 24–5.

19–20 *Fleyes and boyleyun . . . in þe lunges*: The versions of this sign in all **WBw** and **WBp** witnesses reveal a complicated range of variants. It has no clear analogue in **LdH**, but is present—possibly already in a corrupted form—in the early copy of the Middle English text in Cc. In all **WBw** witnesses, the diagnosis is consistently given as *aposteme in the liver and evil in the lungs*; in all **WBp** witnesses, the diagnosis is simplified to *aposteme in the liver*.

As with the preceding sign, however, the symptoms that lead to these diagnoses are more variable. Those variations are most easily presented in tabular form: see Table 3 above (p. 15), with spelling normalized except for forms of *flien* and its reflexes. The sign may have begun with a symptom like 'flies and boil in midward more than above' (as found in Cc) or 'flies and boils in (the) midward (and) thin above' (as in A3 and others), referring to some kind of Foam or Bubbles in the middle of the sample, with less foamy or thinner urine at the top. Over time, the word *flies* (in various spellings) must have been read by some scribes as *flesh*. The subsequent collocation of *flesh* and *boil* could then suggested the standard comparison of Pallidus urine to water in which raw flesh has been boiled, even though the colour associated here is red. Reference to falling rain water may echo comparisons of *ampullae* or Bubbles in urine to bubbles or drops of rain. Other changes may reflect scribes' attempts to make sense of difficult exemplars.

The *-un* ending on *boyleyun* in Cc is a pl. pr. indic. (Benskin in T. Hunt 2001: 228). Because Cc uses the grapheme *y* to represent both the semivowel *y* and *þ*, Benskin interprets the character-string as *boy leyun* ('both lie'). However, given the repeated appearance of forms of *boillen* in other witnesses, it seems more plausible to assign the word to *boillen*, with a spelling related to the forms *boylie, boili, bolyyn* recorded in *MED*. Benskin interprets *fleyes* as a spelling of *flesh*, which may be supported by other witnesses, but the omission of 'Urine that', difficulties with overall sense, and divergence from other versions of the sign suggest some corruption in the textual transmission of Cc.

21–2 Possibly a revision of sign 13 in **LdH**, which deals with urine floating above with a fatty Circle, albeit with a different significance ('angue & lunge enfermite') and no restriction to women. See n. to E.2/29 below.

23 *ray & cler and schynande as siluer*: See m.n. to D/25–6. *Ray/raie* may have its usual Middle English sense of 'striped, having streaks', rather than the more common Old French sense of 'shining, radiant', though the two definitions could overlap in the sense 'having streaks of light'. 'Striped' or 'streaky' urine is often mentioned in English texts derived from a Latin uroscopy attributed to Walter Agilon, in which the second sign is usually *alba* (i.e. clear) urine that is *virgulata*, *radiosa*, or (occasionally) *fenestrata*, rendered in Middle English as *bemy*, *yerded*, and *windowed*. However, the Agilon texts do not link *urina radiosa* with pregnancy. In the French texts, *raie* is very rare; I have only seen it as an emendation in Hunt's edition of the **LdH** from TCC O.5.32 (1994–7: ii. 264).

25 *scom*: The manuscript reading *þe ston* makes grammatical sense and could make medical sense (describing a woman suffering from kidney stones), but is in fact a misreading of *scom* 'foam' in an English exemplar, translating the French *escume* in **LdH** sign 16. Only one other copy of **WBw** agrees with Cc's reading (A3: *a ston*); other variants are *scom(e)*, *skyme*, *skeme*, *som(e)*, and the unique variants *sonyng*, *that semyth*, *that is rede*, *that ys grene*. The analogous sign in **WR** (D/31–2 above), un-usually, is less close to **LdH** than are most **WBw** witnesses, omitting references to Foam, loss of appetite and insomnia, and swelling of the stomach. **WBp** and **JP** omit this sign in connection with women's urines.

26 *nowit*: Here and in E.1/33–6 below, I follow Benskin in taking *nowit* as one word (the adverb 'not'; in T. Hunt 2001: 228). *Nowit* could also be analysed as *no wit* 'not at all', but the absence of intensifiers in the parallel French signs (**LdH** signs 16, 19, 20) suggests that it is meant as a simple negative.

29 *and hat lorn . . . blod*: Probably a reference to the menses, either 'and has begun to menstruate' or 'and is menstruating', although the use of the singular instead of the plural is highly unusual (all *MED* quotations for this sense (s.v. *flour* (n. (1)), sense 6) use the plural). The phrase also occurs in several E.2 witnesses (S24S35YoRo2S28A3A9), but not in Ad2 and nowhere among the witnesses to F.

31 *3ridde*: A rare but not unattested spelling of *þridde* (Benskin in T. Hunt 2001: 208, 228).

35 *golled*: 'Yellowed, made pale' (from *gul(le)*, *go(u)le* 'yellow, pale, sickly-looking', probably the colouration later known as chlorosis; see *MED*, s.v. *gul* (adj.)). Scribal variation in **WBw** suggests some unfamiliarity with the word: *golled* (Cc), *gull(e)* (Ad2 Ro1A8), *golle* (Yo), *goule* (Ro2), *guld* (A13), *gule* (CpS14), *3elow3* (S24S35 S28 A3 S1), *cold(e)* (Ht A9; in error), *om.* Ar S29a S29b, *sign om.* **WBp**. **LdH** and **WR** speak only of the *colur de lin* and urine *lyche flaxe*.

bolned: 'swollen'. Cf. **LdH** *emfle* 'swollen' and ME variants (*y*)*bolned* (Cc Ad2A13 Cp Ro1A8 Ht Yo), *bolne* (S35), *boylled* (S24), (*y*)*swolle* (A9Ro2), *yswellud* (A3), *sygne þat sche bolnyth* (S29a), *blody* (S14), *bonde* (S1), *om.* (Ar S28 S29b).

2

Collated Witnesses: Ad2A13 Ro1A8 S35 A3 A9; Cp S1 S14 selectively; **Uncollated:** S28 S24HtS29b Ro2YoT14Su ArS29a Cu6T13a. Scattered **WBw** tokens are mingled with signs from other texts in T13bPmNm2; three additional witnesses occur in Ro1 and S24, but are copies of earlier **WBw** texts in the same manuscripts. These scattered and repeated witnesses are not reported in the notes below.

4–7 *Vrine thinne and grene . . . Vryne thenne and blak . . .*: One of the additional touchstones by which the Middle English white–brown uroscopies can be distinguished from white–red treatises is the replacement of the two signs based on thick and moderately thick urine (D/7–8) by one or two signs based on thin urine whose upper region or Circle is Green, Livid, or Black (colours associated with adustion and mortification; cf. A.1/8–13, A.2/22–7).

Among witnesses to **WBw**, the first sign, on thin Green and Livid urines, appears only in selected γ (Ad2A13CpCu6S1) and β (Ro1A8ArS29a) witnesses. The second sign, in contrast, linking thin black urine to male sexual desire, occurs in all witnesses aside from those comprised of a few individual signs inserted in other token lists. The **JP** segment of the *Dome of Uryne* incorporates both signs with little substantive change (see I/236–9 below).

Unlike **JP**, **WBp** radically alters these new signs (see F/6–10 below). The only points of similarity that remain in **WBp** are the focus on thinness at the upper level of the flask ('thin . . . above' vs. 'thin . . . under the circle' and 'a great circle') and the colours Green, Livid, and Black. The phrase *talent to womman* drops out and the diagnoses are changed to stomach fever, nausea, and headache caused by water between the meninges and the brain.

5 *botonys of leed*: 'Small pieces of lead, buds of lead', attested in Ad2 Ro1A8S29a. One witness reads *betyn leed* (A13), another *bakyn peyse of leed* (S1), two simplify the phrase to *leed* (CpAr), and one omits the comparison entirely (Cu6). **JP** likewise eliminates the comparison. The sign is missing in the entire α group.

13–18 *Vrine fat in þe botme . . . Vrine blody . . . Vrine fat & flesshy & in þe founsse . . .*: These three signs and their analogues in **WBp** (F/11–16) and **JP** (I/241–5) appear to be deliberate modifications of three signs in **LdH**: fat, white, and moist urine signifying a quartan to come; bloody urine signifying a purulent lesion in the bladder; and fleshy, fat urine signifying disease of the kidneys (**LdH** signs 6–8 in App. II; cf. D/13–16 above).

The terms *botme* and *founsse* in the first and third sign both refer to the lowest level of the urine flask (Lat. *fundus*), and their **WBw** variants provide a miniature thesaurus of synonyms for that level: *bottom* (Ad2A3Ro1), *foundirs/foundres*

(A13S1 Ro1ArS29a Ht A9Ro2YoT14 S29b), *foundyrs of þe bottome* (S29b), *founde/ funde* (Cu6Ar), *founsse/fonce/faunce* (Ad2A13S1), *fenderes/funderes* (Cc), *grounde* (S28 S24S35 Su), and the errors *4nyȝt* (Cp), *sondyrs* (A8), *fome* (S14). **WBp** witnesses consistently spell the term *founderel/fundrell*.

Some **WBw** witnesses omit the sign for cold dropsy (CcS28 CpCu6); S14 omits the sign for hot dropsy, as does the **JP** text in the *Dome of Uryne*.

15 *Vrine blody . . . bladdere is brosed*: A slight abridgement of the *vrine sanglente* sign in **LdH**, dropping the reference to putrefaction (*acune pourture*) within the bladder, followed by the new observation that if the bladder is not bruised, the blood signifies the hot dropsy. The Middle English White–Red uroscopies (**WR**, **ST**, **15D**) preserve the original content of the sign (D/14–15 above; the second sign in both **ST** and **15D**).

24 *as pesyn broth*: Another difficult phrase for scribes. **LdH** refers here to 'vrine sanguente & for mise od peccoies de sang' or 'urine that is bloody and produced with pieces of blood' (sign 11; cf. D/20 'sumdel blody of sekenysse'; E.1/18 'red as fiir or blod'; and possibly F/20 'red lyke old wyn'). Variants among the E.2 witnesses can be divided into those that omit the reference to blood (*as pesyn* (*pese* S14) *brothe* Ad2S14, *as pese bro* A13, *as p⟨?⟩sper broth* Cu6, *as pese blomes* S1, all in the γ family) and those that retain it (*as peses* (*pyse* A8S29a, *pysse ys* T14Su) *of blood* A9YoT14Su Ro1A8Ar S29a, *& posid of blood* S35, *as spottys of blode* A3, *as blood* S24S28, all in the α and β families). It seems likely that the *pesyn/pese broth* variants are corruptions of the *peses of blood* variants, but comparisons of urine to types of broth (meat, fish, gravy) are not uncommon.

24–5 *in þe body of þe menysoun*: Possible misunderstanding of the French original, 'dedeyns le corps & meisment en la vessie', with *meisment* (perhaps in abbreviated form) misread as *menisoun* and 'en la vessie' lost. Some α witnesses add '(&) in the kedneyres (nerys HtS28, feuerys Yo) bothe' (S28S24HtYo) or '(&) in þe arse (ers boþe S35)' (S35T14Su).

29 *gallades*: This word gave scribes great difficulty, and it is hard to know what the original might have been, aside from some disease that affects women, possibly in the gall bladder (note the difference from the parallel sign in E.1/21–2, also restricted to women's urine, which signals 'gret euele in þe body'). The sign appears only in **WBw**, and only in fourteen witnesses. The closest analogue in **LdH** (sign 13) describes a urine with fat or a fatty ring floating above, signalling acute fever and long illness, but does not limit the sign to women or mention any disease term similar to *gallades*. The attempts made on the word are as follows: *galla^{des}* Ad2, *galrades* A13Yo, *galleracles* Cp, *gallerakkis* S14, *figal racles* Ro1, *garecles* A8, *here galle rancles* Ar, *grete sykenes* A3, *a syknese þat women haþe & hyt ys callyde þe galorache* S29a, *galard in þe lyuer and þe bitternes ther of rancours of þe hert* S1, *sign om.* S28 S24S35 A9Ro2, *text ends before sign* T14SuCu6. **WBp** has no equivalent sign. The best translation of *gallades* and its variants is probably something like 'ulcerated gall bladder' or possibly 'bitterness (rancour) of the gall, bitter bile'.

30–1 *mercurye*: Ad2 is unique in its reference to the metal mercury by its planetary name; A13 has *quyk siluer* here, but all other witnesses for texts D and E give *silver*, corresponding to *argent* in **LdH**. Three witnesses add a further dimension to the sign: *and heuy* in Ad2S1, *and hony* A13. **WBp** omits the sign.

41–2 *Et si . . . mortis sue*: The use of Latin for this sentence is unique to Ad2. Elsewhere it is rendered in English, with only minor variations from the reading of S35: '& ȝif sche be noȝt with childe it is signe þat sche may noȝt leue longe'.

46–7 *Vryne . . . longe euel*: Although this sign is omitted in the base text (Ad2), it occurs with minor variants in slightly over half the witnesses that continue to the end of the text (S28 S24S35 HtS29bA3 A9Ro2Yo; *om.* Ad2A13 Cp S1 Ro1A8ArS29a). In its mention of urine that floats like bubbles formed by rain and its diagnosis of long infirmity, it appears to echo sign 12 in **LdH**, though not as a direct translation and despite occurring substantially later in the series and being restricted to women.

50–3 Some γ witnesses to the text (Ad2A13 Cp S1S14) add a pair of signs (24–5) about urines indicating pain on the left and right sides of the body, apparently unique to **WBw**, and useful in distinguishing textual families within the universe of all witnesses.

F. *Urine White and Brown* (Phlegm Variant)

Collated witnesses (all): W12S2A7 S20 Gc1aGc1b Eg3Nw2A14. Gc1 contains two copies of **WBp**, the second of which rearranges the text but otherwise appears to copy the first; it is not reported separately in the notes below.

1 *kenne & dysscryue*: W12Gc1, knowe & discrye S2, dyscern and deme A7, *om.* a2, γ, δ.

35 *mares*: The base manuscript form *mayes* is found only in W12 and the two copies in Gc1; it is not recorded in the *MED* or *OED*. The spelling with *y* may simply be a misinterpretation of long *r*, as the variant *maris* (S2A7Eg3Nw2) is a common enough word for the uterus, used in an extended sense (like its native equivalent *moder* 'womb, uterus') for diseases of the uterus. See *MED*, s.v. *maris* (n.), sense (b), and *OED*, s.v. *mother*, n.¹, sense 9.

41 *wastyng*: Although W12's unique reading *wastyng* ('enfeebling') is not an unreasonable diagnosis, supported by S20's *febill*, the more common variant is *walting* 'rolling, surging' (S2A7Gc1Nw2), perhaps as a description of nausea or rumbling in the stomach. Eg3's *walyng* may be an error for *waltyng*; A14 omits this sign.

44 *stoffyd*: So in W12S2Gc1, but altered to *chafyde* '(over)heated' in A7S20; *om.* Eg3Nw2A14.

TEXTS G–I

Although these texts are indebted at various points to both the Latin and French antecedents of texts A through F, they may be native English compositions. Substantial variants for Texts G and I, from several manuscripts, are given in Apps. III and IV.

G. *Rufus Subrufus*

Collated witnesses: Gc4W10 Di1 T15 A8; **Uncollated:** OmNm1 Ra2 Nm2W11 A10 Ro6JeS29 W1A7Ad6 Ro3

1–4 *Here bigynneþ . . . king Henri þe fourþe*: The 'Royal' prologue ascribes the commissioning of *Rufus Subrufus* variously to Henry IV (Gc4W10), to *þe prairs of þe kyng & of oþer lordis* (Om, with a marginal note possibly in the main scribe's hand reading *kyng hary the v*), and to *the demawnd of the kyng* (Nm1). All versions of this prologue agree in attributing authorship to the 'wisest clerk(s) of physic of England' and in describing the work as being 'translated out of Latin into English', although no direct Latin source for the treatise has yet been uncovered and some of the remedies are well disseminated in Middle English medical recipe collections. 'Translation' may have been understood more generally, in the sense of explaining the Latin colour terms and their diagnostic significance in the vernacular. A second marginal note in Om, in a display script above the beginning of the text, reads *Anno domini m⁰ cccc⁰ xxj Mʳ Johannes & alijs*, which may be a claim of authorship and a date that would be consistent with the note to *kyng hary the v*. However, as the manuscript itself is from the late fifteenth century, the evidentiary value of these notes is uncertain at best.

2 *icontryued*: Devised or composed (by the authors of the treatise). In the variant 'Circle' prologue (App. III below), the twenty colours of urine are described as *nat contryuid*, perhaps with the sense 'true, not (falsely) devised' or 'natural, not artificial'. See *MED*, s.v. *contreven* (v.), sense 4 (including various deceptive purposes), and *OED*, s.v. *contrive*, v.1 ¹, sense 5 ('to make up, concoct, fabricate, invent').

16–17 *Cum dicitur . . . ortis*: This Latin tag is omitted in all witnesses to the δ group, as well as in Gc4 (α) and Ra2 (with mixed α and β features). The three remaining α witnesses and all four β and γ witnesses preserve the phrase, with minor variations.

20–5 *foure watris þat bitokenen indigestioun . . . two bitokenen bigynnyng of digestioun*: Gc4 and Nm2 both follow the usual assignment of four urines to the Indigestion group and two to the Beginning of Digestion, but W10Om T15 Ra2 A8 shift Karapos to the latter group and give the numbering here as three and three. In Nm1A10, the numbers are four (corrected to three in Nm1) and three, an error no doubt caused by the greater familiarity of a four-urine Indigestion group. The three-and-three numbering for Indigestion and Beginning of Digestion may be the original count, susceptible to pressure from the more common assignments of four and two urines to those groups. On further numbering difficulties in the text, see n. to G/71, 89–90.

68–70 *& sey . . . sine dubio*: This charm, with small differences, appears in α-group members W10OmNm1 and the γ witness A8. Gc4 retains only the final clause, translated as '& he schal be hool'. The β-group T15Nm2 probably both contained the abridged instruction '& say v pater nostyrs & v aysse ffor alle crystene sowlys & holle' (Nm2; T15 has two lines heavily cancelled, presumably for religious reasons). Other witnesses drop the charm entirely.

71, 89–90 *foure . . . indigestioun, pre . . . bigynynge of digestioun*: Eleven witnesses, all in the αβγ or acephalous textual groups, report the number of colours in the two digestion groups named in these lines, but the reporting is inaccurate or incomplete in all of them. Nine witnesses (α; T15Ra2 A10 A7Ro3) err in assigning four and three colours respectively to Indigestion and Beginning of Digestion, rather than four and two or three and three, depending on how those two groups were counted at the start of the text (see n. to G/20–5). Nm2 specifies three colours for Indigestion (despite listing four colours for that group earlier), but then gives no number for Beginning of Digestion. A8 says that these two groups have three colours each, but fails to give numbers for the Excess, Adustion, and Mediate Digestion groups.

88 *Turne vp*: Only in Gc4, written in red at the end of a paragraph, with the rest of the line left blank. It may have begun as some form of reading instruction, referring to an earlier point in the text (see *MED*, s.v. *turnen* (v.), sense 19a.(c)), but if so, the antecedent point is no longer clear.

H. *Ten Cold Ten Hot*

Collated witnesses: S10S32 Cu4 H5 Co3; **Uncollated:** Ra6Gc6 H7S20 H4 S1 Nm3 H1Cu3

88 *me most take hede*: 'One must take heed'. This construction, with the indefinite pronoun *me* 'one, they, people in general', appears in S10Cu4S1, but other scribes revise it in various ways, perhaps for greater clarity: *men most take hede* (H5Co3), *me behoues tak heeth* (H4), *take hed* (Ra6Gc6H7S20); in the sixteenth century, John Eames (S32) and the compiler of Wyer's *Boke of Knowledge* (*K*) opt for *yow must take good hiede* and *we must take hede* respectively.

103 *falowe leues fallyng of trees*: So in S10H5H4, but other witnesses read *salow leuys fallyng of treys* (Cu4S32), *fallyng levis falling downe of treis* (S1), *ripe leuys fallyng fro þe tre* (*fr⟨o⟩ trees* S20) (H7S20), or employ the more traditional simile *a cler lanterne horne* (Ra6Gc6).

105 *sammen sothen flesch*: I.e. half-cooked meat, reflecting the traditional simile for

Pallidus, 'the broth of meat half cooked'/'ut succus carnis semicocte' (see *MED*, s.vv. *samsoden* (adj.), *sam-* (pref.); *OED*, s.v. *sam-*, prefix). Neither dictionary records the spelling *sammen*, which scribes may have found obscure as well: variants include *samon sodyn sothyn flesch* (Cu4), *semyng like to soden fleshe* (S1), *ha(u)lf sode / sodin fleshe* (H4S32), *lik (to) well sothin fleche* Ra6Gc6), and *lik sodyn flesch* (H7S20). The sense 'together' (*MED*, s.v. *samen*, adv.(1)) is unlikely, given the standard comparison of Pallidus to the broth of half-cooked meat.

106 *pom syter . . . 3alowe floures*: *Pom syter* (varr. *sither, citer, siter*) is probably a citron (*MED*, s.v. *pome* (n.), ~ *cedre* 'citron'; *OED*, s.v. *pome-cedre*, n.). Two scribes alter the *pom syter* comparison to *ryp appull* (Ra6Gc6), while three drop the fruit comparison entirely to leave only the yellow flowers (H7S20S1). Cu4 retains *pom siter*, but alters *3alowe* to *salow*.

126 *iawnyes*: The letter-forms of *iawnyes* led a couple of scribes astray, probably by a misreading of *j* as a long *r*: *rawnes* (S32), *raynes* (S1). Ra6's *jandandas* is likely simple dittography.

I. *The Dome of Uryne* (Expanded Version)

Collated witnesses: S15Ad4 Ad7 Sj3 W7; Uncollated: H11A6Ra4Se

27 *frothi*: The scribe of W7 frequently replaces the words *froth, frothy* with *broth, brothy* (here and again in the fifteenth colour; several times each in **JP** and **4Con**). This first occurrence of the error may have been triggered by the comparison of Subpallidus/Pallidus colours to 'broth of flesh'. Elsewhere, the confusion may be more attributable to the similar endings of the words, or it may suggest that the scribe was thinking of the foam that rises to the top of broth in cooking.

35 *tastyng*: Possibly an error for *castyng* ('urine thin when it is produced, and without smell'), a reading that is attested clearly in Ad4W7, though *tastyng* is supported unambiguously in Sj3. As can be seen elsewhere in this volume (H/96–7, 111–12; I/184–7), tasting urine could be included in a thorough uroscopic analysis. Even if *castyng* is the correct reading here, the phrase 'wythouten sauour' still points to smell or taste as a feature to be considered. Depending on context, the 'casting' of urine can refer either to the patient who produces the sample, or to the interpretation offered by the uroscopist: cf. E.1/6; E.2/5, 6; H/86; I/81, 92, 204–5, 237–8, 373.

70, 71 *bloo, bloohed*: Some scribes of the *Dome of Uryne* appear to have had difficulty with the word *bloo* ('livid, bruise-coloured') and its derivatives, replacing them with various alternatives: *blo, blohede* S15Ad7Di1; *bloo* corr. from *blood, bloo hede* Di3; *bloo, blodhed* Co3; *blo, blones* Om; *blode, blode hed* Ad4; *blake, blode* W7SeA6; *blody, bloode abouten* Sj3; *bloo, bloude* Ra4. *Blo* is derived primarily from ON *blá* ('livid') , possibly with some influence from OF *bleu/bloi*, which can in turn mean 'livid', 'blue', or—in reference to hair—'blond(e), tawny'. Cf. *MED*, s.v. *blo* (adj.);

AND, s.v. *bleu*, a.; *OED*, s.v. blo, *adj*. On the entrance and semantic development of French *bleu* in English, including 'livid' among other senses, see Biggam 2006.

97 *crullyng*: Rumbling in the bowels. *Crullyng* is well distributed among the versions (Exp.: S15Ad4H11Se; Core: Co3Di1A11; Hyb.: S16; the Abbreviated Version omits **GrCon**), but variants are common, possibly reflecting a range of colloquial terms for the phenomenon and occasional misunderstandings:

> Exp.: grullyng Sj3Ra4, crwelynge A6, brwlyng Ad7, quellyng W7;
> Core: gurgelande Co1OmW9, gurlyng & gulacion Ht, gurlyng A14, crowlyng H6;
> Hyb.: churlyng Hm1, straytnese S29a, clensyng *S*.

100 *8ᵐ*: The marginal numbers from 8 to 10 in S15 (9 to 12 in Ad4, but overlapping with S15 on signs 9 and 10) look like the remnant of an earlier series from 1 to 15, covering the four contents in **4Con** and the eleven in **GrCon**. No other Expanded Version manuscripts contain the numbers, but three of the Core Version witnesses introduce **4Con-GrCon** with a heading that indicates fifteen contents to follow:

> In vnaquaque regione continentur diuersa and þer ben 15 in al Om;
> And eche of these regyonus forsayd ben dyuerse contentes and þer ben xv in all Co1W9.

Other Core witnesses omit the number:

> and yn ylke of þes regions bethe dyuerse contentys Di3A11Di1;
> in lyknes of þe regyon (*add* bene dyuers contentes Ht) HtS29b;
> *heading om.* Co3A14.

The Hybrid Version witness Hg1 retains '10' after the heading 'De lapide' for Gravel in its copy of **GrCon**, but no other numbers. No other Hybrid witness has any numbering in **GrCon**.

105 *webbe of an erayn*: Scribes often modified the word *erayn* (Lat. *aranea*, OF *araigne*):

> Exp.: webbe of an yrayn (*add in later hand* or ethercopp Ad7) Ad4H11Ad7, webbe of a loppe Se, webe of an attyrcope Ra4, webbe of an anay W7, webbe of any vryn as ?cuy Sj3;
> Core: a naran web Di1, webbe of an (*om.* Om) yedercope Co1W9Om, nett off an attercope Co3, webb of a spyder A14, web of a natter coppe nest vel spithe ?ster (*or* spithester?) quod dictum est Ht, bebbe of þan i. tela aranea nescio ego A11;
> Hyb.: webe of an yran S16, webbe of an Irayne or a cobbewefte Hg1, webbe of a spyder S29a, webbe of Erren *Seynge of Uryns* sig. B4r.

The Abbreviated Version omits **GrCon**.

243 *schaddyng*: The most common reading (S15Ad4Ad7H11W7), but also found as *schauyngis* Sj3Se, *stondyng* Ra4, or *om.* A6. See m.n. to E.2/17.

247 *the*[1]: 'they' (so spelled in S15Ad4; Sj3W7 read *þey*).

258 *vmers*: I.e. 'humours'. The spelling *vmers* (with *er* curl above *m*) also appears in H11; other witnesses to the reading (e.g. W7Ra4Ad7Se in the Expanded Version; OmDi1Co1A14 in the Core Version) have the more common *hu-* spellings of the word. Ad4Sj3 read *fyueris* and S16S29a (and the print *Seynge of Uryns*) read *wormys*, readings that could have arisen from different confusions of minims and abbreviation marks. The Abbreviated Version omits the sign.

336 *substaunce of vryne*: Witnesses to the Expanded Version and the Abbreviated Version that include this transition sentence (S15Sj3Ad4H11Ra4; Add2T8Lm2) omit the phrase *and colours* found in the Core Version (after *substaunce*, in A11Di1Di3Co3HtS29b). In other Core, Expanded, and Abbreviated witnesses, the transition sentence is dropped or wanting due to loss of text or is replaced with '& so ssufficient' (once, in the s. xvi witness A14). In the Hybrid Version, all but one of the witnesses either omit the transition sentence or **UMort** or are wanting leaves or text (Hg1Nm3*SU* S29a); the one Hybrid witness with a form of the sentence (S16) reads only 'And this ys for to knowyng of vryne'. See the discussion of structural differences between the versions in section V of the Introduction.

379 *Explicit. Hic intrat*: Also in Ad4 (as *hic intrat. Explicit*). The phrase 'Hic intrat', written within the text by the main scribe in both manuscripts and carrying the general sense 'It enters here', looks like it could be some sort of *signe de renvoi* for a text that should begin at this point. However, there is no corresponding sign at the beginning of **GrCon**, which should follow **4Con** for medical reasons, or at any other point in S15Ad4. The partly illegible marginal note 'Hic v⟨. . . v . . .⟩ on f. 9ʳ (only in S15) is in a lighter ink, a different script from other marginalia, and possibly a slightly later hand than the main text, so it seems unlikely to be related to the more formally written 'Hic intrat' at the end of the text.

MEDICAL COMMENTARY

A. *Twenty Colours by Digestion Groups*

The notes to this text are keyed to text A.1, the unillustrated version of the *Twenty Colours*, but refer as appropriate to readings in text A.1 and text A.2, the illustrated wheel of urines with its two unillustrated derivatives (S29 and the unillustrated copy in W4). Lines in A.2 that correspond to the lemmas from A.1 are given in parentheses.

1 (A.2)

1–2 (A.2/15–16) *crocus occidentalis . . . orientalis*: Bartholomaeus Anglicus, citing Dioscorides, describes two kinds of saffron: 'oon is *ortensis* and haþ þe name of gardynes, for he groweþ þerinne: þe oþer hatte *orientalis* and haþ also þe name of þe place þat he groweþ inne; and is þe beste'; the best saffron *orientalis* is 'somdel reede oþer al rede, and þe whiteshe schal be forsake' (*On the Properties of Things* 17.41, Seymour 1975–88: ii. 934; cf. Dioscorides, *De materia medica* i. 26, trans. Beck 2005: 23–4). The *Twenty Colours* also distinguishes between types of saffron, generally as a contrast between coarser, more common hues and finer or rarer ones, but with *saffron d'orte* usually on the finer side of the contrast: in various copies of the text, Subrubeus and Rubeus are compared to western/*occidentalis* vs. eastern/*orientalis* saffron, false saffron vs. saffron d'orte ('of the garden'=*hortensis*; Ro6), sad ('dull') saffron vs. saffron (S9), saffron not fine vs. fine saffron (T7, with a parallel comparison to watery blood vs. red blood), and saffron 'belynge(r)' (see below) vs. saffron d'orte. A few scribes take garden saffron as the coarser or more common colour, as in Pe3W6 (*saffran of gardyns* vs. *saffran orientell*) and the late T13 (*saffron d'ort* vs. *þe fynest saffroun*), in agreement with Bartholomaeus.

The unusual word *belynger* (varr. *bellynger, belynger, belenger, bylenge, bylyng'*), found in the β group witnesses W8Di2S36T11S6, is not recorded in *MED* or *OED*, but may mean something like uncultivated or wild (saffron), in contrast with saffron d'orte. Cotgrave (1611) records a French word *belinge*, identified as a Norman equivalent of *tiretaine*, a kind of linsey-woolsey worn by French peasants (the latter word may be the etymon of English *tartan*, according to the *OED*). If Cotgrave's *belinge* is the same word as that found in the β group, the sense may be something like 'country saffron' or 'peasant saffron' or may refer to whatever the most common colour of such fabric was (see the 'russet' variants in the m.n. on Karapos below, A.1/17).

6–7 (A.2/20–1) *Ynopos . . . Kianos*: Although etymology might lead one to expect these colour terms to mean 'wine-coloured' (οἰνωπός) and 'dark blue colour' (< κύανος), the Anglo–Latin colour-wheels behind *Twenty Colours by Digestion Groups* are generally consistent in describing them as like liver (*color epatis*) and black wine (*vinum nigrum*) respectively. Some Continental urine wheels apply both similes to Inopos and compare Kyanos to rotting or rotten (*putrescens/putrefactus*) blood. W8Di2S36 compare Kyanos to 'blacke water', but I have not been able to find the simile *ut aqua nigra* for Kyanos in the Latin tradition.

The variants *purpill* and *purpura blak* in Cu5 and Pe3W6 are paralleled in an unillustrated Latin version of *Twenty Colours* in Bodl., MS Ashmole 1438, I, p. 165 ('Kyanos vt purpura'); Ashmole 1438 also gives Latin equivalents to the watery/ good blood variants for Subrubicundus/Rubicundus found in Pe3: 'vt sanguis aquosus' and 'vt sanguis purus'. H8's comparison of Kyanos to 'fowll blood corrupted' corresponds to Latin texts with 'ut sanguis putrefactus/putrescens'. The comparison of Kyanos to *rasspise/rayspys* (T13T7) refers to another kind of wine, ML *raspecia*, *vinum raspatum*, OF *raspé*, glossed in the *Promptorium Parvulorum* as *vinum rosatum*, 'rose-coloured wine' (*MED*, s.v. *raspeys* (n.)). Yet another gloss on Kyanos occurs in Yo: 'a colour of water þat is lyk to blac burnet [*poss. with* win *added below* burnet *in a later hand*]', referring either to the dark brown cloth known as *burnet* or perhaps to the burnet plant, so named for its brownish-red flowers. See *MED*, s.v. *burnet* (n.(1) and adj.; n.(2)).

8 (A.2/22) *Greyne*: The late manuscript T13 adds a twenty-first colour, Subuiridis, after describing the colour Viridis; in S36, Subuiridis replaces Glauca and is described (along with Alba) as being like 'clere welle water'. Subuiridis also appears in the *Twenty Jordans* series, replacing one of the two black colours and described as being light green or like standing or clear water (Tavormina 2005: 52). Pe3W6 add the phrase *or herba violaria* 'or violet' to the colour simile for Green/Viridis, possibly echoing a confusion already found in the Latin translation of Theophilus, where Green urine is described as being both like leeks and *violaceus*; E. Ruth Harvey suggests that *violaceus* is a mistranslation of the word for verdigris in the Greek original (ἰοειδής 'violet-coloured' for ἰώδης 'like verdigris'; personal communication). Besides the *herba violaria* alternative, the γ1 witnesses Pe3W6 add an extra green colour, 'tulye', apparently using the word to mean an emerald green ('as smaragde stone'), although it normally refers to a deep red colour associated with fabrics. See *MED*, s.v. *tuli* (adj.).

10 (A.2/24) *Lyuidus*: The livid colour of urine (also sometimes labelled Plumbeus 'leaden') may be rendered in Middle English texts as *liuidus, -a, blo* or *blue, ledissh*, etc. Both *blo* and *blue* can refer to livid or leaden colours in the human body, including the 'black-and-blue' colour of bruises, though ME *bleu* is somewhat later in showing this sense (cf. *MED*, s.vv. *bleu, blo* (adjs.)). The sense 'livid' is also attested in thirtenth-century Anglo-Norman usage of *bleu*. For discussion of the etymological and semantic development of ME *bleu*, see Biggam 2006, who takes an agnostic stance on whether 'popular confusion with ME *blo*' is the source of 'the senses of BLUE-GREY and DISCOLOURED . . . for ME *bleu*' (p. 168).

In the β1 group, *lyuidus* is altered to *pallida*, competing slightly with the later use of *pallida* in its own right, but the two colours are still distinguished, thanks to the qualification 'as (is) led' in this line, contrasting with the later comparison of *pallida* to half-cooked meat broth. In S36, a later hand corrects *pallida* at this point to *plumbea*.

11–12 (A.2/25–6) *colour of adustion . . . colour of mortificacioun*: Although Inopos, Kyanos, and Viridis normally constitute the Adustion digestion group, while Lividus and the two species of Niger normally make up the Mortification group, the two Black urines could themselves be distinguished in terms of adustion vs. mortification, depending on whether they had been caused by extreme physiological heat (adustion) or cold (mortification). Which extreme was in question could be determined, it was thought, by the urine's colour before it became Black: Green for adustion, Livid for mortification, a distinction that can be traced back at least as far as Theophilus's *De urinis* (Dase 1999: 17).

In *Twenty Colours by Digestion Groups*, the hot Black of adustion is usually compared to ink (or the 'feather of a crow' in the γ1 group), while the cold black of mortification is usually compared to black horn ('earth coals' in γ1; 'brent horn' in Cu5). *Ten Cold Ten Hot* distinguishes the two Blacks with different metaphors, which appear to conflict with those seen in **20Col-Dig**: hot Black urine is like clear black horn, cold Black like dark coal (H/117, 100). *Rufus Subrufus* and *The Dome of Uryne* also describe two kinds of Black urine, but without specifying which is caused by excess heat and which by excess cold: *Rufus Subrufus* compares them to ink vs. black horn (G/15); **DU** to a raven's feather vs. coals (I/ 75, 78).

15 (A.2/2) *Glaucus*: The comparison to 'shining', 'bright', or translucent (Lat. *lucidum*) horn is relatively easy to visualize; some texts refine the simile by specifying the horn used for lanterns or ox-horn or by narrowing the colour to a yellow or white/whitish hue. *Ten Cold Ten Hot* describes Glaucus as 'ȝalowe like to falowe leues fallyng of trees' (H/103), suppressing the sense of translucency or brightness.

17 (A.2/4) *Karapos*: This strictly uroscopic colour term is described by Theophilus as being like the pelt or hair of a camel, a simile that becomes commonplace throughout the Latin (*vellus/pili cameli, pannus camelini*) and Middle English ('flesh/skin/hair of a camel') traditions, though it is unclear how useful it would be for people unfamiliar with camels, outside of biblical, bestiary, and geographical illustrations. A number of English uroscopy texts offer additional or alternative descriptions, including hare's hair (Ra6); camels' *vlijs* (Pe3), meaning either 'fleece' or 'flesh'; various colours of the coarse fabric known as russet, ranging from white to grey to a mix of white and 'blew', probably in the sense of *blo* rather than sky-blue or indigo (Cu5T11S6; see m.nn. to A.1/1–2, 10); ginger (T7); 'fallow', 'white douny', 'doun' (T13W8Yo). Something on the order of beige, light tan, or dun-grey is apparently intended.

19–20 (A.2/6–7) *subpallida . . . Pallidus*: Palish and pale urine, like partially or fully cooked meat broth, already features in Theophilus's *De urinis* (Dase 1999: 15); the later Latin urine wheels usually compare both Subpallidus and Pallidus colours to *succus carnis semicocte* (var. *semicrude*), either *remissus* or *non remissus*. The

English tradition generally preserves the kitchen imagery, varying the descriptions in relatively minor ways: the *remissus* vs. *non remissus* contrast may become 'half sode' vs. 'full sode', 'well sode', or 'not half sode'; less frequently, 'flesh' may be altered to 'raw flesh' (Ra6S9) or the reference to broth may disappear (W8T11S6Ra6Pe3W6), yielding contrasts between well-boiled flesh (Pallidus) and raw flesh or the broth of half-boiled flesh (Subpallidus). In the versified uroscopy 'Urines for the Simple', Pallidus and Subpallidus are compared to meat broth and boiled fish (lines 33–4; Tavormina 2010: 598). Only two *Twenty Colours* witnesses diverge from the cooked-meat comparison: Subpallidus 'of colour as ?asshes' in the late manuscript T13 and Pallidus 'lyk to þe ius of þe eldyr ber[?e]' in Yo.

22–3 (A.2/9–10) *Subcitrinus . . . Citrinus*: Applying the label *citrine* to urine can be traced to Constantinus Africanus's translation of Isaac Israeli's *De urinis* (E. Ruth Harvey, personal communication; see also Visi 2015: 45–58 for Greek and Arabic uroscopic terms for shades of yellow); the term *citrinus* is not found in the Latin Theophilus. The descriptions of the citrine colours generally agree in comparing them to yellowish fruits or fruit juices, though the specific fruits vary and the generic senses of both *pomus/pome* and *apple* to mean simply 'fruit' blur the picture even further. The Latin terms *pomus citrinus* and *pomus citrinus remissus* are fairly stable, albeit general, but the Middle English texts compare the colours to a whole cornucopia of fruits and fruit derivatives: citrines and oranges (*pome citrine/citre, pome orenge, orange apple*); yellow or red-spotted yellow fruits, possibly even apples proper; plum (perhaps an error for *pomme*); pear or the drink 'perry'; 'apples' and oranges of different ripeness; *fistulet* (not in *MED/OED*, but perhaps a light reddish or yellowish medicine or beverage derived from *cassia fistula* 'bastard cinnamon'); cider; orange juice; and juice of celandine (*citrine* may have meant 'celandine' in some medical recipes; see *MED*, s.v. *citrine* (n.), sense (b)). In Yo, the colours are compared to apples 'cler in þe compas' and 'nout cler in þe comp'', perhaps with the sense '(not) bright all round'.

25–6 (A.2/12–13) *Subrufus . . . Rufus*: These colours of 'perfect' or completed digestion are usually defined in terms of less and more refined gold. For Subrufus, the descriptions include gold that is unburnished (so in text A.2), impure, faded, murky, unclean, or 'sad'; white gold, French gold, an alloy of gold and silver, latoun; and gold *remisse*, put out, sent out, etc. For Rufus, they include gold that is burnished, pure or purified, fine, or clear; red gold; and gold not *remisse*, not put or sent out, etc. A visual correlative to these descriptions occurs in some illustrated uroscopies, in the use of gold leaf to colour the flasks representing Rufus and sometimes Subrufus (e.g. the urine wheels in Di1 and in the T15 *Twenty Jordans*); also seen in illustrated Latin texts, such as Bodl. Ashmole 391, Part V, Ashmole 789, Part VIII, and Savile 39; TCC R.1.86.

B. *Urina Rufa*

9–11 *to moche blod . . . Geminorum*: Using phlebotomy to reduce a plethora of blood is a common-sense solution to the problem. The warning against phlebotomy if the moon is in Gemini probably assumes that the phlebotomy would be applied to veins in the arms; if so, then the procedure should be avoided when the moon is in the sign governing the arms (Gemini), so as to forestall an excessive flow of blood caused by the moon's influence in the sign.

19 *secunde degestion*: The second digestion was understood to be the metabolic stage at which urine was produced, so a failure or weakening of the second digestion would yield insufficiently concocted, pale urine.

32 *expulcion of venemosy materes*: There is one important exception to the normally negative interpretation of black urine in medieval uroscopic theory: if black urine occurred at or near the crisis of a febrile illness, it could signify the excretion of the poisons or corrupt humours causing or caused by the disease, accompanied by the return of health. See also texts C/29–31, G/17–19, and I/75–7.

37 *crocea*: The colour-label *crocea* was introduced into the uroscopic tradition in Constantine's translation of Isaac Israeli's *De urinis* (Peine 1919: 20–1, lines 447, 466), where it is used for a colour identical or near to *igneus* and *rubeus*, perhaps under the influence of the description of *rubeus* in the Latin Theophilus, as a colour 'qui assimilatur vero croco'. (For the general reception of Isaac's treatise in the West, see Veit 2015; for Isaac's colour terms, see Visi 2015.) However, Giles of Corbeil, following his teachers Urso and Maurus of Salerno (mid-twelfth-century), does not adopt Constantine's term. Instead, he labels the yellow-to-red spectrum with the terms *citrinus—rufus—rubeus—rubicundus* and their associated subhues. The author(s) and adapters of the Latin *Urina Rufa* text circulating in fourteenth-century England may have considered *rubeus* a slightly different colour from *croceus*, more comparable to a rose or to blood (B/7, 9) than to saffron, despite the common descriptions of *rubeus* and *subrubeus* as being like different kinds of saffron or other shades of yellowish or orangey red (see m.n. to text A.1/1–2).

40 *aboue sumwhat fat signefiep feuere etike*: Hectic fever was believed to consume the solid members of the body, as opposed to bodily spirits and humours, melting or wasting the substance of those members into fats that were excreted with the urine (see McVaugh 1974: 260–5 *et passim*). The urinary content *pinguedo* (ME *fatte, oile, grese*, etc.) is regularly associated with one or another version of hectic fever, as in texts H/129–30 and I/100–8 below.

43–6 *more harm in þe riȝt side . . . in the luft side . . . coldere þan þe riȝt*: Humoral theory commonly associates reddish colours and the right side of the body with heat, white or pale colours and the left side of the body with cold.

47–8 *þynne and pale and clere . . . acetosum flewma*: Acetous phlegm is one of five common types of phlegm in medieval humoral theory, defined in terms of the mixing of phlegm with other humours: natural (or insipid), sweet, salt, acetous, and vitreous phlegm. Acetous phlegm was considered to be a mixture of natural phlegm and the cold dry humour melancholy, so its association with the paleness generated by cold and thinness generated by dryness fits readily into the humoral model. For a brief but influential description of the 'five phlegms', see Johannitius, *Isagoge* (Maurach 1978: 152).

50 *rennyng flewma and of oper humors*: The motion perceived in the urine is associated with the flow of humours in the body.

71–95 The last section of the treatise focuses on women's urines; many of the signs included can be found in similar clusters in other uroscopic texts, as in *Rufus Subrufus* below and the unique treatise *Eleven Manners of Urine for a Woman* ('Guide', item 7.2.4). This set of urines was already circulating together in England by the early twelfth century (Green 2011: 179).

74 *ypostatesie*: The *ypostasis* or sediment found in the bottom of the urine flask. Besides the variety of spellings that this word generates, the term may also be translated with forms of the words *sedimen(t)*, *residence*, *substance*, etc.

78–80 *a ymage in þe glasyne vessel . . . þe ymage of hym þat scheweþ apeireþ*: The 'appearance' of an image in a urine sample (sometimes specified as the reflected face of the uroscopist, as in line B/80) may seem an odd characteristic on which to base diagnosis, but it is commonly associated with a diagnosis of conception in women's urines and with fever, other ailments, or impending death among patients in general (see text I/79, 296–301 below).

C. *Cleansing of Blood*

1 *clansyng*: The canonical description of urine as *colamentum sanguinis* reflects the physiological understanding of urinary formation through a filtering of blood in the liver, with the liquid waste eliminated as urine; several major Latin uroscopies define urine as *colamentum sanguinis* early in their treatment of the subject (e.g. Theophilus, *De urinis* (Dase 1999: 3); Isaac Israeli, *Liber urinarum*, part. 1 (Peine 1919: 10); Bernard de Gordon, *Liber de urinis*, chap. 1 (in *Lilium medicinae*, 1574: 730)). In his verse uroscopy, Giles of Corbeil describes urine as a *cribratio* ('sifting') *rerum* (line 8; Vieillard 1903: 272).

1–3 *properliche . . . inproperliche*: Lat. *proprie . . . improprie*. Uroscopic theory recognized that urine was most reliable as an indicator of organs through which it passed (liver, kidney, bladder, and the veins and other vessels that carried it or its precursor blood). Using the urine to diagnose other organs or disease states, such as the head, lungs, stomach, fevers, frenzy, etc., was justified by humoral theory, but acknowledged to be a less direct reflection of those organs or ailments. See Isaac Israeli, *Liber urinarum*, part. 3, taking urine as most indicative of diseases within rather than 'outside' the veins (Peine 1919: 16). Scribes in both Latin and

English copies of this text occasionally change one or both of these words to the other, probably through inattention to meaning, as in the S6Gc4b reading *propyrly* in line 3.

13–14 *cercle . . . body of eir . . . perforacio . . . grounde*: Representing the Latin terms *circulus*, *corpus aeris*, *perforatio*, and *fundus*, which describe four 'parts' or layers of the urine sample, from the top of the urine flask to the bottom. The two middle parts together are equivalent to the middle 'region' of the next section. The parts or regions of the sample from top to bottom were considered to reflect broadly the state of the body from the head to the excretory and reproductive parts, and can be traced back to the *Regulae urinarum* of Maurus of Salerno (Moulinier 2007: 268); Maurus refers to the four parts as *regiones* and to the second and third layers as *superficies* and *perforatio seu substantia* (De Renzi, iii. 41).

15–16 *spiritual membris*: Organs associated with respiration, especially the lungs and heart; the term *corpus aeris* is probably named for this relation to the breath, although it was also seen as indicating the state of the stomach as well as heart and lungs.

19–22 *pre regions*: Yo, uniquely, translates *regio* as *kyndam* 'kingdom'. Moulinier suggests that the division of the urine sample into three layers was popularized by Giles of Corbeil, though with conceptual roots in Galen (2007: 268). For further discussion of the terms 'regions' and 'parts' in Middle English uroscopic texts, see Tavormina 2014: 70–1.

23–4 *fome . . . ventosite bollyng vp*: Although the Circle or uppermost region of the urine was primarily associated with diseases of the head, Foam (also called *spume* and *froth*) floating in this region could signify ailments elsewhere in the body, based on the relatively mechanical notion that metabolic or disease processes in the lungs, stomach, and other organs could generate gas (*ventosite*, *wynd*, *fumosite*, *bollyng up*, *inflacion*), manifested as Foam rising up to the Circle.

25 *replecion*: Repletion was commonly taken as an imbalanced and thus unhealthy state, caused by some kind of physiological excess or humoral superfluity.

26 *white clude*: A white nebulosity seen in the urine sample. In healthy urine, the middle region should be clear, so a white cloud is 'an yuel signe'; if the patient is already sick, the cloud was interpreted as noxious matter that was in the process of being digested (C/27) and excreted, like the black sediment expelled in the urine of someone recovering from an illness (C/30).

D. Urine White and Red

1–4 *Hyt is for to wete in iiij partys . . . lurne*: The brief prologue to **WR** is also a part of the *Lettre d'Hippocrate* (**LdH**), forming a bridge between a short text on the 'humours' (more accurately, the prime qualities) and the subsequent uroscopy

within the **LdH**, which in turn is often followed by a variable series of medical recipes. For Middle English renditions of the **LdH** including its prefatory materials,
see Tavormina 2007; for the French text, see App. II, lines 1–3.

5–6 *whyt at morwe & rede byfore mete & whyt after mete*: The terms 'white' and 'red'
in the incipit refer to relatively dilute and relatively concentrated urine samples,
translating French *blanche, rouge* literally, although a better sense of the actual
colours intended by the two terms can probably be gained from modern, online colour charts (aimed mainly at athletes) depicting hyper-hydration to extreme
dehydration. See also m.n. to E.1/2 below.

9 *asse pysse*: Compare *Aphorisms* 4.70: *Quibus in febribus urine conturbate uelut subi-
ugalis: hiis capitis dolores aut adsunt aut aderunt* (Harley 3140, f. 25ʳ; Jones in Loeb
iv. 153: 'In cases of fever, when the urine is turbid, like that of cattle, headaches
either are, or will be, present').
　　Comparisons of particularly thick and turbid urine to the urine of asses, horses,
other beasts of burden (Lat. *subiugales*, ME *bestes*), and cattle (ME *nete(n)*) are not
uncommon in uroscopic texts (e.g. here in **WR**; below in the full version of **WBw**;
JP in *Dome of Uryne*; some versions of *Urina Rufa*, in both English and Latin; and
in Henry Daniel's account of the man of Stamford in the Karopos chapter of the
Liber Uricrisiarum, ed. Harvey, Tavormina, et al., forthcoming).

11–12 Cf. *Aphorisms* 4.71: *Quibus .vii.ᵃ terminantur hii nubem habent quarta die. &
urina rubeam & alia secundum racionem signa* (Harley 3140, f. 25ʳ; Jones in Loeb iv.
155: 'In cases that come to a crisis on the seventh day, the patient's urine on the
fourth day has a red cloud in it, and other symptoms accordingly'). This and similar Hippocratic remarks on symptoms observed on particular days during diseases
eventually led to a far more organized theory of 'critical days', traceable through
Galen (*De crisibus*; *De criticis diebus*), Isaac (e.g. *De febribus* 4.6–7), some Salernitan
texts, Bernard de Gordon, and others. See O'Boyle 1991; Alonso Guardo 1997.
　　The French adapter apparently understood the preposition *secundum* as an ordinal number, and modified the sign to match that misapprehension, with con-
sequences for both the French and English traditions. For discussion of the variation and associated confusions in Latin forms of this sign, see nn. to D/11–12
and E.1/8–9.

14–15 *Vryne pat is blody . . . withinne*: Though blood in the urine may seem an obvious indicator of a problem elsewhere in the urinary system, even without written
authority, cf. *Aphorisms* 4.75: *Si sanguinem aut pus minxerint renum aut uesice ulcera-
cionem significat* (Harley 3140, f. 25ʳ; Jones in Loeb iv. 155: 'Blood or pus in the
urine indicates ulceration of the kidneys or bladder').

17–18 *Ho-so pessyth blody . . . raynys*: Cf. *Aphorisms* 4.78: *Quicunque sanguinem sponte
mingunt hiis de renibus uene rupturam significat* (Harley 3140, f. 25ʳ; Jones in Loeb iv.
157: 'When a patient has a spontaneous discharge of blood and urine, it indicates
the breaking of a small vein in the kidneys').

22 *bolnys*: 'Bubbles', possibly as a variant form or modification of the more common ME term *bollys* (attested for this sign in R03), under the influence of the verb
bolnen 'to swell' and other words related to bubbling, swelling, and boiling and beginning with *b-* in English, French, and Latin. Cf. OF *ampules* 'bubbles' in most
witnesses to the **LdH** (HYCNVT), sometimes replaced by *boulonne* (WF) or *borboille* (S), and the Middle English *ampulettes* in Nw1. Conversely, compare *bolle* in
line D/41 below, translating *emfle* 'swollen', in place of *bolne* or *bolni*.

The whole sign derives from *Aphorisms* 7.34: *Quibuscumque in urinis ampulle su-
pernatant nefreticam significat & longam egritudinem fore* (Harley 3140, f. 28ʳ; Jones
in Loeb iv. 199: 'When bubbles form in the urine, it is a sign that the kidneys are
affected, and that the disease will be protracted'). The **LdH** original of this sign
speaks of urine that *chet par gutettes* ('falls in droplets') and that *noe desure cum
ampules* ('floats above like bubbles'). In Middle English uroscopies, descriptions of
ampulle in urine often liken them to bubbles, droplets, rain water, or the dimpled
surface of 'water (puddles) when it rains'; terms used include *ampul, burble, froth*,
and *creme*. Cf. Henry Daniel, *Liber Uricrisiarum* 3.3 (BL, MS Royal 17 D.i, f. 89ʳᵇ;
ed. Harvey, Tavormina, et al., forthcoming).

25-6 *schynnyng in þe vrynal as siluer*: Like the later sign of gold urine in women
signifying desire for men (D/33–4), this sign achieves a remarkably wide dissemination through the several derivatives of the **LdH**: both signs occur in **ST**, **15D**,
WR, and **WBw**, while gold urine as a sign of 'talent (liking, lust) to man' also appears in **WBp** and the **UMul** segment in the *Dome of Uryne*. See E.1/23–9, E.2/
30–7, F/28–9, and I/283 below.

31-2 *blody above . . . hed ache*: This sign is a truncated version of **LdH** sign 16,
on women's urine that has bloody Foam above but is otherwise clear, signifying
headache, loss of desire for food and sleep, and swelling of the stomach. For more
complete translations, see E.1/25–7 and E.2/33–5. Omitted in **WBp**.

41 *colde menson*: The **LdH** reading 'la tuse & la menisun' (sign 20) is better reflected
in Nw1A8's *þe cowʒhe and þe menson* and T12's *chowhein and the menysoun*. It is
possible that *colde* (S42Ra3A9) is an early scribal misapprehension of archetypal
coughe. (Although a number of diseases are described in the Middle Ages as hot or
cold—e.g. the hot dropsy and the cold dropsy—I can find no evidence that dysentery or the menses, the two primary medical senses of *menison* in French and
English, were so characterized.)

E. *Urine White and Brown* (Woman Variant)

1

2 *brown*: Brown is the less literal but more common ME translation of OF *rouge* to
describe the darker, more concentrated urine in a healthy patient before eating. As
noted above for *white* and *red* in the opening sign of D/5–6, the word *brown* should

not be understood in its modern colour sense, but rather as an indication of greater intensity or concentration.

brown at afteremete: In contrast to the **LdH** and its **WR** reflexes in Middle English (when they are not textually corrupt), the **WB** texts regularly alter the time of more intense colour from before to after eating. They also reduce the number of uroscopic inspections from three to two.

4–5 *singne of water in þe boweles*: The diagnosis of water or phlegm in the bowels in this sign appears only in English texts, and only in **WBw**, **WBp**, and **JP**. The latter two texts omit the phrase inherited from **LdH** about 'no god hele', and **WBp** further modifies the sign by diagnosing phlegm rather than water.

8–9 *on þe firste day . . . al but feuere etik*: On the numbering of days in this sign, see n. to D/11–12 above. The proviso *al but feuere etik* is apparently an English addition, found only in **WBw**. **WBp** drops the entire sign. For *feuere etik*, see m.n. to B/40 above.

12 *Vrine of bloid . . . þe bleddere is brised*: See m.n. to D/14–15 above.

16–17 *He þat pisset . . . in þe lendes. . . . þat spewit . . . in þe herte or in þe lunges*: For the first of these two signs, on blood in the urine, see m.n. to D/17–18. For the second sign, on spitting blood, see n. to E.1/17.

23 *ray & cler and schynande as siluer*: See m.n. on D/25–6.

25–6 *singne of blod in þe sercle . . . heued werck*: The Circle was taken to signify illnesses of the head and brain (see C/14–15, 24–5, H/122, I/362–9). Giles of Corbeil refines the general principle along humoral lines, associating particular colour–density pairings with the four humours and the four quadrants of the head (front, back, right, and left sides), so that thick white urine signifies pain in the back of the head caused by excess phlegm, thick *purpureus* (dark reddish) urine signifies pain in the forehead caused by excess blood, and so on (*De urinis* 220–5; Vieillard 1903: 289).

29 *lorn a flour of hire blod*: A diagnosis added, in **WBw** only, to the reflex of the **LdH** sign on women's urine like gold. See also textual note on this line.

38 *as burbeles . . . in reyn*: See m.n. to D/22.

2

4–5 *thinne and grene . . . cold conpleccioun . . . bloo abouyn as botonys of leed . . . ptysyk*: The association of Green urine with cold complexion is somewhat unexpected, given that green colour is usually said to indicate adustion through an excess of heat and choler. Less surprising is the linkage of *bloo* or lead-coloured urine with phthisic: *consumptiua ptisis* is one of the many illnesses signified by lead-coloured urine according to Giles of Corbeil (*De urinis* 46; Vieillard 1903: 275). This sign and the following one, Black urine indicating male sexual desire, are new in the

WBw texts, though the early Cc only gives the latter sign, which also appears in a modified form in JP.

16 *hote dropesye*: a form of dropsy (the morbid buildup of fluid in the body) thought to be caused or dominated by heat. The *Tractatus Magistri Bartholomei*, a translation of the 'Cum secundum auctores' adaptation of Walter Agilon's *Summa medicinalis*, says that the species of hot dropsy, *tympanites* and *ascites*, are incurable, while the species of cold dropsy, *leucofleumancia* and *yposarca*, are curable (Sloane 121, ff. 44ᵛ–45ʳ; see Norri 2016: 73, 317–18, 594–5, 1127–8, 1279; 'Guide', item 16.1).

17 *schauyngges*: possibly one of the contents like small or large flakes (Bran/*furfura*, Scales/*squame*, and Crinoids/*crinoides*). The French text here has *& cum ele fust uelue* ('and as if it were velvety'), which the English translator ignores. Some English variants opt for forms of *changeth/changed* (mostly in the α2α3 groups), perhaps through a misreading of *schauing(es)*. WBp changes the uroscopic characteristics for this sign to 'red os watyr þat flesch is waschyne in & fatt abowue', but retains the cold dropsy diagnosis, adding that it betokens death. JP hews more closely to the reading in WBw, but usually renders 'be drubly as schauyngges' as 'hath drest(s) in the bothum as schaddyng (*varr.* schauyngis, stondyng)'. The sense in JP is probably still flakes of skin shed into the urine from internal vessels.

21 *lendes*: the loins (lower back, buttocks, kidneys, etc.). Blood in the urine (hematuria) often indicates some kind of trauma to the kidneys and urinary system.

50–3 *reed . . . on þe ryȝte syde . . . lyuere; whyth . . . left syde . . . splen*: The lateralization of the diagnoses in these two signs corresponds to the standard humoral associations between the liver and blood (warm and moist) vs. the spleen and melancholy (dry and cold), reinforced by the general medieval privileging of warmth and the right side over cold and the left.

F. *Urine White and Brown* (Phlegm Variant)

Although WBp derives from the LdH, like WR and WBw, it replaces nearly half of the signs found in those texts with new ones (signs 3–4, 12–13, 15–17, and 19–21).

8–9 *a grete cercule . . . hed ache*: See m.n. to E.1/25–6 above. In its attention to changing colours, the sign is reminiscent of the first sign in the UMort segment of the *Dome of Uryne* (I/317–18). *Blew* is equivalent to *blo* '*lividus*, lead-coloured', and all three colours listed here and in UMort—green, leaden, and black—are associated with mortality, as might be expected for fluid pressing on the brain. The differences in colour may also suggest movement of the excess water to different sides of the head, like the different humoral causes of headaches signalled by variously coloured circles (see I/362–9).

9 *fylmyne*: 'dura mater'. This relatively rare term for an animal or vegetable membrane (e.g. the retina, the tay or dura mater, the membrane within a walnut or an

egg, etc.) derives from OE *filmen*, but gradually evolved into ModE *film* (see *OED*, s.v. *film*, n.; *MED*, s.v. *film* (n.)). Variants include both the older and newer forms: felmyn S2S20, filmen Gc1, fylme A7Eg3Nw2A14.

15 *Uryne red os watyr þat flesch . . . & fatt abowue*: This sign in **WBp** corresponds to signs of fat and fleshy urine in **WBw** and **JP** (E.2/17–18, I/243–4). All three texts read the symptom as a sign of cold dropsy (an evolution of **LdH/WR**'s sickness in the reins), but the compiler/translator of **WBp** appears to have taken 'fleshy' to refer to colour rather than the texture suggested in the French original (*charnuse & crase & cum ele fust uelue* 'fleshy and fat and as if it were velvety'), no doubt influenced by the common comparison of Pallidus and Subpallidus urines to the broth of boiled or half-boiled flesh.

24–5 *Uryn þat schynys lyk a lanterne horne . . . ingleymyd*: This new sign in **WBp** introduces a colour from the Latin rather than French tradition, *Glaucus*, almost universally described as shining like bright, lucid, yellow, or lantern horn. The 'no dygestioun' diagnosis fits with the digestion group to which Glaucus belongs: Indigestion 'lack, failure of digestion'.

26 *small grauell*: I.e. a sandy sediment, one of the Aegidian contents (Arena/Gravel), regularly taken as a sign of kidney or bladder stones, depending on its colour and consistency. See H/134, I/114–16, and cf. *Aphorisms* 4.79: *Quibus in urinis harenosa substant uesica aut renes litiasim habent* (Harley 3140, f. 25^r; Jones in Loeb iv. 156–7: 'When the urine contains a sandy sediment, there is stone in the bladder [*var.: add* καὶ οἱ νεφροί "and the kidneys"]').

30–1 *Uryne . . . lyke wheye . . . a cloud in þe bothome . . . whyte flourynges . . . with chyld*: The 'cloud' is probably the 'suptil body' in the urine of pregnant women described by Avicenna, John of Gaddesden, and Henry Daniel, and compared by them to carded cotton wool or raw silk (*cottum carminatum, bombax vel cotum carminatum vel lana carminata, rawe silke i. vnwroght silke*). In the context of pregnancy, the white 'flourynges' are probably the mote-like contents that can mean gout or (in women) pregnancy, but may mean a larger, flake-like content (*Canon medicine* 1.2.3.2 c. 10 (1486: 51vb); *Rosa anglica* 2.17 (1502: 82vb); *Liber Uricrisiarum* 3.16, BL, MS Royal 17 D.i, f. 102vb; ed. Harvey, Tavormina, et al., forthcoming).

32–3 *red lyk blod . . . hyr flourys be to heuy*: This common-sense sign of an excessive menstrual flow is paralleled in *Urina Rufa*'s 'Wymmen þat beþ menstruat makeþ blody vryne' (B/93).

34 *blake flourys*: Black 'blossoms' or particulates in the urine, distinguished here from black 'matter', which may simply be a clumping of the *flourys* at the bottom of the urinal.

38–9 *Uryne of a womane þat has smale grauell . . . chawd pysse . . . renysse*: The lower frequency of kidney and bladder stones in women presumably led medieval uroscopists to seek a different explanation for Gravel in women's urine than the generic Hippocratic diagnosis of sandy sediment as a sign of the stone (F/26–7). On the relative rarity of stone in women, see Constantine's translation of ibn al-Jazzar's *Viaticum* 5. 18: 'In mulieribus vero raro [lapis] nascitur: quia materia vnde lapis concreatur: non adunatur multis ex causis in mulieribus: quia collum vesice earum curtum est & foramina sunt larga & non multum tortuosa sunt: & minus bibunt aquam quam pueri' (*Omnia opera Ysaac* (1515: ii. 163ʳ): 'The stone arises in women infrequently, because the material from which the stone is formed does not coalesce in women for many reasons: because the neck of their bladder is short and the openings are large and not very convoluted and they drink less water than children').

G. *Rufus Subrufus*

1–2 *vrine or watir, þat we take for oon*: Three witnesses to the 'Ipocras' prologue to *Rufus Subrufus* have a fuller comment on English words for urine, identifying *water*, *state*, *piss*, and *urine* as 'al one', but highlighting *urine* as the more common (Di1S29) or certain (Je) and 'fairer' term, suggesting distinct sociolinguistic registers for the words. See App. III.

7 *parfiȝt digestioun*: 'completed digestion'. For the seven digestion groups of medieval uroscopy, see the Introduction (§III, pp. lx–lxi).

16–17 *Cum dicitur . . . in ortis*: The second, qualifying half of a couplet on the healing power of sage from the *Flos medicine*: 'Cur moritur homo, cum salvia crescit in orto? / Contra vim mortis non est medicamen in ortis' (lines 372–3 in Frutos González 2010a: 186; also in De Renzi, i. 469, v. 31; Walther 3346, 4695b–4696). The next four to six lines of *Flos medicine* list specific virtues of sage, but only after the reminder of death's ultimate inevitability.

32–40 Similar remedies may be found in Heinrich 1896: 65–6; Müller 1929: 50–1, 116–17; Dawson 1934: 18, 333; Ogden 1938: 1; T. Hunt 2001: 163.

40 *on warantise*: I.e. (it is) guaranteed; assuredly. A formula similar in purpose to the more familiar *probatum est* (see G/96 below, where both are used). *On warantise* appears in a few Middle English recipe collections and herbals but is far more common in legal contexts, with suggestions of a guarantor who stands behind a claim. See *MED*, s.vv. *warantise* (n.) and *warantisen* (v.).

41–3 *for clensynge of þe heed . . . teeþ in þe gomes*: Cf. Heinrich 1896: 66; Müller 1929: 51, 109, 117; Dawson 1934: 18; Ogden 1938: 2 (using mastic); T. Hunt 2001: 163. See also Henslow 1899: 130 and Heffernan 1993: 316 (peleter of Spain for migraine and dizziness in the head).

44–6 *for vanite of þe heed . . . & þi templis*: I.e. for dizziness; cf. Heinrich 1896: 66; Müller 1929: 51, 109, 117; Ogden 1938: 2, 6; T. Hunt 2001: 163.

47–8 Jaundice was often associated with Foam in the urine; see, for example, Giles of Corbeil, *Carmen de urinis* 253–4: *Indicat ictericum vel hepar portendit aduri / Si nigra vel viridis vel quasi tincta croco* 'If [foam is] black or green or saffron-coloured, it indicates jaundice or predicts that the liver will be overheated' (Vieillard 1903: 292) and cf. I/44–5, 62–3, 352–5 below. The colour of the Foam signalled the three types of jaundice, yellow, green, and black, which were attributed to increasingly intense heat in the liver.

55–70 Since adustion is a kind of overheating, it is not surprising that the two ailments listed in this section are a *hoot agu* and *pe axesse* (i.e. a febrile attack).

69 *archidriclini*: Saying Paters and Aves (the Lord's Prayer and the Hail Mary) and the Creed for the souls of the faithful departed could be seen as a simple pious act, possibly with psychosomatic benefits, but the mysterious addition of 'the souls of the father and mother (?and) of *archidriclini*' tilts the prayer instruction in the direction of medieval charms that invoked the pseudo-saint Archedecline. The name is derived from the Latin noun *architriclinus* 'master of the feast, steward', found in the gospel narrative of the marriage at Cana; medieval readers took it as a name, and then bestowed sainthood on the character. 'Archedecline' appears in French gospel paraphrases, in John Gower's recapitulation of Christ's life in the *Mirour de l'Omme* (line 28395; Macaulay 1899–1902: i. 316), as well as in Latin, French, and English charms against fever, splints, and at least once for sprains in horses. See Müller 1929: 121 (French charm from Stockholm, Royal Library, MS X.90); Trotter 1987; Roper 2006: 71; T. Hunt 1990: 87 n. 115, 93, 97, 98 (English and Latin charms); Manual 10: 3870, citing occurrences in five manuscripts.

94 *turmentyne*: 'turpentine, an oleoresin derived from pine trees'; though attested in several witnesses (Gc4OmNm1A10), this may be an error for *turmentylle*, the plant tormentil (*Potentilla erecta*), the reading of W10T15Nm2A8Ro3, especially given the reference in the next sentence to boiling 'these herbys'. The earlier mention of *turmentille* in a fever medicine (G/58–9) is common to all witnesses that include that remedy.

96 *Probatum est*: 'It is proven; it has been tested.'

103–8 Analogous recipes for provoking a sweat (using cumin and bed rest under covers, but not the patient's own urine or suffumigation): Heinrich 1896: 145; T. Hunt 2001: 173.

123–34 The signs in these lines are drawn from the Latin or English *Urina Rufa* treatises: see B/71–9, 85–6, 93 above. The variant form of *Rufus Subrufus* found in the δ group adds several more signs from *Urina Rufa*, some specific to women's health and others non-gendered (see App. III).

124 *reed grauel stoonys*: The emendation of Gc4's *greete* to the majority reading *reed* is further justified by the common uroscopic distinction between red Gravel (i.e. sandy particulates) and white Gravel in urine: red indicating kidney stones, white indicating bladder stones. See text I/114–16 and the variant *Rufus Subrufus* text in Digby 29 (App. III, text d, lines 97–8).

135–55 The text offers remedies for three types of gynaecological maladies: excessive menstrual bleeding, retention of the menses, and suffocation of the womb. Analogues to some of these remedies occur in the following collections: Heinrich 1896: 169 (comfrey/white wine plaster); Heinrich 1896: 169, Müller 1929: 81–2, 139, Green and Mooney 2006: 513 (dung plasters); Heinrich 1896: 168, Green and Mooney 2006: 546, Frisk 1949: 101 (gladden-root suffumigation and decoctions); Green and Mooney 2006: 489, 503–4 (suffumigation with herbs or sweet things; inhalation of stinking things).

H. *Ten Cold Ten Hot*

25–7 After describing the pairs of prime qualities associated with the four elements, the text moves to six secondary characteristics, which also fall into binary pairs (sharp/corpulent, subtle/dull, and movable/unmovable). Unlike the simple symmetry of linking two prime qualities with each element, however, the members of each pair of secondary qualities are associated with one, two, or three elements: Sharp (Fire) vs. Corpulent/Thick (Air, Water, Earth); Subtle (Fire, Air) vs. Dull (Water, Earth); Movable (Fire, Air, Water) vs. Unmovable (Earth).

27–36 In an earlier chapter of the S10 compendium, readers learn that there are nine spheres above the four elements—the seven planets listed by name, the fixed stars, and the 'nynte spere es heuene of heuenes, ioy of ioyes, and blisse of alle blisses departed in 9 ordres of aungels', above which 'es no thyng bot only ineffabel god' (f. 115rb)—an arrangement that apparently conflates the crystalline and empyrean heavens. On the spheres and heavens, see Simek 1996: 9–12; Grant 1996: 308–23, 371–8; Bartholomaeus Anglicus, *On the Properties of Things* 8.4 (Seymour 1975–88: i. 454–5); and *The Wise Book of Philosophy and Astronomy* (Griffin 2013: 8–11). For the comparison of the elemental spheres to an egg, see Simek 1996: 20–3.

46–59 These lines and couplets about the complexions translate two extremely widespread sets of Latin verse (cf. Walther 10945, 13474), and are similarly well disseminated in Middle English. For Latin examples, see Thorndike 1955: 178–80. In Middle English, see the *Four Elements* treatise extant in twenty-one manuscripts (Esteban-Segura 2012: 39–43, from Glasgow, University Library, MS Hunter 509, f. 1^{r-v}(bis)); for other witnesses, see 'Guide', item 8.2); Henry Daniel's *Liber Uricrisiarum* 1.4 (BL, MS Royal 17 D.i, f. 15vb; ed. Harvey, Tavormina, et al., forthcoming); and the *Wise Book of Philosophy and Astronomy* (Griffin 2013: 11–12), which gives the 'desires much/little . . . can do much/little' qualities for the complexions.

57–8 *mekil spittyng*: Lat. *in sputamine multus* 'great in spitting, very productive of spittle'.

60–80 The interest in temporal and spatial correspondences of the complexions has important clinical dimensions, as both diagnosis and therapeutic prescriptions were seen to be affected by when an ailment commenced, the age of the patient, and the direction of sun and wind, similar to strictures on letting or not letting blood depending on the zodiacal position of the moon.

82–3 *souled lymmes . . . spirituale lymmes*: These two common terms (Lat. *membra animata*, *membra spiritualia*) are physiological rather than theological: the first refers to organs of cognition and sensation in the head, the second to organs related to respiration in the chest (including the heart) and throat. The nourishing limbs are the digestive system, while the fourth part of the body, or the 'generative' limbs, include both reproductive and excretory systems.

96–7 *swete taste . . . oper taste*: *Swete* in this context means 'fresh, salt-free', possibly 'natural', not 'sweet' in the sense of 'honeyed, sugary'. Association of a sweet ('honeyed', *mellitus*) taste in urine with diabetes appears to have been an early modern development in Western medicine, attributed to Thomas Willis (1621–75), although it was noted centuries earlier in Chinese and Indian medicine (Guthrie and Humphreys 1988).

Relatively few uroscopic authorities speak of actually tasting urine, though they do mention smelling it or taking note of a fetid or putrid odour, signalling corruption or infection.

98–118 *twenty culoures*: The essential information in this list of colours is the same as that given in Text A, the *Twenty Colours by Digestion Groups*, with the usual Aegidian list of colours and classification by digestion groups. Minor differences include the further division of the colours into cold and hot, the conflation of the four pale and citrine colours into a single group labelled Beginning of Digestion, and the invention of several uncommon and more homely similes for some of the colours (e.g. fallow leaves falling from trees, gray russet, yellow flowers).

The distinction between the two kinds of Black urine, based on whether they are preceded by lead-coloured urine or Green urine, is only implied in Giles's *Carmen de urinis*, in its lines on black Circles (233–4; Vieillard 1903: 290). The distinction is made explicit in Maurus of Salerno's *Regulae urinarum* (De Renzi, iii. 6) and in the Standard Commentary on Giles's poem (BL, MS Sloane 282, f. 21ʳ). (This Standard Commentary is often misattributed in catalogues and scholarship to the fourteenth-century physician and commentator Gentile da Foligno (d. 1348), but it is attested in thirteenth-century manuscripts and probably pre-dates the more scholastic commentary on Giles by Gilbertus Anglicus. See Sudhoff 1929.)

119–46 *18 contentes*: The list of contents here, as in most other Middle English uroscopies that discuss contents, derives from Giles of Corbeil, with some minor reordering between Furfura and Sperma: 'Circulus, ampulla, granum, nubecula, spuma, / Pus, pinguedo, chymus, sanguis, arena, pilus, / Furfura, crimnoides, squamae, partes atomosae, / Sperma, cinis, sedimen, spiritus alta petens' (*Carmen de urinis* 216–19; Vieillard 1903: 288–9). The *Ten Cold* list, like most others, omits the final content, the vapour that rises from the urine, and glosses *sedimen* as *ypostasis*, both indicating the matter deposited at the bottom of the urinal.

122 *Cerkel*: The uppermost layer or surface of the urine sample.

123–6 *Ampul . . . creme . . . Graynes . . . Scume*: Bubbles (*burbles, bolles*; Lat. *ampulle, ambulle, bulle*), Grains (*grana*), Foam (Froth; *spuma*). The gloss *creme* is an unusual word for Ampul/Bubbles, but must refer to the way cream floats to the top of raw milk, with a foamy consistency.

All three of these contents are like bubbles of Foam hanging together or floating separately at or near the surface of the urine sample, and signify different kinds of windiness, rheuminess, or heating within the head, lungs, or liver. Methods for differentiating among types of Froth (bubbly, grainy, and *continuata* 'like the foam of a boar') are given in the *Liber Uricrisiarum* 3.3–3.5 (BL MS Royal 17 D.i, ff. 89rb–91rb; 91vb–92va, esp. at 91vb–92rb).

125 *Cloudes*: Lat. *nubecula* or *nubes*; often translated into English as *sky*. The misty look of a 'cloud' of suspended matter floating in or throughout a urine sample makes its association with the respiratory organs understandable. Two other terms were often used to describe clouds in the middle or near the top of the urinal: *eneorima* and *nephilis*, both of which gave scribes a great deal of difficulty thanks to their unfamiliarity and the frequent miscounting and misdivision of minims in *eneorima*. *Nephilis* and *eneorima* were understood to be forms of the Ypostasis that had risen to unnatural locations in the urinal, indicating illness; the Ypostasis itself was sometimes presented as being like a cloud at the bottom of the urinal. See also I/135–43, 357–61.

127 *Atter, þat es to say quyter*: I.e. pus (Lat. *sanies, putredo*). How to distinguish Atter, Raw Humour, and Ypostasis, all of which could be similar in colour and could sink to the bottom of the urinal, concerns a number of uroscopic authors. For diagnostic procedures used to accomplish this goal, see Henry Daniel, *Liber Uricrisiarum* 3.9; BL, MS Royal 17 D.i, ff. 95va–96vb; ed. Harvey, Tavormina, et al., forthcoming.

129 *Fattenes as oyle dropes schewes wasting*: I.e. tuberculosis or other consumptive disease, understood as a 'melting away' of the bodily tissues; once melted, they would be excreted as an oily or fatty substance. See also the *Dome of Uryne* I/100–1. On medieval explanations of wasting diseases and the role of the *humidum radicale* in such explanations, see McVaugh 1974.

131 *Humur . . . glet . . . drestes of blode . . . roten galle*: Humur (raw humor, humor crudus, chimus) is any incompletely digested bodily fluid, especially one or more of the four humours.

134 *Grauel*: Small particulates like sand (Lat. *arena*), which were taken to be eroded bits of kidney or bladder stones. If red, they were understood to come from the kidney; if white or black, from the bladder; if red and soft to the touch, they were taken as a sign of a liver sickness.

135 *Heres*: Modern medical texts assert that the hair-shaped renal casts found in urine cannot be seen by the naked eye, except possibly clumped together, but both the Western uroscopic tradition and traditional Tibetan medicine, which relies significantly on visual and osmic inspection of urine (Donden 1986: 113–30; Rapgay 2005: 62–6), describe hair-like particles among the contents to be seen in urine.

137–9 *Scales & branne . . . Crynoydes*: Three flake-like contents, distinguished mainly by size and diagnostic implications. According to Henry Daniel, *crinoides* (*crypynes*) are the largest, *branne* (*scuddes*, Lat. *furfura*) of a medium size; *scales* (*shales*, Lat. *squame*, *petaloydes*, *petala*) the smallest (*Liber Uricrisiarum* 3.15; ed. Harvey, Tavormina, et al., forthcoming). All three suggest shedding of tissue, but with different points of origin and subdiagnoses, depending on other symptoms such as fever or its absence.

141 *Sperme . . . man kynde*: *Man kynde* 'man's semen' in the urine was widely taken as a sign of lechery, as here, but could also be read as an indicator of involuntary emission of seed, which was known to have various causes.

142 *Dust*: Fine suspended particles, often called Motes in English and *partes athomose* in Latin, traditionally said to 'sparkle like motes in a sunbeam'. Motes are notoriously difficult to interpret, especially in women, because they can signify gout for both men and women, but are also the most important uroscopic indicator of pregnancy.

143 *Askes*: Like the sandy particulates known as *gravel* (Lat. *arena*), ash-like particulates sink to the bottom of the flask. Whereas *gravel* signifies calculous maladies of the urinary system, whether of the kidney or bladder, *askes* (*cineres*) were usually deemed to signify haemorrhoids and similar problems in the anal region.

144 *cloddes*: Probably 'clouds', but possibly 'clods, clots (of matter)'. The Sedimen/Ypostasis was sometimes described as being like a clump of combed cotton or silk, more like a slowly settling, cloudy suspension than a solid mass of particles. See also m.n. on F/30–1 above.

I. *The Dome of Uryne* (Expanded Version)

21–2 *neuere knyt wyth thykke substance*: The obligatory association of Glaucus urine with thin substance plays a key role in Henry Daniel's discussion of the man at Stamford with thick yellow urine, whose illness baffled doctors (*Liber Uricrisiarum* 2.7; BL, MS Royal 17 D.i, ff. 53[vb]–54[rb]; ed. Harvey, Tavormina, et al., forthcoming).

36, 38 *tercian, double tercian*: Tertian fevers spike every forty-eight hours, an interval counted in medieval numbering systems as the third day. A double tercian is effectively two tertian cycles, offset by twenty-four hours, leading to a daily fever spike. For the many types of tertian fever, see Norri 2016: i. 391, 401–2 (s.vv. *febris, fever*).

57–8 *sinocha inflatiua, sinecha putrida*: The fevers described here are both associated with blood, but *synocha* (*inflativa*) was seen as arising from an excess of otherwise normal or merely distempered blood; *synochus*, in contrast, was said to be caused by rotten blood in the blood vessels. **DU** 's *sinecha putrida*, found in all versions, may be a miswriting for *synochus putridus* or a conflation of *synochus* and *putrid fever*. See Norri 2016: i. 399, ii. 1065–6 (s.vv. *fever, synocha, synochus*). The absence or presence of stench in the urine corresponds to the non-rotten and rotten quality of the blood in the two fevers.

71 *so that no residens . . . may doon awey the bloohed*: I.e. the lividity remains even after the sediment has settled to the bottom of the flask.

105 *webbe of an erayn*: Comparisons of surface oil on urine to a spider web can be traced at least as far back as Isaac Israeli: *Urina oleagina in superficie quasi araneae tela consumptionem pinguedinis significat* (*Liber de urinis*, part. 10: 'Oily urine on the surface like a spider's web signifies the wasting away of fat'; Peine 1919: 71).

130 *post suppositum*: I.e. 'after sexual intercourse, after having lain down (with another)'. See *DMLBS*, s.v. *supponere*, v.(2), sense 1(c).

137–8 *whit & brood . . . warsschid*: A good Ypostasis was defined by Giles (partially following Isaac, *De urinis*, part. 8; Peine 1919: 49) as 'Album, continuum, residens, constans, pineatum' [white, smooth, settled, unchanging, pine-cone-shaped] (*Carmen de urinis* 311; Vieillard 1903: 297). The first two qualities correspond to *whit* and *wythoute brekyng*, while the last two correspond to *long lestyng* and *brood in the bothum & scharp vpward*.

141 *nefilis*: Ultimately derived from Greek νεφέλη 'cloud(s)', cognate with Lat. *nebula*. Most uroscopic treatises apply the term *nefilis/nephilis* to the highest of three forms of Ypostasis, which rises to the top of the urinal, employing the term *eneorima* (Greek ἐναιώρημα 'suspended matter in urine') for Ypostasis that hangs in the middle of the flask, and *sedimen* for Ypostasis proper, resting (*residens*) at the bottom of the urinal. Thus, the Standard Commentary on Giles of Corbeil glosses *Carmen de urinis* 322: '*Si pendeat*: ut fiat enormia, *aut petat altum*, ut fiat nephile' (Sloane 282, f. 45ᵛ). The **DU** author may be confused about the position of *nefilis*, or a clause about *eneorima* may have dropped out of the text early on.

146–53 *Ad sciendum gradus*: Quantifying the four degrees of heat (and *mutatis mutandis*, the other prime qualities) as cold/hot ratios of 1:2, 1:4, 1:8, and 1:16 is the invention of the ninth-century Arabic philosopher Ya'qūb ibn Ishāq al-Kindī, elaborated in the West by Arnald of Villanova and others. Being able to calculate degrees was particularly important in medieval pharmacology, and contributed to larger philosophical and scientific developments (McVaugh 1969; 1975a: 53–156; 1975b). For English versions of this and the next two Latin texts, see App. IV.

199–214 Short texts and sections of texts on distinguishing the urines of men, women, and beasts are common in medieval medical writing, from Avicenna and the *De urinarum cautelis* attributed to Bernard de Gordon to the *Flos medicine* and anecdotes about physicians who were undeceived (or deceived) by substituted samples.

See McVaugh 1997: 201–4; 'Guide', item 7.3 and nn. 42–3. The source in Avicenna is probably *Canon* 1.2.3.2, c. 10 (1486: f. 51vb): women's urines 'habent . . . supra summitatem suam spumam rotundam' ('have a round froth on their surface'); 'oblong' froth on men's urines is not in Avicenna, but may have been inferred from the female feature.

223–73 Several of the signs in **JP** originate in the *Lettre d'Hippocrate* tradition, presumably by way of English texts like *Urine White and Red* and the variant forms of *Urine White and Brown*.

255–6 *palseye, paralisis*: These two words are usually interchangeable in Middle English, referring to paralysis or numbness in part or all of the body, but at least one recorded instance of *palsy* refers to quaking of a limb (see *MED*, s.v. *palesi(e* (n.), sense (d)). Henry Daniel frequently uses *palsy* as a word for a weakness in the bladder or penis (particularly common in the old, he notes) that causes involuntary and sometimes unwitting urination (*Liber Uricrisiarum* 1.4, 2.8, 3.17; ed. Harvey, Tavormina, et al., forthcoming). Most copies of **DU** (all Abbreviated and most Expanded witnesses, plus one late Core witness) read *palsy . . . paralisis* here, but some (Core: Co1W9A14; Exp.: W7Ad7; Hyb.: S16Nm3*S*) read *palsy . . . palsy*, and one (Di1) has *polucyon . . . palysy*, which may derive from the mention of male *kynde* or sperm in the first clause of the sign.

274–301 Several signs in **UMul** are drawn from other well-known women's urine texts, with signs 11 and 13 similar to signs 38 and 39 in *Urina Rufa*; 3, 4, 8, 9 similar to signs 14, 16, 18, 19 in **WR** (and parallels in **WBw** and **WBp**); sign 5 in **UMul** similar to sign 15 in **WBw** (E.2). Some of these signs are also incorporated into *Rufus Subrufus*.

275–6 *clere stripis*: See n. to E.1/23 above.

344–79 *the 4 that longeth to vrynys*: I.e. the fourth thing to be considered in judging urine, namely the contents. In the Expanded Version, apparently also taken as the number of contents to be included in this segment. **DU** conflates the usual Aegidian contents *ampulle* and *spuma* under Froth, and *furfura*, *squame*, and *crinoides* under Bran; it also orders its contents somewhat differently from the Aegidian list (see H/119–21), though still proceeding roughly from top to bottom of the urine flask when **4Con-GrCon** are read together in their original order.

355 *ȝyf hit be yelewe, swot*: 'If the patient suffers from yellow jaundice, there is sweat (as a symptom)', parallel to the association of green and black jaundice with swelling of the gall bladder in the preceding sentence.

362–72 Although all the content and colour signs of **DU** are indebted more or less to Giles of Corbeil, the diagnoses associated with the Circle are particularly close to those in the *Carmen de urinis* 220–34 (Vieillard 1903: 289–90).

GLOSSARY

The Glossary focuses mainly on words and forms that are obsolete or archaic in modern English, unusual dialect forms or orthographic variants, technical terms and senses, *materia medica*, and forms that may be difficult in other ways. The headwords and forms are drawn from texts A through I and Appendices III and IV. The four texts in Appendix III are abbreviated Ap3a through Ap3d; the two texts in Appendix IV as Ap4a and Ap4b. For the sake of readers outside the field of Middle English language and literature, the Glossary includes a wider selection of words and forms than appears in most EETS editions.

Illustrative instances of individual grammatical and orthographic forms are cited by text letter and line number, or for words from Appendices III and IV, by text abbreviation and line number. Asterisks indicate emended instances of words. Latin words and forms, identified by their retention of non-English morphological features or their occurrence in Latin phrases (e.g. *color vrine*, *suffocacio matricis*), are included in the Glossary but marked with a dagger (†). Forms that employ standard Latin nominative inflections and for which anglicized equivalents exist (e.g. *rufus* vs. *rufe*, *ypostasis* vs *ypostas*, *ypostatosis*) are normally taken as Latin, even if used in combination with English words, as in such phrases as *rufus colour*, *vrine . . . rufa oper subrufa*, *a whit ypostasis*, etc.). It should be noted, however, that a case could be made that these words are beginning to be adopted into English. The only exceptions to this practice are occurrences of the hard-to-translate and hard-to-anglicize terms Karapos, Inopos, and Kyanos in texts where all other (A.2, H) or all nearby (G) colour words are rendered in English.

For headwords with multiple spellings, those spellings are listed in alphabetical order for each distinct grammatical form, aside from a few eccentric spellings and the forms of the verb **be(n)** . The headword is followed by the part of speech, definition, and illustrative citations in the order in which they appear in the texts. Nouns are entered under their singular form(s), if extant in the texts; plurals are listed after all singular forms. Adjectives and adverbs are entered under their positive form, if extant, followed by comparative or superlative forms if any. For verbs, the headword is the infinitive, if extant, followed by present indicative, present subjunctive, imperative, present participial, past, and past participial forms in that order. When both English and Latin cognate terms occur, the Latin forms are listed after the English. Only one or two illustrative citations per text are reported for any given form or spelling, although for many words this exhausts all occurrences. Repetitions of headwords within the entries and in phrases are represented with a swung dash (~). The abbreviation '(n.)' after a text reference signals a note to that line in the Textual Commentary; '(m.n.)' signals a note in the Medical Commentary.

The letters *i*, *j*, *y*, *u*, and *v* are alphabetized according to their vocalic or consonantal phonetic value. Thus, vocalic uses of *y* and *j* (e.g. *yvel* 'evil', *jwe-beris* 'ivy berries') are alphabetized under *i*, vocalic *v* (e.g. *vrynal* 'urine flask') under *u*. Consonantal uses of *i* for *j* (e.g. *iaundis* 'jaundice') are alphabetized under *j*. Thorn (*þ*) is treated as *th* for purposes of alphabetization; yogh (*ʒ*) is alphabetized with *gh* or *y*, depending on its phonetic value. Cross-references for variant spellings are given when the variant is relatively remote from the main entry (e.g. **caropos** *see* **karapos** *adj.*, **culour(e)** *see* **colore** *n.*[1]).

Uncertain senses are indicated by a preceding question mark. Definitions of herbal *materia medica* are further glossed with their most likely Linnaean binomial classifications, with the acknowledgement that one cannot always be certain of the specific botanical identity of some common plant names. In some cases, only a genus name can be given.

116 GLOSSARY

ABBREVIATIONS

adj. adjective
adv. adverb
art. article
comp. comparative
conj. conjunction
corr. correlative
dem. demonstrative
fem. feminine
fig. figurative
imp. imperative
inf. infinitive
Lat. Latin
marg. margin(al)
masc. masculine
n. noun
nom. nominative
num. numeral
obj. objective

ord. ordinal
pa. past
pa. p. past participle
phr. phrase, phrasal
pl. plural
poss. possessive; possibly
ppl. participial
pr. present
pr. p. present participle
prep. preposition
prob. probably
pron. pronoun
rel. relative
sg. singular
subj. subjunctive
superl. superlative
vbl. n. verbal noun, gerund
1, 2, 3 first, second, third person

A

a *see* an *prep.*
access, ax(c)esse *n.* fever, illness characterized by fever G/65 (*marg.*), G/65,
I/100, *hoot* ~ I/317, I/319
***accidentes** *n. pl.* sicknesses, disorders
*C/17
†acetosum *adj.* of phlegm: sour, acetous
B/47
ad *see* **haw(e)** *inf.*
adustio(u)n *n.* intense heat within the
body that morbidly alters humours
A.1/9, A.2/23, B/12, G/56, H/116
afteremete *n.* the time after a meal
E.1/2
agu(e) *n.* acute fever G/57, I/78
aymers *see* **emeris** *n. pl.*
ayre, are, eir *n.* air G/153, Ap3d/125;
the element air H/19, H/20; *body of*
~ , *body* ~ the second layer, counting downward, of a urine sample (Lat.
corpus aeris) C/14, C/15
†alba, †albus *adj.* of urine: clear A.1/14,
B/20, B/71, *I/12 (*marg.*)
ampul *n.* bubbles at the top of a urine
sample H/119, H/123
a(n) *prep.* of time: on, at, in G/95, G/96
and *conj.* if I/85, I/133, & I/361
anise *n.* anise (*Pimpinella anisum*), *poudir
of* ~ ground aniseed G/80-1

apostym, apostume *n.* morbid swelling,
inflammation, or abscess E.1/19-20,
G/110 (*see also* **postem(e)**)
appel, appil, appyl *n.* an apple or other
fruit A.2/10, G/49, I/33, Ap3d/90,
Ap3d/91; ~ *citrin, citryn(e)* ~ a yellow
or orange fruit (poss. citron, orange, or
other citrus fruit) A.2/9, G/26; *3onge*
~ an unripe fruit (poss. apple or citrus
fruit) Ap3d/115
aprest *ppl. adj.* afflicted, weighed down
(with illness) G/148
apruwyd *pa. p.* approved, endorsed
Ap3a/3
†archidriclini *n. poss.* of the master of
the feast G/69 (m.n.)
are *see* **ayre** *n.*
arn *see* **be(n)** *inf.*
asaiynge *vbl. n.* of medicines: dosing,
administration, application G/54
askes, askis *n. pl.* ashes H/121, H/143,
I/131
asur *n.* lapis lazuli Ap3d/99
atte *prep. +art.* at the I/258, I/358
atter *n.* pus, putrid matter H/120,
H/127
aumbre *adj.* having the colour of amber
F/43
auance, auence *n.* avens (genus *Geum*)
G/73, G/121, Ap3d/50
auelong *adj.* elongated I/124, *I/205

ax(c)esse *see* access *n.*

aȝanys, aȝens, aȝenys *prep.* against G/49, Ap3a/2, Ap3d/106

aȝen *adv.* again G/35, G/51

B

battoum *see* bothem *n.*

bemeneth *3 sg. pr.* signifies E.2/19

bemys *n. pl.* beams, rays (of light) I/14

be(n) *inf.* be D/19, D/40, G/11, I/205; es *3 sg. pr.* is F/9, F/44, H/5 (also is throughout); arn *pr. pl.* are I/58, I/94, I/313; are H/5, I/315; be G/34; ben A.2/27, G/5, I/11, I/113; buþ B/23 (n.), B/33, C/5, Ap4a/11; beþ B/ 93, C/9, G/23; *hit* ~ there are I/109; be *pr. sg. subj.* B/6, C/30, D/5, E.1/35, E.2/5, F/30, G/30, H/90, I/19, I/85, ben I/113; beyng *pr. p.* I/132; was *pa. sg.* B/78, I/67, I/130; were *pa. sg. subj. as (h)it* ~ as if it were, like D/22, I/80, I/103, Ap3d/106-7

bene *n.* bean (as a measure of quantity) G/63, Ap3d/62

benet *see* eerbe benet *n.*

betayne, biteyne *n.* betony (*Betonica officinalis*) G/32, G/121, Ap3d/7

bychgyng *vbl. n.* buying Ap4a/14

†bipartita *adj.* of astrological signs: of mixed nature, between movable and fixed (='mutable' in modern astrology) I/166

biteyne *see* betayne *n.*

blak *n.* of wine: dark red A.1/7, A.2/21

blew *adj.* lead-coloured, livid F/8, I/237, I/318 (see n. to I/70, 71, m.n. to A.1/10)

bloo *adj.* lead-coloured, livid E.2/5, I/70 (n.), I/88 (see m.n. to A.1/10), I/123

bloohed *n.* lividity, leaden colour I/71

body *n.* ~ *of eir,* ~ *eir* the second layer, counting downward, of a urine sample (Lat. *corpus aeris*) C/14, C/15

boyleyun *pr. pl.* ?boil, bubble E.1/19 (poss. corrupt; see n.)

bolyth *3 sg. pr.* bubbles, froths F/22; bollyng *pr. p.* C/23

bolle *adj.* swollen D/41

bolned, bolnyd *ppl. adj.* swollen E.1/35, E.2/43

bolnyng(ge) *vbl. n.* swelling, distention E.1/27, E.2/35, I/263

*bolnys *n. pl.* bubbles *D/22 (m.n.)

bornyd *ppl. adj.* polished Ap3c/8

bothem, bothom(e), bot(t)hum, botme, bottoum, battoum *n.* the lowest part of a urine sample or urine flask, bottom E.2/13, E.2/33, F/30, G/128, I/24, I/64, I/93, I/98, I/121, I/132, Ap3d/67, Ap3d/102

botonys *n. pl.* buttons, button-sized pellets E.2/5

braie *imp.* stamp, grind, or crush into pieces G/98

brayn(e), brane *n.* brain C/15, F/10, H/123, I/359, Ap3d/2; braynes *n. pl.* H/149, I/362

brake *inf.* vomit F/7; braketh *3 sg. pr.* D/26

brane *see* brayn(e) *n.*

bran(ne), bren *n.* bran, husks of grain G/36, H/120, H/137, I/109

brede *n.* breadth I/341

breed *n.* bread G/73, G/87

bren *see* bran(ne) *n.*

brend *ppl. adj.* burned, overheated I/116, I/351, I/353; of gold: refined, pure I/273

brenny *adj.* branny, bran-like I/109

brestyng *vbl. n.* rupture, breaking I/68

brised, brosed *ppl. adj.* injured, bruised E.1/12, E.2/15, E.2/16

brystyne *ppl. adj.* ruptured F/13

bryth *adj.* translucent, shining I/19

brith *adv.* of colours: bright, light I/369

brosed *see* brised *ppl. adj.*

broun, brown(e) *adj.* of urine: dark, concentrated (in contrast to 'white'=pale or clear) E.1/2, E.1/40, E.2/1, F/3, I/225

burb(e)les *n. pl.* bubbles E.1/38, *E.2/46

buþ *see* be(n) *inf.*

C

camune *adj.* common Ap3a/6

caropos *see* karopos *adj.*

cast, castis, castys *v.[1] 2 sg. pr.* of urine: excrete, void E.2/5, E.2/6; ~ . . . *vp* excrete, void E.1/6; cast *pa. p.* H/86, I/81, I/107

caste *v.[2] imp.* add (to) G/81; throw G/150, G/151

casteth *v.[3] 3 sg. pr.* vomits E.2/31; caste *pr. sg. subj.* E.1/23

castyng *vbl. n.* excretion, voiding I/92, I/204; ?examination I/373 (see n. to I/35)

caule, cawle, cole *n.* cabbage or cabbage-like plant, green leafy vegetable A.1/8, A.2/22, H/117

cawled *pa. p.* called Ap4b/4

celydon *n.* greater or lesser celandine (*Chelidonium majus* or *Ranunculus ficaria*) Ap3d/95

cercle *n.*[1] circular diagram Ap3c/2

cerc(u)le, cerkel, cerkyll, s(c)ercle, cirkyl *n.*[2] the upper region or surface of a urine sample B/4, C/13, E.1/25, E.2/33, F/6, F/40, G/31, H/86, I/122, Ap3d/69; *medyl* ~ the middle region in a urine sample Ap3d/73 (cf. *myddel region* in B/25-6)

chawd pysse *n.* excessive or painful urination F/39

chauffyng *vbl. n.* heating, inflammation I/361

che *see* **s(c)he** *pron.*

chere, *n.* facial expression H/50

citrin(e), citryn(e), sitryne, *adj.* (also as *n.*) of a yellow or yellowish colour, like the colour of a citrine fruit *A.1/22, A.2/9, G/26, G/27, H/106; †citrina, †citrinus, †setrinus A.1/23, B/4, I/37 (*marg.*), Ap3d/36

claye *adj.* of colour: clay-like (Lat. *luteus*) H/56

clansyng, clensyng(e) *vbl. n.* filtration C/1; purging G/41, Ap3d/17; *stable* ~ ?the sweepings of a stable D/35 (n.)

clense *imp.* strain Ap3d/47

cleped, clepid *pa. p.* called G/154, I/57, I/58

clernesse *n.* of urine: clarity, absence of cloudiness B/14

cleueth *3 sg. pr.* adheres I/346

cloddes *see* **cloud** *n.*

cloos *ppl. adj.* enclosed G/106

cloud, clude *n.* nebulosity suspended in a urine sample C/26, F/30; **cloudes, cloddes** *n. pl.* H/119, H/125

clowe *n.*[1] clove from a bulb (of leek or garlic) I/306

clowis *n.*[2] *pl.* the spice cloves (*Caryophyllus aromaticus*) G/115, G/151

clude *see* **cloud** *n.*

cod *n.* scrotum G/78, I/99

coffre *n.* ~ *of the galle* the gallbladder I/191

cole *n.*[1] *see* **caule** *n.*

cole *n.*[2] *see* **co(o)le** *n.*

coler, colore, colre *n.* the humour (red) choler, bile H/41, H/70, I/181, I/185, I/228

coleryk, colerike *adj.* characterized by choler H/47, H/53

†colica passio, †colica passyoun *n. phr.* severe abdominal pain I/24-5, Ap3d/102

†color vrine *n.* colour of urine A.1/25, A.1/26

colore, col(o)ur(e), culour(e) *n.*[1] colour A.1/6, A.1/8, H/15, H/16, H/51, I/10, I/289; **colour(e)s, colouris, culoures, colourus** *n. pl.* A.2/14, C/6, E.1/1, F/8, G/5, H/98, I/2, I/11, Ap3a/8

colore *n.*[2] *see* **coler** *n.*

coloure *pr. sg. subj.* take on the colour (of) Ap3d/113

colre *see* **coler** *n.*

colur *see* **colore** *n.*[1]

comande, comyng *pr. p.* occurring D/11 (n.); about to occur, impending E.1/11, E.2/14

combynaciones *n. pl.* (allowable) combinations, pairings H/18

comferie, *confirie, confery *n.* comfrey (*Symphytum officinale*) G/84, *G/136, Ap3d/120

comyn *n.* cumin, seed of the plant *Cuminum cyminum* G/80, G/104, Ap3d/53

comyng *see* **comande** *pr. p.*

commyned *pa. p.* had intercourse (with) I/303

compleccion, complexioun, conpleccioun *n.* the balance of humours within a person's body, usually with one humour predominant E.2/4, H/3, H/62, I/208, I/214; **compleccion(e)s, complexciouns, complexio(u)n(e)s** *n. pl.* H/1, H/60, I/184, I/189, I/221

conceyued *ppl. adj.* (to have) conceived, (to be) pregnant H/142

confery, confirie *see* **comferie** *n.*

conpleccioun *see* **compleccion** *n.*

consoud *n.* daisy (*Bellis perennis*) G/84

conteyned *pa. p.* *pat is* ~ urinary content(s) C/6

content *n.* material suspended or settled out in urine H/89, I/91, I/135; **contentes, contentis** *n. pl.* H/112, H/119, I/2, I/17

contyned *ppl. adj.* contained (in a text), mentioned Ap3d/33

contryuid *ppl. adj.* ?falsely devised Ap3c/2 (see n. to G/2); **icontryued** *ppl. adj.* devised, composed G/2

co(o)le *n.* coal or charcoal, a piece of (char)coal H/100, I/54, I/78, I/272; **coolis, colys** *n. pl.* G/151, I/246

corpulent(e) *adj.* thick, dense H/26, H/27

corrupciouns *n. pl.* infections, putrefactions G/112

corrupte *adj.* infected, diseased B/29; of women: having had sexual intercourse *D/09

costyfnesse *n.* constipation I/262

cotydyan *adj.* of fever: recurring on a daily basis I/30; **cotidian** (as *n.*) a cotidian fever I/39, I/47

cottyng *vbl. n.* an excised part Ap3d/91

courchef *n.* kerchief, cloth to cover the head Ap3d/12

creme *n.* a layer of bubbles at the top of a urine sample (Lat. *ampulla*) H/123

crynoydes *n. pl.* of urine: large scale-like contents H/121, H/139

†**crocea** *adj.* saffron-coloured (either the reddish-orange colour of the spice or the yellower stain produced by saffron) B/37

†**crocus** *n.* saffron (*Crocus sativus*); † ~ *occidentalis* 'Western' saffron, a duller-coloured and possibly less valuable form of saffron A.1/1; † ~ *orientalis* 'Eastern' saffron, a brighter and possibly higher-quality form of saffron A.1/2 (m.n.)

crodded *ppl. adj.* coagulated, clotted B/94

croppis *n. pl.* buds, shoots, or tops of a plant G/98

crullyng *vbl. n.* abdominal rumbling I/97

culour(e) *see* **colore** *n.*[1]

D

daies y3e *n.* daisy (*Bellis perennis*) G/84

declynyng *vbl. n.* ~ *of þe yuel* the fourth and final stage in the progress of a disease (Lat. *declinatio*) B/14-15

ded(e), deid *n.* death E.1/31, H/80, H/118

ded(e), deed *adj.* dead D/38, E.1/33, E.2/41, F/37

deedli, *adj.* deadly, fatal A.2/27

defeccion *n.* weakness, defect (Lat. *defectio*) B/18

defye *inf.* process nutriment, digest I/140

degestion *see* **digestio(u)n** *n.*

deid *see* **ded(e)** *n.*

delit *pa. p.* dealt, had intercourse B/92 (n.)

delyuryng *vbl. n.* relief (from an illness) I/76

departed *ppl. adj.* divided (into groups) H/36

differyd *ppl. adj.* deferred, suppressed Ap3d/122

digestio(u)n, dygestioun, degestion *n.* metabolic coction of food, digestion by physiological 'cooking' A.1/5, A.1/21, A.2/8, F/5, G/7, H/107, I/32; *secunde* ~ the stage in the metabolic process that occurs in the liver B/19; ~ breaking down of noxious matter in the body C/27

dym *adj.* dark, dull I/231

dirke *adj.* dark Ap3d/73

dyscrecyoun *n.* differentiation, judgement, discernment F/45

discryue, dysscryue *inf.* describe F/1, G/29

disposicion *n.* state (of health) B/1, ~ *of* predisposition to B/36

dissolution *n.* of bodily tissue: melting away, wasting H/129, H/135

dissolued *pa. p.* of clotted blood: broken up, dispersed B/95

distried *pa. p.* destroyed, suppressed G/141

distrucioun *n.* ~ *of kynde* destruction of (a person's) nature, undoing I/143

dolour *n.* pain C/25

done *ppl. adj. ful* ~ inclusive, completely H/78

doome *n.* judgement, interpretation I/1, I/145

d'o(o)rt *see* **o(o)rt** *n.*

draven *inf.* draw, move I/280

drawyng *vbl. n.* extension, prolongation B/82

dredefull *adj.* timorous H/56

drest *n.* waste material I/243; **drestes** *n. pl.* dregs H/43, I/212, I/246

dresty *adj.* like dregs *I/64, I/327

dropes, dropys *n. pl.* drops, as a content in urine B/58, D/22, H/129

dropes(e)y(e), drop(e)sie *n.* dropsy, edema, a pathological accumulation of fluid in the body B/26, B/27, E.1/13; *hote* ~ dropsy caused by excessive heat E.2/16; *cold(e)* ~ dropsy caused by excessive cold E.2/18, I/244, I/245

droubli *see* **drubly** *adj.*

drouie *adj.* turbid E.2/26

drubled *ppl. adj.* turbid E.2/8

drubles *n. pl.* turbidity I/279, I/280

drubly, dr(o)ubli *adj.* turbid *E.2/17, I/17, I/66, I/226, I/240

drublihede, drublyhede *n.* turbidity I/201, I/202

drublynesse *n.* turbidity I/276

dul, dull(e) *adj.* heavy, not sharp or subtle H/27, H/27; mentally dull H/59

durye, durre *inf.* last, remain Ap4a/13, Ap4a/18

dust *n.* motes suspended in a urine sample (Lat. *partes athomosi*) H/121, H/142

duellyng *n.* location, (*fig.*) place of residence I/192, ~ *place* I/191, I/195

E

†econtra *adv.* conversely I/163

eerbe benet *n.* common or wood avens, herb bennet (*Geum urbanum*) G/65-6

e(e)rbis, herbis *n. pl.* herbs G/34, G/60, G/95, Ap3d/9, Ap3d/78

†effimeram *adj.* of fever: transient, ephemeral B/7

eghteth *adj.* eightieth H/79

†egritudo, †egritudinis, †egritudinem *n.* illness, sickness I/160, I/161, I/162; **†eppaticam** ~ illness of the liver B/81

ey *n.* egg H/28

eyn, ene *n. pl.* eyes I/315, Ap3d/4

eir *see* **ayre** *n.*

elde *n.* old age H/77, H/79

eldertre *n. medyl barke of þe* ~ the moist cambial layer, between the outer bark

and the wood, of the elder (*Sambuca nigra*) Ap3d/77-8

ele *n. kynd* ~ an eel that is 'natural' (=wild, not farmed in an eel-pond?) Ap3d/31; *elys grece* rendered fat of an eel or eels Ap3d/25

elike *adv.* alike, in the same way H/4

emeris, aymers *n. pl.* embers G/52, Ap3d/92

emorautys, emorodis *n. pl.* haemorrhoids I/133, Ap3d/110

endywe *n.* a prickly wild lettuce, poss. sowthistle (genus *Sonchum*) Ap3d/77

ene *see* **eyn** *n. pl.*

enke *see* **ynke** *n.*

epilensie *n.* epilepsy I/366

†eppaticam *adj.* hepatic, pertaining to the liver B/81

erayn *n.* spider I/105

eryn *n. pl.* ears Ap3d/5

es *see* **be(n)** *inf.*

eth *adj.* easy I/211

etik(e), etyk *adj. feuer(e)* ~ , *feuyre* ~ hectic fever, a chronic wasting fever B/40, E.1/9, E.2/12, H/140; **etyk, etik** *adj.* (as *n.*) I/102, I/110, I/112

etynk *vbl. n.* eating I/216

euel *adv.* with difficulty I/315

euel(e), euell, yuel *n.* disease, illness B/15, B/42, C/27, D/20, D/29, E.1/14, E.2/24, G/120, I/60; *ȝelowȝ* ~ jaundice G/47-8; **eueles** *n. pl.* E.2/11

euen, ewyn *n.* evening G/85, G/96, Ap3d/49, Ap3d/83

euene, ewen *adj., adv.* ~ *porcioun*, ~ *proporcionde* (with) an equal amount of each G/63, G/73, Ap3d/62

ewere *adv.* ever Ap3d/114

ewery *n. see* **yuery** *n.*

ewyn *see* **euen** *n.*

excesse *n.* excess, plethora (of blood) I/57, ~ *of degestion* (*digestioun*) the continuation of metabolic coction beyond its proper end, leading to overheating of the alimentary material A.1/5, A.2/19, G/9

excoriacion *n.* shedding of the skin or membrane lining an internal organ B/68-9

F

falis *3 sg. pr.* fails Ap3d/123

fallyng *vbl. n.* ~ *of floures* flow of the menses I/285-6

falowe *adj.* fallow, the colour of autumn leaves H/103

fare *adj.* clean, 'fair' Ap3d/81

fastne, festen *inf.* fasten G/43, Ap3d/19

fat, fatt(e), ffatte *adj.* fat(ty), greasy, oily (Lat. *pinguis, crassus*) B/40, B/54, D/7, D/13, E.1/4, E.1/10, E.2/13, E.2/29, F/4, F/15, I/103, I/106; ~ *visage* fat-faced H/59

fathed *n.* oiliness, fatness I/100, I/102

fat(te)nes *n.* oiliness, fatness H/120, H/129, H/135

fatty, fetti, fetty *adj.* fat(ty), greasy, oily I/66, I/79, I/319

†febrem *n.* fever; ~ *effimeram* ephemeral fever, a transient fever B/7; **†febres** *n. pl. interpollatas* intermittent fevers B/81

fenderes, funderes *n. pl.* the lowest part of a urine sample, where the dregs appear E.1/10 (n.), E.1/26

festen *see* **fastne** *inf.*

fetti, fetty *see* **fatty** *adj.*

feuer(e), feuyr(e), fewer, fyuer, fy-uyr *n.* fever B/71, F/41, F/44, I/57, I/66, I/227, I/298, Ap3d/59; **feueres, feuerys, feuers, fyueres** *n. pl.* B/21, C/27, I/58, I/297, Ap3d/71; ~ *etik(e)* hectic fever, a fever associated with chronic wasting diseases (esp. tuberculosis) B/40, E.1/9, H/140, ~ *etyk* E.2/12; ~ *quart(e)yn*, ~ *quart'*, ~ *quarta(y)ne* quartan fever, a fever that reaches crisis every three days D/13, D/36, E.1/11, E.1/30-1, E.2/14, E.2/39, F/12, Ap3d/88; ~ *continual* fever that remains steadily above normal temperature B/8; *cotydyan* ~ an intermittent fever with daily recurrence I/30; *vrine of feueres* urine of a feverous person (poss. understood as 'urine accompanied by fevers') E.1/8

fewerfu *n.* feverfew (*Tanacetum parthenium*; also as *Chrysanthemum parthenium*, *Pyrethrum parthenium*) Ap3d/75

†feuerosus *adj.* febrile, accompanied by fever D/11

feuerouse *n.* a person with fever E.2/8, E.2/10; **feueres** (poss. understood as 'fevers') E.1/8

ffatte *see* **fat** *adj.*

fier, fiir *see* **fire** *n.*

fylmyne *n.* a membrane between the brain and the skull, one or more of the meninges (*dura mater*, arachnoid *mater*, *pia mater*) F/9

fire, fyre, fier, fiir, fuyr(e) *n.* fire A.1/3, A.2/17, E.1/18, G/45, H/19, H/30; ~ *coole* a burning coal I/67

fyuer(es), fyuyr *see* **feuer(e)** *n.*

†flaumatico *n.* a phlegmatic person, someone in whom the humour phlegm is dominant B/30

fleete *pr. sg. subj.* float I/92

fleyes, fleyeth *3 sg. pr.* ?floats, drifts E.1/19 (poss. corrupt; see n.), F/22

fle(i)sch, fles(s)h *n.* meat A.1/19, A.2/6, E.2/26, F/15, G/23, H/105, I/26, I/29, I/251; skin, hide A.1/17, G/22; the flesh of the human body G/113

fleschy, flesshy *adj.* fleshy, containing particles like flesh *E.2/17, I/243; fleshy, not lean (Lat. *carnosus*) H/52

flesly *adj.* fleshy, containing particles like flesh D/16

fleteth, fletith, fletyth, fletut, flotud *3 sg. pr.* contains floating matter (fat, bubbles, etc.) E.1/21, E.1/38, E.2/29, E.2/46, I/284; **fletyngg** *pr. p.* floating I/127

fletyng *vbl. n.* floating matter I/325

fleumatik(e), fleumatyke *adj.* characterized by the humour phlegm H/49, H/57, H/67

fleume, fl(e)wme *n.* the humour phlegm F/4, H/44, H/72, H/75, I/31, I/182; **†flewma** B/50, **†acetosum** ~ acidic phlegm *B/47-8

flewrys *n. pl.* see **floures** *n.[2] pl.*

flotud *see* **fleteth** *3 sg. pr.*

flour *n.[1]* flour (of wheat) I/112

flour *n.[2]* a ~ *of hire blod* a portion of a woman's menses? E.1/29 (m.n.)

floures *n.[1] pl.* flowers, blossoms H/106

floures, flouris, flourys, flewrys, flowres *n.[2] pl.* a woman's menses F/32, G/133, I/64, I/134, I/286, Ap3d/118, Ap3d/122; *blake* ~ (?flake-like) particulates in the urine F/34 (m.n.)

flourynges *vbl. n. pl.* a nebulosity or sediment in urine, poss. similar to flour?

flake-like particulates in the urine?
F/31 (m.n.)

flwme *see* fleume *n.*

flux *n.* morbid flow or discharge of bodily
substances (esp. blood or excrement)
I/18, I/125, I/292; ~ *of the wombe*
diarrhoea, dysentery, or lientery B/57

fome *n.* foam, bubbles, or froth on the
surface of a urine sample C/23, H/126

fomie, fomye *adj.* containing foam,
frothy *B/37, B/43, B/45, B/83

founderel *n.* the lowest part of a urine
sample F/11 (cf. funderes *n. pl.*)

founsse *n.* the lowest part of a urine
sample E.2/17 (n.)

frankencense *n.* frankincense G/79,
G/151

frenesy *n.* madness, a fit of madness
I/368

froth *n.* foam I/45, I/63, I/204

frothi, frothy *adj.* foamy I/27, I/255,
I/269

frustris *n. pl.* flakes appearing in a urine
sample (Lat. *frustra*) B/68

fumiter *n.* fumitory (*Fumaria officinalis*)
G/59

funderes *see* fenderes *n. pl.*

fuyr(e) *see* fire *n.*

G

galyngale *n.* galingale, the root or
rhizome of various plants (*Cyperus
longus, Aristolochia rotunda, Alpinia
galanga,* etc.), powdered to create a
culinary and medical spice G/115

gallades *n.* an illness associated with
women, possibly ulceration of the
gall bladder or bitterness in the bile?
E.2/29 (n.)

gal(le) *n.* the gall bladder H/42, H/152,
I/9, I/191, I/355; bile (the humour
produced by the gall bladder) H/131;
the gall bladder (of animals) used as a
medicinal ingredient Ap3d/30

garland, garlond, gerlond *n.* a bandage
for the head in the shape of a wreath
G/37, G/38, Ap3d/12

garleek *n.* garlic (*Allium sativum*) G/87

gendryng *pr. p.* ~ *lymmes* the reproductive and excretory organs H/148,

H/153; gendred, ygendred *pa. p.* en-
gendred, produced H/41, H/42, I/189,
I/194

gerlond *see* garland *n.*

gyf *imp.* give I/306

gyngeuer *n.* ginger, the root of *Zingiber
officinale* G/74

gladen, gladwyne *n.* a plant in the genus
Iris G/142, Ap3d/123

glas *n.* a (glass) urine flask B/9, Ap3d/59

glasyne *adj.* made of glass B/78

*†glaucus *adj.* of a pale, translucent
yellow colour *A.1/15, *I/19 (*marg.*)

glet *n.* mucus, phlegm G/92, H/44,
H/124, H/131

gobet *n.* a small piece G/50, I/121;
gobet(t)is, gobettes *n. pl.* (Lat. *frustra,
frustula*) B/62, I/87, I/246

golde *n.* marigold (*Calendula officinalis*)
G/59, G/121; goldys *n. pl.* Ap3d/50,
Ap3d/107

golled *ppl. adj.* yellowed E.1/35 (n.); cf.
gulle *adj.*

gomes *n. pl.* gums G/43, Ap3d/19

goutous *adj.* producing gout G/86

graynes, graynys, greyn(e)s *n. pl.*
grain-like bubbles or bits of foam
near the top of a urine sample H/119,
H/124, I/257, I/351

gratter, grettere *adj. comp.* greater,
larger H/139, I/113, I/213

grauel(l), grauil *n.* gritty particles in
a urine sample F/26, F/38, H/120,
H/134, I/24, I/114; ~ *sto(o)nys* gritty
particles or somewhat larger con-
cretions in a urine sample G/124,
Ap3d/97

grauely *adj.* gritty, sandy, gravelly C/28

grece, grese *n.* grease, rendered fat
G/79, Ap3d/25, Ap3d/108; grees *n.*
fat (inside the body) I/100

gree *n.* gradation (of heat, cold, moisture,
or dryness) Ap4a/2, Ap4a/4; greys
n. pl. Ap4a/1

greyne *see* grene *adj.*

greyn(e)s *see* graynes *n. pl.*

greynes *n. pl.* grains of paradise (seeds of
Aframomum melegueta) G/115, G/151

greys *see* gree

grene, greyne *adj.* green A.1/8, A.2/22,
E.2/4, F/8, H/117, I/73, I/236

grese *see* grece *n.*

greuaunce *n.* pain F/39

greueþ *3 sg. pr.* afflicts G/146; **greuede, greuyd** *ppl. adj.* afflicted F/49, H/143

grynddyngg *vbl. n.* abdominal griping, twisting pains I/96

ground(e) *n.*[1] the lowest region or bottom of a urine sample B/64, B/77, C/14, F/27, F/34, H/87, H/144; the Ypostasis, the material that settles to the bottom of a urine sample H/145

gr(o)unde *n.*[2] floor, soil, ground G/143, Ap3d/124

gulle *adj.* yellow E.2/43; cf. **golled** *ppl. adj.*

H

had *see* **haw(e)** *inf.*

ham *see* **hem** *pron.*

hany *adj.* any Ap4a/2

harde *adj.* ~ *of witte* obtuse, slow-witted (Lat. *hebes est sensus*) H/59

harm *n.* arm I/311

harnes *n. preuy (priuy)* ~ reproductive organs H/143, H/153

has *n.* European ash (*Fraxinus excelsior*) Ap3d/23

hat *see* **haw(e)** *inf.*

haw(e) *inf.* have Ap3d/67, Ap3d/83, Ap3d/122; **ad, had, hat** *3 sg. pr.* has E.1/6, E.1/17, E.1/28, E.1/36; ~ *pr. sg. subj.* Ap3d/66, Ap3d/68; **hauende** *pr. p.* having I/325. (Also occurs in more common forms **haue, have; has(e), hath, haþ, haueþ; han** *pr. pl.*)

he *pron. masc. sg.* he B/7, D/6, E.1/6, E.2/21, F/19, G/53, H/46; (*fig.*) it I/52; *fem. sg.* she E.1/26, E.1/35 (*see also* **sche**); *fem. sg.* she or *3 pl.* they B/73, B/76, B/94

hede *n.* bulb or 'head' of a plant's root Ap3d/112

he(e)te *n.* heat (as a prime quality or as a characteristic of individual things) B/17, B/83, C/9, G/106, G/117, H/99, I/259, I/356; *kyndeliche* ~ essential heat generated within an organism, necessary for life B/31, *vnkyndely* ~ unhealthy heat caused by illness G/56

heye, hy(e) *adj.* of colour: intense, bright, 'high' (as opposed to low or dull)

I/129, I/267, I/365; **hyest** *superl.* highest (in space or position) H/36

hele *n.* health E.1/3, E.1/4, E.2/1, E.2/11, F/3, F/29, H/97

hem, ham *pron. 3 pl.* them B/73, C/26, G/98, G/135

her(e), hir(e), hyr(e), hure *pron. fem. sg. poss.* her D/29, E.1/29, E.2/41, E.2/43, E.2/49, F/32, G/129; *fem. sg. obj.* B/89, D/34, E.1/33, G/139

here *n.* hair H/103; ~ *syf* sieve made of woven hair Ap3d/81; **heres, heris** *n. pl.* hair-like contents in urine H/120, H/135, I/124, I/126

heryn *vbl. n.* hearing Ap3d/23

herte *n.* ~ *of þe erth* centre of the earth H/33

herte *see* **horte** *adj.*

hertis tunge *n.* hart's-tongue fern (*Phyllitis scolopendrium*) G/94

het *see* **hit** *pron.*

hete *see* **he(e)te** *n.*

heued(e) *n.* head E.1/26, E.2/9, E.2/34, H/122, I/60, I/240

hy *pron. 3 pl.* they C/10

hy(e) *see* **heye** *adj.*

hil(e) *imp.* cover G/107, Ap3d/57

hynder *adj.* back, situated in the rear B/51

his(e), hys *pron. masc. sg. poss.* his D/7, E.2/15, F/7, F/19, G/78, G/106, I/21; *neut. sg. poss.* its G/154, H/87

hit, het *pron. neut. sg.* it B/4, C/1, D/9, D/12, D/31, H/42, I/3, I/6

hoil *see* **hole** *adj.*

hold *adj.* old I/48

holdynge, holding *pr. p. hard & fast* ~ *of persons:* tenaciously grasping (Lat. *dextreque tenacis*) H/55; *long* ~ *of disease:* persistent Ap4b/19

hole *n.* hole H/29

hole, hool, hoil *adj.* whole, healthy B/20, C/26, D/6, D/41, G/40, G/96, I/68, Ap3d/15

hoofe *see* **hove** *inf.*

hore-hofe *n.* ?colts-foot (*Tussilago farfara*) Ap3d/77

horhowne *n.* horehound (*Marubium vulgare*) G/98

horte, herte *adj.* hurt D/14, D/19

hous *n. pl.* houses Ap4a/13

hove *inf.* float I/279; **hovyth** *3 sg. pr.* I/102; **hoofe** *pr. sg. subj.* I/139

huche *see* **w(h)ich(e)** *rel. pron.*

humur *n.* a bodily fluid or secretion, esp. but not exclusively one of the four fluids of medieval physiology: blood, phlegm, choler (bile), and melancholy (black bile) H/120, H/131; **humo(u)rs, humouris, humures, vmers** *n. pl.* B/29, B/50, E.1/41, I/258, Ap3d/1-2; *raw* ~ undigested bodily fluids or secretions I/91, I/94

hundes-tong *n.* hound's-tongue (*Cynoglossum officinale*) Ap3d/107

I

icontryued *see* **contryuid** *ppl. adj.*

†ydropico *n.* a person with dropsy B/30

ydropyk *adj.* dropsical, having the dropsy I/273

ygendred *see* **gendryng** *pr. p.*

yke *adv.* also I/354

ilk(e), ylke *pron.* as *adj.* each, every H/2, H/13, I/342

ilkone *pron.* each one H/4

ylokid *see* **lok(e)** *imp.*

ymedlid *see* **medle** *imp.*

ymellid *see* **mel** *imp.*

indigestio(u)n, indygestioun, yndygestyon *n.* absence or failure of the process of digestion, non-digestion A.1/18, A.2/5, G/20, G/71, H/104, I/13, I/347

indisposicion *n.* unhealthy state, predisposition to illness Ap3d/71, *n. pl.* B/35

inflacion *n.* production of gas in the body or swelling caused thereby C/24

*†inflatiua *adj.* causing or characterized by swelling *I/57

ingleymyd *ppl. adj.* covered by or containing viscous matter, made sticky, ?constipated F/25

ynke, enke *n.* ink *A.1/11, A.2/25, G/15

inopos, ynopos *adj.* of a dark reddish colour A.1/6, A.2/20, H/115; †**ynopos, *†inopos** G/12, *I/62 (*marg.*)

inordinances *n. pl.* unhealthy states, disorders B/23

†interpollatas *adj.* intermittent B/81

ypostas, ypostatecis, ypostatesie *n.* the material that settles to the bottom of a urine sample, urinary sediment B/74, B/77, H/121, H/145; †**ypostasis** I/135, I/141

yput *see* **putte** *imp.*

ysend *pa. p.* ~ *out* duller or lighter in colour, reduced in intensity (Lat. *remissus*) A.1/3, A.1/4

jwe-beris *n. pl.* ivy berries Ap3d/99

yuel *n. see* **euel(e)** *n.*

yuel *adj.* bad, harmful G/113; of a diagnostic sign: bad, indicating disease B/34, C/26

yuery, ewery *n.* ivory G/51, Ap3d/91

y3e *see* **daies y3e** *n.*

J

iaundys, iaundese, iavndes, iawndys, iawnd(is), iaundise, iauneys, iawnyes, iaunys *n.* jaundice B/38, E.1/15, E.2/20, G/48, H/126, I/45, I/63, I/353, Ap3d/89; *blake* ~ a form of jaundice thought to be generated by excess black bile or overheated humours I/353

iete *n. blacke* ~ black jet (lignite) Ap3d/99

ioyntis *n. pl.* joints I/5

iuys, iuse, jus *n.* juice, sap (of herbs) G/44, G/67, Ap3d/20, Ap3d/95; ~ *of flessh* (*fleisch*) broth, 'juice' of cooked meat A.1/19, A.2/6, G/24

iuste *adv.* properly Ap3d/82

K

*kaynos *see* **kianos** *adj.*

karapos, caropos *adj.* of a light brown, yellowish brown, or brownish grey (camel-like) colour (also as *n.*) A.1/17, A.2/4, G/22, H/102; †**karapos, *†karopos** B/29, *I/23 (*marg.*)

kepen *inf.* retain I/21; **kepyn** *pr. pl.* remain in I/198

kerchir *n.* kerchief, veil, headscarf G/37

keuerid *ppl. adj.* covered G/106

kianos, kyanos *adj.* of a dark red or purplish red colour in urine (also as *n.*) A.1/7, A.2/21, H/116; †**kyanos, *†kaynos** G/12, *I/65 (*marg.*)

kynde *n.*[1] semen I/128; ~ *of a man, man* ~ semen H/141, I/254-5; ~ *of man* desire for man D/34 (n.); *lust of* ~ sexual desire I/238-9

kynde *n.*[2] nature I/143, *of* ~ naturally I/82; **kyndes** *n. pl.* natures, characteristics H/6

kynd ele *see* **ele** *n.*

kyndeliche *adj.* natural; ~ *hete* essential heat generated within an organism, necessary for life B/31

kitte, kutte *imp.* cut G/49, G/50

knaf, knave, knawe *n.* ~ *child* a boy I/122, I/279, I/311

knyt(te) *imp.* combine H/17; *pa. p.* combined, joined I/21, I/377

knyttynges *vbl. n. pl.* combinations H/18

kutte *see* **kitte** *imp.*

L

†**lactea**, †**lacteus** *adj.* whey-coloured or milky A.1/16, B/22, B/25, *I/16 (marg.)* (cf. A.2/3, B/54, *B/56, B/58, translating *lactea* as *milky/mylky*)

lactike *adj.* milky H/102

lagheng *pr. p.* laughing H/50

langdebeef, langedebefe *n.* one or more species of bugloss (Anchusa, Echium, Lycopsis *spp.*) or hawkweed (Hieracium, Pilosella *spp.*) G/121, Ap3d/51

large *adj.* sizable, of quantity: great, sizable H/15; generous H/50

latyn *see* **let** *pa. p.*

leche *n.* the ring finger (Lat. *digitus medicus*) I/169

leche *conj.* like D/33

led(e) *see* **le(e)d(e)** *n.*

ledy *adj.* lead-coloured, livid B/52

le(e)d(e), leid *n.* the metal lead A.1/10, A.2/24, D/37 (n.), E.1/32, E.2/5, E.2/40, F/36, G/14, H/101, I/56, I/70

l(e)ek(e) *n.* leek (*Allium porrum*) I/306, I/307; *vnset* ~ leek that is not yet rooted or established Ap3d/112; **lekys** *n. pl.* Ap3d/26

le(i)ndes *n. pl.* the loins, the kidneys (OF *reyns*) E.1/16, E.1/40, E.2/21, E.2/49

leid *see* **le(e)d(e)** *n.*

lemes *see* **lymmes** *n. pl.*

let, latyn *pa. p.* be ~ *blod(e)* have blood drawn, be bled B/10, Ap3d/60

lette *pr. sg. subj.* hinder, prevent; ~ *not . . . to wyrche* allow (sth.) to work Ap3d/16

lettyng *vbl. n.* hindering, blockage (Lat. *impedimentum*) B/18

leuk *adj.* lukewarm G/99

lewer *n.* the liver Ap3d/42

leues *n. pl.* leaves (of plants) H/103

licorice, liquoris *n.* licorice root (*Glycyrrhiza glabra*) Ap3d/43, Ap3d/44

licour, lycour, liquour *n.* fluid in which herbs have been cooked G/36, Ap3d/11, Ap3d/11; **licours** *n. pl.* Ap3d/82

lift, lyft, luft *adj.* left (as opposed to right) B/44, B/45, I/311, I/364

lykyng(ge) *vbl. n.* ~ *to* desire for F/29, *wythoute* ~ involuntarily I/129

lile rote *n.* the underground part of a lily, including bulb (*see* **hede**) and roots Ap3d/112

lymmes, lemes *n. pl.* bodily limbs or organs H/82, H/83, H/154

lynse(e)d, lynseid *n.* linseed (poss. referring to the light yellow colour of linseed oil or the light brown colour of linseeds proper) E.1/36 (see n. to D/40), E.2/44, I/292; *poudre . . . of* ~ ground linseeds G/80

liquoris *see* **licorice** *n.*

lyuerwort, lywerworte *n.* liverwort (*Marchantia polymorpha*) G/93, Ap3d/77

lyuyd *adj.* (also as *n.*) lead-coloured, livid; a leaden colour H/100, H/101; †**liuida**, †**lyuidus** A.1/10, B/85, *I/70

lok(e) *imp.* make sure, see to (sth.) G/145, Ap3d/123; determine I/184; ~ *to* consider I/3; **ylokid** *pa. p.* considered C/5

longes *3 sg. pr.* belongs, pertains F/46, F/47; **longeth** *pr. pl.* I/1, I/145

long(g)es, longys, lung(e)s, lungge, loungis, longon *n. pl.* lungs C/24, E.1/17, E.1/20, E.2/23, E.2/28, F/19, H/44, H/150, I/260, I/359, Ap3d/42

longhed *n.* length, long duration I/142

longon *see* **long(g)es** *n. pl.*

lorn *pa. p.* lost E.1/29

lothe *pr. sg. subj.* is nauseated I/333

loungis *see* **long(g)es** *n. pl.*

loueache *n*. lovage (*Levisticum officinale*) Ap3d/43

low *adj*. of colour: dull or faded I/131, I/133; **lowere** *comp*. ~ *parties* the genital and excretory organs of the body H/146; **lowest** *superl*. (as *n*.) deepest position H/37

†**lucida** *adj*. translucent B/35

luft *see* **lift** *adj*.

lung(e)s *see* **long(g)es** *n. pl*.

lust *n*. ~ *of kynde* sexual desire I/238-9

M

maisters *n. pl*. learned authorities I/11

malencolie, melancoly *n*., the humour melancholy, black bile H/43, H/71, I/39, I/183

malwys *n. pl*. mallows, prob. the common mallow (*Malva sylvestris*) Ap3d/108

***mares** *n*. a disease of women, possibly of the uterus *F/35 (n.)

mastik *n*. resin of the mastic tree (*Pistacia lentiscus*) G/79

mater(e), matyr *n*. subject matter Ap3a/4; substance, material F/35, G/129; *venemous* ~ a morbid substance in the body G/18 ~ *of þat* (*þe*) *yuel* the substance of a disease C/27, Ap3d/87; **mater(e)s** *n. pl. venemos* (*venemosy*) ~ morbid substances B/32, C/30

matfeloun *n*. knapweed (*Centaurea spp.*) G/59, G/83

matrice *n*. uterus, womb B/61, C/17, E.1/34, E.2/49; †**matrix** G/154; **matrices** *n. pl*. B/23; †*suffocacio matricis* a sensation of internal pressure believed to be caused by movement of the uterus G/147

maw *n*. stomach Ap3d/99

me *indef. pron*. (some) one H/88

mechel, mekel, mekil, mychel, mykel *adj*. much E.1/18, E.2/24, H/91, I/76; (as *n*.) a great deal H/46, H/47; *in as* ~ *as* to the degree that, because I/213-14; ~ *spittyng* spitting often or much H/57-8 (m.n.)

med(d)el, medyl, med(d)il, myd(d)el, myddil *adj*. middle, at the centre H/34, I/170; (as *n*.) centre H/29, Ap3d/69; of regions in urine samples:

middle, between the top and the bottom (also as *n*.) B/25, B/52, C/19, C/21, F/47, G/90, G/101, H/87; of urinary density or quantity: intermediate (between thick and thin, between much and little) B/4, H/90, H/91; of the digestive process: partially completed A.1/24; (as *n*.) the middle, the mean (between two things) Ap4a/17; ~ *barke* the moist cambial layer between the outer bark and the wood of a tree Ap3d/77; ~ *cirkyl* the middle region in a urine sample Ap3d/73 (cf. *myddel region* in B/25-6); ~ *signe* the middle degrees of a zodiacal sign (Lat. *medio signi*) B/10

mediat *adj*. ~ *digestioun* partially completed metabolic coction A.2/11, G/28

medle *imp*. mix G/80, I/209; **(y)medlid** *ppl. adj*. mixed, blended G/63, I/331

mekel, mekil *see* **mechel** *adj*.

mekel *adv*. much I/214

mel *imp*. mix, blend Ap3d/31, Ap3d/63; **melled** *pa. p*. mixed I/195, ~ *þykke* ?mingled thick, ?thickened D/8 (n.); **ymellid** *ppl. adj*. mixed B/16

melancoly *see* **malencolie** *n*.

melancolius, melancolyus *adj*. characterized by a preponderance of black bile H/48, H/55, H/65

mele *n. smal* ~ finely ground or refined meal E.1/30, *E.2/38

membre *see* **preuy** *adj*.

membris *n. pl*. members, organs, limbs B/59, C/15-16, C/18; reproductive and excretory organs F/48

mene *adj*. intermediate H/93, H/94; (as *n*.) middle, intermediate state H/9, H/11, Ap4a/18; of zodiacal signs: neither cardinal nor fixed, mutable, common Ap4b/27

menysoun, menisoun, menson *n*. excessive flow of bodily fluids (due to dysentery, diarrhoea, the menses, etc.) E.1/36, E.2/25, E.2/44; *colde* ~ excessive flow caused by or accompanied by cold D/41

menstruat *adj*. menstruating B/93

mercury(e) *n*. mercury (the metal) E.2/30-1; a herb (*Mercurialis annua, Mercurialis perennis*, poss. *Chenopodium spp.*) Ap3d/108

mesurable *adv.* moderately, temperately I/218

mete *n.* food, a meal D/5, D/6, E.1/24, E.2/1, E.2/31, F/3, I/98, I/225; **metis** *n. pl.* G/86

meu(e)able, mevabel, mevable, movable *adj.* of elements: able to move H/25, H/26; of zodiacal signs: cardinal, associated with change from one season to another (i.e. equinoxes and solstices) Ap4a/11, Ap4a/13, Ap4b/18, Ap4b/20

miche, myche *adj.* much A.1/9, A.2/23, G/13, G/55; *as* ~ the same quantity, an equal amount G/63, G/93

mychel *see* **mechel** *adj.*

myd(de)rif(e) *n.* diaphragm H/83, H/84, H/132

myddes, myd(d)ys, myddis *n.* middle, central part E.1/10, E.2/13, E.2/27, I/96, I/139, I/202

midward, mydword *n.* middle, central part E.1/19, F/22

mykel *see* **mechel** *adj.*

mykelhed *n.* abundance I/287-8

mykke *adv.* much I/213

mylfoil *n.* yarrow (*Achillea millefolia*) G/98

milky, mylky *adj.* like milk, whitish A.2/3, B/54, *B/56, B/58

mylt(e) *n.* the spleen *H/43, *H/152, I/15

mynte *n.* mint (Mentha *spp.*) G/73, G/120; **myntys, mynten** *n. pl.* Ap3d/50, Ap3d/107

mysse *adj.* duller or lighter in colour, reduced in intensity G/27

mythy *adj.* heavy, oppressive, ?pungent D/33 (n.)

moder, modir *n.* the uterus G/154, I/282, I/291

mold(e) *n.* the crown of the head G/34, G/37, Ap3d/9

mo(o)tis *n. pl.* motes, specks of dust I/92, I/117, I/249

mortificacio(u)n *n.* the destruction of natural heat through extreme cold A.1/12, H/101

most(e) *3 sg. pr.* must B/10, F/45, H/88

most(e) *superl. adj.* most, greatest H/146, I/276

most(e) *superl. adv.* most F/48, F/49

motie *adj.* having very small particles (Lat. *athomosa*) B/70

motis *see* **mo(o)tis** *n. pl.*

mulan *n.* mullein (*Verbascum thapsus*) Ap3d/111

murmale *n.* a dry sore or ulcer on the surface of the body Ap3d/106

musty *adj.* moist Ap4a/9, Ap4a/10

N

nath *3 sg. pr.* does not have I/195

nauele, nauil, nauyl, nawyl *n.* navel B/84, G/137, I/314, Ap3d/104, Ap3d/121

ne *adv. and conj.* not I/315; *in double negative construction:* ~ *may not* may not F.2/44; *in correlative constructions;* ~ ... ~ ... ~ neither ... nor ... nor E.2/34; *correlative and double negative constructions:* ~ *traueile not* ~ *ete no potage* ~ *no sewis* and neither work nor eat stew nor sauces G/87-8

neeris *n. pl.* the kidneys I/100

†nefilis *n.* a nebulous form of the Ypostasis found in the middle of a urine sample I/141 (m.n.)

negh *inf.* approach, come near H/9, H/11

ney *adv.* nearly, almost I/40

nessch *adj.* soft I/116

neþer(e) *comp. adj.* ~ *parties* (*membris*) reproductive and excretory organs B/51, *C/18; (as *n.*) lower (region) C/21; **neþmest, neþ(e)most(e)** *superl. adj.* (as *n.*) ~ *region* the lowest of three parallel portions of a urine sample C/28; ~ (as *n.*) lowest (region) C/19, C/20

†nigra *adj.* black B/31; *†niger *I/75 (*marg.*), *I/78 (*marg.*)

nynch *n.* inch (*redivision of* an ynch *as a* nynch) F/47

nyppyng *vbl. n.* ~ *of the splene* pinching or biting pain in the spleen I/96

no3t *see* **no(u)3t** *adv.*

norischand(e) *pr. p.* ~ *lymmes* organs of nourishment or digestion (liver, spleen, gall bladder, intestines; prob. also the stomach) H/84, H/148, H/151 (see m.n. to H/82-3)

notemuge *n.* nutmeg G/116

notyd *ppl. adj.* used Ap3d/79

O

no(u)ȝt, noutȝ, now(i)t, noght *adv.* not A.1/4, A.1/23, B/2, B/23, D/7, D/38, E.1/26 (n.), E.1/33, E.2/16, H/4, H/8, I/7, I/21

occidental *adj.* western A.2/15, †occidentalis A.1/1

onys *adv.* at ~ at once, immediately Ap3d/83

onmevable *see* vnmeuable *adj.*

o(o)rt *n. saffro(u)n d' ~* saffron 'of the garden', possibly safflower (*Carthamus tinctoria*) H/113, I/40 (see m.n. to A.1/1-2)

oriental *adj.* eastern A.2/16, †orientalis A.1/2

orpyn *n.* ?orpine or stone crop (genus *Sedum*), ?ground ivy (*Nepeta hederacea*) Ap3d/108

ort *see* o(o)rt *n.*

os *conj.* as, like E.1/32, F/6, F/8

osmond *n.* royal fern (*Osmunda regalis*) G/84

other, oþer(e), oþir *adj.* (also as *pron.* and *pron. pl.*) other(s) B/30, B/50, C/3, C/24, G/14, G/55, H/6, H/10, I/210; second E.1/8; *conj.* or B/27, B/32, I/4; ~ ... ~ ... ~ ... ~ either ... or ... or ... or C/2-3

oþerwhile, oþirwhile *adv.* sometimes B/71, B/72, C/28, G/17, G/18

our *prep.* over F/44

ouemest *superl. adj.* (also as *n.*) ~ (*region*) the highest of three parallel portions of a urine sample C/19, C/22

ouerpassid *pa. p. is* ~ of heat: has begun to cool, has abated G/117

ouerthaward *adv.* wrongly, nonsensically I/334

oweth *3 sg. pr.* owns, produces (urine) I/216

P

pal(e) *adj.* pale, of a light colour A.2/7, B/47, B/60, G/23, H/105; *litil ~ , noght ful ~* of a lighter pale colour (= Subpallidus) A.2/6, H/104

†pallida, †pallidus *adj.* (also as *n.*) pale, of a light colour A.1/20, B/18, I/29 (*marg.*)

palseye *n.* various kinds of neuromuscular impairment, such as numbness, tremor, and paralysis I/255 (m.n.)

†paralisis *n.* paralysis I/256 (m.n.)

†paralitism *n.* paralysis or palsy B/53

parfit(e), parfiȝt *adj.* ~ *digestioun* coction that has been completed A.1/27, A.2/14, G/7, H/110-11; ~ excellent, ideal B/6

parti(e) *n.* part, region C/13, I/94, I/317; *in* ~ partially, somewhat I/358; **part(e)ys, parties, partyes** *n. pl.* D/1, D/3; of urine: ~ , ~ *of his body matyr* stratified regions in a urine sample or flask B/58, C/13, F/46, I/94, I/139; *hynder* ~ dorsal parts of the body B/51, *neper/lowere* ~ lower parts of the body, esp. reproductive and excretory organs B/51, H/146; *by* ~ in separate pieces I/103

partie *inf.* separate, part I/210

passyng *vbl. n.* emission I/128; ~ *of digestion* coction that goes on too long (Lat. *excessus digestionis*) H/115

passion *n.* disease C/2

†pedacrito *n.* someone suffering from podagra, gout in the feet B/30

peionys *n. pl.* pigeons Ap3d/100

***peys** *n.* weight *D/37 (n.)

peleter, peletre *n.* ~ *of Spayne* pellitory of Spain (*Anacyclus pyrethrum*) G/41, Ap3d/17

pepir *n. poudir of* ~ ground pepper G/74

percyl *n. see* perseli *n.*

perforacion *n.* the third of four parts of a urine sample, counting downward, where signs related to the liver and spleen are seen C/16; †perforacio C/14

peritori *n.* pellitory (*Parietaria officinale*) or a plant of similar use and appearance Ap3d/103

perlous, perloce *adj.* perilous B/23, Ap3d/71

perseli, persely, percyl *n.* parsley (*Petroselinum nigrum*) G/73, G/120, Ap3d/43

pese *n.* piece G/52; **peses** *n. pl.* E.1/32, E.2/40

pesyn *n. pl.* ~ *broth* pease broth E.2/24

pessyth *see* pisseth *3 sg. pr.*

pety moryl *n.* black nightshade (*Solanum nigrum*) Ap3d/75

philipend *n.* the dropwort (*Spiraea filipendula*) Ap3d/43

philofer *n.* philosopher Ap3d/38

phisik *n.* medicine G/2

pyn *n.* a lesion of the cornea Ap3d/32

pipes epatis *n. pl.* vessels of the liver (bile duct, hepatic artery, portal vein) I/252-3

pisse, pysse *n.* urine D/9, E.2/8, G/103, I/240, Ap3a/6, Ap3d/53; *chawd* ~ painful ('hot') urination F/39

pisseth, pisset, pessyth *3 sg. pr.* urinates D/17, E.1/16, E.2/21; pisse *pr. sg. subj.* urinate B/7; pissed *pa. p.* B/12

plantayne *n.* a member of the plantain family (Plantago *spp.*) Ap3d/103

plantes *n. pl.* shoots, sprouts (of a tree) Ap3d/43

plaster, pla(y)stre *n.* a medicinal poultice or compress, usually made of ground herbs, meal, or other substances and bound over the affected part of the body with a piece of cloth or leather G/33, G/37, Ap3d/8, Ap3d/121

plenily *adv.* fully Ap3b/2

pokyt *n.* a small cloth bag used to hold a poultice of medicinal herbs Ap3d/104

pom(me) *n.* a fruit A.1/23; *citrine* ~ , ~ *syter* a yellow or orange fruit (poss. citron, orange, or other citrus fruit) A.1/22, H/106

ponderouse *adj.* heavy, thick F/17 (see n. to D/19)

postem(e), postim, postyme, postom, postume *n.* morbid swelling, inflammation, or abscess B/65, E.2/27, F/19, F/23, G/93, I/14, I/63 (*see also* apostym)

potage *n.* a thick stew, soup, or porridge G/87, G/120, Ap3d/50

potel *n.* a half-gallon measure G/114

pouderouse, poudrows, pudruse *adj.* powdery D/19 (n.), E.1/14, E.2/19

poudir, poudre, powder *n.* powder G/61, Ap3d/100; ~ *of pepir* (*gyn-geuer/gynger, comyn, lynseed, anise, fenel, galyngale, greynes, clowis, notemuge*) ground pepper (ginger, cumin, linseed, anise, fennel, galingale, grains of paradise, cloves, nutmeg) G/74, G/80, G/115; poudris *n. pl.* G/117

powne *imp.* ~ . . . *togidere* pulverize and mix together G/83

preuy, priuy *adj.* ~ *membre* genitalia G/144; ~ *harnes* genitalia H/143, H/153

prime, pryme *adj.* ~ *qualite* one of the four fundamental qualities in medieval cosmology (heat, cold, moisture, dryness) H/3; *pl.* ~ *qualitees* H/6

priuy *see* preuy *adj.*

priuy *n.* privy, toilet I/333

priuite(e) *n.* the female genitalia G/152, Ap3d/126

proued, pruuid *ppl. adj.* tested and found efficacious G/58, G/75, Ap3d/49

ptysyk *n.* phthisic, consumption E.2/5

pudruse *see* pouderouse *adj.*

purpill *adj.* reed ~ dark, purplish red I/363

purpure *adj.* dark crimson or purplish red I/133

†putrida *adj.* rotten; *sinecha* ~ a fever caused by rotten or corrupted blood I/58 (m.n.)

putte *imp.* put, add G/67, G/84; (y)put *ppl. adj.* ~ *out* duller or lighter in colour, reduced in intensity (Lat. *remissus*) A.1/19, *A.1/22, A.1/23; expelled, discharged B/33

Q

quan, qwan, qwen *conj.* when E.1/6, E.2/6, Ap3d/9, Ap3d/64

qware *conj.* where Ap3d/92

quart(e)yn, quarta(y)n(e), quart' *adj.* of fever: reaching crisis every three days D/13, D/36, E.1/11, E.1/31, E.2/14, E.2/39, F/12; ~ (as *n.*) a quartan fever B/36, I/35, I/48, I/242; †quartana B/33

quey *n.* whey H/102

queynte *adj.* cunning (Lat. *astutus*) H/54

qwen *see* quan *conj.*

qwete *see* whete *n.*

qwhit, qwit, qwyt(e), qwythe *see* whit(e) *adj.*

qwyche *see* w(h)ich(e) *rel. pron.*

quytour. *n.* pus, putrid matter I/81, I/83, quyter H/127, whitter *B/64, B/66

R

radiche, radyche *n.* radish (*Raphanus sativus*) Ap3d/43, Ap3d/44

rafnys *n. poss.* raven's I/75

ray, *raie *adj.* streaked, exhibiting rays or stripes E.1/23 (n.), *E.2/30

raynes, raynys, reyn(e)s, reynys, renys(se) *n. pl.* the kidneys B/60, B/63, C/3, D/16, D/18, F/39, G/124, H/84, H/153, I/68, I/88, Ap3d/121

rasyng *vbl. n.* material shaved or scraped from something I/252

raw *adj.* uncooked E.2/26; crude I/128, I/208; ~ *humouris* undigested bodily fluids I/91, I/94

rawnesse *n.* incomplete digestion (Lat. *cruditas*) B/20

red(e), reed *adj.* red A.2/18, B/12, C/11, D/5, D/11, E.1/8, E.2/11, F/11, G/114, *G/124, H/15, I/44, I/52; the urinary colour Rubeus H/113; ~ *gold* gold alloyed with copper I/49; *litil* ~ a lighter red colour of urine (= Subrubeus) A.2/17; ~ *suart* dark red I/62

regio(u)n *n.* one of three parallel layers in a urine sample B/25, B/52, C/21, I/93, I/119; **regions, regionys, regyouns** *n. pl.* C/6, C/19, F/45, I/2, I/145

regnes *3 sg. pr.* rules, influences H/2, H/4; *pr. pl.* H/68, H/73

reyn *n.* rain E.1/38

reyn(e)s, reynys *see* raynes *n. pl.*

remis *n.* loss of intensity, dimming A.2/18

remisse, remys, remysch *adj.* duller or lighter in colour, reduced in intensity (Lat. *remissus*) A.2/6, A.2/17, G/26

remouyd *ppl. adj.* far, distant B/14

renys(se) *see* raynes *n. pl.*

rennyng *pr. p.* flowing, fluid B/50, I/196

replecion *n.* of a humour: fullness, esp. to excess C/25

reseyith *n.* uterus *D/29 (n.), D/38

residence, residens *n.* the material that settles to the bottom of a urine sample, urinary sediment C/8, C/29, I/93; ?the process of sedimentation I/71 (m.n.)

resolucio(u)n(e)s, resolutions *n. pl.* particles suspended or settling out in a urine sample B/39, H/139, I/127, I/132

reu *see* rue *n.*

rewmatik *adj.* ~ *goute* gout caused by watery humours flowing from the head I/119, I/120

rewme, reume *n.* watery humours originating in the head, rheum H/124, I/264, I/352

rygbons *n. poss.* of the backbone I/372

rody *adj.* ruddy, reddish H/50, I/59

rosyn *n.* rosin or some other resin G/79

roten, rootyn *adj.* rotten, putrefied H/116, H/131, I/65, I/291

rotet *3 sg. pr.* rots, putrefies E.1/33; *pa. p.* putrefied, necrotic D/39

rotyng *vbl. n.* putrefaction, decay *B/65, B/66, D/15

roumest *superl. adj.* (as *n.*) most spacious region, region of greatest extent H/37

†rubea, †rubeus *adj.* (also as *n.*) of a colour ranging from yellow-orange to red (variously compared to saffron, roses, and blood) A.1/2, B/7, B/9, G/10, I/44 (*marg.*) (cf. **red(e)** *adj.*)

rubicunde *adj.* (as *n.*) of a fire-red or blood-red colour H/114; **†rubicunda, †rubicundus** A.1/4, G/10, I/54 (*marg.*)

rue, reu *n.* rue (genus *Ruta*, esp. *Ruta graveolens*) G/65, Ap3d/103

ruf *adj.* (also as *n.*) of a bright golden colour H/110; **†rufa, †rufus** A.1/26, B/1, B/27, G/6, I/49 (*marg.*)

russet *adj.* (as *n.*) of a light or muted greyish-brown colour: *gray* ~ H/102; *whit* ~ I/23

S

saffro(u)n, saferon *n.* the yellowish-orange to reddish-orange spice derived from the dried stigmas of the saffron crocus (*Crocus sativus*) G/47, G/51, I/44, Ap3d/91; ~ *occidental* Western saffron, possibly from Spain or France A.2/15; ~ *oriental* Eastern saffron, probably from the eastern Mediterranean or Middle East, normally of a finer quality A.2/16; ~ *d'o(o)rt* saffron 'of the garden', possibly safflower (*Carthamus tinctoria*) H/113, I/40 (see also m.n. to A.1/1-2)

sall *see* **xal** *2 sg. pr.*

saltere *comp. adj.* saltier I/207

sammen *adv.* half, partially H/105 (n.)

sanguyn(e), sangwyn(e) *adj.* (also as *n.*) dominated by the humour blood, especially in relation to a complexion dominated by blood H/40, H/46, H/50, H/74

sauge *n.* the herb sage (*Salvia officinalis*) G/72, Ap3d/76

sauour *n.* taste I/35, I/38; odor, smell G/150, I/86

saxifrage *n.* saxifrage (Saxifraga *spp.*) Ap3d/43

scabbe *n.* scaliness on the surface of an organ (e.g. the bladder, the skin); crusting over of a sore H/137

scales *n.* the urinary content Squames, similar to small flakes or flsh-scales H/120, H/137

scercle *see* **cerc(u)le** *n.*

schaddeuyngg *pr. p.* darkening, overshadowing I/357

schaddyng *vbl. n.* a shedding or scattering (of particles, precipitates) I/243

schadueth *3 sg. pr.* darkens, obscures I/360

s(c)hadwyd *ppl. adj.* dim, obscured I/41, I/50, I/245

scharp(e), shaarp *adj.* of fever: intense, high (Lat. *acutus*) B/21, B/24, Ap3d/71; of elements: piercing, penetrating H/25; pointed, conical I/136, I/137; rough I/59

schauynge, schawyng *vbl. n.* material shaved or scraped from a larger piece of material G/51, Ap3d/91; **schauyngges** *n. pl.* E.2/17 (cf. **rasyng**)

s(c)he *pron. 3 sg. nom. fem.* she D/26, E.1/24, E.2/34, F/28, G/124, I/289; **che** E.2/31, E.2/32; **he** (*some instances may be 3 pl.*) B/73, B/76, B/94, E.1/26, E.1/35; **se** E.1/33

scheynet *see* **schineth** *3 sg. pr.*

schetis, schetys *n. pl.* sheets (bedclothes) G/107, Ap3d/57

schineth, schyneth, schynys, scheynet *3 sg. pr.* is bright, shines E.1/28, E.2/36, F/24, I/323; **schyne** *pr. sg. subj.* I/323; **schyn(n)yng, schynande, schinyng, scynend** *pr. p.* bright, shining (like silver or quicksilver; Fr.

relut cum argent) D/25, E.1/23, E.2/30, Ap3d/68; of horn: translucent (as in a lighted lantern; Lat. *lucida*) A.1/15, A.2/2

schire *adj.* clear H/102

schyvys *n. pl.* the woody refuse from beaten flax, splinters I/251

schoon *n. pl.* shoes G/149

schoore *n.* the groin I/88, I/89

schorthed(e) *n.* ~ *of breth* difficulty breathing, breathlessness I/95, I/358

scynend *see* **schineth** *3 sg. pr.*

sclep *n.* sleep I/307

sclepe *inf.* sleep E.1/27

scom, scume *n.* a scum or frothy substance on the surface of a liquid *E.1/25 (n.), E.2/33; the urinary content Foam H/120, H/126

se *see* **s(c)he** *pron.*

sedymen *n.* the urinary content Ypostasis, the material that settles to the bottom of a urine flask H/121, H/144

se(e)d(e) *n.* semen B/87, B/90, Ap3d/116; seed (of plants) G/59, Ap3d/76; **seedis** *n. pl.* G/60

se(e)k(e), sijk, sike, syke *adj.* sick I/61; of body parts: affected by disease G/33, G/37, I/139, Ap3d/8; (as *n.*) sick person, patient G/38, I/20, I/138, Ap3d/13

semy *inf.* seem, appear (to be) B/94; **semys(se), semet(h), semeþ** *3 sg. pr.* seems, appears E.1/14, E.2/19, F/17, F/20, G/148

sercle *see* **cerc(u)le** *n.*

sethes *pr. pl.* boil Ap3d/47; **seþe, sethe** *imp.* G/32, G/103, Ap3d/17, Ap3d/53; **sode(n), sothen, sothyn, soþyn** *pa. p.* A.1/19, A.2/6, G/23, G/24, H/105, I/26, I/29, Ap3d/10, Ap3d/47

setrinus *see* **citrin(e)** *adj.*

sewis *n. pl.* sauces or gravies G/88

shaarp *see* **scharp(e)** *adj.*

shadwyd *see* **s(c)hadwyd** *ppl. adj.*

she *see* **s(c)he** *pron.*

syche, swich *adj.* such B/91, I/360

sy3te *n.* viewing, examination F/2

sijk *see* **se(e)k(e)** *n.*

syne, singne *n.* sign E.1/2, E.1/4, F/4, F/20, Ap3d/60; **syngnys** *n. pl.* Ap4a/13

†sinecha putrida *n.* a fever caused by corrupt blood I/58 (m.n.)

syngrene *n.* the houseleek (*Sempervivum tectorum*) Ap3d/25

†**sinocha *inflatiua** *n.* a fever caused by excess of blood *I/57 (m.n.)

syter *n.* pom ~ a citrus fruit (Lat. *pomum citrinum*) H/106

sithes *n. pl.* times (indicating comparison, e.g. *ten* ~ *more*) H/30, H/31

siþþe *conj.* because, seeing that (Lat. *cum*) C/9

sitryne *see* citrin(e) *adj.*

skalis, skalys *n. pl.* scales (of fish) I/109; scale-like flakes in a urine sample B/54, B/56, I/123

sky(e) *n.* the urinary content Clouds (Lat. *nubes*), a cloudiness or darkening usually seen in the upper portion of a urine sample but sometimes in the middle or bottom I/259, I/323, I/327

skyn(ne) *n.* skin A.2/4, G/113; membrane H/28, H/28

skyppyngg *vbl. n.* the act of leaping I/68

sleuthfull *adj.* slothful H/56, H/57

slomery *adj.* somnolent H/57

smalache *n.* smallage, wild celery (*Apium graveolens*) Ap3d/42

smylleth *3 sg. pr.* smells, gives off an odor I/208

smytyng *vbl. n.* beating, pulsing I/169

so *adv. and conj.* so that, as long as, assuming H/111

sode(n) *see* sethes *2 pr. pl.*

sory *adj.* sorrowful (Lat. *tristis*) H/55

sotel *adj.* light, fine H/25 (m.n.), H/26

sothen, sothyn, soþyn *see* sethes *pr. pl.*

souled, sowled *ppl. adj.* of bodily organs: animate (i.e. producing and controlling movement, perception, and thought) H/82 (m.n.), H/147, H/149

sowneth *3 sg. pr.* sounds, makes a noise I/107

spermatik *adj.* like semen, sperm-like I/127

sperme *n.* the urinary content Semen H/121, H/141

spewit *3 sg. pr.* spits, coughs, or vomits out E.1/17

spice *n.* type, kind H/140, I/102, I/104

spigirnel *n.* a medicinal plant, poss. spignel (*Meum athamanticum*) G/94

spinagre *n.* a medicinal plant, poss. spinach (*Spinacia oleracea*) G/58

spiritual(e) *adj.* ~ *membris* (*lymmes*) the respiratory organs and the heart C/15, H/83, H/125, H/150, Ap3d/41

spotti *adj.* of more than one colour, variegated I/87

spourge *n.* spurge (Euphorbia *spp.*) Ap3d/76

spume *n.* the urinary content Foam Ap3d/89

sqwames *n. pl.* the urinary content Squames, small flakes in a urine sample Ap3d/102

stable *n.* ~ *clensyng* ?the sweepings of a stable D/35 (n.)

stable, stabel *adj.* of astrological signs: fixed, not associated with a change of season Ap4a/21, Ap4b/26; †**stabiles** I/165

stalke *n.* stem of a fruit G/49

stanmarche *n.* horse parsley (*Smyrnium olusatrum*) Ap3d/43

sta(u)mpe *imp.* pound, mash G/66, G/84, G/136, Ap3d/45

stedfast *adj.* of persons: constant, steadfast B/86, H/52; of zodiacal signs: fixed, stable, unmovable Ap4b/19

sternes *n. pl.* stars H/35

stoffyd, stuft *ppl. adj.* obstructed, blocked F/21, F/44

stok *n.* stem of a plant H/117

ston(e) *n.* þe (*the*) ~ kidney or bladder stones B/55, B/70, F/26, H/134, I/114, I/115; **stones, stoonys** *n. pl.* small, sandy particulates in urine or the urinary system C/28, C/29, G/124

stoppyng *vbl. n.* obstruction, blockage I/252; ~ *of floures* amenorrhoea I/134

straytest *superl. adj.* (as *n.*) narrowest, most restricted place H/38

streit *adj.* of breath: constricted, impeded G/97

streythede *n.* constriction, congestion I/95

streitnesse *n.* constriction, congestion G/89 (*marg.*)

stride *inf.* stand astride, bestride G/143, Ap3d/125

stripis *n. pl.* streaks, rays I/276

strok *n.* of the pulse: a beat I/175, I/177; **strokis** *n. pl.* I/174

strong(e) *adj.* having a pungent odor, stinking D/7 (n.), D/28; high (of a fever), powerful, intense F/44, H/114,

I/86, I/170; **strongere** *comp. adj.*
I/169

stuft *see* **stoffyd** *ppl. adj.*

subcitrin, subsitryne *adj.* (also as *n.*) of
a light or dull yellowish colour A.2/9,
H/105, †**subcitrina**, †**subcitrinus**
A.1/22, B/6, B/85, I/33 (*marg.*)

subpale *adj.* of a light or dull pale colour
H/104; †**subpallida,** * †**subpallidus**
A.1/19, *I/26 (*marg.*)

subrede *adj.* (also as *n.*) of a colour ranging from light or dull yellow-orange to
red (=Subrubeus) H/112

†**subrubea,** †**subrubeus** of a colour ranging from light or dull yellow-orange
to red A.1/1, B/43, G/10, G/30, I/40
(*marg.*)

subrubicunde *adj.* (also as *n.*) of a light
or dull fire-red or blood-red colour
H/113; †**subrubicunda,** †**subrubicundus** A.1/3, G/10, I/52 (*marg.*)

subruf *adj.* of a dull or pale golden colour H/109; †**subrufa,** †**subrufus**
A.1/25, B/2, B/27, G/6, I/46 (*marg.*)

subsitryne *see* **subcitrin** *adj.*

substa(u)nce, substauns, sustaunce *n.*
the consistency or relative thickness of
urine B/4, B/22, C/7, F/40-1, G/90,
H/13, H/88, I/2, I/47; **substaunces**
n. pl. H/90

sues *3 sg. pr.* follows H/1; **suynge** *pr. p.*
G/6

†**suffocacio matricis** *n. phr.* a sensation of internal pressure believed to
be caused by movement of the uterus
G/147

sumdel *adv.* somewhat D/20

superfice *n.* the second highest region of
a urine sample H/86

†**suppositum** *pa. p. post* ~ ?after coitus
I/130 (m.n.)

suart *adj. reed* ~ dark red I/62

suete, swete *adj.* sweet G/152, H/13,
H/96, I/185

swete *inf.* sweat I/230; *pr. sg. subj.* sweat
G/106

swich *see* **syche** *adj.*

swythe *adv.* swiftly, vigorously I/309;
swythere *comp.* I/311

swot *n.* sweat I/355 (m.n.)

talent *n.* desire, appetite D/26, E.1/6,
E.1/24, E.2/7, E.2/31, E.2/36, I/283

tastyng *vbl. n.* ?tasting I/35 (n.)

tele *see* **tijl** *n.*

temper(e) *imp.* combine, mix G/35,
G/74, Ap3d/10

temperure *n.* balance (of humours)
H/92, H/95

tercian *n.* an intermittent fever that recurs every other day I/36, I/42; *double*
~ an intermittent fever that recurs
every day but with greater violence
every other day I/38 (m.n.), I/48

tesyke *see* **tisyk** *n.*

thanne *n.* tanwater, water used in tan-
ning I/277

the *pron. 3 pl.* they I/247

þe *conj.* that E.1/6

þee *pron. 2 sg. obj.* thee, you (*sg.*) G/122

thenne, thinne, thyn(ne), þinne, þynne
adj. thin B/42, C/12, E.2/4, E.2/6,
E.2/27, E.2/50, F/6, F/22, G/101,
H/14, H/41, I/3, I/9; *comp.* **thynnere**
H/30, H/31

þera3en(s) *adv.* against that, as a remedy
for that G/103, G/149

there, þere *adv./conj.* where G/50,
I/341; ~ *as* where C/21

þereageyne(s), þereagayne *adv.* in
contrast to that H/14, H/34, H/37

þerouer *adv.* over that, above that
G/105, G/144

þethen *adv.* thence, (from) that point
H/78, H/79

þies, þise *dem. pron.* these F/45, F/48,
H/6, H/17

þilke *dem. pron.* that B/79

þi(n), þy(n) *pron. 2 sg. poss.* thy, thine,
your (*sg.*) G/46, Ap3d/48, Ap3d/78,
Ap3d/82

thynnehed *n.* thinness I/5

þise *see* **þies** *dem. pron.*

tho, þo *dem. pron. and adj.* those G/11,
H/99, I/345

þoru3, þorw, thourgh, thro3t *prep.*
through G/99, I/5, I/7, Ap3d/81;
throughout B/66

þou, þow, thou, thow *pron. 2 sg. nom.*
thou, you (*sg.*) D/3, E.1/1, E.2/50,
F/1, G/64, H/2, I/1, I/79, Ap3d/63

þow *conj.* though B/6

þriddendel *n.* one-third, a third part (of an initial quantity) G/95

þries, *þriyse *adv.* thrice, three times G/64, G/68, *Ap3d/63

þriste *n.* thirst B/84

þroȝt *see* þoruȝ *prep.*

tijl, tele *n.* tile G/104, Ap3d/54

tymes, tymys *n. pl.* times G/39, Ap3d/14, Ap3d/28; *wiþinne foure ~ asaiynge* within four attempts or applications G/54; *within sex ~* within six doses or applications Ap3d/94

tynkt *adj.* coloured I/217, I/219

tirdlis *n. pl.* dung G/138

tisyk, tesyke *n.* phthisic, consumption I/237, Ap3d/41

†tysicus *adj.* suffering from phthisic, consumptive I/233

to *prep.* until H/78, H/79, Ap3d/56

to *adv.* too, in excess, overly A.1/9, B/9, C/25

to *see* to(o) *num.*

tobroste *ppl. adj.* ruptured, afflicted by hernia G/78

tofoorn *adv.* previously I/67

tok(e)n(e), tokyn(e) *n.* sign E.2/1, E.2/2, F/6, F/12, G/56, G/77, I/236, I/277; tok(e)nes *n. pl.* H/124, I/59, I/206, I/313

tok(e)neth, tokenyth *3 sg. pr.* signifies E.2/6, E.2/8, I/9, I/28; tokne *pr. pl.* I/375

to(o), tuo *num.* two B/73, C/1, C/5, H/8, H/10, I/206, Ap4a

toþir *adj.* second E.2/10

tourne *pr. pl.* return I/375

trauaylyng *pr. p.* moving, quivering (Lat. *tremulus*) B/49

traueile *inf.* work; travel G/87

tremell *pr. sg. subj.* quiver, tremble I/369

tretrus *adj.* faithless, traitorous H/53

triacle, triakyl *n.* theriac, an antidote to poison or venom G/63, Ap3d/62

trie *imp.* refine, separate out impurities Ap3d/48

trobele, trub(e)le, tr(o)ubli, trubul(e), turble *adj.* turbid, murky B/62, B/87, B/90, E.1/4, E.2/2, F/4, Ap3d/116 (cf. **drubli** above)

trobulyd *ppl. adj.* turbid, murky F/49

turmentille *n.* tormentil (*Potentilla erecta*) G/58-9, turmentyne G/94 (m.n.)

turned *pa. p.* changed E.1/8 (n.), *E.2/10

twies *adv.* twice G/68

tuo *see* to(o) *num.*

U

vmers *see* humur *n.*

vmgos *3 sg. pr.* surrounds, encircles H/29, H/30

vnbornyd *ppl. adj.* unpolished Ap3c/8

vnkyndely *adj.* unnatural G/56

vnmeuable, vnmevabel, onmevable *adj.* of elements: physically fixed, solid H/27; of zodiacal signs: fixed, not associated with a change of season Ap4a/11, Ap4a/12

vnset *pa. p.* of leeks: not yet transplanted Ap3d/112

vreynes *n. pl.* urines A.1/5, A.1/9

vrinal, vrynal(l) *n.* flask for inspecting urine C/20, D/25, F/27, G/130, I/338

V

valypere *see* voliper *n.*

vanite, wanyte *n.* ~ *of þe heed/hede* dizziness, lightheadedness G/44, Ap3d/20

veyn(e), vein(e), vayne *n.* a blood vessel B/63, D/17, E.1/16, E.1/17, E.2/21, I/68, I/86; veynes, vayn(e)s *n. pl.* C/2, I/193, Ap3d/39; *vrine veynes* ducts carrying urine B/33

venemo(u)s, venemosy *adj.* infected, morbid B/32, C/30, G/18

ventosite *n.* gassiness in the body B/83, C/23, H/126

ver *n.* the season of spring H/61

verte sauce *n.* a sauce made from green herbs and spices G/75

verueyne, ueruayne *n.* vervain, verbena (*Verbena officinalis*) G/32, Ap3d/7

vessel *n.* flask for inspecting urine B/41, B/64

vice, vyce, vise *n.* disease, disorder H/125, H/127, H/131; vices *n. pl.* B/16, B/61, C/24

vicious *adj.* diseased E.2/49

†viridis *adj.* of urine: green B/12, G/12

visage *n.* face, countenance H/59

vise *see* vice *n.*

voliper, valypere *n.* a bandage for the head G/39, Ap3d/14

W

wa(a)n *adj.* leaden, pale, discoloured A.2/24, G/14, I/70

waybrede *n.* a member of the plantain family (Plantago *spp.*) Ap3d/107-8

waische *see* wesche *imp.*

waistyng *vbl. n.* a wasting disease, such as consumption or hectic fever I/28

walwort *n.* a term applied to a number of plants, including dwarf elder (*Sambucus ebulus*) and (possibly erroneously) dropwort, chicory, elecampane, etc. G/44, Ap3d/20, Ap3d/76

wan *see* wa(a)n *adj.*

wanhed *n.* leaden or pale colour, paleness I/50

wanyte *see* vanite *n.*

warantise, warantyse, warandise, warandyse *n.* surety, guarantee: *on* ~ , *of* ~ assuredly, guaranteed G/40, G/53, G/96, Ap3d/15, Ap3d/57-8, Ap3d/95-6

warsschid *ppl. adj.* healed, cured I/138

wasche(n) *see* wesche *imp.*

wastyng *pr. p.* weakening, being enfeebled F/41 (n.)

wastyng *vbl. n.* the process of wasting away, being consumed by disease H/129, H/137, I/100

water(e), watir, watyr *n.* water A.1/14, A.2/1, B/20, D/31, E.1/4, F/6, H/20, H/26, I/12; urine D/31, F/2, G/1, I/207, Ap3a/6, Ap3c/2; sap Ap3d/24; ~ *of vrine* liquid part of urine G/47; ~ *weies* urinary ducts G/19; water(e)s, watris *n. pl.* waters, fluid(s) E.1/41; waters (of the firmament) H/35; urines F/45, G/20, G/27

waueryng *vbl. n.* unsteadiness, dizziness I/367

wax, wex *n.* wax G/45, G/79, Ap3d/21

web *n.* white film over the eye, cataract Ap3d/32

weel *adv.* well G/45, G/46

weyys *n. pl.* ~ *of vrine* vessels that carry urine out of the body (i.e. the ureters and urethra) C/24 (compare **vrine veynes** B/33, **watir weies** G/19)

wel-cryssys, wel-kyrsyn *n. pl.* watercresses (*Rorippa nasturtium-aquaticum*) Ap3d/77, Ap3d/84

wer(c)k, werch *n.* pain, ache E.1/26, E.1/40, E.2/9, E.2/34, I/240

wesand(e) *n.* the esophagus H/83, H/150

wesche, wa(i)sche *imp.* wash G/33, G/136, Ap3d/8, Ap3d/78; wa(i)schen *pa. p. new* ~ freshly washed G/107, Ap3d/57; waschyne, wasschen rinsed, soaked E.2/26, F/15

wete *inf.* know (that) D/1

wex *see* wax *n.*

whech *see* w(h)ich(e) *rel. pron.*

whete, qwete *n.* wheat G/36, Ap3d/11

w(h)ich(e), w(h)ych, whilk, whech, whoche, qwyche, huche *rel. pron.* which D/62, *B/64, F/48, G/9, G/71, H/98, I/91, I/93, Ap3a/3, Ap3a/8, Ap3c/3, Ap3d/116, Ap4a/1

whit(e), whi(3)t, why(3)t(e), whyth, qwhit, qwit, qwyt(e), qwythe *adj.* of urine: clear A.2/1, B/45, *C/11, D/5, E.1/2, E.1/9, E.2/1, E.2/48, E.2/52, G/20, I/12 (compare *MED*, s.v. *whit*, *adj.*, sense 4a.(f)); (milky) white I/16, Ap3d/70; of contents or sediments in urine: white B/74, B/76, C/26, E.2/19, I/17, I/113, Ap3d/67, Ap3d/97; ~ *wyne* pale or clear wine Ap3d/8, Ap3d/80; ~ *gold* gold alloyed with silver or another lightening metal I/46

whyth *prep.* with I/17

whyth *adj. see* whit(e) *adj.*

whitter *see* quytour *n.*

whoche *see* w(h)ich(e) *rel. pron.*

wych, wiche *see* w(h)ich(e) *rel. pron.*

wicke, wyk *adj.* harmful, wicked E.1/41, I/171

wyckyd *adj.* diseased I/378

wynd(e) *n.* abdominal gas I/7, I/97, I/269

wyrche *inf.* work, have effect Ap3d/16

wite *inf.* know C/6, G/6, G/86; *imp.* H/2

wmman *n.* woman E.1/7 (n.)

wol(le) *1 & 3 sg. pr.* will (indicating futurity) G/29, G/42, I/345, I/346; wilt, wolt *2 sg. pr. subj.* want to, desire to I/184, I/189

wombe *n.* belly D/2, G/139; *flux of the* ~ diarrhoea, dysentery, or lientery B/57

woned *pa. p. hit was* ~ there was accustomed to be B/78

woorts *n. pl.* plants, herbs, greens I/73

wormod(e) *n.* wormwood (*Artemisia absinthium*) G/33, G/65, Ap3d/7, Ap3d/75

wort *n.* ~ *þat is not changed* wort, an as yet unfermented infusion of grain or honey, used in making beer or mead Ap3d/80

wowle *n.* wool Ap3d/28

wrethe *n.* wrath I/354

wryeth *3 sg. pr.* covers I/104

X

xal, xalt *2 sg. pr.* shall E.2/50, E.2/52; **sall** F/1; **sall** *3 sg. pr.* F/26

Y

ȝalowe, ȝelow(ȝ), ȝel(e)w, ȝolw(e), yel(e)w(e), yelow *adj.* yellow A.2/2, A.2/15, G/21, H/103, I/19, I/33, I/33, I/40, I/355, I/361, Ap3d/89

ȝe *pron. 2 pl. nom.* you G/5

ȝelde *inf.* result in, produce H/18

ȝerde *n.* penis Ap3d/40, Ap3d/87

ȝolw(e) *see* ȝalowe *adj.*

ȝridde *ord. num.* third (with rare substitution of ȝ for þ) E.1/31 (n.)

INDEX OF PROPER NAMES